With best Wishes

THE GENTLEMEN TALK OF PEACE

THE MACMILLAN COMPANY
NEW YORK · BOSTON · CHICAGO · DALLAS
ATLANTA · SAN FRANCISCO

MACMILLAN AND CO., LIMITED
LONDON · BOMBAY · CALCUTTA · MADRAS
MELBOURNE

THE MACMILLAN COMPANY
OF CANADA, LIMITED
TORONTO

THE GENTLEMEN
TALK OF PEACE

WILLIAM B. ZIFF

THE MACMILLAN COMPANY · NEW YORK

1944

FOREWORD

UNDER examination the problems of peace are seen to be highly complex. They are no longer rooted in the familiar motivations of high politics, but are an expression of the perplexing social questions of our times, and do not lend themselves to cure by the use of mild political medicines.

Events have moved rapidly since this book was completed in the early summer of 1944. Our European enemies are on the verge of collapse. The end of the war in Asia cannot be far off. These eventualities make it necessary for us to appraise the coming power equilibrium and determine the type of institutional structure in which the future peace is to be housed.

A number of preliminary conferences have been held by representatives of the principal United Nations, seeking to arrive at an agreement on questions of oil, food, and currency control. Still others are planned to deal with the regulation of international flight, the control of raw materials, the allocation of world markets, and the establishment of a World Court. As this is written, conferences are going forward at Dumbarton Oaks with a view to setting up a world organization capable of organizing and maintaining the peace.

Whatever the merits of the different schemes suggested, or of the means by which they are to be placed into effect, they all possess the fatal flaw of ignoring certain basic facts. Without exception, their authors wish to eat their cake and have it too. They seek the benefits of a new and peaceful world, but are unwilling to abandon the conditions which make struggle inevitable.

The parties to the deliberations seek a formula which will preserve unimpaired the absolute sovereignties of their respective States and yet at the same time will provide for the use of sufficient force to keep would-be aggressors within bounds. The smaller States are to retain their complete independence and presumably their freedom of economic, political, and ideological action. Thus the antique world of political fragments is to be guaranteed against change despite the social, industrial, and military changes which already make it inoperable.

The larger nations, confronted with widely varying temptations and opportunities, differing radically in territorial position, military and economic power, in psychology, ideals, material needs, and levels of development, and committed to opposing sets of objectives, nevertheless are to police one another by a mutual consent which presupposes the non-existence of these factors.

It is assumed also that an international peace organization can be organized, independent of the terms of the coming peace settlement. This separation from the stream of power facts which dominates the physical affairs of the world must confine the deliberations within a vacuum and condemn them to sterility. The discussions, then, will be little more than diplomatic shadow-boxing and can only reflect the exigencies of underlying power politics. The delegates must make an effort to protect the vested interests of the nations they represent. There will be little done which will bear reference to the changed political, social, and economic conditions under which the world of tomorrow must operate.

Each of the major States involved will be concerned with a totally different set of national problems and goals: England, whose power position in the material world is rapidly deteriorating, attempts to bolster that position by using her influence with America. Both nations are nervously watching Russia, and look with apprehension at the prospect of a renascent Orient, which they fear might overrun the world.

England cannot give up India without volcanic results in her material situation. China cannot yield on the question of industrialization of the East. The Soviets must seek outlets on warm water. The United States must gaze with frank misgivings on Soviet control of the Balkans, whether by military occupation or by the indirect domination of so-called "friendly" governments. The instant the Soviet Union sits on the blue waters of the Adriatic it occupies an impregnable military position, outflanking all that remains of Europe. Europe then would be impossible to hold, should the Soviets determine to devour it. Britain, itself, would be ultimately doomed. The United States would be compelled to remake its entire view of the political and economic universe and to conduct itself accordingly.

No commitments arrived at under these conditions can survive the scrutiny of time. They will be doomed by their own contradictions and will be in no real sense different from the pacts, alliances, and arrangements which have preceded them. The hope of building a lasting peace edifice independent of the conflicting needs, ambitions, and power positions of the nations, is a vain one. It is only by a complete settlement all around, which takes into recognition the real character of the basic issues involved, that a semblance of enduring peace can be secured.

It may be accepted that the basic problems of the world will survive the present conferences intact; disguised and obscured for a brief moment, but unchanged. If these problems are to be met and overcome and are no longer to lurk as a terrible menace in the twilight shadows of civilization, they must be properly assessed.

The nature of these problems, and the kinetic stream of forces which arises from them, constitute the scope of this book.

WILLIAM B. ZIFF.

New York, August 23, 1944.

ACKNOWLEDGMENTS

The author wishes to thank the editors of *The Economist, Free World,* and *Reader's Digest* for permission to quote from articles originally appearing in their magazines; and for permission to use copyrighted material in this book, grateful acknowledgment is made to the following authors and publishers:

The John Day Company, for quotations from *Toward Freedom,* by Jawaharlal Nehru; Doubleday, Doran and Company, Inc., for a quotation from *Pattern of Conquest,* by Joseph C. Harsch; Harcourt, Brace and Company, Inc., for excerpts from *Grandeur and Misery of Victory,* by Georges Clemenceau; Houghton Mifflin Company, for excerpts from *The Intimate Papers of Colonel House,* by Charles Seymour; Sanford Jerome Greenburger, for excerpts from *The Voice of Destruction,* by Herman Rauschning; Reynal and Hitchcock, Inc., for quotations from *German Economy,* by Gustav Stolper; Alfred A. Knopf, Inc., for quotations from *Decline of the West,* by Oswald Spengler; and Ziff-Davis Publishing Company, for excerpts from *Free Men of America,* by Ezequiel Padilla.

CONTENTS

THE GENTLEMEN TALK OF PEACE

I

WORLD DILEMMA

IN victory our Republic will be confronted with the most serious situation in its history. We will stand at one of the great turning points of human society, oppressed with problems, irresolute and uncertain of our way.

No one of the riddles which our generation is committed to answer is of more pressing importance than that of preventing the ruinous recurrence of war.

If the past is any criterion of the future, when our statesmen sit down at the peace table with the gentlemen from the chancelleries and foreign offices for the final settlement which is to determine the fate of the world, no fundamental issues will be settled. What is to be will have been determined by hidden councils in which the various national interests, racial prides, greeds and class and group prejudices will have been brought to bear against each other in a mad scramble for priority and advantage.

While these gentlemen pay reverence with their lips to justice and democracy, their cold passionless eyes will survey the dismal remnants of this war in the light of spoils which are to be equitably divided according to the immediate interests and power position of the various nations engaged.

Yet it will be for these gentlemen, trained more in manipulation and cold sagacity than in insight, to determine whether there shall be future and more terrible wars on this planet, or whether they are to be avoided. Seated with the nations at the conference table will be irradicable prejudices and suspicions. States and groups

1

of States will be pledged to widely varying and irreconcilable objectives. Behind the smooth façade of words will be a bitter haggling for advantage accented by the usual type of bland international blackmail and power threats.

Together with this traditional jockeying for position, the gentlemen may be relied upon to take with them to the conference table the fierce partisanships and closed hearts which have made, of what should be the simple common cause of humanity, an ugly art called diplomacy.

Today the masses of mankind are, for the moment at least, recoiling in disgust from the kind of world these gentlemen and others who have preceded them have made. It is only in some terrible crisis such as that through which we are passing, that man is able to shake the chains which bind him to his brutelike past and see the problem outlined in all its grim unpleasantness and dark horror. In this illumined moment he perceives the sorry truth of war. He sees depicted in all its grisly reality the senseless slaughter of millions of our finest young men and the pathetic wasting of the patient labor of generations. He discerns the epic horrors of war no longer sketched in terms of the chivalrous and heroic, but in all their savage destructiveness.

It is only in this single inspired vision when the scales of blindness are momentarily thrust from his eyes that man is able to appraise the terrible cost of the ceaseless and increasingly ghastly conflicts in which he has been engaged since the dawn of history.

A bare glance at the collective chart of these figures is appalling. Professor Hannibal Duncan estimates that more than fifteen billion persons have sacrificed their lives to the God of War in historic times.[1] Other authorities, such as Professor Quincy Wright and Professor Sorokin compute far smaller, though still impressive, totals. It is believed that for every soldier butchered on the battlefield, at least four civilians have died of starvation, disease, massacre, or other causes attributable to war.

In World War I, itself, ten million are known to have met death

[1] Hannibal Gerald Duncan, *Race and Population Problems,* p. 284.

on the battlefields, 21,250,000 were wounded, and somewhere between five and ten million were listed as prisoners or missing. To these numbers must be conjoined an additional thirteen to thirty million because of increase in the death rate of the civilian population brought about by wartime conditions. Other population losses running far into the millions may properly be added to these figures to cover the resulting decrease in birth rate.

The economic and physical costs of this orgy of bloodletting are incalculable. Since the period of the Middle Ages alone, they must be well over a thousand billion dollars, with the figures rising steadily as new and more deadly instruments of destruction coincide with advances in technology and the physical sciences.

Bogart estimates the total cost to humanity of World War I alone to have been $338,000,000,000.[1] It obviously would take centuries for the Western World to recover from these catastrophic losses. Nevertheless it was pitched head foremost almost within a generation into a second and infinitely bloodier and costlier conflict.

In addition to the millions who will have been killed on the battlefields when the present struggle has terminated, untold legions will have been permanently crippled. Great masses of men will emerge maimed in mind and spirit, as well as in body. In military casualties the Germans alone already have lost close to five million men, the Russians perhaps as many as 7,500,000, the Chinese 4,500,-000, and the Japanese somewhere around two million. The civilian deaths due to the war are upwards of thirteen million for China and eleven million for the Soviet Union. Over three million Jews have been exterminated by Germany in the abattoirs of Poland. The Poles must have lost among all classes of citizens as many as four million.

At least forty million people of all nationalities have been torn up by their roots in Europe and perhaps as many as thirty million in Asia. Uncounted millions will have been destroyed by epidemics and disabled by disease and starvation. In France alone during the year 1940-41 the excess of deaths over births resulted

1 Quoted in Quincy Wright, *A Study of War*, Vol. I, footnote p. 219.

in a net population loss of 366,648. The figures for those afflicted with soul-sickness and dangerous psychoses will dwarf completely those of any other war in history.

Broad areas once flourishing with industry and commerce will have been reduced largely to rubble. Without taking into account imponderable losses of economic destruction the actual cost of the present war was probably over five hundred billion dollars by the beginning of 1944. The United States alone was spending money at the rate of $276,000,000 a day.

If the pre-war costs made necessary by the rise of Hitler are added in, the figures become astronomical. Since July 1940, the United States Congress has appropriated $350,000,000,000 for war, or at the rate of thirteen times the cost of World War I. The outlay for the United Kingdom in the way of indirect as well as direct military expenditures must be close to $200,000,000,000. The corresponding investment on the part of the Soviets was well over $400,000,000,000 by the beginning of 1944. Even Canada spent over $3,000,000,000 during that period.

Beyond these required expenditures there are unseen costs which virtually are measureless. We cannot replace, for example, the minerals from our soil which are now sent so freely to Europe and Asia in the shape of food products, plastics and other materials derived from agriculture. In Western Russia the work of an entire generation has been blown into heaps of junk. Destruction to greater or less degree has taken place in almost every one of the European countries, throughout the South Seas, Africa, Asia, and, presumably before the struggle finally comes to an end, Japan.

If the all-over global cost of World War II in the destruction of property, stoppage of production, and money spent for armaments, were added together, the figure would spiral close to the fabulous sum of $2,000,000,000,000.

Warfare no longer possesses even the ideals and chivalry which once added a certain luster to the profession of arms, attracting energetic and adventurous men when hand-to-hand combat was the rule. Wars are not decided by such incidents as the wild dash of Marshal Ney's cavalry at Waterloo. The courtly punctiliousness which caused Gustavus Adolphus to send a trumpeter to challenge Tilly and his army on the fields of Breitenfeld before the battle was joined,[1] now appears ridiculous. So does the immortal comedy of Fontenoy where the gallant invitation was extended: "Gentlemen of France, fire first." [2]

Today attack is based on the tactics of treachery and overwhelming military advantage. The strategy is apt to be one of a surprise transition from peace to war in an effort to deal the enemy a lethal blow while he still is off guard. With the exception of the rapidly passing dog-fight stage of air combat, the picture has changed to one of heavy long-range demolition machinery, supply lines and competing propaganda offices. Warfare has descended to a grubby and barbarous business concerned with the employment of great contending masses of proletarian robots who in the main never see each other, or who may not be in the fighting forces at all but regimented behind the lines into great producing collectives. As far as the science of murder, rapine and plunder can be said to have deteriorated, it has lost whatever dignity and romance that once adhered to it.

II

A study of these facts should convince anyone of the need for a world structure capable of preserving the peace. The question is, of course, what kind of structure—and how is it to be achieved?

In the crystal globe in which man sees his future written, the longing for some strong and paternal authority which will end this senseless turmoil forever, is vividly though briefly etched. In this moment of immeasurable pain and misery man sees in a blinding flash of intuition the road he must take if he is to fulfill his destiny. He sees that eventually there will have to be one State—the World, and one race—Man.

1 1631.
2 Capt. B. H. Liddell Hart, *Great Captains Unveiled*, p. 102.

At that time the doctrines of race and class and nation, as we know them, will disappear. They will be outmoded, not by virtue of some new and irresistible nobility and morality, but because, as concepts, they will no longer serve the interests of man.

The only things which will matter will be intelligence, health, strength and utility. Man will turn his attention to the great inanimate universe around him, and from its illimitable wealth will seek to create a new golden age of universal culture and happiness to last until this planet grows old and shrunken in its orbit and can no longer support human life.

It is this superb destiny which mankind in the far and unpredictable future must inherit and make its own.

But that time is not now. It has been only some five thousand years since the first small tribal groups emerged from the gloom and anonymity of their forests and mountain caves to construct the first rude cities and begin the course of human progress in the valleys of the Indus, the Euphrates and the Nile. It was not more than eight hundred years ago that the races of Northern Europe found their savage beginnings modified by conversion to the universal creed of Christ, thus entering for the first time the stream of history.

It is clear that peace cannot be organized by lofty phrases written into the international statute books, nor the hidden causes of war removed by outlawing them in a legal document. It will not be sufficient to create an international police force or to bring into existence world courts. Superficial adjustments in the way of peace treaties or constitutional devices will prove brittle and unavailing as long as they bear on the problems which confront us but do not liquidate them.

It seems equally certain that society as it now exists has failed and that it is no longer capable of functioning within its present political and social boundaries.

If a workable solution cannot be found for this dangerous dilemma, it is evident that mankind will be projected into other and still more terrible conflicts. These are no longer obscure, but are measurable and may be predicted with certainty.

If in this constantly changing and explosive situation humanity is not to be exposed to newer and constantly mounting dangers, the nature of the essential problem which confronts society must be understood. That problem is a complicated one with a myriad of complex cross-currents adding to the difficulties of resolving it into simple terms. It has to do with the realities, pressures, hungers and prejudices of life as well as with its ideals. It cannot be dis-associated from the revolutionary character of the times, and the altering picture of the instruments of power and the techniques by which it is maintained. In short, the machinery of peace must be concerned directly with what is going on in the world and with the controls by which human life is galvanized and directed.

In general, one can say that the problem which will face our peacemakers has little to do with the claims and counter-claims of the political organisms we know today as sovereign States. Neither is it decisively anchored in the so-called struggle between Fascism, Communism and Democracy. As long as we conceive of the present war in terms of a mere perfidious attack on Pearl Harbor dictated by the militarist element of Japan, or as an effort by Germany to acquire territory or to evade the strictures of the Versailles Treaty, we can have no adequate idea of the titanic forces which actually are at work.

Under examination it will be seen that the central problem of our civilization is not the problem of capital and labor, nor of national boundaries, religion, adventurous ambition, or competitive finance. The question is the far more fundamental one of adjusting the aging political and social forms of society to its new economic and industrial needs.

The conquest which will have the most decisive bearing on the affairs of men will not be of some nation at arms, but of science. The revolution in living habits which has sprung from the test tube, the microscope, the laboratory and the drafting board will induce a conforming revolution in economic procedures and political institutions. The violent disturbances which have resulted from the scientific and technical achievements of this century and which are altering the entire equilibrium of existing power facts, form the central reality of today.

The chronicle of the present era is one of convulsive and sweeping adjustments on the part of both man and his institutions to the new tempo and conditions of life. The radical demands these have placed on the constitution and nature of organized community life are greater in extent than those which would have been evolved normally during entire millenia.

In a century man has advanced farther along the path of material evolution than he has in five thousand years of written history. The problem of peace bears an immediate identification with this fact. It must remain a completely unanswerable riddle unless the contemplated solution succeeds in adjusting the emotional and political outlook of man to the new world of mass production, air transport, electronics and technological wizardry.

If, for example, we were to think in terms of reconstituting the politically independent States of Europe, or of recovering Burma for the British colonial system, or the Dutch East Indies for Queen Wilhelmina, we would find ourselves, like the Bourbons and the exiled White Russian aristocracy, dedicated to the failing past. These obsolete political systems will not be able to function in relation to the new technology or the altered economic structure of the world. They are not evil and undesirable—they are simply meaningless. They bear no relation to modern military facts, to the movement, production and marketing of goods, or to the existence of resources required for the welfare of their citizens.

We are compelled to recognize that power factors which were perfectly rational in their time are now anachronisms, and that situations which were altogether reasonable yesterday will be fantastic tomorrow. The day is past when a small island kingdom can control the commerce and political destiny of the world by possession of half a dozen key gateways between the seas. Comparatively small nations such as Belgium, Holland, France and Italy never will be able to occupy as disproportionate a share of the world's wealth and influence as they have in the past. Their places will be taken by tremendous national entities with illimitable resources, such as China, India, Brazil and the Soviet Union.

We cannot enter into a contemplation of permanent peace conditions until it is realized that all social aggregates are shifting and realigning themselves to conform to the new realities. It is with these realities alone that any enduring peace can be concerned.

The circumstances are sufficiently grave to warrant a forthright analysis of all the facts and questions involved. Instead of approaching these gingerly and handling them by diplomatic suggestion, we should start calling things by their right names.

III

It is useless to ignore the revolutionary nature of this conflict by pointing to the numberless wars which have afflicted the human race throughout time. If during these centuries civilization did not collapse completely due to the general lawlessness, it was because of the lack of instruments which made global control possible. Today, modern technology has shrunk the world to manageable proportions. We are all locked together in the same small room and no longer can escape the consequence of each other's existence.

What is destined to succeed the present fluid stage will depend upon the wisdom and resource with which we move to create the future. If we do not do so consciously and by plan, the march of the Caesars is as inevitable tomorrow as were the Middle Ages when the flame of Roman civilization, having drawn on its last resources, began to splutter in the winds of destiny.

If we cannot create government capable of adjusting itself to the complexities of the industrial revolution, the mechanization of life will destroy us. It will place at the disposal of dictators the methods by which all humanity may be controlled, and will reduce men to faceless serfs whose bodies and souls alike will be coordinated in the future blueprints of managerial masters.

The new age of light metals, of chemicals, of swift communications, of breath-taking discoveries, of managerial competence, lends itself favorably to bureaucracy. Discovery and invention facilitate this drift. The mercantile era with its system of free enterprise and its separate principles of political rule and independent control of capital has found itself in fundamental conflict with the mechanics on which modern civilization depends. The money power symbolized by such outstanding figures as Jay Gould and J. Pierpont Morgan has tended to decrease in influence and become unimportant. In the place of the free capitalist is the anonymous corporation with its many stockholders, its close supervision by government, and its rule by all-powerful executives.

The rise of this system of industrial managers has seen a coincident rise of horizontal labor unions. The consequence has been to force the Government itself to become a partner, tending to regulate increasingly both industry and the conditions of labor. Thus a tri-cornered competition has ensued between management, labor, and government, each covertly seeking to merge the powers of the triumvirate into its own hands.

In one guise or another we see the familiar drive toward authoritarian rule, and the irresistible emergence of a society ruled by the efficiencies of the machine. In this phase the rights of man no longer appear to count. They do not seem to be an asset as they were in the essentially mercantile and rural world of two hundred years ago. They do not serve to maintain the efficiency of the central power form. The more logical and able the officials charged with the handling of modern social problems, the more impatient they grow with what appear to them to be intolerable obstacles in the path of progress.

Thus, authoritarian enterprise finds its way ready-made everywhere. The inconsistencies, the contradictions, the irreconcilable divergencies which distinguish the present decade from the classic forms and traditions which previously regulated human existence, are forcing entirely new conceptions on the world, giving rise to new drives, new demands, new desires and new loyalties. Out of this matrix new political configurations are bound to take shape and new legitimacies rapidly form, to take the place of old institutions which are dissolving themselves.

This is a gigantic international revolution, which to more or less degree affects all nations. It is the outgrowth of inexorable forces which, for good or bad, are at work and no longer can be stamped back into the old molds.

The new age of social organization can come about in one of two ways. One is by a succession of explosions which gain force as repression is applied to them, and which will succeed finally in blowing the lid off the kettle and splattering it in pieces against the walls and ceiling of civilization. The second, and most improbable, will be the application of wisdom to the affairs of men in this crisis.

When historians of future millennia peer back into the history of our time as those of today pore over the chronologies of fabled Babylon and Egypt, it may be written that World War II was the second phase in a trinity of mighty struggles which marked the end of a fragmentary world divided by oceans, mountains and river barriers, and the beginning of a totally new concept of society.

In this respect it is difficult to pierce the black veil of the future with prophecy. Who in the middle of the Eighteenth Century would have dared to predict the industrial revolution and its concomitants, the airplane, the motion picture, the radio tube and the totalitarian horde? Or who could have ventured to foretell during the bright day of Carthaginian greatness that in time to come the Bedouin would herd his goats in the noble ruins of the temples of Astarte! It is conceivable that Europe, sickened of all forms of authoritarian control, may reject the Russian type as well as the German, and may swing back in a wide arc to still other and newer kinds of revolutionary society.

It is certain that from any dislocation as great as that which now afflicts the world, new principles will arise to struggle with the old, which will become relegated to history as archaic and false. The views of such men as Trotsky might find a mass following. Even more certain of popular support in some countries will be the doctrines of political anarchism and syndicalism which will seek the abolition of centralized government as coercive, as well as the liquidation of the privileged classes.

This possibility may appear fantastic but it is no more so than the eagerness with which collectivization theories which were looked on with unconcealed contempt less than a generation ago, are now accepted by whole sections of the population. In pre-war France the Syndicates had several hundred thousand members. In Spain, among the Catalonian Loyalists in particular, they were actually a political power. In Northern Italy there is every indication that only military repression keeps them under control.

These ideas could grow with astounding rapidity as a reaction to the failures of totalitarianism unless a better order immediately is provided as an alternative.

In this tragic hour there is no flaming figure around whom humanity may gather; no Moses, or saintly Jesus or inspired Napoleon. There is only a Churchill with a rare gift of phrase and an obsession with traditional British power politics; a Roosevelt who must please many diverse and straining factors to assure the future acceptance of his policies; a Stalin who sits like a gnome in the midst of his own faraway world; and a Chiang K'ai-shek in whom the pulse of glory is just beginning to beat. Who else? Beneš, a great man who unfortunately represents nothing in the way of power and has no color? Eden who is the very epitome of mercantile psychology and diplomatic acuteness? Willkie, a noble man without a State to back him? Or De Gaulle, an impassioned patriot and great general without an army? None of these can attain universal leadership enabling him to hold and form the surging revolutionary forces which are moving to make a new world—the world of tomorrow.

IV

It should be accepted as axiomatic that there are no problems on earth which cannot be solved if the proper willingness and skill are applied to them. The key to their solution lies in an exact understanding of the nature of the problem, plus a willingness to regroup the facts of today in those known terms toward which the future is driving.

If the gentlemen of the chancelleries, the state departments and the foreign offices are to settle these questions on a sane basis, they will have to draw on their last resources of courage, sagacity, tolerance and insight. They will have to dispose of the essential contradictions which today disfigure human relationships. They will have to understand that not a thousand treaties nor a million declarations of faith—such as those contained in the Atlantic Charter—will have the slightest effect on the ultimate sequence of events.

It will be necessary for them to weigh many questions and abandon many national conceits. There will have to be much give and take based on that implicit understanding, rare in men, that the world changes and that power forces in particular are not static but compounded of illimitable and resurgent dynamisms.

They will be compelled to study many questions to determine the inner practicalities, viewing them anthropologically, socially and economically, as well as by the historic facts of convention and geography, if they are to come to any sort of reasoned and workable conclusion.

It will be necessary for them to reach behind the curtain of official explanations to search in German and Japanese history, living space, personality and social organization for the real causes of the present conflict. Otherwise the entire pattern of thought and scheme of operation which actuates these peoples will be hidden from their eyes, and the world will be victimized again by a peace which will be but an interlude between two wars.

The peacemakers will need to estimate the differing levels of industrial and political competence of the various States, their position in space, their numbers, the quality of their leadership, the national tradition, appetite and will, their collective hatreds, frustrations, and the quality, quantity and situation of the human element out of which the national body is composed.

To these estimates must be added the need for creating a balanced world economy which will allow the participation of all States, relieving their population pressures, satisfying the expansion of their industry as well as the need for raw materials and markets.

In this most difficult of situations, requiring the shrewdest discernment and the most indomitable will to act, the terrible certainty exists that the captains and rulers of the world will be governed entirely by the hope of saving their present regimes intact. When the immediate crisis is over they will tend to look at all plans for effective world reorganization as being so many crackpot dreams advanced by unrealistic and dangerous men. Long before the peace meetings have been officially convened they will have juggled the fate of millions of men and scores of nations, which under the appraisal of their cold eyes will have been robbed of humanity and pulse and have become impersonal markers in the ancient game of statecraft.

It will be this precarious and insecure result which will be offered to the world in a suffusion of highly colored words as a lasting peace.

Just as after the last war, we are entering into a stage of society in which the lack of courage and vision of the peacemakers will be covered by a cloak of beautiful phrases and illusive hopes. The first flush of idealism will be over. Though prepared earnestly to seek an end to these shooting scrapes, the Western peoples will be tired, and consumed by that utter weariness of spirit which will prevent them from taking the one last brave step forward which could insure it.

At that moment, the peoples will see transcendent beauty in the tiresome pronouncements of statesmen who are entirely wanting in inspiration and humanity, who are incapable of looking beyond the immediate vested interests of their States, and who have no more real conception of the kind of world humanity will live in tomorrow than a fly has of the planet Mars. They will be typical in type of the uninspired military technicians who labelled General Billy Mitchell a wild visionary, or the suspicious French academicians who coldly disposed of Pasteur's wonderful discovery as a fraud.

It is always the conservative, aging mind which finds recourse in the petty wisdom provided by experience, and which is unable to see the gigantic revolutionary changes which are even now convulsing the fabric of society.

One observes this melancholy truth in all the crises of history. We see the Czarina and her court preoccupied with the question of Rasputin, as if that were the principal question, at the very moment when the earth was shaking under the feet of all the Russias. It was the same when Hanno debated nonsense among his peers at Carthage and prevented the immortal Hannibal from receiving those supplies and reinforcements which would have altered the entire course of history. It was the same when the shaggy Mongol conquerors fell like a blight on the proud and seemingly invincible Chinese civilization whose scholars had "proved" to a mathematical certainty that such a result was impossible.

It was the same at Versailles and it will be the same again; always the same lack of foresight, the same play for advantage and the same application of poverty-stricken wisdom. Civilization appears never to have the genius and good sense voluntarily to undertake the new terms in which its future is being written, or to grasp the new pattern of power by which events unfailingly must be dictated. It is always the traditional and conservative, the failing and the aging, which prevails and which in a moment of great human weariness passes under the banner of prudence and sagacity.

There must be in the United States at the present time more than a thousand organizations concerned with various panaceas which will allow a peaceful postwar settlement with a minimum of disturbance to the political forms and economic interests which now exist. Some of these, like the conservative banking and clerical bodies which supported the Fascists throughout Europe in the hope of creating a bulwark against impending change, simply would succeed in creating counter-revolutionary explosions infinitely more terrible than the dangers they were originally designed to circumvent. Others are based on various political schemes and social doctrines, and still others on scholastic dogma. Such panaceas as education are advanced by some thinkers as the universal solvent for all ills. Others believe confidently in the remedy which, would be provided by the cooperative State.

In regard to these beliefs, it is only necessary to point out that the personification of the mechanized and material State was the Republic of Germany. Here was the socialized State with the best educational facilities and most highly developed industry in Europe, which nevertheless turned savagely on the world in an orgy of lust and conquest.

In the general view toward panaceas it may not easily be forgotten that the nationalist movements of the last century were once esteemed to be the hope of the world. They proved instead to be the womb in which racialism was born. Though it was the French Revolution which created the urge for unification among the German States, it remained for the Prussian armies to realize this ideal and to pervert it to their own peculiar psychology. It was only yesterday that the world of free men applauded the passionate dreams of *Italia irredenta,* and watched with eager eyes the entry of Garibaldi at the head of his revolutionary troops into the Holy City of Rome, applauded Kocziusko, or suffered with the nationalist dreamers of the German States who were resisting Napoleon's domination. Today when nationalism is at last triumphant it stands itself revealed as a bloody threat to the entire structure of civilization.

None of these ideas are proof against war since they are incapable of remedying the fundamental conditions from which military struggle arises. The mere act of concentration of power, as in the case of the Welfare State, may not destroy the liability to conflict but may strongly increase it.

The possibility of war, as we shall see, depends on opportunity, profit, human needs and on an increase in those psychological abrasions which are the outcome of continued maladjustments. The actual predisposing cause to aggression may be pure temptation and the opportunity for quick victory. It may be long continued race hatred stimulated by the violent cries of demagogues, or the desperate need for food, markets, natural resources or room to live. Irrespective of social convictions, war will be the inevitable consequence of the attempt by an antiquated political economy to maintain itself in an age which has long since outgrown it.

Until the social and political adjustments demanded by the machine age are complete these doctrinaire schemes can have little effect on the ultimate outcome.

There are still other political designs which have an appearance on the surface of great plausibility. We find one well-known and lovable public figure speaking of "one world" which presumably would be a politically united world. He does not, however, indicate how the seemingly impossible mechanics of such a project can be blueprinted. Still another calls for a world of regions surmounted by a reinforced League of Nations with teeth in it. This solution runs headlong into the sovereign nature of the State itself, which cannot occupy any intermediate status, and is compelled either to exist as an independent power form, or be relegated to a provincial status in some larger empire.

Another influential figure urges on the nation an alliance with Russia, Britain and China, despite the fact that the entire power relationship has changed due to the airplane and modern machine industry; that consequently Britain is no longer mistress of either the counting-houses or the seas, and an alliance with her would ultimately drag us into wars all over the earth; or that the same factors which have metamorphosed Russia and will do the same for China, have developed fundamental conflicts of interests between those nations and ourselves. In the coming decades the relationship will no longer be one of two backward, agrarian Nations to an enlightened industrial State, but rather of two expanding and aggressive industrial States to a third which may be past its peak and which rejects issues, essential to the two, such as race equality and the classless society.

V

All of the Western nations will face vast and perhaps desperate internal problems connected with the process of demobilization of both industry and men. This dangerous transition phase will further be complicated by the acknowledged stresses straining the aging mercantile capitalist structure, whose remaining degree of resiliency is an open question.

Everywhere mankind is restless. It has been inured to the belief that force is the final expression of logic and the final instrument of political action. Our boys will come roaring home as the mightiest power in our Republic. They will have been exposed to the political radicalism of a fermenting Europe and Asia, as well as to the schemes of native demagogues. They will be impatient, vaguely radical, and half of the opinion that self-seeking politicians, plutocrats and labor leaders have taken advantage of the wartime situation for their own benefit.

It seems plain that men in the Western World no longer believe in the slogans which are engraved on their banners. The old claims of liberty and democracy hold few illusions for them. They do not fight with the passion of belief, but only to save themselves from the consequences of defeat, viewing the future with unconcealed misgivings and cynicism. They indeed see none of the basic questions confronting our nation settled as a result of the present war. They observe, instead, a deepening of these fundamental conflicts rather than their disappearance.

Western men observe a world hopelessly divided against itself, occupied by races, individuals, cults and nations all of different levels of civilization, understanding and wealth. They observe in the peoples most responsible for bringing humanity to its present stage of culture a singular neuroticism, a growing apathy and cynicism toward the entire body of principles on which Western civilization has been based.

They see class and race, as well as nations, turned against each other in a savage and unrelenting civil war. They see a wave of radicalism, intolerant of ethics, capitalist and parliamentary system alike, rapidly rising among all classes of the population.

They see a far-reaching breakdown in all social relationships everywhere. They observe a brittle and dangerous struggle rising between unregenerate capital making a final, determined, last ditch stand, and great amorphous labor unions concerned primarily with their own welfare. They view with concern the problems created by the vastly increased production of our industrial plant as well as the competition which will be provided by other States which are just coming out of the agricultural into the industrial age, and which our arms will have helped to free.

They observe that at a certain point the body of contradictions and inconsistencies with which society is burdened can only be expurged by sweeping away the entire superstructure which contains them.

They see that Europe, mother of Western civilization, has been permanently weakened as a result of the two ferocious wars imposed on her by Germany—that Europe is no longer mistress of the world and may be culturally as well as materially bankrupt.

They observe that no plan for the postwar organization of the world possibly can be conceived without reference to the forces unleashed by the Axis efforts to dominate the globe. In addition to the destruction of physical property there will have been the liquidation of whole traditional ruling classes and the demoralization of cultural forces which have been painstakingly erected by centuries of human effort. One of the consequences of the German and Japanese efforts to impose their New Order will be a sweeping revision of institutions, concepts and views which have stood the test of centuries.

The shattering of the *ancien régime* will have resulted in the complete reorganization of the Continent's economic life on regional rather than national lines. Economic Europe will not easily be broken down and regrouped again.

Europe has been melted down in fire and recast from a new mold. Its old institutions and traditions have been smashed beyond recognition. The effect will be far more radical than that which attended the appearance and departure of Bonaparte from the stage of history. Though the little Corsican finally was defeated at Waterloo, the decisive result of the crushing victories of his armies over the old feudal system was never to be undone. Feudal Europe was dead forever.

Western men view with deep skepticism the lofty professions contained in the Atlantic Charter. They wonder if it is our intention to impose constitutional government upon the world, and how we intend to do so in relation to Russia, or for that matter, Greece, Portugal and Brazil. They wonder what we intend to do about India and China.

They wonder what we are going to do about Germany, about Europe, about the vast colonial systems of Britain, France and Holland from whose continued existence they can see nothing but ceaseless embroilment, tumult and disturbance for the next generation.

Above all, they do not wish to fight another war. They believe that the illustrious age through which we have passed is dying before their eyes and will soon be part of the obscuring haze of history. The phrases which dignified it—"Freedom," "Democracy," "Fraternity," "Equality"—are fading into empty words robbed of the human will and experience which gave them vitality. Today these ideas have lost their inward meaning. They are no longer stalwart principles throbbing with life, part of the essential nature of social existence, and seem to bear no real relation to the problems posed by modern industrial concentration and sociological complexity.

Everywhere, Western man sees civilization in travail and apprehends that the present disequilibrium could as easily end in a new and universal dark age as in a golden period of prosperity and culture.

Western man surveys with frank misgiving the major political questions provided by Germany, Japan, Russia and the Orient, and sees no answer to any of them.

A century ago Japan was a little feudal kingdom of no consequence in the world and seemingly in imminent danger of being added to the colonial spoils of Europe. By 1943 she had become the hub of a vast empire and openly flaunted her intention to rule the earth.

A generation ago the German Reich was a defeated and disillusioned nation, deprived of its arms, subject to huge reparations with which to pay the cost of the war it had imposed on the world, and staggering under an internal social problem which seemed to threaten it with dissolution. By 1941 Germany had succeeded in rising again for the third time in a century. Smashing with ridiculous ease through the walls which had been carefully erected to contain her, the Reich consumed almost all Europe to the gates of Moscow before her course of conquest was halted.

What view shall we take, operating as sensible men determined to acquit ourselves with solid reason as well as decency, toward these avowedly predacious States? Both the Nazi and Japanese movements are revolutionary developments peculiar to this century and rising directly out of its character. Their programs are made possible by the tools which industrial maturity has made available. Merely to carve these States up or to saddle them with reparations will accomplish nothing.

It seems clear that in the hands of a highly industrialized people such as the Germans, the forfeiting of arms no longer means the automatic imposition of peace. Quite the contrary. Though they give up their weapons and melt down the dies and presses with which these are made, the possession of basic heavy industry would enable the Germans on the briefest of notice to create new and improved methods of military manufacture and, presumably, the altered concepts of strategy which go with them.

If there is revolution in a weakened and destroyed Europe, will not Germany once more seize the reins and stand poised again for another attempt at world rule? If we allow the Reich to be absorbed by Russia, will not Russia proceed to roll irresistibly over all Europe, facing us with the nightmarish possibility of an all-powerful revolutionary State on our very northern boundaries in the new round world of the air age?

If traditional Slavic phlegm disinclines the Russians to move, is there not the possibility that the German enzymes might promptly digest the more impassive Slavic mass rather than the other way

around? In such an amalgam, the Germans immediately would possess an unlimited field of operation, which would allow them to
continue onward in their march to power essentially unopposed.

The potential quarrel of the West with Soviet Russia is based on
our instinctive dislike and suspicion of what we regard as an actively
subversive political creed aimed at the final ruin of our institutions.
When the truce which is based on the present emergency is done,
the open, naked conflict of psychological and economic warfare will
replace the present quiescent tensions.

Added to these intrinsic discordancies is the disturbing fact that
the balance of industrial power is shifting to cheap labor countries
with whom we will have great difficulty in competing. Soviet Russia,
once an important world market, is rapidly becoming self-sustaining. At some future period when faced with the problem of her own
surpluses she may be expected to enter the world markets as an
aggressive competitor.

The same soon will be true of China and perhaps India. The
Argentine, Brazil and South Africa, with cheap labor and power
sources, are certain to become formidable industrial rivals within
the coming decade.

The tide of the future also would seem to be carrying us directly
into conflict with the great surging masses of Asia whose emergence
as a fundamental power form will be one of the leading phenomena
of this century.

The so-called unchanging East is changing before our eyes and
no longer may be safely ignored. It has already disposed of the myth
of white superiority and is reaching out like some great lumbering
giant vaguely aware of the irresistible nature of his strength, for
social and industrial equality and for elbow room.

More terrifying still to the prejudices of the Western states,
the East is demanding free movement—the right to move around the
world and to occupy its favored spaces. This development is the
most significant fact of the present generation and presages a thrust
for power which completely would alter the character and history
of the world.

In the vast contradiction of logic to which we are committed we will continue to subject the peoples of Asia to the stigma of social inferiority while at the same time setting them up as competitors by assisting them in the creation of centralized forms of government, as well as heavy industry. Our quarrel with this billion or more people is one, as we shall see, of racial exclusiveness, which cannot be contained within the confines of the future peace since it merges with problems of migration, free movement, economics, natural resources and human pride.

Against the huge regeneration of the East, the scarecrow of armed colonial power will not serve. The East can be repressed only by total and continuous war, a type of peace by power which would require all of our forces and at least the tacit consent of the Soviet Union.

The central question in whatever variant or guise it appears is this: can civilization survive the radically changed conditions brought about by the machine age, without a series of violent and bloody upheavals which will leave the world finally a shambles, and perhaps put an end to the white race?

This dreadful question can be settled only by an act of courage and nobility of which Western civilization has given little indication.

If our peacemakers are to think in terms of a sane post-war world, obliterating the circumstances which have led to the havoc of war in the past and threaten to do so in even more terrible form in the future, they cannot shrink from the radical·action such a cure would necessitate.

The belief that we can secure peace and prosperity by not earning it, or through the intercession of magical methods, is a tragic delusion. It results in half-measures which throw a concealing veil over the realities, but do not change them. Soothing syrups doped with minor concessions will not tranquilize or subdue the situation. They will only put off the day of reckoning, when open furious warfare will burst forth once again on a scale hitherto unprecedented.

If we temporize on this question without settling it, or attempt to cover its ugliness with a camouflage of worthless treaties and agreements, we shall place ourselves in the greatest eventual jeopardy. We will buy a precarious peace for a few short disturbed years as did Chamberlain and Daladier at Munich. Then the heavens will fall.

A century and a half ago, an American legislator stood in his homespun clothes before the Continental Congress. Evidently inspired by the words of the prophet Jeremiah,[1] he declared in his cool, clear voice:

"Mr. President, it is natural to man to indulge in the illusions of hope. We are apt to shut our eyes against the painful truth and listen to the song of that syren till she transforms us into beasts. Is this the part of wise men engaged in a great and arduous struggle for liberty? Are we disposed to be of the number of those who having eyes see not, and having ears hear not the things which so nearly concern their temporal salvation?

"For my part, whatever anguish of spirit it may cost, I am willing to know the whole truth, to know the worst and provide for it . . . It is in vain, sir, to extenuate the matter. The gentlemen may cry Peace! Peace! But there is no peace! . . ."

This somber warning delivered by Patrick Henry of Virginia to his peers of the Second Revolutionary Convention on March 23, 1775, applies by reference today with unabated power. The gentlemen may proclaim peace; they may shout it from the housetops; they may sanctify their deliberations by all the holy rites of diplomatic convention. It will be in vain. Until we know the whole truth and provide for it, there will be no peace, but only the shattered promise of one.

1 "But, behold, the false pen of the scribes hath wrought falsely . . . from the prophet even unto the priest everyone dealeth falsely. And they have healed the hurt of the daughter of my people slightly, saying, Peace, peace; when there is no peace." Jeremiah 8: 8-11.

II

THE MARCH TO GLOBAL WAR

WAR represents simply the application of unlimited force to the settlement of questions which may not be favorably determined by other means. The use of cannon and shot as an argument in settling problems is the ultimate political means by which the organized State achieves its objective.

This process involves recognized rights which accrue to the State by virtue of its sovereignty. The principles of conduct which govern it are considered to be a normal result of the intercourse of States with each other.

There is no element of condemnation involved as would be the case where an individual citizen brings on himself the wrath of society because of some shameful misconduct. The impropriety has not been in fact to fight a war, but to lose one.

These are circumstances which must be understood before any of the problems affecting war and peace can be seen in their proper relationship.

Men have fought each other for every conceivable purpose and reason, ranging from a simple quest for wives as in the Rape of the Sabine Women, ambition as in the case of Alexander, religion as in the wars of the Protestants, Catholics, and Mohammedans, or for the sake of pure deviltry and plunder as in the case of Timur the Lame, or the Mongol, Temuljin, who was called Ghengiz Khan. There have been bloody conflicts involving the question of the divine right of kings, social philosophies, trade routes, water holes, markets and sources of raw materials.

There has been in fact hardly a question in human history in which one side or the other has not finally had recourse to violence.

There is, therefore, nothing unique in the effort by the Germans and Japanese to impose their will on the world. The uniqueness lies only in the fact that it was we who were the projected victims; the consequent disturbances which have overtaken our way of life, the serious losses we have sustained in property and men, and the dread foreboding that despite impending victory this is not the end, but only prolegomena for other and still more terrible conflicts to come.

There is no hope of establishing an enduring foundation for peace without a clear understanding of the nature of modern wars and, in particular, the antecedents of the present one. Conventional peace means, such as treaties and agreements between the existing States, will not suffice unless there is a definition of causes, and of the nature of power as it applies to the means by which States make war on each other.

Much of the genesis of the present conflict will be found in the revolutionary character of our times. This feature will be referr d to at length later as part of the world-wide earthquake of change proceeding from the industrial revolution. What we shall consider for the moment are the political events in which the present war is rooted, and the character of the two States, Germany and Japan, immediately responsible for bringing it about.

II

During the days of Rome, Europe had been an orderly empire bordered by the sands of the Sahara on the south and an equally mysterious barbarian fringe on the north. On the east it was separated from the collective *terra incognita* by mountain ranges, deserts and fearsomely arid plateaus.

The fall of Rome split Europe up into many contending segments which alternately swelled, grew and contracted, fed on each other, and were fed on in turn. Little States like Holland, Austria,

Prussia and Sweden alternately became powers to be reckoned with, and grew small again. Under the first Bonaparte, France threatened to become a universal State and as rapidly subsided. The Sublime Porte reached its long arm almost to the gates of Vienna, then slowly disintegrated. Poland expanded and contracted like an accordion. A myriad of States whose names are now forgotten came and went as the European map kept changing with dizzying rapidity.

The little island kingdom of Britain which once had its hands full in occupying Scotland, Ireland and Wales, finally found the key to world power. This discovery was symbolized by Britain's ability to attain complete control of the narrow channel of water which separated her green island from Europe.

A host of Goliaths rose to challenge her—Spain, France, Russia, Prussia, Austria, Holland and, in this century, Germany. They all left off, baffled by the slender moat of sea which protected the castled might of their doughty adversary.

Here was a phenomenon unique in military annals—a comparatively weak island which could not be conquered from a strong adjacent continent; and a continent split into innumerable fragments engaged in an almost continuous cycle of armed adventure against each other, yet which could not be consolidated by the strongest of these Powers into a single empire as had been the case when Europe was ruled by Rome.

The invention of superior weapons had in the beginning contributed much to this strange situation, making it possible for the determined burghers and shepherds of the Swiss Alps to hold back great armies, or for the people of the Lowlands successfully to challenge, first Spain, then Austria, then France. It was not until the power of weapons was matched by the power of communications that the reverse tendency of consolidation into larger spatial groupings became visible.

This continual kaleidoscopic reshuffling of States seeking final supremacy brought into being a policy which came to be known as the Balance of Power system.

The balance wheel in this arrangement was Great Britain. The apparatus itself was designed to protect her naval supremacy and with it the great trade routes by which her far-flung empire was held together.

Where in the past the peace had been kept by the vast inertias of distance, or by the resistless legions of some Caesar, the principal concern of British policy was to weigh the balance against the strongest nation on the continent of Europe and thus prevent it from acquiring dominance.

This system of power politics became significant as the most potent guarantor of peace as well as the major cause of wars.

The great fault in the balance of power theory was the existence of such a multitude of complex and changing factors as to make the balance extremely difficult to weigh. Always at some point it has proved sufficiently inexact as to offer irresistible temptation to one of the parties. This was the case in 1914 and again in 1939 when the German Reich decided that the balance was sufficiently in its favor to risk a war.

It was this instrument of policy which made Great Britain the automatic enemy of every ambitious Power on the Continent, of Alexander I of Russia, of Louis XIV of France, of Napoleon, of the German Kaiser, and now of Adolf Hitler. A whole series of wars based on shifting coalitions and alliances was fought to keep it intact. To the makeshift treaties, expedients and accommodations aimed at preventing the Continent from falling under the hand of a single strong ruler, the present world war can be traced.

We see the shifting uncertainties of this crotchety equipoise running like a crimson thread through the entire registry of European wars, from the Treaty of Utrecht in 1713 which provided that the Spanish and French thrones should never be united, to the Treaty of Versailles which interdicted the *Anschluss* of Austria and Germany. The Treaties of Baden, of Aix-la-Chapelle, of Berlin and Vienna, all were proof that no absolute balance could ever be established. England became the traditional champion of the weak and also of turmoil—all in the interests of that peace she so desperately needed to enjoy the fruits of her vast acquisitions the world over.

This attempt to maintain a permanent equilibrium in an inherently fluid and unstable situation had the effect of keeping Europe in a state of embroilment and dissension long after it was ripe for unity.

At the Congress of Vienna in 1814-15 and in the Berlin Congress of 1878, the global explosion known as World War I was made inevitable. This first of the great global struggles was the direct outgrowth of the political ferment brewed by a two-hundred-year application of the balance of power principle.

The immediate tinder-box of trouble was the Balkans which were just beginning to slip out of the clutch of dying Turkey. They were a seething hotbed of conflicting hopes, hatreds and ambitions in which both the Hapsburgs and the Hohenzollerns on the one hand, and the Romanoffs on the other, saw an extension of their primary interests. The Balkans were the gateway to the lush East which Britain jealously guarded as its own particular sphere of interest. The great peninsula fronted on warm water. It possessed important mineral and agricultural, as well as strategic, assets.

With the breakdown of the Sultan's power the upper half of Ottoman Europe consisting of Hungary, Transylvania, Bukowina, Northern Moldavia and part of Serbia, had by successive treaties been surrendered to Austria. The great White Czar appropriated the Black Sea coast as far as the Dniester, and after the Treaty of Bucharest in 1812 had reached out as far as the River Prut. A series of wars and patchwork treaties resulted. These for the most part were concerned with London's effort to prevent the Russians from achieving that historic goal of Slav ambition, the Dardanelles, and with it an outlet directly on the teeming traffic of the Mediterranean. To enforce this decision Britain became party to a series of coalitions, each of which led to another.

At various times in this game of shuttlecock, both Russia and Austria were forced to disgorge a portion of their gains but remained in the position of the Roman feasters who patronized the vomitarium only to return to the table hungrier than ever.

Within the Balkans themselves, a crazyquilt of conflicting exigencies, hopes and ambitions gradually raised a number of national States, Rumania, Bulgaria, Greece, Albania, Montenegro and Serbia, which contested with each other with an incessant and almost canine appetite.

Other areas without political independence developed bold revolutionary movements seeking it. Wallachia, Moldavia and Transylvania gave up the ghost finally, and disappeared from the world scene. Little Macedonia, divided between Greece, Serbia and Bulgaria for generations, provided the powder keg which threatened hourly to blow Europe into a shambles.

Between all of the little nations of the Balkans, bitterly disputed territory continued to change hands. To national minorities were added religious minorities. Roman and Greek Catholics as well as Mohammedans struggled and fought with each other for control.

It was in the midst of this rancor, hatred, ambition and suspicion that the Archduke Franz Ferdinand, heir apparent to the Hapsburg throne, was assassinated on June 28, 1914, in the Bosnian town of Sarajevo by a Serb patriot named Princeps.

This incident while the actual reason for World War I was not its principal cause. It coincided unfortunately with the German belief that the balance of power had tilted sufficiently in the Reich's favor to risk a showdown fight with her ancient Slavic enemies to the east as well as her rival for world commercial hegemony, Great Britain.

The major issue was the rapidly maturing industrial revolution which was making Germany the workshop of the Continent, and her rising ambitions, which centered in the Balkans though they embraced great areas in Asia and North Africa. The Reich already was permeated with the conviction that it was her destiny to become the chief Power of the world.

Within this planetary system of ripe antagonisms there existed other and serious counter-gravitational pulls. The difficult problems of the decaying Ottoman Empire carried over from the previous century, continued to show themselves in an Anglo-Russian rivalry which centered on Constantinople and the Straits. Britain also was anxious over Russian ambitions in Asia in the direction of India, Afghanistan and Persia.

The main question, however, centered in the aspirations of Berlin which slowly but certainly became the central issue.

Previous to the actual military outbreak, this silent tug-of-war had been on the point of breaking out into open struggle more than once. As early as 1896, Kaiser Wilhelm offered the implied suggestion in a cablegram to President Kruger of the Transvaal that if the Boers had appealed for help to the foreign Powers in their struggle with Britain they would have received it. However, nothing came of this incident. Germany was not ready, the Transvaal was far away, and the omnipotent British fleet lay watchfully between.

Again in 1906, Wilhelm sent a gunboat to the Moroccoan port of Agadir with a coincident message to the Sultan assuring that gentleman that any attempt to challenge him as "an absolutely independent sovereign" would be a *casus belli* for Germany. Since France and Spain had just intervened in the Sultan's dominions to quell alleged disorders there, this message was in the nature of a direct challenge.

Despite this defiance, Germany did not yet feel strong enough to carry through its bluff, and the partition of Morocco proceeded without any share being given to the Reich.

Germany's open truculence had succeeded in virtually isolating her. Her ambitions in Asia and North Africa had forced France and Japan into a working alliance. The alarmed English who felt their interests immediately threatened, were at pains to smooth out their troubles with Russia. Austria-Hungary was the only reliable friend Germany had on the Continent. Italy, the third member of the Triple Alliance, was regarded by its partners as a jackal posing as a wolf, whose assurances counted for nothing.

The entire program of Britain, France and Czarist Russia, the so-called democratic Allies, during World War I, was simply that of resisting German pretensions. The French statesman, Georges Clemenceau, admitted this aspect of the conflict quite frankly in his subsequent memoirs. It was only after the surrender of Russia and her withdrawal from the conflict that there had gradually unfolded around the Allies a grouping of elements striving for national restoration. "We had started as allies of the Russian oppressors of Poland with Polish soldiers of Silesia and Galicia fighting against us," wrote Clemenceau. "By the collapse of military Russia, Poland found herself suddenly set free and recreated, and then all over Europe oppressed peoples raised their heads and our war of national defense was transformed by force of events into a war of liberation." [1]

III

Though World War I was the springboard from which World War II was launched, the latter proceeded from a transmuted and not identical set of causes. It was again the unrequited ambitions and tormented appetite of the Germans which unloosed the Pandora's box of horrors on the world. This time war represented not the usual slugfest between conventional adversaries but the unlucky mischance of the coevality of a powerful predatory State and a revolutionary movement.

World War II represented the culmination of a process of organic failure on the part of European civilization. It was not only a war in the true sense but a revolution in human affairs, in which inflexible and determinative forces were pitted irreconcilably against each other. It was the end point in the blind alley in which the Western World finally had found itself.

Europe was no longer mistress of the world. In the East, Japanese military strength and economic power were swelling to formidable proportions. Across the ocean, the United States by mass produc-

[1] Georges Clemenceau, *Grandeur and Misery of Victory*, pp. 171-198.

tion methods had seized the industrial as well as financial hegemony of the globe.

The old principle of balance of power had settled into a pure figment with the United States instead of England the real balancer, but unwilling to function in the role history had assigned to her.

In Europe the dynastic empires had split into a number of national States. The ethnological conception took on exaggerated form and everywhere became increasingly pathological. The age of machine industry, of science and invention, lashed like a thundering and angry sea against the antique political framework of the Continent. The entire relationship of production to distribution, of city to countryside, of rulers to governed, began to flounder and show signs of impending failure. Beneath the conventional restraint of which the Old World still was capable, many confused, angry and disorderly forces jangled and elbowed each other in an effort to make adjustment to a situation which rapidly was becoming intolerable.

In the Czar's domains the most massive upheaval in history had swept out the old institutions with brutal thoroughness, so that nothing whatsoever remained of the old regime, neither its traditions nor its people. Russia became the focal point for tremendous, aggressive and universalist policies which were seeking to remake the world into completely new and unrecognizable shapes. In a speech on April 3, 1917, Lenin had roared: "The world revolution is at hand. The bourgeoisie are about to be overthrown in all lands. Comrade workers! Take the factories from your exploiters! Comrade peasants! Take the land from your enemies, the landowners!"

Italy was seething with strikes and was on the verge of violent social upheaval. In Hungary a Communist State came into existence but was overthrown by an invasion of Rumanian troops. The Far East was turning over uneasily in its sleep. Everywhere the established legitimacies were under decisive attack.

The traditional world was in a funk. Institutions which only yesterday were proud and imperious now appeared to be hollow, decayed and in querulous conflict with each other.

In Russia, the White Guard led by Denikin, Wrangel and Semenoff, and backed by the Western countries, was soundly beaten. Europe itself managed to breast the first convulsive impact of this storm without difficulty, but remained with the uneasy conviction that it had gained only a temporary respite. A terrible neurasthenia remained as a legacy of its grim ordeal, affecting all portions of the population.

The Continent became the prey of ambitious and masterless men, of passionate zealots, of strange prophets, demagogues and inspired lunatics. All of these were devoted to sweeping innovations in the conventional social order. They regarded capitalist and parliamentary Europe as having outlived its usefulness and as tottering on the verge of complete collapse.

Thereafter the Communists were to attempt by legal means what they had formerly envisaged as a series of *coups d'état* accompanied by the ruthless application of force. At the opposite pole, opposing them, was a miscellany of elements including the great oil, steel and munitions kings, the fantastically reactionary White Russian emigres, the alarmed business and financial oligarchies, the ubiquitous "bureaus" of the various countries staffed with their dangerously competent civil service personnel, the Junker landlords, reactionary clericals, military adventurers, politicians and intellectuals. These who originally organized themselves to protect the classic order, proved even more violent, more brutal and extreme in their determination to crush it. Their ideal was a modernized cooperative State modeled on the social usages and convictions of the Middle Ages.

Hatred of bourgeois society was hence by no means restricted to the proletariat, but ran deep in all classes. In particular there rose a disregard, a contempt and a true resentment toward the processes of free government for which in the past men had fought with all the passion of which the race is capable. This cynicism toward the very fundamentals of the Western way of life ran deep in whole classes and in one aspect or another pervaded the entire population.

There likewise was introduced into the internal political competition of nations techniques of aggression based on strategies formerly reserved solely for military operations. One was the principle of unlimited duplicity to attain an objective; another that of mass shock tactics, and the will to make victory decisive by a literal obliteration of the opposing forces. Against these disruptive activities the constituted authorities seemed helpless to defend themselves. Everywhere except in Communist Russia they found themselves in retreat.

Powerful tensions and dislocations developed between all classes of the population. The signs of serious dislocation were everywhere. They showed themselves in physical clashes between races, in sharp tensions between capital and labor, as well as in increasing irritations, distrusts and suspicions among the States themselves.

As the situation progressively deteriorated it became complicated with questions of wickedly stimulated national egos which heightened the already existing animosities to dangerous dimensions. Europe was going through a severe psychic crisis. It stood on the very edge of demoralization, while still maintaining a surface display of its normal institutions and accustomed habits.

The Germans, who themselves were affected forcibly by these boisterous and apparently insuppressible currents, watched events with keen appraising eyes. The Reich possessed a leadership which was at the one time logical and without compunction. Though heavily distorted by devotion to dark Teutonic mysticism, German leaders were faithful in their devotion to the art of *Realpolitik*. Revengeful, bitter and frustrated, they surveyed the situation endeavoring to measure it with cold, clear insight. It was the Nazi firebrands especially who were able to pierce the fog of confusion which hid the rising tide of events from sight, and to plan with sagacious thoroughness for a new attempt at world conquest.

Above all, the Germans who had sent Lenin and Trotsky through the Reich in a sealed car on the mission which ended in the destruction of traditional Russia, understood the dynamics of revolution. They saw that this era was doomed to come to an early end, that it already had outlived its present form. The lesson of Russia, where both the Czar and the subsequent Kerensky government ignominiously had collapsed before the determined onset of a small group of professional revolutionaries, was not lost on them. They saw the world as a great jungle inhabited by overfed, armored monstrosities which could be devoured at leisure once these were turned over on their backs.

The German leaders regarded the chaos which must result from the inherent conflicts of the industrial revolution as providential to the mission they conceived for Germany. They endeavored thus to make their nation the catalyst of a new order, accelerating the general process of dissolution by which they conceived the Western world was spontaneously destroying itself.

Long before Hitler came to power the Germans had been obsessed with a sense of divine ordination, and with the belief that the inhabitants of neighboring States possessed degenerate qualities. The mere fact of world-wide revolutionary change was not regarded by them as an essential obstacle to their plans, but rather fitted in with these perfectly. German destiny was now viewed as that of a tightly knit racial horde operating in an area without boundaries, and subsisting as an eternal privileged caste over all others.[1] Rauschning, Hitler's leader in the Danzig Senate, informs us that *Der Fuehrer* "was convinced that only world revolution would bring Germany to leadership among the Powers. Therefore it was his task to drive this world revolution forward, and, as it were, to put on his payroll the destructive and disintegrating forces in all nations." [2]

In addition to the conception of the racial State operating in a

---

[1] The German writer, Ernst Rudolf Huber, in his book, *Constitutional Law of the Greater German Reich*, states that "the German people forms a closed community which recognizes no national borders . . . it represents an independent community which reaches beyond such limits [that of national States]." pp. 157-158.

[2] Hermann Rauschning, *The Redemption of Democracy*, p. 40.

Lebensraum without precise boundaries, there evolved another and coordinating theory, that of geopolitics.

This much-heralded German thesis was developed from the philosophical views of the great English geographer, Mackinder,[1] and a later German oceanographer, named Friedrich Ratzel, who maintained in his *Politische Geographie* that "the decay of every State is the result of a declining space conception."

The outstanding modern German prophet of geopolitics is the general, Karl Haushofer, who in the German system is not only a thinker, but a man of unchallenged authority. In Haushofer's adept hands the Germanic predatory complex was rationalized to agree with the new conditions which bore upon the science of conquest, and provided it with a philosophy.

The Germans made the study of geopolitics the horn-book of their foreign policies. Geopolitics was the natural corollary to practical politics, to historic German ambition and to the national mood of frustration. It was the logic which explained the world in the light of German personality and position.

The German people were taught that they were rooted within a cultural space of expanding dimensions and that their mission was by successive stages to unify their own society on a national socialist basis, purge its culture of alien elements, and march to control first of Europe, then of the entire Eurasian-African land-mass, and then of the world.

Haushofer saw only one power possible on a globe where rapid communications had made all nations neighbors—a world power. He regarded the total conquest of the globe as being both the task and result of any possible grand strategy.

He concluded that in the center of the struggle for living space was not the nation but the race, which by its existence had been given a role which it must fulfill. The essence of life, he taught, was struggle, and the *Kultur*-race-society must expand with growing

1 Sir Halford Mackinder. See his paper, *The Geographical Pivot of History;* also his book, *Britain and the British Seas.*

force over all boundaries until its dynamics were spent. Therefore, it was the will to power, or will to rule, which principally differentiated one great competing horde from another, and which enabled it to make the most effective use of its industrial and geographic position.

The geopoliticians were persuaded that for the purpose of conquest and rule, master races must be pure races, that is, races with one common blood and purpose. Race mixture was considered to be fatal and was regarded as the cause of the decay of all great Powers from the time of Assyria, Greece and Rome to the era of Charlemagne and Britain. Thus the earlier Germanic obsession with class, as symbolized by the teachings of Marx, was wiped out to make class and race synonymous, the master race becoming automatically the master class.

The German geopoliticians believed the world ripe for conquest. They saw only one possible rival, Japan, which they felt they could neutralize until, in the fullness of time, they were ready for the final test of strength. The reins of the British Empire, they believed, were held in the nerveless fingers of men who had lost the will to empire. The countries of the Continent they considered decadent, corrupt, and easy prey to a determined and well-organized conqueror. China and India they wrote off as power vacuums long estranged to practical military politics. The United States was believed to be incurably pacifist, addicted to political unreality, racially disunited, and interested only in a mad pursuit of money and creature comforts.

The Soviet Union was regarded as a clumsy and vastly over-rated giant with a glass jaw, who would not survive the first flurry of attack. This monstrous land-mass was considered to be the special German field of reference, a source of endless supplies, and the open thoroughfare to world dominion.

Revolutionary Fascism is generally believed to have been conceived with the *Fasci di Combattimento* of Mussolini. Actually this is not altogether true. Italian Fascism did not represent a true mass revolutionary movement, but a reaction on the part of conventional institutions endeavoring to save themselves from the revolutionary process.

Mussolini moved on Rome in 1922, yet parliamentary government did not disappear to give way to government by corporations until 1928. It was still later that Italian Fascism took a strong military trend and concerned itself with the possibility of vast external adventures. Its difference from the German military State is one of revolutionary intent. The German State professes actually to liquidate basic contradictions implicit in the present European order, and to substitute for it an entirely new order based on a new rationale.

Despite the propaganda it has utilized on its road to power, the Nazi credo demands not separatism, but universalism, though under a racial hegemony. It is revolutionary as well as predacious, and proposes to reorganize society on a continental, and perhaps a global scale, rid of the constricting boundaries of small States.

Like a buzzard who with uncanny instinct waits for a great strong beast to die that he may feast on its bones, outstanding German thinkers for half a century have sensed the fact that the present phase of world organization was drawing rapidly to a close, and that the day of German destiny was approaching. Nietzsche, Von Treitschke and a whole string of lesser lights harped on this theme interminably. Oswald Spengler in his massive *The Decline of the West* made it clear that the traditional world was in its death throes. "The democratic nations," he warned dourly, "must disappear because they put their faith in illusions, more particularly the illusions of truth and justice. There is only one reality in the world—force. If you listen closely, you can already hear the tramp of the Caesars who are coming to take over the world."

Western leaders, secure in their possession of the greater part of the earth's resources and culture, have failed to grasp this essential fact which the Germans understand: that society is in the midst of a new period of reformation dominated by a radical alteration of its industrial potential. In the wake of this cataclysmic upset the

Germans conceived a total reconstruction of the known political and economic world.

IV

In the German New Order there would be no problems of industrial relationship, no trade barriers, unstable currencies, or unemployment. No national prejudices would interfere with the free functioning of trade or with ready access to required raw materials. There would be no sectional strictures to prevent the easy flow of commerce, no tariffs, no social disorders, no ruinous depressions in which millions of workers would be unable to find work and plants have to shut down for want of the essential markets which the wages of these workers should themselves provide.

In this German blueprint for the future there would be no surpluses which would have to be burned while millions starved. Wasteful competition would be eliminated. There would be only production for use and distribution according to plan.

This propitious condition would be achieved in a simple way: by the creation of a totally new type of society in which the present nations would be reorganized into what would be tantamount to corporations feeding directly into a center which would be the German parent corporation.

These corporations would each specialize in the production of some essential product, the whole to be coordinated from the German power center. This military and industrial power house would be the actual pivot of the universe, around which all the national planets and their satellite moons would revolve.

The populations would be well fed and tended according to their needs, but would possess no political or social rights in the sense of the present social order. They would be anonymous serfs, tied to their occupations and directed by a military elite who would act in the combined sense of custodians, judges, managers and directors.

This is a magnificent and bold, though from Western standards a brazen, wicked and misbegotten dream. Where did it come from? Whose is it?

It did not happen by some spontaneous mutation, mysteriously brought into existence full-born. It is not the result of the criminal mesmerism of a small group of men. It is a growth which developed symmetrically, like a plant whose roots reach down beyond the memory of those who loll in its shade. It is part of the ethos of a singular, vainglorious, efficient and paranoid people.

This vision to which the Germans are inseparably chained, was watered and fed by the mills and furnaces of the Ruhr, demanding guaranteed markets and access to a continually widening catalogue of raw materials. It stemmed from the rapid growth of Rhenish Westphalia, from the applied weight and incessant demands of German heavy industry. To a degree it was fashioned by the position in space occupied by the German people. This though restricted in area was the best military situation in Europe, that of a centrally located industrial nation surrounded by semi-agrarian States lacking the heavy manufactures necessary to create modern weapons, less populous, possessing few natural defense boundaries, torn by social troubles, nervous, flaccid and subjected to increasing disfunction in reference to the central problems affecting nations everywhere.

These were tempting conditions to any nation already affected by the call to glory. The German military position at the beginning of World War II was an ideal one. The Reich was a vast producing workshop criss-crossed with a complex and highly organized network of roads and railroads enabling her to concentrate her armies with crushing strength against any of the smaller and less well-armed opponents on her borders. France was in disorder, England was aloof and living in the spiritual past of omnipotent navies, finance systems and power equilibriums. Russia had been temporarily immobilized by treaty. Japan was now allied with the Reich so that for the moment the interests of the two nations were grooved in identical channels.

In the hands of German leaders were new and terrible mechanical weapons which already had been carefully tested on the preliminary battlefields of Spain. There had been tested, too, the will and stamina of the opposing democratic powers, which from the German view were found to be pathetically wanting.

By the use of threat alone, Germany had gained fantastic political successes by which it had remilitarized the Rhineland, and seized Memel, Austria and Czechoslovakia. The West was seemingly in disastrous retreat and on the verge of collapse.

The Reich was confident and ready, and nervously poised for the kill, when in the early Fall of 1939 World War II was officially ushered into existence.

III

THE NEW ORDER

NO clear picture of the future can be gained without an understanding of the character of the German people, who more than any other have been responsible for the violent crisis with which we are confronted.

Though the Germans claim to be a pure race of *Herrenmenschen,* a people of superior blood to whom all other nations are destined to bow, they appear to be quite as mixed as any other.

The inhabitants of the Reich are a melange of original Danish, Teutonic, Celtic and Slavic tribes admixed with Latin, Jewish and some Oriental blood, and strongly modified in the east by nomadic Mongols of the Ural-Altaic group who roared into Europe under Attila during the Fourth Century.

In contemporary Germany the so-called Nordic type is heavily in the minority, and in the South is rare altogether, as has been proved by a census of hair and eye color of German school children taken in 1880 at the instance of Professor Virchow.[1]

Many peoples crossed this territory and left their stamp. In the Rhine provinces the Romans built a whole group of cities. During Caesar's time the entire west bank of the Rhine had been Celtic, with a strong Celtic infusion still visible deep to the east. Levantine blood was brought back from the Near East with the families of the Crusading Knights, and during the Middle Ages whole communities of Jews are known to have abjured their ancient religion, and became Christians.

[1] Friedrich Hertz, *Race and Civilization,* p. 103.

43

In his famous *Twelfth Century Chronicle of the Slavs,* Helmold informs us that the Wends and other Slavic tribes were settled as far as the Oder. Up to the end of the Middle Ages, Slavic dialects were still spoken as far as Leipzig, Dresden, Vienna, Magdeburg and Luebeck. In Prussia not only was the great majority of the population of Slavic origin, but a large portion of the working classes spoke a Slavic dialect until late in the Eighteenth Century. The very name of Berlin is a corruption of Barlin, an old Slav fishing settlement located on the present site of the capital.

II

It is important to an understanding of the German State to know that the composite of peoples from which it was formed, possessed originally neither racial nor national consciousness. For the most part they were barbaric tribes whose historic business was war and loot and who were guided by no other overriding considerations. The great Charlemagne could hardly have regarded his "Germanism" as being of any more significance than did Theodoric the Ostrogoth who overran Italy and Byzantium, or the Visigoths and Vandals who scourged the Western Mediterranean, or the Angles, Jutes and Saxons who swarmed over Celtic England. All of these were absorbed and molded by the superior cultures they encountered, though not before such tribes as the Vandals had wrought such havoc and devastation that their very names have lived as synonyms for wanton destruction.

In the main the German tribes remained outside of the boundaries of history until Rome began to decay and by its weakness invite invasion. Until a late date the hostility of the tribes to civilization was so great that the missionaries and builders of cities had constantly to be protected against them. The Frisians and Saxons were not Christianized until the Seventh Century. Pomerania remained pagan until the Twelfth and Thirteenth Centuries.

The haunted effort to become homogeneous and to identify the nation with the coming of superman, derives from a unique inspiration. This was the advent of the Teutonic Knights, a religious order of military adventurers organized in the early twelve hundreds for the purpose of converting the remaining pagans of Central Europe, the carrying on of trade, and freebooting.

In 1226 the Polish prince, Conrad of Masovia, committed the most disastrous mistake in Polish history when he invited the Teutonic Order which had just been expelled from Hungary, to lend its arms in a war against the Prussi, a heathen Slavic race inhabiting what is now East Prussia.

This task the Knights performed with a brutality scarcely exceeded in military annals. They not only converted the entire area by the sword, appropriating the land and property of these people, but took over their name as well.

No one who has read the history of this Order, of the savage man-hunts it conducted against the unfortunate population of the Eastern Baltic, can fail to understand the tradition of relentless cruelty, fanatic sense of mission, and unrelieved excesses indulged in by the German nation since.

When the Knights attacked pagan Lithuania in 1309 they massacred the entire population of the Lithuanian city of Danzig. Enforcing a relentless policy of blood and iron, they turned the Baltic regions into a charnel house, where they forgot their oath as soldiers of the cross and became a landed aristocracy. For six hundred years a Lett or Esthonian was to tremble in his mean cottage like a hunted animal at the very sight of the descendants of these ex-Crusaders, who now exercised their rights as members of a divinely decreed elite.

The Prussian State did not exist until the year 1701. Two centuries previously, in 1511, Albrecht of the Hohenzollern-Ansbach family had been elected Master of the Order. Later Albrecht decided it was more profitable to become a Protestant, and caused the ancient monastic Order which by now had lost most of its fanatic fighting zeal, to be secularized. He accepted the title of Duke of Prussia under Polish overlordship. It was not until the beginning of the Eighteenth Century that the strange inheritance of the

Teutonic Knights of the Cross evolved into a kingdom under Frederick I.

During all of the period in which Prussia struggled to emerge from a small State, vassal to the Kings of Poland, to control of German-speaking Europe, she never forgot the tradition of the sword in which she had been conceived. The military character of this inheritance led Mirabeau to remark acidly that "Prussia is not a State which has an army—she is an army that has a nation."

The savage application of unmitigated force, the squeezing of profits by exclusively organized commercial bodies, and the religious zeal of mission, derive their primary impulses from this early record. All the German principles of power, ruthlessness, absolutism, calculated brutality, commercial avidness and arrogance had their period of gestation here.

Later, Hitler was to make obeisance to these facts, proclaiming that "We take up again at the halting place of six hundred years ago. The principle," he declared, "which once made the Prussian army the most wonderful instrument of the German people will be the basis of the structure of our whole State—authority of every leader over those below him and responsibility to those above him."[1]

In thus turning the clock back to the days when the Grand Master, Hermann von Salza, led the Teutonic Order as a solid, crushing phalanx against the unfortunate peoples of the Baltic, we see an old and terrifying vision reintroduced into European life—the sense of divine errand, the stern unyielding discipline, the brutal crushing of all opposition, the lauding of the military form as a way of life, and the concept of every citizen as a soldier marching behind an omnipotent and inspired leader whose word is final.

The development of Prussia is a slow motion counterpart of the morbid genius which propelled the Turks and Mongols from their steppes in Central Europe and sent them on a whirlwind campaign to devour the world. In the Prussian case, the course of conquest was lost to view in the slow, painful and methodical generation of

1 Adolf Hitler, *Mein Kampf*, p. 501, 1933 edition.

forces. Nevertheless, it was just as intractable and fully as demonic and all-engulfing.

The history of this State is one in which the arts and sciences were paid little concern, but where rigid emphasis was given military organization and efficient statecraft. Prussia has had no other flowering. It was led by a group of men familiarly known as the Junkers, who combined in a single body the land-owning, commercial, administrative and military classes.

The spirit of the State has shown a singular genius for long-range purpose and for accommodation to new circumstances which stood in the way of its ambition. In the Nineteenth Century, Prussian absolutism absorbed the nationalist vision as its own after having opposed it for ninety years. When the Liberals were crushed in the revolution of 1848, it was the Prussian armies of Otto von Bismarck which "realized the dream of the national unification that the Liberals had longed for in vain." [1]

In our own time we have seen the Nazis take over May Day and the slogans of Socialism in order to meet the circumstances created by a failing industrial society. We have beheld a surface modification of the traditional icy sobriety and cool calculation of Potsdam in favor of the theatrically violent character and wild stentorian oratory which fascinated the peoples of the German South and West.

It was Napoleon Bonaparte who acted as the unwitting ally of Prussia in creating the first effort at unification among the German States. Until that time Germany had been a geographical expression, not a nation. The area now covered by the Reich had been divided into some three hundred and sixty states, principalities and free cities, which made war on each other and allied themselves with Slavs, Latins and others, indiscriminately.

By the Act of Mediation put through by Napoleon in 1803, the number of States was reduced to one hundred and eighty, and the imperial cities to six. Bonaparte felt that in simplifying the map

[1] Gustav Stolper, *German Economy*, p. 11.

of Germany it would be easier for France to deal with the newly enlarged State.

After the defeat of the French Emperor in 1815 the Congress of Vienna reduced the one hundred and eighty German States to thirty-five, and the free cities to four. Prussia was one of the principal beneficiaries of this process.

By 1863, after a series of wars, Prussia succeeded in annexing sufficient territory to allow her to stretch continuously from the Rhine to the Baltic. The next year Bismarck formed the North German Confederation in which all of the remaining States north of the River Main were loosely joined under Prussian leadership.

After the Franco-German war in 1870, Baden, Bavaria and Württemberg entered the Confederation, leaving Austria as the sole German State outside the folds of this scheme.

Theoretically, no Imperial German crown existed. Nor was there an hereditary sovereign. The States composing this union retained their rulers and could maintain their own embassies in foreign capitals as well as levy their own taxes. The control of the army, however, passed to Prussia.

The King of Prussia by virtue of his presidency of the North German Confederation became Emperor, exercising his rights through the *Bundesrat,* a federal council composed of representatives of the various States, where sovereignty technically was vested.

In addition to the *Bundesrat,* a *Reichstag,* or Upper House, was provided to which representatives were sent by common suffrage.

Whatever appearance of liberalism this gave was deceptive. The Reichstag was never more than a sounding board for the Prussian Emperor and his chancellor, the sole federal minister. The chancellor, himself, had assistants but no cabinet and was the sole responsible official of the Empire. Only the Kaiser could remove this.

Occupying a completely independent position was the omnipotent German General Staff in which the real leadership of the State was vested. It was responsible neither to a war ministry nor to a parliament and acknowledged only one master, the Prussian Emperor.

III

The German record shows that States as well as individuals can suffer from an abnormal psychology and even a type of dementia. As in individuals this may be induced by a long continued series of events which for practical purposes are irreversible. To attempt to reason otherwise, on the basis of purely mechanical definitions, is to reduce all explanations for human conduct to absurdity.

Among the complex elements which have contributed to the shaping of the German character, only one ranks in importance with the emotional legacy left by the Teutonic Knights. This is the exposed position occupied by the Germans on the central plains of Europe, and the dark fears and obsessions to which this fact subjected them.

Germany is a favored country whose physical position makes it the very hub of Europe. In the day of the railroad and mechanically equipped armies, its military situation is incomparably superior to any other on the Continent.

The country lacks, however, natural frontiers such as the mountains which wall Spain and Italy off from France. Existing as a disorganized group of principalities, it was always in danger of being overrun. During the Middle Ages, when the early German period of ferocious tribal assaults had abated, Germany lived in continual dread, caught between the pyramiding population growth of the Slavic East and the military proficiency of the West.

During almost the entire period in which they have been conjoined with European civilization, the German States have been involved in innumerable wars. One of these, the Thirty Years War, reduced the German population by a full third, and left Central Europe almost a wilderness.

Under these pressures the Germans developed certain signs of morbidity and hysteria not common to the other peoples of Europe, a circumstance which, combined with the phenomenon of Prussian absolutism, goes far to explain their subsequent history.

No one who has studied the German people at close range can doubt the painful instability of their character and the demonic obsessions which periodically take command of souls which would appear otherwise to be kindly, gentle and steady. The German suffers from a strange set of warring complexes that is part of the whole system of grossness and vulgarity which allows him to reach forward to the state of *Uebermensch*. Wallace Deuel refers to the German as being essentially unsure of himself. "He lacks poise . . . he is chaotic and violent. He is the creature of constant *Sturm und Drang*, of storm and stress and striving, of self-consciousness and self-examination." [1]

Mass neurasthenia has shown itself in strange forms from the earliest times. In 1374 assemblages of men and women were seen in Aix-la-Chapelle who had come out of Germany, united by a single common delusion which caused them to form circles, hand in hand, and to execute wild dances "for hours altogether until at length they fell to the ground in a state of exhaustion . . . While dancing they neither saw nor heard, being insensible to external impressions through the senses, but were haunted by visions, their fancies conjuring up spirits whose names they shrieked out; and some of them afterwards asserted that they felt as if they had been immersed in a stream of blood which obliged them to leap so high. Others during their paroxysm saw the heavens open and the Savior enthroned with the Virgin Mary." [2]

Similar visitations occurred in the Fifteenth Century. During every destructive pestilence a singular paranoia seemed to affect these people. They would first come to believe that the wells were poisoned. Seized by a dreadful panic arising from this supposed poisoning, the inhabitants of many towns and villages would use

1 Wallace Deuel, *People Under Hitler*, pp. 24-25.
2 Justus Friedrich Karl Hecker, *Epidemics of the Middle Ages*, pp. 80-84.

only river and rain water.[1] During the period of the Black Death it was the Jews who were accused of having poisoned the wells, just as they were accused of being responsible for Germany's troubles following World War I. This people was pursued with merciless cruelty, torn to pieces, or officially burned alive. In the city of Mayence alone, twelve thousand were put to death.

Periodically there has been a frenzied effort to rid the German social body of all liberal, or dissenting elements. A great portion of those capable of checking the German tendency to sadistic extremes fled the Reich after the revolution of 1848. This sick passion for coordinating all members of the State into one unreasoning, marching, militarized unit received its highest personification in the present Nazi regime. The greatest part of what was left of independent liberal Germany died in the concentration camps, or fled in hopeless, heart-broken weariness to any land which would receive them.

By this selective process, swiftly accelerated by Nazi indoctrination, these inheritances have molded the collective German character into something implacable and frightening, which finds its epitome, perhaps, in Hitler's amazing statement that "conscience is a Jewish invention—it is a blemish like circumcision." Or in the German Fuehrer's savage declaration: "I deliver men from the humiliating chimera that is called culture. Culture as well as education cripples men. I have this advantage, that I am not deterred by any theoretical or moral considerations."

A recent medical writer calls attention to the German pattern of behavior as typical of the paranoid picture. He lists the retrospective falsification of history, the projection of all blame onto everyone else, the almost desperate fear of criticism and opposition, the characteristic absorption in mystic bombast, the tendency toward plotting and conspiring, the megalomania, suspiciousness, feeling of persecution, complex rationalization, sense of mission, exaggeration, and above all, Germany's topsy-turvy insistence on claims of "unjust treatment." These, coupled with the martyr

[1] *Ibid.*, p. 339.

phraseology unremittingly used, "make them appear typical, and by definition, insatiable paranoid demands . . ." [1]

In no other country would it be possible for the supreme political head to declare publicly that a little lie should never be told, but only a big one, since the big one will be believed; or could a national hero be made out of such a man as Horst Wessel, a street brawler and pimp who died in a squabble over women.

This perversion of normal human attitudes is discerned over a long period of German history. Hitler's system is only a terrible fulfilment of doctrines preached by the State and written by philosophers, historians, bankers, business men and clergymen for many generations.

The historian, Hegel, states that civilization is spread only by war, and that the triumph of culture demands the suppression by the higher races of races less capable or less advanced. A whole line of Prussian historians led by such figures as Von Ranke, Von Treitschke and Mommsen ardently championed this view.

A century ago, Fichte taught that Germany was predestined to rule the world. We find General von Bernhardi telling his people early in the Twentieth Century that "war is not merely a necessary element in the life of nations but an indispensable factor of culture in which the truly civilized nation finds the highest expression of strength and vitality." We discover the philosopher, Oswald Spengler, preaching that "man is a beast of prey" and that "all of the paragons of virtue and social morality who want to be, or get beyond this, are only beasts of prey with broken teeth who hate the others on account of the attacks which they prudently avoid."

Over the course of centuries we descry the same tendency to unrestrained excesses, the identical worship of the cult of deceit, the same fanatic belief in the divine mission of the German people. We find Frederick the Great observing frankly that "he is a fool and that nation is a fool who having the power to strike his enemy

[1] Dr. Richard M. Brickner, "The German Cultural Paranoid Trend" *American Journal of Orthopsychiatry*, October 1942.

unawares, does not strike and strike his deadliest." We see Von Treitschke declaring that since Germany will never be able to understand the world "the world must be conquered and reformed so that it will be able to conform to German thought." We observe Kaiser Wilhelm II urging his soldiers departing for the war against China to "Give no quarter—take no prisoners—kill all who fall in your hands."

Reading the proclamations and doctrines of the Pan-Germans of the latter Nineteenth Century, one encounters all of the principal ideas which are now associated with Nazi ideology. They include the project for colonization in South America, the mass evacuation of Slavic peoples so as to make room for German expansion in the south and east, the persistent anti-liberalism, State Socialism and anti-Semitism, and even a budding reliance on psychological warfare, mainly to be used to immobilize the United States. Then as now Germany saw in the ambitions of the Asiatic East an instrument which could assist her in crushing her Western competitors for power.

Throughout officialdom, in the schools and in the homes, the idea of German hegemony bubbled and grew. It was part of the outlook of the banks and reflected itself in the churches. It spoke from the voices and pens of an imposing list of philosophers, teachers, historians and statesmen.

Underscoring this entire line of reasoning in pulpit, school, book and newspaper, has always been the ultimate world domination of the *Herrenmensch*, the final coming of Superman into his own.

In any other nation such men would have been considered crackpots. In Germany they were national teachers whose words were received with reverence, acclaim and enthusiasm.

These vainglorious obsessions to which the German soul was committed were observed by the thoughtful poet, Heine. In his *History of Religion and Philosophy in Germany* he declares with far-seeing, wise eyes that "when the cross, that restraining talisman, falls to pieces, then will break forth the frantic berserker rage whereof Northern poets have said and sung so much . . . The old stone gods will then arise from the forgotten ruins and wipe from their eyes the dust of centuries, and Thor with his giant hammer will arise again and he will shatter the Gothic cathedrals . . . When you hear a crash such as never before has been heard in the world's history, then know that at last the German thunder-bolt has fallen."

The time of the fulfilment of this prophecy is now.

We observe a nation powerful in numbers and industry and oc-cupying a favored position in the center of the European Conti-nent, challenging the entire world, and threatening to drag it down in flames with the Teuton armies if they are defeated. We see a pathological development of race attributes which causes an en-tire State to regard itself as being selected by Providence to rule the world, considers itself the carrier of all culture, and which does not disdain to relegate all other races to various brackets of subhumanity.

We observe a nation turned into a shambles, beating in the heads of its liberals, dissenters and Jews, and denouncing foreigners, Communists, Capitalists, Freemasons and Catholics alike. We note martial music and displays everywhere exalting unrestrained vio-lence, together with a new form of government in the nature of a socialist military society. At the head is an ex-painter with a funny, small mustache, who would have been laughed off the stage of history in any other country. Ecstatic women give up their free-dom, and return to the cookstove and the home on the theory that woman is made to bear children and for the recreation of the tired returning warrior.

As if hypnotized, men yield all pretense to liberty. All powers are vested in a supreme ruler who is at the same time the highest legislator, the highest judge and the head of the administration. He commands the Party, the State and the Army. In his name cabinet officers, national governors, officials and officers are ap-pointed and dismissed. All officials and soldiers must swear per-sonal allegiance to him. As defined by Dr. Frick, "All powers of government are concentrated in his person while he, himself, is responsible only to the nation." Law has become, in the words of Karl Schmitt, "no longer an objective norm but a spontaneous emanation of the *Fuehrer's* will."

We behold the burning of books as in the days of the Inquisition. We see a deliberate return to bestiality and to paganism, not proceeding from a few disordered minds, but as an orderly conversion of society, read from the pulpit, legal bench, university platform, and government house. We observe the official League of German Maidens marching through the streets singing, "We have given up the Christian life for Christ was just a Jewish swine; as for his mother, what a shame, Cohen was the lady's real name."

We hear General von Ludendorff demand the rejection of Christianity "because it is Jewish, because it is international, and because, in cowardly fashion, it preaches Peace on Earth." We see Dr. Theodore Lewald, President of the German Olympic Committee, remark in what passes for Germanic humor, that "Catholics cannot be recognized by the shapes of their noses in the same way Jews can be recognized, so that if they keep their mouths shut they even can be housed with Aryans." Or we view Hitler admonishing his people: "You can be a German or a Christian. You cannot be both."

We hear Gauleiter Greiser aver of the tortured Poles that "If God exists, it is He who has chosen Adolf Hitler to drive this vermin hence." [1] Or, Sauckel, Nazi governor of Thuringia, proclaiming that "in the name of this [Nazi] Germany, I command you now to show intolerance against all others." Or the amazing fantasy of the mayor of Koenigsdorf, Bavaria, solemnly avowing that "cows and cattle which were bought from Jews, directly or indirectly, may not be bred with the community bull."

We observe the dedication of an entire State to the worship of war as being the noblest endeavor of man. We see the amazing spectacle of little children taught militarism and brutality "un-

[1] Speech at Kalisz, Poland, October 6, 1939.

relieved by any of the virtues which modern civilization has come to place above brute force." [1]

We find a theory evolved in which the individual is allowed only cherished duties toward the State, but no fundamental rights. Except as he becomes a participant in the supreme will of the State, the individual has sunk to zero.

Running parallel with this principle has been the complete destruction of the judicial system by which the citizen could protect himself against official violence. Now he may be seized without warrant, thrown into a concentration camp, or shot, substantially without trial, all in the name of the common purpose. The greatest police system ever envisaged by man, functioning with a network of spies and *agents provocateurs,* operates everywhere, building up *dossiers,* carrying on an invincible and all-pervasive espionage, and terrorizing all free expression of opinion.

We perceive the consolidation of small peasant holdings into large estates more or less along the Communist model, with the peasant permanently frozen to his land, so that it no longer can be sold or mortgaged and becomes in effect "the property of the German people." We note all business enterprise more and more closely "coordinated" and linked to the State by commissars whose omnipotence cannot be challenged.

We discover a leadership which possesses an unparalleled grasp of the mechanics of revolution, capable of implementing it on a world-wide scale, and which holds a complete contempt for conventional society. "I came early to realize" writes Hitler in *Mein Kampf,* "that the proper employment of propaganda is a real art, one that can always remain almost unknown to the bourgeois parties."

The German leaders realized that society was divided along social, economic and racial, as well as along vertical national and religious lines, and that the horizontal divisions were perhaps the more powerful of the two. They made a profound study of the psychological weaknesses of human beings out of which traitors

[1] *Peace and War,* Paper printed by State Department, 1942.

and saboteurs are formed. We witness an unceasing agitation, scientifically designed to create confusion and civil war in the bosom of national societies everywhere. We observe an unrelenting use of these principles, by which man is to be kept in that continuous ferment which the Germans regard as the first leg in the journey to world domination.

We find an intense, almost pathological longing for power, and a wild jealousy of nations which possess it. This hatred is particularly extravagant in relation to Britain which from the German view has usurped the place in the sun rightfully reserved for the Reich. As early as 1911 Von Bernhardi asks: What is the precise significance of German destiny? It is, of course, he replies, war. Who, he asks again, is to destroy England, this abominable Venice-Carthage of the Twentieth Century—and replies that to those who see in Germany "the nation of nations, which God has chosen for the accomplishment of His inscrutable will, the answer is obvious."

We observe millions of unfortunate Jews butchered in cold blood in a coolly stated determination to exterminate the entire race. We see the whole intellectual class of the Slavic East slaughtered as part of a plan to brutalize the Eastern masses and turn them into a perpetual race of helots. We find looting and extortion systematized into a science, and malevolence and barbarity exalted as the finest attributes of the warrior race.

We see a Nazi youth which has been systematically taught that it is the elite of the world, destined to rule it and to make all other nations and peoples their slaves. With stark realism the Nazi recognizes the contradictions and failures of our present society. His solution as expressed in a tremendous body of literature is based simply on a non-recognition of the rights of man.

The significant alterations in character and psychology this radical new approach involves, is difficult to grasp. When the *Uebermensch* takes the girl children of the Poles for his brothels he sees nothing unusual or reprehensible in this act. The immorality if anything is on the other side if it is resisted by the Poles, since he regards this action as simply his due as the representative of the higher race which all others must serve. When he reduces these sub-races to slavery he commits no act not in conformity with decency and natural law, since he conceives these races, like the lower primates, to be limited by nature to tasks and functions to which their inheritance forever binds them.

In this extravagant mishmash we observe a peculiarly wanton view of man's destiny such as a generation ago would have been regarded by the West as unutterably monstrous and odious. We see this phenomenon reaching out in wide eddies from its nesting ground in Germany and rapidly becoming a concurrent element in the great world upheaval.

IV

The race doctrine to which we shall refer later at length, is not a minor conceit incident to the peculiarities of our times. It is the very core of German life, as much so as Christianity was to Byzantium.

These beliefs are the product of a completely altered interpretation of history, and represent a deeply implanted social conviction. As an evolving religious form they already possess their shrines, their dogmas, their liturgical values, their saints and heroes, and their devils against which the universal struggle is conducted.

In the new racial science the classic egoism which has characterized German history found the perfect binding agent with which to cement its structure into a tremendous, inspired and indissoluble force.

The Teutonic race-gospels are the present-day key to all German action. Neither the German plans for the future, nor our own relations with a defeated Reich can be understood without reference to them.

The founder of this new and revolutionary belief was a French count, named Arthur de Gobineau, whose *Essai sur l'Inégalité des Races Humaines* must rank with Marx's *Das Kapital* and Paine's

Age of Reason as among the most influential and epoch-making documents of modern times.

Gobineau maintained that there was a fundamental inequality between races, and that civilization was due entirely to the superior energy and gifts of one of them, the fair-haired Aryan people. This race he identified with the long-headed Teuton invaders of practically every European country, though he was careful to state that these aristocrats were scattered in a thin stratum of masters and leaders in every modern nation. Despite the confusion of the word Teuton, he declared, this people were not more numerous in Germany than they were elsewhere.

According to Gobineau the question of race overshadowed all other problems of history. "Societies perish," he asserted, "because they are degenerate and for no other reason." "Degeneracy" meant solely the watering out of the "precious blood" possessed by the original Aryan makers of civilization.

The theories of Gobineau were adjusted to the developing Pan-German megalomania by the composer, Richard Wagner. In the hands of a whole group of German philosophers and historians, the Aryan myth was absorbed bodily into the Pan-German system. It took over the restless ambition, iron discipline, aggressive plan of aggrandizement and sense of mission which had characterized the lives of the Teutonic Knights. It became the creed *par excellence* of the warrior. To such men as Fichte and Von Treitschke it provided an ethic and explanation for an otherwise insoluble contradiction, the simultaneous existence of the scientific ideal and the Pan-German creed.

The Germanized Englishman, Houston Stewart Chamberlain, whose book *Grundlagen des Neunzehnten Jahrhunderts* appeared in 1899, further sharpened this theory and made it distinctly Teutonic in character. He reconciled it to the conviction of Hegel, Mommsen, and other Prussian historians, that civilization demanded the suppression of the lesser races by those most advanced, and that the natural expression of a virile national existence was war.

Chamberlain added the further ingredient of anti-Semitism, with the assertion that the Jews were the source of all evil and lacked all creative capacities. The Germans on the other hand, he alleged, were the authors of all progress and the sole custodians of the world's culture. With a sense of awful prophecy, he predicted that "what has happened is only a preview . . . True history begins from the moment when the German, with mighty hand, seizes the inheritance of antiquity."

Chamberlain's theories took all Germany by storm. The myth became fixed in the German mind until it became coincident with a complete explanation for life itself.

Under this gospel, the characteristics of races are alleged to be fixed biologically without the slightest possibility of alteration. The great error of civilization has lain wherever this precious blood has been adulterated or lost. Without it civilization cannot continue, and then only in direct proportion to the amount of Nordic blood flowing in its veins.

In a torrent of similar explanations we find as early as 1903 the claim by the anthropologist, Ludwig Woltmann, that "it is susceptible of proof that all European civilization, even in the Slavonic and Latin lands, is a product of the German race." We see this conceit repeated over and over again by an unending list of German scientists and scholars who had hypnotized themselves into the conviction that as long as the other nations "had pure German blood in their ruling families, they were unequalled in politics, art and science," but that since this supply from the Teutonic homeland ceased, these nations "became sterile and impotent—pygmies, bandits, robbers of the people and of the world."

This view is restated with dogmatic assurance by Hitler in *Mein Kampf*. "Whatever we see before us of human culture today," he writes, "the results of art, science and technique, is almost exclusively the creative product of the German man. *Just this fact admits of the not unfounded conclusion that he [the German] alone was the founder of higher humanity as a whole, and thus the prototype of what we understand by the word 'man.'* "

The central principle which rules existence is stated by Langbehn, as that of a superior Aryan blood which for its own defence cannot live in peaceful communion with others. "It is necessary," he declared, "that Aryan blood revolt, and it will revolt victoriously against all other bloods." [1]

These images are an integral part of the glorification of the *Volk* and the autocratic totalitarian State. They involve concepts which reach as far back as Gottfried Herder, in the latter Eighteenth Century, who first developed the idea of the organic folk-nation as opposed to the conventional political State.

The logic of course is plain. If all achievement is anthropological, and all spiritual values and culture are determined by inheritance, men must think with their blood or with their biological instincts rather than with their brains. If it is the racial constitution alone which determines culture it is obvious that there is "no such thing as a universally valid science, truth, justice or other value.[2] These are all dependent on the race genius." [3]

By setting up inner conflicts, the mixture of races is alleged to do great mischief, and all "mongrel" races are doomed to permanent inferiority. The task of the pure Nordic race is to keep itself from being swamped by the inferior sub-races around it, and to fulfill its mission by taking over political and military control of the earth.

Thus ethics are justified on scientific grounds and the theory of the higher or racial ethic evolved which cannot escape considering pity and compassion in the light of weakness, and democracy as an abjuration of the supreme value, which can only relate to increasing *Lebensraum* for the superior races and the checking of the growth of the lower ones.

This in fact the Germans regard as the command of civilization

[1] Julius Langbehn, *Rembrandt als Erzieher—von einem Deutschen,* 38th Edition, Leipzig.
[2] This was in fact claimed as early as the year 1800 by the German philosopher, Karl Friedrich Schlegel.
[3] Dr. I. Zollschan, *Racialism Against Civilization,* p. 34.

itself. "To lead civilization onwards is, they say, the highest moral law, standing above all conventions of lower origin." [1] The obligations of race thus supersede all other loyalties—whether of religion, geography, or State. These responsibilities are based on a racial universalism on which all other problems are dependent.

Since life consists of a struggle between the various racial groups for ascendancy, all ethics unconnected with the ability to rule, are vain and a symbol of degeneracy. Humanism, itself, represents a complete misinterpretation of history and a watering out of the task of the ruling race—which is, in short, to rule.

The major factor which applies in existence therefore is unrestrained force which must be unhesitatingly applied, as one would to ferocious animals. The great task is the mandate to protect the precious blood by those privileged to be its custodians.

These necessities force the need for still another, the purification of Nordic blood within the Nordic groups themselves, which in the past have had their inheritance fouled by contact with the inferior sub-races. This has become an *idée fixe,* causing the Germans to speak incessantly of breeding a new pure race of leaders in which only the tall, rangy, narrow-headed and allegedly superior blond type will be left.

In a frank exposition of the future, Hitler told Rauschning: "There will be a *Herren*-class, an historical class tempered by battle and welded from the most varied elements. There will be a great hierarchy of Party members. They will be the new middle class. And there will be the great mass of the anonymous, the serving collective, the eternally disfranchised, no matter whether they were once members of the old bourgeoisie, the big landowning class, the working class, or the artisans . . . Beneath them there will still be the class of subject alien races . . . And over all of these will stand the new high aristocracy, the most deserving and most responsible *Fuehrer*-personalities." [2]

[1] *Ibid.,* p. 63.
[2] Rauschning, *The Voice of Destruction,* p. 41.

The Germans subscribe to the idea that races are organisms and not merely collections of individuals, that therefore some races are in biological decay whereas others are young, vigorous and growing. The latter condition is the case in the East, unfortunately, from the German view. Here the grave danger is that the heroic Nordic race will be swamped by the enormous philoprogenitiveness of the inferior but biologically fertile Slav women.

Because of this high birth rate the Slavic question is far more pressing than that of the Gallic Latin to the west, who is assumed to represent a deteriorated and rapidly declining organism.

The answer to the Eastern problem is twofold. One is to detach the Slav farmer from the soil, making him a landless laborer working on great estates held by the German *Herrenmensch*, and to confine the entire race to unskilled industrial labor. The other is a policy of depopulation, and where desirable, extermination.

The latter policy has actually been followed in regard to the Jews, whom the Germans rank lowest on the scale of their catalogue of races. In the propaganda of the Nazis this small scattered people is identified as the omnipresent power against which all Aryanism struggles for ascendancy, the eternal enemy of the Nordic race. No canard has been too extreme to be refused credence, the Germans even going so far as to assert that the secret meaning of the Book of Job was that the Jews were the product of the miscegenation of apes and a Semitic tribe.

Europe became a torture chamber for its Jewish population. Jews were deprived of food cards, prevented from engaging in business or the professions, humiliated, beaten, reviled, crippled and ostracized from community life. Throughout the Continent they were seized, herded into cattle cars and transported, often in the dead of winter, to Poland which became the official Nazi slaughterhouse. Untold thousands were packed standing up into sealed cars without food or water. Much of this human freight arrived dead.

Poland became an abattoir in which an entire people who have been responsible for much of the glory of the human race were systematically butchered. Jews were machine-gunned, asphyxiated in gas chambers, or lined up before Nazi doctors who introduced air bubbles into their veins. At Treblinka there were constructed special lethal houses, hermetically sealed, into which condemned Jews, men, women and children, were forced stark naked, and gassed to death. Many hundreds of thousands were buried in mass graves at this camp alone. The total number of Jews who have been murdered by these methods is said to reach a figure of more than three million.

The attitude toward the Slavs is defined by Herr Ueberhor, the German President of Polish Lodz. "We are the masters," he declared. "So we must behave as masters. The Pole is a *Knecht* [hereditary servant] and must serve us."

The idea of human slavery is not new to German thought. As early as 1905, Ernst Hasse, member of the Reichstag and director of the German Statistical Office, asks: "Who in the future is to do the heavy dirty work which every national community based on labor will always require?" He replies that it is, of course, unthinkable that any part of the German people should be involved with such helot's occupations. "The solution," he states baldly, "consists in our condemning alien European stocks, the Poles, Czechs, Jews, Italians and others who will live under us, to these slave tasks." [1]

Just as the Romans held Gallic and Greek slaves, the Nazis saw nothing unusual in the holding of Slavic, French or English slaves. The only novelty was to be that of gradation of servitude according to a caste system, measured by racial inheritance. The Poles, Czechs and other Slavs were to be allowed only heavy labor occupations. Their schools and industry were to be destroyed and they were to be relegated to the position of serfs on the land, which was to be owned entirely by great German lords as in the days of the conquering Knights of Livonia. The Western peoples were to fare better, but were not to possess the full rights of Germans.

1 *Deutsche Politik;* c. f., Coole and Potter, *Thus Speaks Germany,* p. 342.

These races, too, would be serfs but would be able to order their lives to some degree.

What was meant may be gathered from the words of Richard-Walther Darre, German Minister of Agriculture, in an address before a group of Nazi officials on December 5, 1940. "We will introduce into our 'living space' completely new methods," he declared. "All soil and industrial property of inhabitants of non-German origin will be confiscated without exception and distributed primarily among the worthy members of the Party and soldiers who are accorded honors for bravery in this war. Thus a new aristocracy of German masters will be created. This aristocracy will have slaves assigned to it. These slaves will be their property and will consist of landless, non-German nationals."

By withholding food and vitamins whole races were to be reduced to the level of churls. Others were to die of famine and disease. The birth rates by these means were to be kept low and the death rates high.

The races were rationed according to scale. The Frenchman obtained a little more than half of the calories which went to Germans. The Jew received the least, being entitled only to a handful of black bread, with neither fats, meat, fruits or vegetables allowed him. Next to the Jews, the Slavs and in particular the Poles were given the roughest handling.

The entire intellectual and ruling class of the Slavs was to be destroyed. In Czechoslovakia all universities, colleges and secondary schools were closed. Their faculties were placed in concentration camps together with priests, labor leaders and intellectuals. In the camps of Poland were placed all of the political, social, educational, religious and economic leaders of that country. Even the stiff-necked Polish noblemen and landowners, who had toyed with Nazism as an alternative to the hobgoblin of Communism, found themselves interned and their property confiscated. All Polish schools were closed. The more valuable scientific equipment of the universities was transferred to Germany, as were the contents of museums, libraries and art galleries. The rest was destroyed.

The Germans set out not only to liquidate the future of the Poles but also their past. They attempted systematically to destroy all Polish learning, as well as historical and cultural shrines. Cathedrals were turned into garages and brothels for the use of the German army. Church hymns in Polish were forbidden. The government as a matter of principle admitted no marriages between Poles, who henceforward might mate only as did animals.

The methods utilized in the West against the French were concerned principally with the retention of the French war prisoners, whose forced separation from their wives could be relied on to create a changed relationship in the population ratios applying between Germany and France.

A more direct measure was that of mass depopulation. This was applied to areas adjacent to the Reich into which the Germans, for strategic or other reasons, wished their own nationals to overflow.

This method was utilized in Alsace-Lorraine, where by October 1942 almost half a million of the 1,900,000 inhabitants had been deported, to be replaced by German colonizers. The reverses in Russia caused these expulsions to be slowed down to a trickle, presumably to be resumed after German victory.

All of Bohemia and Moravia was earmarked for settlement by Germans. The Czech nation later was to be removed to some indeterminate place in Siberia. The task of colonization was entrusted to the *Deutsche Siedlungsgesellschaft* (German Society for Colonization). Cooperating with this body was an "Institute for Shifting Czechs" which was entrusted with the task of removing Czech families from the land.

As a preliminary step, the Nazi authorities specified five large areas from which all Czechs must move to make way for German colonists. The deportees were not allowed to take with them anything but hand luggage. All of their possessions, tools, stocks, businesses and even household furniture, had to be left for the incoming German settlers. It is said that more than 700,000 Germans have already been settled within the borders of Bohemia and Moravia. As was the case with other areas intended for colonization this policy was slowed down by the unexpected turn of the war.

A similar treatment was meted out to the Poles. Posen, Pomerania, Silesia and part of Congress Poland were directly annexed to the Reich. The remaining territory, referred to as the Government-General, was to house a reservoir of slave labor. It was to become what Strzetelski refers to as a *Nebenland,* or a country that "adjoins" a country but has no will or law of its own, and no intelligentsia, an area inhabited by a docile, crushed people who can be expected to serve their masters with doglike servility.[1]

The incorporated provinces became the scene of great mass expulsions. An example of how these deportations were carried out is afforded by occurrences at the port of Gdynia. At six o'clock one morning it was announced that the entire Polish population of 130,000 would be removed that day. They were permitted to take with them only small parcels of personal belongings. Their houses and all other possessions had to be left in good order with the keys hanging on the door handles. They were then packed in cattle trucks and sent to areas in Central Poland where no provision had been made to receive them. Identical procedures took place all over Western Poland.

It is estimated that to date two million Poles and half a million Jews have been expelled from the incorporated provinces. Some four hundred thousand Germans have been brought in as colonizers. Postwar German plans for colonization of the East contemplated the early establishment of four million settlers from the Reich, mostly recruited from demobilized soldiers.

The German blueprint also involved removing the entire Dutch nation and settling with Germans these provinces, which guard the strategic mouths of the Rhine. The Netherlanders were to be sent to the Ukraine where they were to be located on great cooperative farms. Actually only a few thousand families were transferred

1 Stanislaw Strzetelski, *Where the Storm Broke,* pp. 124-129.

before an automatic stop was put to the process by the precipitate German retreat from Russia.

Despite their hatred for the British, the Germans reserved for this people what they considered to be one of the highest destinies in the New Order. A widely discussed official plan involved the transfer to the Continent of all able-bodied British men in work gangs. One or two million British women "of the finest Nordic characteristics" were to be brought to Germany and placed in camps. Turned loose on these women would be 200,000 Germans "of the purest blood." The resulting progeny conceived each year were to be given "a strict National Socialist education" after which they would be sent to Britain to populate the island.

There is some evidence that as revolutionary a future was planned for the United States. There is much literature on this subject, a great deal of it formerly distributed through the German-American Bund. One of these volumes written by the German expert on America, Colin Ross, titled *Unser Amerika,* is a frank projection of the theme that America is rightfully German, that it is now a vulgar, corrupt land clinging to a degenerate form of government and inhabited by a bastardized racial conglomeration who must be crushed and evicted from power by the final triumph of the German supermen.

The original Nazi plan had been for a Northern, Eastern and Central European-Germanic empire. Under this prospectus the various regions were to enjoy a certain limited autonomy in which chosen Quisling personages were to operate with a required minimum of authority. The proposal, however, showed serious deficiencies in practise. It elicited poor cooperation from the subject peoples and invoked contradictions of its own. It was therefore modified in favor of dependent slave States which from the German view had one great quality to recommend them—they functioned.

Europe was to be reorganized into regions under German overlordship. "The coming peace economy," wrote the Reichsminister for Economics, Walther Funk, "will have to guarantee Greater Germany maximum economic power and the German people maximum consumption in those commodities required to increase their national prosperity. This is the goal that the European economic system will have to direct itself toward." [1]

There was to be a rationalization of industry and consolidation of small land holdings into large collective farms under German control. A minimum subsistence consistent with health and ability to perform the tasks assigned to them, was to be allowed the various subject races. Each, however, was to have a different standard of living and to be subjected to a differentiated price policy in the exploitation of its products and labor. Funk states bluntly that "the standard of living cannot and must not be the same in the countries belonging to the European clearing system, because the economic and social conditions are not equal . . ." [2]

There was to be a strict monetary control, proceeding from a central headquarters in Berlin. Only the Reich was to possess arms, or have access to the processes by which critical materials were fabricated for war purposes. All heavy industry and the greatest part of light manufacture was to be transferred to the *Grossdeutsche* Reich which was to be the strategic center of commerce and wealth.

The balance of Europe was to become mainly agricultural, with the exception of those industries which it was desirable to locate near raw material sources.

Reaching out into all the conquered territories were to be prosperous compact German islands inhabited by the *Herrenvolk* and separated from the surrounding inferior peoples by a rigid caste system. All commerce and skilled labor finally was to be concentrated in German hands. The Reich would determine the amount and type of all trade, not only between the various countries and herself, but between these countries and each other.

All essential services throughout the Continent would be operated by Germans. Plans for the electrification of Europe provided

1 Walther Funk, *The Economic Future of Europe,* p. 12.
2 *Ibid.,* p. 12.

that central stations of the system be located in the Reich, mainly in the Ruhr.

Germany at the present time is approximately sixty-eight per cent urban. This already top-heavy condition was to be greatly increased, without draining Germany's own national health in heavy or undesirable work. Required labor was to be recruited through a deindustrialization of conquered areas. The present use of war prisoners and indentured foreign workers was intended to become a permanent measure.[1]

Whole nations were to be set to such routine tasks as the Germans considered them best fitted for. All intensive farming was to be concentrated within the borders of the Reich. The other agricultural States were to specialize in large-scale grain and stock raising in which a lower standard of living is indicated.

Holland and Belgium were to be deindustrialized. Norway was marked off as a large-scale producer of fish, ores and woodpulp. The Norwegian shipping interests were to be transferred to Hamburg. Britain in which the building of boats was to be centered, otherwise would become, in the words of Dr. Ley, "once more that unknown green island that she was centuries ago."

France was to be semi-industrial, but to possess a limited proportion of light industry. Under a ten year plan for French economy drawn up by Reichsmarshal Hermann Goering, all industry in Northern France with the exception of mining was to be abolished for "strategic reasons" with the rights of the liquidated concerns transferred to German firms. Poland, Russia and the Balkans were to be purely agricultural hinterlands, supplying the Reich with raw materials and receiving manufactured products in return.

It was only after matters took a bad turn for the German war-machine that Hitler gave over his policy of stripping machinery from the conquered countries. In places, the unceasing air raids

[1] The Berlin correspondent of the *Sydsvenska Dagbladet* estimated on January 11, 1943 that the number of foreign workers in Germany at that time was over six million. The Polish workers alone constituted a force in excess of one and a half million.

forced a reversal of this process, factories moving from the Reich itself into Polish and Czecho-Slovak territory.

It was intended that the entire continental economy be collectivized. Germany itself was to be run as an enormous socialized business, controlled by commissars, with the State participating in industrial profits.

All important raw materials and basic processes of the conquered areas have become German monopolies. Some have been taken over outright without pretense. Others have been "purchased."

The gargantuan Hermann Goering combine, controlling a labor force of three million workers, has become the greatest industrial empire in the world. As this is written it owns the entire heavy industry of Austria, iron and coal mines in Poland and Norway, lignite companies in Greece, smelting works in France, and oil wells in Rumania. It holds almost the entire French automobile industry as well as its steel, and an assortment of giant munitions works. Compared to this towering behemoth the United States Steel Corporation is a minor concern.

Another tremendous corporation, the Kontinentale Oel Akt. Ges., has taken over directly or indirectly, the entire oil production of Europe. The German dye trust, I. G. Farben, has absorbed most of the chemical industries. Some have been taken by outright confiscation, others, like the great Norwegian concern, Norsk Hydro El Kvaelstof, through stock control. The three largest chemical concerns in France were merged into one monopoly called Francolor. Though a collaborationist Frenchman is president, I. G. Farben controls fifty-one per cent of the shares.

Germans also hold over fifty per cent of all the stock of banks, insurance companies, industrial and commercial firms of France. In Poland practically all private property was taken over. Its administration is centered in the *Haupttreuhandstelle Ost,* a corporation charged with "the conscription, seizure and exploitation of the property of the former Polish State, and trade and urban properties of former Polish citizens."

The Deutsche Bank, together with the Dresdner Bank, the Commerzbank A.G., the Berliner Handels-Gesellschaft and the Bank der Deutschen Arbeit, control and administer directly or indirectly, almost every financial institution in Europe. The Germans have been careful to go through an elaborate pretense of legality in erecting this hidden structure, with the evident intention of withstanding any change in political leadership. The economic and business structures of all Europe have been "coordinated" with the German cartel machine, with all production or sales quotas determined by Berlin.

Even the laboratory and scientific equipment of the great research institutes of Europe have been seized. Public galleries and private collections have been rifled of art objects, together with the contents of museums and libraries. Those not wanted were destroyed by methodical vandalism, as in the deliberate burning of the priceless manuscripts of the University of Naples, and the firing of the great libraries of the universities of Warsaw, Smolensk and Prague.

The Continent further has been pauperized by a direct tax chargeable to "occupation costs." It is estimated that in these levies Germany receives about $4,800,000,000 a year, an estimate which is exclusive of confiscated gold stocks, businesses, rolling stock and factory production. The yearly occupation rate of fifteen billion francs charged to little Belgium is more than the entire Belgium pre-war budget.

In addition to outright seizure, various types of legalized looting existed. One was the "Aryanizing" of Jewish property. Another was the use of "occupation marks," a special kind of money printed on the spot, which had to be accepted at a definite rate of exchange by the conquered countries, yet which was valueless in Germany itself.

Another expedient which easily could be continued into peacetime, has been the manipulation of currency and the overvaluation of the Reichsmark. The official exchange rates pegged for each country, are made to operate for the benefit of German buyers, the price control being fixed from time to time at different levels as required. A typical example is the Czech crown, which before the war was valued at four to one in relation to the Reichsmark. In 1941 the Germans pegged it at ten to one.

Under such a system of currency control the usual preoccupation with the question of a balanced foreign trade is of no consequence. The most rational operation would be one in which the value of imports far overbalanced the exported materials, which would be held to the barest minimum. It is only in a free mercantile economy that some sort of exchange is required in order to balance the transaction. The German slave system neither requires a stable price system nor any concern over the question of being a creditor or debtor country. The matter of debts is largely one of bookkeeping, or of placating and keeping mollified the subject populations.

Europe has gone through an endless night of horror which must leave its effect in permanent psychic as well as material changes. It has been tortured, humiliated and brutalized in an orgy of defilement without parallel since the dreadful days when the Mongol Khans and Turkoman nomads wrecked entire civilizations in their path of conquest. For the wild ferocity of these simple horsemen the Nazis have substituted a hard contemptuous malice in which not a single item of human compassion, or remnant of the French Revolutionary Enlightenment is visible.

This is the new Europe with which our conquering armies and the future must be concerned. When the Nazis leave we will find a continent with whole areas depopulated, industry ruined, traditional cultural classes destroyed and civilized life demoralized. Cultural forms it has taken many centuries to build will have been annihilated. In their place will be despair, brute anger and the promised chaos of revolution.

When the German flood has receded, the Nazis may be found to have left a legacy more terrible even than their armies.

IV

THE CO-PROSPERITY SPHERE

ON the opposite side of the globe, the Empire of Japan has been following a course roughly parallel to that of the Reich, though of less immediate gravity to the future of the Western races.

The main significance of the spectacular Japanese attempt at world conquest lays in the fact that Japan unwittingly has made herself the incubus which has impregnated the great slumbering body of Asia with what may be a demonic fetus.

Tokyo has become the catalyst which is transforming the immutable, unchanging East into a new and frightening force in which the issues are sharply drawn—those between Caucasian might, bumptiousness and domination of the world's wealth, and the almost reptilian hatreds which will accompany the emergence of the yellow and brown races from their former pliant servility. This change in position involves in itself a revolutionary process of formidable proportions, even though uncomplicated by the radical political convictions which will ride by its side.

It is in these facts that the true genesis of World War III finally may be discovered.

The Japanese have been more ambitious and more logical than the white colonial Powers, who have been merely attempting to hold on and make an archaic, moldering system work. They have sought to modify the old imperial suppositions on a basis congruent to the machine age. As is the case with the Germans they have endeavored to make their home territories the physical hub

74

of a tremendous territorial wheel, as well as the spearhead of a revolutionary social movement.

The Japanese describe themselves as the *Yamato* race, which means "great and peaceful." They believe themselves to be descended from the sun-goddess, who by some hermaphroditic trick gave birth to the god Izanagi and his consort, the goddess Izanami. The Nipponese Empire was allegedly founded by the first progeny of this Ptolemaic marriage, Jimmu Tenno (the Illustrious One) who according to conventional Japanese history was born on the island of Kyushu in 660 B.C. It is from Tenno that the present ruler of Japan claims descent in a straight line.

From the purely anthropological view there are marked differences in Japanese racial type, indicating not only Mongolian and strong Malayan admixtures, but considerable Caucasian and Negrito elements as well.

The indigenous inhabitants of the islands were known as the Hairy Ainu because of their profuse body hair, and are thought to be Caucasian aboriginals. Some few are still left in the northern island of Hokkaido.

The basic Japanese stock seems to have been Tungus, a Mongoloid-Turanian people from the steppes of Asia. There is probably also some infusion of Chinese blood as well as a strong strain from Southeast Asia and Melanesia.

Japan was the first of the Asiatic nations to abandon the feudal order and to re-enter the hurly-burly of history as one of the major contending parties. When Commodore Perry sailed into Uraga Bay in 1853 and succeeded at the point of his cannon in inducing the Japanese to open their country to foreign trade, the Japanese Empire was a medieval remnant consisting of a small group of islands practically without industry or contact with the modern world. The chief concern of the nation had been the fear of absorption by Russia which had already seized Sakhalin Island, and was only deterred by the presence of the British fleet from moving toward the warm waters of the South.

It was the insular position of this ancient kingdom, as well as the remarkable intelligence of its people, which enabled it to abandon centuries-old isolation and leap with unsurpassed eagerness and capacity into the whirlpool of Western science, industrial know-how, and political competence. Japan's growth since, both politically and industrially, has been one of the marvels of our time. In 1895 she fought a successful war with China and took over Formosa and the Pescadores. A decade later she had beaten the Russian Goliath in a swift series of actions, had annexed the lower half of Sakhalin, and had begun her penetration of China. In another few years she had swallowed Korea whole.

Moving with unparalleled rapidity she added the strategic Marshalls and Carolines to her bag as her portion of the spoils of World War I. Following her adventure in China, and the assault on Southeast Asia and the Indies, this once antique Asiatic kingdom has emerged with an empire almost as large as that of Britain itself, and infinitely better situated.

The growth of Japanese industry was almost as extraordinary. Not only was Japan able to compete with Britain, Germany and America, but on many categories of goods was able to undersell them even on their own internal markets.

Japan consists of a string of rocky, ill-favored islands occupying something of the position in relation to continental Asia that Britain does to the subcontinent of Europe, but without Britain's physical resources.

The total land space occupied by Nippon proper is 147,328 square miles, an area roughly comparable to that of the State of Montana. No more than one-eighth of this expanse is cultivable.

The population which must receive its support from these islands is in the neighborhood of seventy-five million. In 1920 it was 55,-963,000. Prior to the Meiji Restoration in 1868 it was thirty million. This phenomenal rate of growth shows no signs of diminishing and is one of the factors which gives impelling force and pragmatic necessity to Japanese policies.

Neither the situation nor the peoples of Nippon and the Reich possess much in the way of apparent likeness yet there is a striking similarity of pattern between the persuasions, drives and impulses which have guided the destinies of the two countries.

Both peoples regard themselves as races set apart, as differing from other men not only by virtue of their psychology and the mission they conceive for themselves, but anthropologically as well. While this obsession is fastened especially on the German mind, it is by no means wanting in the Japanese. It is an essential part of the force which has flung them forward like a rain of nettles against the other peoples of the earth, whom they regard as their collective appointed enemy.

Both peoples are actuated by the fanatic sense of divine appointment. Both possess a curious blend of a feudal social philosophy and the most modern scientific efficiency. Both show great capacity for minute organization as well as infinite patience and will.

The course of Japanese foreign policy bears a striking similarity to that of the Reich. It is guided by a long-range view, by the shrewdest of political appraisals, and by a clear conception of the future. Its essence is given briefly in the words of Viscount Tani in 1887: "Make our country secure by adequate military preparation. Make us strong at home. Then wait for the time of confusion in Europe which must come eventually, sooner or later. At this time, even though our country be aloof from the matter as far as Europe is concerned, we may become the leader of the Orient."

As is true with the Germans, endurance, fortitude, infinite application to detail, cautious duplicity, and the capacity for ruthless concentration of striking force when the moment for decision is deemed to have arrived, will remain Japanese characteristics even in defeat.

The Japanese capacity for secrecy is indicated in the building of the great underseas tunnel linking the port of Shimonoseki on the island of Honshu with Moji on the northern tip of Kyushu, without the world being aware of the project until it actually had been finished, though its completion required the employment of a million laborers and six years of work.

Though the Japanese also worship the machine and make a cult of science, they are governed, like the Germans, by a strong national mysticism which affects a supreme disdain for any material interpretation of the universe. The Japanese add an emotional and metaphysical principle which can no more be translated for the logical appraisal of Western minds than can its German counterpart.

Against the miraculous German word, *Kultur,* the Japanese pose the mesmeric term, *Kokutai,* an untranslatable reference to the entire scheme of Japanese civilization by which the superior destiny of the divinely ordained Japanese people is expressed. Like *Kultur, Kokutai* voices more than culture and more than the essence of superior being. It is the touchword by which the entire system and mythology, the laws and mystical ordination of the Superman, are described.

The modern makers of Japan have turned Emperor worship into a cult, which like the fanatic pagan exercises in Germany, is a genuine binding agent in the national social system. Most Japanese are Buddhists of the Zen sect, yet they manage to conform at the same time to the Emperor worship of *Shinto,* thus combining religion with an entirely opposing mystique.

Shinto itself is hard to define. According to the official definition it is not a religion, "but rather an aspect of patriotism." Nevertheless it has certain rites whose observance is required of every Japanese subject whether he be a Buddhist, Christian or agnostic. *Shinto* images referring to the Emperor, his ancestors and the pantheon of gods who created Japan, may be found in every farmhouse. Every village has a local *Shinto* shrine. Thus the Japanese is tied to the omnipotent State by an attachment to national ghosts and spirits, in many of its aspects as primitive as the dark belief in Obi which pervades the backward reaches of the Negro Caribbean.

Among this highly intelligent and mechanized people the idolatrous worship of the State has reached the point of narcissism. As the supreme representation of the authority of the State, the words of the Imperial Household must be printed in capital letters in Japanese newspapers. When His Imperial Highness rides through the streets "all shutters must be tightly drawn . . . and no one may even stand on a doorstep above a sidewalk." [1]

Like the Germans the Japanese are essentially unsure of themselves, emotionally unstable and given to sudden explosive expressions of violence. Their business and political standards are no higher than those which have distinguished German dealings with the rest of the world. Like the Germans, the Japanese regard every means to the end as being justified. Like the Germans, too, their most prominent characteristic is a capacity for teamwork. They do best when working together as a machine rather than as individuals. Also like the Germans, beneath a surface placidity they possess a dour and melancholic attitude toward life itself.

Much like their Teutonic counterparts, the Japanese right wing radicals have not hesitated to enforce their will by political assassination. A crime roughly comparable to the murder of Walther Rathenau in Germany, was the assassination of Prime Minister Inukai together with Finance Minister Junnosuke Inouye in 1932.

There are various powerful secret groups through which these military chauvinists enforce their will. One is the well-known society of the Black Dragon. Others are the Blood Brotherhood, and the National Foundation Society of Baron Hiranuma. They have as their purpose the rigid implementation of the national destiny. They are the watchdogs who will see that there is no weakening in the internal will and determination to continue to the end.

The Japs are nevertheless gentle in their personal relationships and possess a deep-seated love of natural beauty as well as an immaculate cleanliness of person. Like the Germans, the individual Japanese is apt to be mild in appearance, stolid and plodding. Japanese women are faithful, patient wives and devoted mothers.

1 Sydney Greenbie, *Asia Unbound*, p. 275.

Combined with these qualities the race possesses remarkable energy, foresight and capacity for technological achievement, as well as a fanatic pride and national ego. As with Germany, the Japanese devotion to the cult of force is unlimited, and reaches the proportions of a pathology.

Similar to Germany, Japan is ruled by fears and hatreds in which the British prominently figure. Both Axis States regard Russia as their predestined enemy. Both are dedicated to the complete destruction of the old order, and are convinced that their destiny requires the ultimate annihilation of Britain and America. Though there are almost no Jews in Japan, the Japs have adopted anti-Semitism as part of their credo, and like the Germans have been agitating Arabia with anti-Zionist excitations.

The mass espionage practised by the Germans is strikingly like the methods utilized by the Japanese. The beating and killing of helpless American prisoners and the wholesale rape and murder of Chinese civilians by Japanese soldiers, may be compared with the equally savage tactics of the Germans against the civilian populations of Europe. Even the techniques employed have been so alike as to suggest a close exchange of views. The public stripping and humiliation of English men and women by the Japs finds its counterpart in standard Teutonic practice in the Slavic East, the idea being that of demolishing the dignity and prestige on which leadership rests.

The very industrial concentrations of the Reich in the Ruhr valley are matched by the solid factory belt of Japan which runs like a huge sooty sash, forty miles wide, from Tokyo to Kyushu Island, and from Nagasaki to Fukuoka. This teeming, crowded district, belching an unending stream of flame and smoke, contains the steel mills, engineering shops, munitions manufactories, dockyards and principal industrial plants of the nation.

The Japanese industrial structure represents another of the anachronisms peculiar to the country. It is largely a banking capitalism in the hands of a number of monopoly groups, fifteen of which rule seventy per cent of Japanese trade and industry. Eight of these, headed by the great family houses of Mitsui, Mitsubishi, and Sumitomo, control over fifty per cent of Japan's business.

These mountainous monopolistic concerns have vastly increased their power by mutual cartel agreements, creating what is probably the most impressive capitalist control structure of a single national economy in the world. As might be expected, Tokyo treats these immense trusts as if they were extensions of the government itself. The industries which are identified with the national defense and with the political schemes by which the national future is to be advanced, are directly subsidized and controlled. The government now directs all economic life by methods which are closely related to those of state socialism, though in important ways they may be indirectly applied.

Thus, though Japan represents the very epitome of big business, as does Germany, both States veer sharply over to radical philosophies. The tendency is toward both totalitarianism and equalitarianism, a fact plainly evident in the welfare policies of the German State, where the free trade order has been all but liquidated.

Today one of the favorite claims of Nazism is that it has broken the control of international finance. We behold Hitler referring to the Americans as "those capitalistic hyenas," and Dr. Ley demanding at a labor conference that the workers of Europe "unite to smash the rule of English and American capitalism, the common enemy of all workers." What is not realized is that the Japanese have been progressing as steadily to the left. When the Kwantung army seized Manchukuo it broke completely with the feudal and commercial traditions of Japan and embarked on what is primarily an experiment in military state socialism.

The Army has turned Manchukuo into a testing station for its social and economic theories. Agriculture has been largely collectivized. Where the State does not directly operate industry it rigidly controls it under a five year plan which bears striking similarities to that of the Russians.

The Japanese War Department in a significant pamphlet issued in 1934, did not hesitate to declare "that the people should abandon their individualistic economic conceptions. Instead they should recognize the importance of a collective economy."

The Army is the real ruler of Japan. It has sprung mostly from sons of peasant stock, hence of the old feudal economy. The younger of these men especially, have been impressed by the theories of Marx which they have turned into a typical national socialist program whose core is the superior destiny of the *Yamato* people.

Just as the Germans believe that whatever promotes the welfare of the Third Reich is moral and whatever does not is immoral, irrespective of any other applying consideration, the Japanese army is convinced that whatever stands in the way of the mission of the Japanese people and the divine role of the Emperor must be ruthlessly extirpated.

The military has inherited in a direct line all of the traditions of the *Samurai*, or warrior class. We find beneath the entire framework of modern rationalism, scientific skill and industrial competence, of which the army is perhaps the chief exponent, the ancient cabalism of a powerful and still vibrantly live feudal system.

The *Samurai* as a class disdain commerce as demeaning to men, and like the old Prussian officer caste, long possessed special privileges. Under the Hundred Articles of the Tokugawa Government (1615-1868) a *Samurai* was permitted to cut down a commoner on the spot wherever "common people behaved unbecomingly to members of the military class or . . . showed want of respect to direct or indirect vassals."

The code of these men, who have played a leading role in Nipponese history from the day of the Shogun Iyeyasu to the fall of Singapore, is in many respects as high as that of King Arthur's knights. Yet at the same time it authorizes the most despicable treacheries and brutality. It is known as *Bushido,* and governs every element in the warrior's life including his dress and social behavior. The *Samurai* was taught rigid self control, stoicism and absolute fidelity. He prides himself on having "no second word" and on never drawing his sword without using it.[1]

Despite the classic gentleness of Japanese civilization the Japanese soldier is capable of implacable cruelty and truculence. Until comparatively modern times, when the various feudal clans fought each other, all prisoners, men, women and children alike, were beheaded. Up to 1870 it was the usual Japanese procedure to collect enemy heads after every battle. "The official tally of casualties was always rendered on this basis." [2]

Characteristic of the Japanese soldier is a remorseless sadism which, as in the case of the German, becomes much more intensified as he is organized in the mass than when he functions as an individual. The revolting sex turn this has taken in the case of German crimes on the continent of Europe is also characteristic of Japanese actions against the civilian populations of Asia.

As in Germany, military training begins as the child enters kindergarten. At the age of twelve he is already carrying a rifle and is participating in light maneuvers including the use of hand grenades. At nineteen he is a full-fledged soldier, inured to hardship and practised in the arts of battle.

As in the Nazi army, promotion in the Japanese forces is strictly by merit. Its leadership possesses one of the youngest age averages of any army in the world. Its rate of literacy is probably unsurpassed.

The Japanese army must be considered more than a military machine. It is in part a *Bund* of proletarian origin and national socialist view. Like the art of *Judo* it is an expression of the inherent traditions, the will-to-the-future, the inflexible cultural concepts which rule the Japanese nation. Until 1943 it had an unbroken record of victories which was the pride of every man, woman and child in the country.

The consequent prestige of the army has enabled it to maintain an unbroken hold on the nation. When the fighting services de-

1 Lieut. Col. Warren J. Clear, *Infantry Journal,* 1942.
2 *Ibid.*

cided that the time had come to join the Axis, the Army was able to dismiss a Prime Minister "with little more ceremony than a corporation would use in changing its janitor." [1]

Despite the drift to collectivization, there is no dictatorship in Japan in the current Fascist sense. The Japanese are too cagey to allow the usurpation of power by a single individual. As far back as the Tokugawa dictatorship the governmental system was characterized by a careful rotation of responsibility so as to avoid the possibility of one person acquiring a monopoly of power. Today certain features of this system still remain in existence.

At the moment the three most powerful men in Japan are General Kuniaki Koiso, General Sugiyama and the Chief Secretary of the Cabinet, Naoki Hoshino. The Emperor himself exercises very little actual authority. He is the universal symbol from whom all law unfolds. In practice authority flows through his name and office but is exercised by others as was the case with the German State when Hindenburg was alive.

II

The Japanese believe that their Emperor, a rather mild near-sighted scholarly man, is destined eventually to be the ruler of all nations, and to bring eternal peace to the world. This expectation may be read in General Nonaka's stern observation: "The ultimate conclusion of politics is the conquest of the world by one imperial power. The Japanese nation is bracing herself to fill her appointed role."

As was the German, the Nipponese dream of world empire is a development from old causes.

The ambitious little country long has been painfully conscious of the grave weakness of her physical situation. The bulk of the resources on which her industry depends had to be imported, an infirmity which exposed the nation to recurring dangers. The military position was as unassuring. Foreign Minister Komura warned

1 Hugh Byas, *Government by Assassination*, p. 136.

his countrymen in 1909 of the serious position of the nation, caught in the jaws of four hundred million Chinese, 160,000,000 Russians and 100,000,000 Americans. The mere weight of this galaxy of opponents he alleged was one day bound to crush Japan unless she could find expansion on the mainland, and a compensating growth in population. The goal set by Komura was 100,000,000.

These reasoned fears, suspicions and hopes were grafted onto the old dream of world errand, and a warrior tradition which is integral with Japanese existence itself.

In 1592 the Emperor Hideyoshi, who is to Japanese tradition what Frederick Barbarossa, Bismarck and Frederick the Great are to the German, conquered Korea, slaughtering nearly three million people, and bringing with him for burial beneath the famous Ear and Nose Monument of Kyoto [1] the severed ears and noses of forty thousand Koreans slain during the last week of the war. The Japanese army completely gutted the country, destroying what they could not take with them, and putting an end to a glorious period of Korean art and ceramics from which the nation never recovered.

After the conquest Hideyoshi outlined his plans for the further subjection of the Asiatic mainland in a set of "Articles to be presented to the Imperial Envoy of Tai-Min [China]." In this memorandum he asserted: "Japan is a divine nation. Our divinity is the Heavenly Emperor, there being absolutely no difference between them. Our nation having thus been created by the Divinity, our national customs were originally molded as those of the Divine Age."

When he was born, Hideyoshi relates, his mother was informed in a miraculous dream that "just as there was but one sun in the heavens there would soon be born to her a male child who would have no duplicate and who would become the sole ruler of the world."

Though Hideyoshi's inspired purpose of founding a supreme world empire was never fulfilled, it became the subject of

---

1 The old capital of Japan.

Japanese song and tradition. For more than three centuries every Japanese schoolboy has been taught that this glorious plan, frustrated temporarily by the inscrutable will of Heaven, would finally have its fulfilment and that the divine race of *Yamato* under the leadership of its god incarnate, the Son of Heaven, would rule the globe.

After Commodore Perry had performed his historic mission in opening Japan to foreign commerce, the Court Chamberlain, Baron Hotto, in submitting to the Mikado the text of the first commercial treaty with the outside world, described the glittering destiny which ultimately was to befall the Royal line. "To have such a ruler over the whole world," he said, "is doubtless in conformity with the will of Heaven . . . In establishing relations with foreign countries, the object should always be kept in view of laying a foundation for securing the hegemony over all nations."

The chance disclosure and publication of the now famous Tanaka Memorial was an event whose significance was not fully realized at the time. In this document presented by Baron Giichi Tanaka to Emperor Tenno on July 25, 1927, the procedure was outlined by which Japan was to seek first the subjection of Asia, and then of the globe.

Tanaka asserted that Japan must adopt a policy of "blood and iron. In the future," he declared, "if we want to control China we must first crush the United States, just as in the past we had to fight in the Russo-Japanese War. But in order to conquer China we must first conquer Manchuria and Mongolia. In order to conquer the world we must first conquer China. If we succeed in conquering China, the rest of the Asiatic countries and the South Sea countries will fear us and surrender to us. Then the world will realize that Eastern Asia is ours and will not dare to violate our rights. This is the plan left to us by the Emperor Meiji, the success of which is essential to our national existence."

Tanaka warns his countrymen against the day when "China becomes unified and her industries prosperous," at which time the classic ambitions of the *Yamato* people would be at an end. China's industrial development must be halted at all costs, as must the penetration of Asia by European Powers, whose superior capital resources would result in the eventual defeat of Japan.

Tanaka advises his monarch that "final success belongs to the country having raw materials," and that "the full growth of national strength belongs to the country having extensive territory." In a sound, salty estimate of the nature of power in its relation to the future, Tanaka details the magnificent resources of Manchukuo and Mongolia and outlines a method for their proper exploitation. As Hitler was to advocate later, Tanaka urges a policy of deceit, of grandiose lies, of forced marches and *faits accomplis*. He saw with uncanny insight the connection of modern industrialization with the waging of war, and anticipated fully the use of the modern fifth column. He judged with contemptuous disregard that so long as foreign capitalists were permitted to share in the spoils no one would interfere until the Japanese design had been completed.

There seemed ample justification for this assumption. Japan grudgingly was looked on by the Imperial Powers as a sort of partner whose coinciding interests prompted it to police the turbulent Far East. This provided what seemed to be a reasonable compensation for the crude power of Japanese mercantile competition, which the Western nations found little to their liking.

III

As far as the record goes, the Tanaka plan would seem to be the blueprint which has been faithfully followed by Tokyo since the day it was prepared.

Even the briefest examination makes it evident that the Japanese are dedicated to the identical course in Asia as are their German allies in Europe. Their program calls for unlimited expansion on the Continent under the name of the "Co-Prosperity Sphere" of Eastern Asia. They intend eventually to reduce all Asia and later the world to a vast colony which will supply raw material to the Japanese power center for manufacture and distribution. Though certain light industries would be permitted on the adjacent continent, the manufacture of precision instruments and heavy machinery would be concentrated in the Nipponese Islands themselves.

As in the German plan, whole regions would be given over to the production of single items. Canada would produce wheat, India cotton, and Australia, livestock, under Japanese commissars. The entire global economy would be coordinated into a gigantic Japanese-dominated system.

The likeness of Japanese methods to those employed by their Prussian analogues in Europe is so startling as to suggest that these parallel characteristics were not the result of accident. The Japanese have made looting a precise science. Immediately upon the conquest of a city, the Japanese Special Service Corps moves in. This is composed of experts—appraisers and transportation men who make an exact inventory of everything, raw materials, art treasures and other possessions. Nothing is overlooked in the systematic plundering which then goes forward. When the industrial centers of China were taken, stockyards, factories and plants, mines, public buildings, utilities, and even dwellings, were seized and allotted to Japanese interests.

Wherever it moved in, the Japanese military took monopoly control over all production and distribution, and introduced a type of currency control similar to that initiated by the Germans in Europe.

In the early days of the occupation the Japanese evinced an utter contempt for human life, and a lust for murder which showed itself in the indiscriminate machine-gunning of refugees on the roads, the clubbing to death of Chinese women and children and the use of Chinese civilians as dummies for bayonet practice. German sources estimate the cases of rape at Nanking alone at twenty thousand.

Activities directed at reducing the moral fiber of the exploited peoples and with it their resistance, also have been part of the Japanese system. The Japs made the opium and heroin trade an instrument of State policy in China, as Germans made use of liquor and obscene exhibitions in Poland. These drugs are supplied by the public authorities conveniently and cheaply, and made available even to little children. Over one-eighth of the population of Nanking is said now to be addicted to the use of drugs.

All of the variations of policy employed by Germany in handling the different populations under her rule, may be seen in the Japanese attitude toward the nations she has taken.

In Formosa the 5,400,000 Chinese who constitute ninety-four per cent of the population, have been degraded into hewers of wood and drawers of water. They have no place in business, the government or civil service, and their whole economy is geared to Japanese needs.

Korea is permitted a limited amount of light industries, but these are all Japanese-owned. The Koreans themselves have been consigned to an inferior status, becoming almost exclusively workers and producers for Japanese enterprise. One-third of the arable land is held by absentee Japanese landlords, and something over another third is owned by resident Japanese. It is estimated that eighteen million out of Korea's total twenty-three million population have become tenants or squatters.

In the entire peninsula there is not a single newspaper published in the Korean language; while all utilities, banks and other major businesses, together with almost all of the shops, are in the hands of Japanese.

Japan has brought grim poverty to Korea, though it must be said the efficient Japanese public health service has rid the peninsula of smallpox, cholera and other endemic diseases which formerly were prevalent.

On the whole, the Japanese have had better luck in attaining the cooperation of their new subjects than have the Germans. The Japanese have been cunning. After it was apparent that the war would be long, and that the usual methods of repression could not successfully be applied, Tokyo introduced a gigantic campaign of pro-Asiatic fraternization.

Puppet regimes were set up which by contrast with previous white rule had all the look of independence. Thailand was flattered with the title of "ally." As a reward for its assistance it was given four provinces of the Malay States and two provinces of Burma. The Philippines and Burma were granted "independence" under Japanese "advisers."

A provisional "free government" for India was set up in Singapore. French Indo-China was cajoled by cultural missions and loans, as were the Indonesians.

In strategically situated Indonesia the iron hand was well concealed within the velvet glove. A Home Defense Corps was established by which the inhabitants of the archipelago helped to police their own islands. Farmer's training centers were established together with the usual trappings of the welfare State, all designed to bind these people to Tokyo during the period of the war in an appearance of close-working harmony.

In Manchukuo, on the other hand, all life is dominated by the Japanese and their interests. The universities were closed in 1939, after a design similar to that followed in Korea and Japanese-occupied China. If higher education is desired natives must go to Japan for it and, in short, lend themselves to Japonization.

Faced with the realization that the war was not to be won quickly and easily, Japan has moved with great shrewdness. Where the Germans have brutally announced their determination not to Germanize but to rule the conquered populations as serfs, Tokyo has adopted the role of a big brother whose vision, financial resources, and talent for organization will lead the people of Eastern Asia to a happy future, free from the enslavement of the white man.

In its effort to tie the conquered countries closer to her, Tokyo has even encouraged native leaders to go to Japan for the purpose of marrying Japanese girls, while Nipponese soldiers are induced to marry women of the leading native families.

The customary looting is now conducted on carefully disguised lines. It functions through an inundation of Japanese "experts," "specialists" and "advisers" who in the name of the Co-Prosperity Sphere establish banks and corporations which soon obtain a monopoly on the exploitation of key raw materials and the distribution of consumer products. The issuance of worthless military money and the pegging of local currencies at arbitrary rates, completes the pattern of indirect exploitation.

Simultaneously, Japan has moved forward in line with the most advanced social jargon in an effort to win over the native proletariat. Lands of absentee owners have been confiscated and divided up by the Army among the suppressed, landless peasantry.

The difference in handling of the conquered populations by the Germans and Japanese largely delineates the difference in the nature of the problems which will face our statesmen in Europe and Asia. Where the ancient civilized community of Europe has been debauched and rocked to its foundations, and will be ready for any radical adventure, Asia for the moment has felt the illusion of freedom. The peoples of the Orient have been stimulated to believe that they are engaged in a mighty crusade for equality and freedom.

The liege regime of Wang Ching-wei in North China, together with the governments of Burma, Thailand and Manchukuo, is in a declared state of war with the United States and Britain. It involves not only a struggle for Asiatic freedom, but an emotional approach perilously close to that of vicious race war.

Japanese official opinion controls the sole news and information agencies for this entire section of creation. Tokyo has handled the propaganda instrument with an extraordinary ability not surpassed even by the Germans. In Japanese hands it has become one of the principal agencies of political action. It covers from view the merciless Nipponese exploitation of these countries, even making these acts appear to be an economic blessing. It has amply succeeded in diverting the native suspicion and hatred of the Japanese themselves to the white slave-master who has been represented as responsible for all of Asia's ills.

Fed on self-righteous pride and well-controlled jingoism, this challenging propaganda asserts that the regime of Chiang K'ai-shek, and all others who favor cooperation with the white man, is that of a puppet in the hands of the exploiting Anglo-American powers. The effect has been to compel the Kuomintang [1] itself to adopt an anti-foreign stand out of pure self-defense.

Tokyo has explored every propaganda possibility with consummate shrewdness, creating everywhere a powerful Pan-Asiatic solidarity built on hate for the Caucasian. The slogan "Asia for the Asiatics" has come to mean "Down with the White Man."

The Japanese have done a cunning job of stimulating this movement and following it to its final goals. It exists wherever the yellow and brown races exist, ready to burst into a pyrotechnic display at the first favorable opportunity.

Neither in India, Africa or Arabia has the effect of the white man's early defeat by the Japanese might been lost. The tradition of white invincibility has been shattered by a blow from which it will not readily recover. The Japanese have gone to the length of distributing among the nations of the East and South, lascivious photographs showing nude white women in various indecent poses in order to destroy the last illusion of Caucasian authority and prestige.

More than a billion people have been in one degree or another, exposed to this pitiless spate of anti-white propaganda. In the territories under Japanese control it has done to the Caucasian in Asia what the Germans have done to the Jew in Europe—it has made him an outlaw personality, the source of all mischief and author of all articulate evil.

Many thousands of the Asiatic intelligentsia have been indoctrinated to the hilt with these beliefs. In addition to the territories she dominates, whose inhabitants hear nothing else, Tokyo consistently broadcasts to the Chinese, the Arabs and the Indians, spurring their anger against the Caucasian, and agitating them to hatred. The

[1] The ruling party of Free China.

Chinese and Indians are told that though whites are free to live in Asia, Asiatics cannot enter the United States. They are told that their nationals are forced to live in segregated areas and are able to take only the most menial and humiliating types of employment. With a malevolence comparable only to that utilized in German anti-Semitic propaganda, falsehood, distortion and fraud are combined with a smattering of truth with devastating effect. The Caucasian is shown to be completely unmoral, unworthy, depraved, conscienceless, decadent and false. His civilization is represented as an improvisation dangerous to the true culture of the East.

Though Japanese efforts have applied equally to Americans, the hatred is especially venomous against the English. Here the seeds of Japanese propaganda struck fertile ground.

After her ultimate defeat in this war, Japan, as we shall see, can never hope to be a first-class Power again. She will collapse and become either a helpless vassal State, or a province in some large empire.

What will be left behind as the result of her desperate and exhausting adventure will not be the problem of Japan but the far mightier problem of Asia.

THE ETERNAL PROBLEM OF WAR

THE key to war and peace is not one of moral intent or legal definition, but rather of the balance of conditions which at any given moment governs organized society. It is impossible to find a cure by the introduction of fine principles of "law" for troubles whose real roots are sunk not in some ostensible criminality but in the unresolved problems of daily existence.

Even in the case of the Germans, the moral intent is not the essential control factor. The Germans, who suffer from an abnormal psychology, do not see the course they have pursued as a wicked and reprehensible one. On the contrary, they believe it to be completely justified by Providence, which has appointed them to play out their role of the Chosen People in the future affairs of mankind.

The questions which apply to the problem of world peace are no longer simple but highly complex. They are affected by the collective global organization of economic life, and the industrial potential and position in space occupied by the individual nations, as well as the quality, history, temper and material needs of their peoples. They are influenced, above all, by the relative power positions the States occupy in relation to each other.

Any important alteration in the world's industrial outlook can be expected to force a corresponding change in its political structure which otherwise immediately becomes antiquated. It is a presupposition of life that a political order must be of such a nature as to allow the performance of the vital functions of existence, especially those of manufacture, trade and defense. Any serious disturbance to this balance involves an immediate threat to peace.

Under any analysis the primary basis for all aggression is power. Whatever the reasons for conflict may be, it is the capacity to strike with swift, lethal savagery which determines the course of events and makes the assault inevitable. In rough outline, therefore, it may be said that wars result not only from hungers, provocations and abnormal quirks of psychology, but from a primary disequilibrium of forces which provides the incentive to attack by the stronger upon the weaker.

This will be found to be true universally whatever the complaint to be redressed. It applies with equal validity to the primitive man and wolfpack whose weapons are no more than clubs and teeth, as to a military age whose central problem is measured by the amount and velocity of steel which can be put into motion and massed against the enemy's vulnerable points.

Every relationship of organized, competitive existence is thus dominated by the capacity of weapons to achieve concentrated striking force, and by the properties of effective resistance which can be offered against them. Every change in economic or social conditions brings with it a change in the nature of power and the methods by which it can be employed. Every new invention or discovery automatically creates new problems and new areas of contention. If the imbalance which results is sufficiently great it leads to only one possible result—war.

It may be taken for granted that wherever new instruments of control exist, military leaders will arise to make use of them. Wherever political institutions are unable to adjust themselves to the new social forces which appear in the world, they will succumb to the active pressures exerted on them, a failure which will be just as factual whether it passes under the name of revolution or war.

This is part of the conventional design of history. Its outline may be seen in the collapse of Rome to the Northern barbarians in the Fifth Century, in the fall of Byzantium to the Moslem Turks in

1453, or in the death of the fossilized royal absolutism of France at the hands of the Revolutionary Commune.

In modern times a similar relationship of cause and effect may be observed in the crumpling of Romanoff Russia in the Red revolt of 1919, or in the ignominious collapse of Western Europe to the Nazi hordes in 1940.

However dissimilar the causes of these disturbances might have been, it will be observed that they possessed one absolute characteristic in common—in almost every case they proceeded either from an actual decay of the State itself, or from an imbalance of power. In every case the aggressor believed himself to be in possession of a superiority of forces.

It should be observed that none of the prescriptions by which wars were to have been outlawed have been of any material value. The abysmal failure of treaties and agreements to be effectual is evident to all eyes and will be discussed in detail later. The hope that either religion, science or social philosophy would provide the basis for a lasting peace has proved as illusory.

At one time it was confidently believed that as kings, princes and other hereditary rulers were disposed of and the universal ballot came into being, peace would be the automatic result. This was considered to be especially true wherever equal suffrage was granted to women since they of all others, it was alleged, understood the hurt and pain of war. Notwithstanding, we find the principal war government of Europe to be the German Republic, seated in power by constitutional means and largely through the devoted help of spellbound women.

It was also presumed that as improved communications and scientific achievement made the world smaller, the nations would grow to know each other better and thus automatically demolish the more ridiculous elements of national prejudice and hatred. It was assumed that in the hot sun of mutual interdependence the causes of war would evaporate. The machine age which was to have done away with war and want at the same time, actually increased both by concentrating workers in the cities and by increasing the maladjustments between production and distribution. Science which was to have made wars impossible, actually made them more terrible. What had been considered to be the beginning of a new and unparalleled golden age of progress in which reason was to be enthroned as the guiding principle of mankind, turned out to be quite something else—a tyranny of inarticulate forces which lent themselves to bloated and constantly shifting consolidations of power.

Universal education was another remedy which, it was claimed, would bring sanity to the world and provide a prophylactic against the bloody business of war. Science, scholarship and research were to be the short cuts to Utopia.

Nevertheless, it has been the universities themselves, once held to be the stronghold of liberalism, which incubated and nourished the blackest and most reactionary of the current designs for living. It was precisely here that Nazi philosophies found their strongest support, and prejudices which once were shamefacedly hidden as being the legacy of the gutter, were dragged out, rationalized and made respectable.

Even the sacred cause of pacifism by which the Holy Grail of peace was to be secured forever, is now conceded to have been one of the causes of war. It acted as a direct encouragement to the aggressor and caused the democratic countries to evacuate step by step the strong positions by which the dictator nations could have been confined within bounds. The pacifism of the West strongly encouraged the predatory States in their dreams of easy slaughter, and stimulated them in the prosecution of their schemes.

The assumption that protective social legislation would erase the conditions which foster war proved equally unsound. Such plans as those advanced by Beveridge in London, and which seem so radical to American eyes, have long been part of the commonplace operations of the Reich. The Weimar Constitution under which Germany still theoretically exists, was the most liberal document it was possible to compose. It provided for a system of proportional representation which allowed all groups to be heard in the government according to their strength.

The effect was to force on the nation a system of government by coalition in which no one ever had a clear majority, and to open up the path to power to the most radical elements. Instead of providing that equipoise which existed in the more experienced democracies, it created a set of angry disparities which resulted in the flight of power from the *Reichstag* to the *Reichsrat,* and thence to the Executive Branch and the Chancellor.

When finally in 1933 the Republic which had begun with the Socialist, Friedrich Ebert, ended with the National Socialist, Adolf Hitler, it was the result of a sequence of orderly processes all of which had kept nicely within the law.[1]

II

Modern wars derive from quite a different set of conditions than those which existed in the past. The present causations are linked to the overwhelming changes in the power formula brought about by the machine age, and to the even greater changes which are impending. The impetus to war now finds itself in social problems and in the conflicts which exist between the expanding industrial order and the fixed political divisions in which the world is carved.

The present political order is like an obstinate old man who has outlived his usefulness but who still insists on his prerogatives. It has become an antique and rapidly stratifying form of authority, containing such consistently widening fissures and repugnancies as to be soon inoperable altogether.

It is in the efforts to resolve this impossible situation that the wars and revolutions of tomorrow will be nurtured.

The familiar political framework with which we are acquainted has emanated from the needs and political ideals of a more or less

---

[1] The Weimar Constitution has yet to be repealed. The Nazis operate directly within its framework by virtue of an Enabling Act transferring emergency powers from the Reichstag to the Cabinet.

rural world dominated by maritime communications. Today it no longer conforms to either the pattern of economic or military logic. This may be seen clearly in an examination of the critical transformations which have periodically affected the power pattern, and which are now again revolutionizing it totally.

Among primitive peoples war was the result of simple needs and emotional drives. Such factors as revenge, fear, the quest for women, plunder or better grazing grounds, regulated the incursions of one tribe upon the settlements of the others. Marauding had its irresistible fascinations also in the way of plunder and sheer sport. It was a testing ground for heroes and leaders, much as the headlong battle of males during the rutting season has been the classic means by which the mammalian female has selected her mate.

The factors which dominated aggression were hardihood, fierceness, mobility and recklessness in battle. Martial qualities and the genius for conquest have in the past run concurrent with privation and a wild, nomad life. These eruptions against organized society were based primarily on the motive of gain and the restlessness which proceeded from a poor climate, a poor soil and a poorly organized social structure.

Wherever we have seen the eruptions of fierce desert and prairie tribesmen against their vegetative and more civilized neighbors, we observe a conflict in which the table of numbers, organization and material possessions has always favored the defender, whereas the dynamics of ferocity, mobility and will have been on the side of the attacker.

The picture is painted in clear pigments in the Mohammedan assault on the great helpless populations of India, Asia and Africa, or the ease with which Temuljin, Sabutai and the other Mongol captains rode their yaktails across the length and breadth of the Eurasian Continent.

We see these untamed primitive forces at work in the periodic storming of all the rich and civilized areas of history almost up to modern times. The process is observable in the fall of the great opulent Hittite Empire in 717 B.C. before the screaming armies of

Sargon of Assyria, as it was in the attacks by the Vikings on suffering Europe during the early centuries of the Christian era.

These conditions were obviously irremediable to the settled communities which found themselves assailed. The causes involved would not yield to a papal bull or to the moral denunciations of a constituent assembly. They were forces which not only led to war —they required war before their destiny could be fulfilled. Hence they were to remain until the leavens which produced them had left the stage of history.

The incentive to war has passed through many successive modifications; but at all times it reflected the social order and the needs of the era in which it operated. The Crusades mirrored not only the religious impulses of the Twelfth and Thirteenth Centuries but the anarchy and political disorganization which had engulfed Europe with the fall of the Roman Imperators. They gave opportunity to impoverished noblemen, knights and adventurers who had been ruined by the general decay which characterized the times, to sack the rich cities of the fabled East and to escape from the famine, poverty and monastic life of Europe.

It did not appear incongruous for the newly established Christian Levant States to find themselves in economic conflict with the Church itself, or even to form alliances with various Moslem rulers in their mutual struggles against Christian rivals. Indeed, during the Fourth Crusade the Westerners did not hesitate to besiege Constantinople, then the keystone to Christian Europe, and to sack and burn it.

The end of the power of the Medieval Church coincided with a totally new group of wars. Thus the events of the Fifteenth and Sixteenth Centuries could have been predicted with accuracy from the anxieties which were proclaimed by the institution of the Inquisition. The universal church as the supreme political authority had already begun to lose its function and the heresy trials were evidence of this alarm.

Until this time, race, color and nation played small part in the quarrels of Christendom. Men were divided as between Christians and heathen, and differences in nationality were synonymous with differences in dynastic loyalties or language.

The beginning of the era of science and free trade saw large sections of Europe, particularly in the north, break from the Church, evolving a decentralized ecclesiastical system which attempted to reconcile the conflicts between the old religious societies and the new mercantile age. It saw also the small beginnings of the principle of political nationalism which later was to unfold itself as the dominating influence of the period.

A series of desperate struggles followed the resistance of the Church to this challenge. The War of the Spanish Succession involved almost all of Christian Europe, the two sides being divided along religious lines. The Thirty Years War fought between the Catholic Powers under the leadership of Austria and the Protestant States led by Sweden, almost turned the Continent into a desert.

If one refers to the map, Northern Europe will be seen to consist of a long, narrow, irregular plain stretching from the Pyrenees to the Pripyat marshes of Eastern Poland, and from the Alps and Carpathians to the sea. It is drained by a number of excellent river highways which favor easy communication, and possesses few natural barriers to free intercourse among its peoples.

To the north this plain surrounds the large salt water lake of the Baltic. On the northeast it extends through the green rolling fields of Britain to the uplands of Wales and Scotland, an area separated from the parent mass by a waterway only twenty-eight miles wide.

This unbroken stretch of territory contains excellent harbors, considerable mineral riches, and in particular, great resources in coal and iron. It has been continuously inhabited by a talented, numerous and energetic people who had received from their contact with Rome an introduction into the classic arts and sciences.

The countries of this plain, possessing little in the way of topographical protection from each other, remained almost uninterruptedly in the war-making phase, much as did the old Hebrews, Edomites, Moabites and Philistines who had been situated on a similar though diminutive land-bridge.

As a result of this interaction of factors this region became the seat of an extensive development of industry and the material sciences, destined to have a decisive effect on the affairs of the world. Coincident with these transformations occurred a steady improvement in the efficiency of weapons and in the methods of their use. At this anvil of Mars was fashioned the traditional European Imperialism with which the world has been familiar. It was accompanied by the swift maturing of political nationalism, based no longer on religious or dynastic considerations but on common boundaries, interests, language or culture.

The process reached its half-way mark in the stirring events of the French Revolution. Rising in triumph out of the ashes of the old order came the bourgeois trader, a tendency toward urbanization, and an almost religious trust in the omnipotence of science and objective knowledge. This formula demanded markets and free movement of goods independent of the suzerainty of the little city-States, the manorial courts and the myriad of independent enclaves into which the Continent was divided.

The required reforms were carried through Europe by the bayonets of Napoleon's armies. They led to a simplification of political geography, and vast constitutional changes. They put an end to medieval land arrangements and to the privileges of the Trade Guilds whose operations were hindering the growth of industry. With these were abolished the feudal dues and the innumerable tolls and customs lines of the many city-States, dukedoms and baronial fiefs.

These smashing innovations resulted in a period of feverish world-wide commercial activity. Raw materials were transported from the farthest reaches of the earth and markets began to exist wherever there were human beings. Coincidentally the progress of science and the technical skills led to the blast furnace, the electric power plant, the steam engine, the gasoline motor and the long list of corollary inventions by which man began to take control of his environment.

Each new advance in the industrial revolution reflected itself in anatomical changes which pyramided the power of weapons and reordered the nature of national competitions. The invention of the musket and the harquebus made modern infantry tactics possible, and enabled the substitution of the highly drilled national army for the militia-type troops and mercenary bands which had served Europe previously. The organization by Napoleon of the first field artillery regiments reintroduced the war of movement by which the feudal era of Europe was irretrievably shattered.

The accession of the steam engine and the rapid industrialization of cities made possible the invention of the Prussian general staff system with its carefully planned designs of logistics and strategy. The invention of the steam-driven armored vessel, the discovery of high explosives and the rifled gun barrel, altered, each in turn, the blueprint of military operations.

The discovery of new processes for hardening and manufacturing steel, the maturing revolution in transportation, and the giant strides forward taken by the science of engineering, created altogether new powers and causations in war as well as a radically revised succession of objectives.

Power is no longer governed by the massed fire action of marching men led by an alert and quickly responsive generalship. It is now a composite from many contributing sources. It is based on superiority of transportation and communication. It involves a complexity of conditions and motives which relate to the industrial and economic position of the State.

The consequence of the printing press, the radio, the internal combustion engine, mass production and the urbanization of life, has been to extend military action into entirely new dimensions, as well as to create new centers of authority. Wars are now fought in their first stages far from the battlefield by the use of invisible methods and without formal declaration of hostilities. The economic and propaganda elements may themselves be decisive without further recourse to arms, a matter we shall discuss in detail later.

Whether in the fields of economic struggle, psychological attack or in the actual theaters of combat, wars no longer are conducted by the classic strategies employed by such captains as Alexander, Hannibal and Napoleon. The military potential of the modern State relates not to any historic grit, toughness and fighting quality, but to blast furnaces, scientific laboratories, and mills for the advanced processing of metals. Mass production and mass military organization have become synonymous.

The core of the war machine is not individual brilliance of command but the industrial power apparatus. Strategy is no longer an improvisation by some military genius whose decisions are made on the evidence his field glasses give him. Modern military technique consists, instead, of a system of carefully related shock tactics and the concentration of pure, naked, merciless killing power directed not only at the enemy's armies, but at his cities, railways and industrial apparatus. The object involves a large-scale destruction of the physical properties of the State itself in an effort to subdue it totally.

Only a large industrialized nation, populous in numbers and possessing guaranteed access to required raw materials, can fight a modern war successfully. Only such a State is capable of organizing, equipping and servicing the huge mechanized armies which must be employed.

The Military itself has become an almost completely autonomous society with its own engineers, scientists and experts in virtually every human skill. Back of these in turn are the millions who are laboring in the mines, offices and shops of the civilian economy back home, offering a constantly rising ratio which today may be as high as six essential civilian workers for every man in uniform.

The startling nature of this revolution in power may be seen in the reversed relationship existing between nomad societies and settled communities. It is no longer possible for the wild tribes of the Asiatic steppes to burst in a flood over the frontiers of Europe. Nor may patriots rise spontaneously like the Orangemen against

Spain, or the American settlers against their British cousins and overlords. Men no longer grab their squirrel rifles from the wall and rush to battle in the heat of emergency as they did in the early days of American life. Wars today are meticulously prepared with all the carefully systematized method involved in the most gigantic enterprise. It is the tank, the flame thrower and the airplane which dominates combat, plus a carefully calculated system of transport and supply, and a total organization of the national raw material and industrial potential behind the lines.

The fundamentals which have dictated these changes give promise of still more startling rearrangements for the future. A generation ago it was sufficient to establish supervision over the trade routes to obtain control of world affairs. The capture of the Rock of Gibraltar in 1704 and the purchase in 1875 of the controlling shares of the Suez Canal, proved acts of immeasurable consequence in their political as well as military effects.

Today possession of an atoll in the South Pacific may be fully as decisive. We have come centuries in time from the day Neville Chamberlain made his famous observation that after all the Czechs were "a faraway people of whom we know nothing."

The world has shrunk to such proportions that no significant event can take place on any portion of its surface without the effect being felt immediately everywhere. There is no longer such a word as neutrality or sanctuary in the language of military realities. There are no longer spectators in war or civilian onlookers. There are only participants.

There is no longer such picture as that of D'Erlon, confused and out of touch with his commanders, marching his corps futilely back and forth between Waterloo and Ligny at the very moment when its appearance on the field might have decided the fate of Europe. Armies today have at their disposal a system of communications by radio, telephone and cable which for all practical purposes may be said to be instantaneous.

There are no longer mountain and ocean barriers or impregnable fortified points which may be relied on to turn back a determined enemy. There are no shores or front lines capable of protecting the national nerve centers against a sudden and paralyzing onslaught. The great ocean of air bathes on all portions of the universal economy and offers a medium through which attack may be facilitated on any single point of the compass.

Warfare now can be conducted in this third dimension with all the concentrated lethal fury which in the past had been the property of massed armies of men alone. As a result the grand strategic conception of centuries, that of the protected rear, has disappeared. On the opening of hostilities every installation, machine and communication point in the enemy system is instantly exposed to destruction.

III

The great air armadas of the future not only will consist of mounted artillery on wings, but will also be the principal means of military transport. Air fleets in coming decades will move complete armies together with their equipment in a matter of hours across entire continents.

Armed with the remarkable power the offensive grants under these circumstances, issues would be decided actually before the victimized country could mobilize.

As the air arm matures, control of this medium will be found to lend itself to even more dazzling blitz operations based on superior mobility and power. It will create a new and heartless strategy of which all nations are uncomfortably aware—that of attack by surprise, without previous notice, the war being declared by bombers, paratroopers and sky-borne infantrymen.

This will be found by all successful generals to be a necessary part of strategy. The entire character of surprise essential to war is now concerned with the unexpected transition from peace to war. This was the case with the Japanese at Pearl Harbor, and with the various attacks by Germany on her neighbors. Otherwise, today, in the presence of mass armies and even more massive supply problems, no major operation can be undertaken without warning and without being noted long before by the prying eyes of reconnoitering planes.

It is the opinion of many American military men acquainted with the potentialities of the chemical arm, that the next war will be fought and won by exactly such a sudden incursion, in which great gas barrages will be laid down on the cities and factory centers of the enemy as a prelude to smashing aerial bombardments and troop landings.

Plans for the distribution of gas from airplanes are already well developed in the secret military projections of every nation. The evolvement of the strategies emanating from these possibilities would bring about fantastic changes in the art of war. The attack would be intensively prepared and would propose to bring about an unqualified decision within a few days, to obviate the possibility of a retaliatory stroke.

It is essential to the peacemakers to realize that the means of military action for the next decade will be infinitely more terrible than anything which yet has been seen. The potentialities are utterly frightening in a tactical outline of giant submarines, super-explosives, rocket-propelled bombs, and propellerless planes approaching the speed of sound.

The coming age of chemistry, light metals and electronics will be the age of great discovery and consequently the age of great danger from those who seek to conspire against the future peace. A single major step forward in the quality of known weapons could make the powerful armies of today as vulnerable as were the helpless multitude of Incas to the armored horsemen of Pizarro.

Any material advance in the speed, carrying power or maneuverability of aircraft immediately would alter the prospects of battle and provide irresistible temptation to some would-be world conqueror. New engines capable of utilizing higher octane gasolines, or alloys of such metals as beryllium and magnesium to form lighter, tougher sheets, would add fabulous striking power and speed to present-day battle planes.

No one knows what will result when the problems connected with rocket propulsion are fully solved or what will come out of any of the countless experiments which are taking place daily in field and laboratory. Great dreadnoughts of the air equipped with pressure cabins and turbo-superchargers, hurtling through space at 750 miles an hour or more and capable of carrying loads of one hundred tons on a circumglobular range, are a distinct possibility. New types of explosives many times more efficient than any now used could immediately change the balance of military power among the nations.

The key to war and defense of the future is not in known armaments alone but in the workshops of scientists and technicians, and in the throbbing heart of foundries, mills and factories. These give vitality and fluidity to military processes which are far from fixed and permanent.

The chemical age may force a general alteration of the concepts now held toward military adventure. By it a great industrial nation will be enabled to emancipate itself from many sources of bulk supplies not readily available, and needed for the purpose of continued hostilities. Rubber may be made of alcohol, and oil of coal. Textiles can be fabricated from sea water, or even finely spun glass. Ordinary wood has become a source of edible sugar and of a substitute for cotton and wool. An enormous supply of cheap materials can be drawn from sea water, from the air, or grown on farms.

The picture of technological achievement has not ended. It has scarcely begun. There will be miracles ascribable to the new monumental discoveries in electro-magnetism, to new types of electric furnaces, to chemical processes which are now just unfolding in the world's laboratories. There will be incredible developments in electronics and the vacuum tube, a total pattern of new power sources and methods into which we are now getting only a breathless insight.

Any nation possessing space, resources, skilled workers, scientists and engineers, given a brief period of peace can create a war machine of deadly striking power.

It may be seen that the problems of war and peace are no longer in the ordinary sense anthropological or political, but are instead harnessed to those factors which are transforming agrarian and primitive communities the world over, to massively organized industrial societies.

One of the most significant facts of this century has been the ability of the United States to shift suddenly from a pacifist community torn by many internal strains and contrarieties, to become the world's greatest military power, furnishing mechanical weapons not only to its own armies but to those of its allies as well.

The explanation of this marvel obviously lies in the great peace-time factory concentrations which have turned out quantities of automobiles, trucks, refrigerators and other types of machinery required by a high-speed mass production civilization. The relationship is established by the fact that out of a total world registration of motor vehicles of 45,376,891, the United States possessed 32,-452,861.[1] In a normal year she manufactures two million electric refrigerators, one and one-half million washing machines and a million vacuum cleaners. She produces three times the amount of high octane gasoline of all Europe combined.

The conversion of industry to military use was found to be comparatively simple where it was directed by a firm and determined will. The problem of mass production of war machinery, parts, guns, shells, casings and other paraphernalia which go with mechanized warfare was easily met by swift retooling and the planned allocation of raw materials. The training of necessary workers and mechanics proved to be little more in the way of an obstacle.

The automobile industry was turned over almost one hundred per cent to war work, and at the end of 1942 was employing fifty per cent more hands than in its highest pre-war year. A single aluminum sheet mill was able to produce one and one-half times as much high-strength alloy sheets during 1942, as the entire country had made before the war. The farm implement industry turned out tanks, ordnance, and other apparatus. Sewing machine manu-

[1] As of January 1, 1941.

facturers were converted to rifle and pistol parts. Cooking utensil makers turned to hurricane lamps, engine cowlings and bomb parts. Builders of stoves shifted to aircraft parts, radiators, smoke bombs and land mines. Even makers of fountain pens found themselves manufacturing igniters and fuse parts.

IV

By causing industrial power to become in the largest sense synonymous with military preparedness, these developments have given the economic question a central role in politics. The invention of the refrigerator, making it possible for Argentine meats to be shipped to European or North American markets, establishes a political as well as an economic fact. Modern farm machinery and transport methods which make it possible for Canadian grain and Cuban sugar to compete on advantageous terms with small, backward producers, establish an altogether new relationship of power.

The implications of the present age are momentous. A simple factor such as the act of subsidizing a failing railroad system could possess determining consequences, leading the nation into a state of competitive unpreparedness at a time when others were reconstructing their transportation network along the most efficient modern lines.

Any one of a series of unspectacular attainments could have immeasurable weight. New inventions and processes to be used in metallurgy or chemistry, new engine designs or processes for cracking gasoline, would bring a whole train of conundrums in their wake.

These improvements more likely would be taken advantage of by rising new Powers such as Russia and China than by established industrial States such as the United States and Britain. New methods involve the excising of old habits which of necessity die hard. They also make necessary the abandonment of extensive investments, costly plants and established markets. In the democratic countries with their banking interests and widely held stocks and bonds, basic innovation is likely to find itself confronted by the most disheartening obstructions.

In an era of progressive discovery there is no permanence which may be assumed for either the military or economic power of any nation. At the very moment a superior instrument is born it is on its way to obsolescence; new and improved types are already on the drafting boards. This is pre-eminently true of the critical communication and transport mediums, and only less so of manufacturing methods.

The accustomed processes and accumulated wealth to which the industrialized Western Powers are tied, may be a fatal encumbrance in the final competitive sense, just as England's commitment to the superior industrial machinery of the Nineteenth Century served to handicap her against the more effective competition of the United States, Germany and Japan in the Twentieth.

Something of the same prodigy may be seen in the recent astonishing military growth of the German Reich which had been left, as it was thought, permanently disarmed. It was precisely the fact that the slate had been wiped clean, which enabled Germany to investigate and accept new and more efficient methods at a time when the military staffs of the Western countries were bogged down in the complacent smugness which is the price all conquering States ultimately pay for victory.

We should not be deceived by the present lack of wealth and know-how in any of the great populous areas of the globe. The capacity to produce wealth is not the product of some mysterious necromancy. As has been observed in the case of once seedy and stagnant Russia, it results from basic resources, stabilized political conditions, and the intelligence and industry of a persevering and tenacious people.

Less than three generations ago Siberia was just a word in the geographies and China was an unknown far-off place which might as well have been on the moon as far as most men were concerned. These giant backward regions, which normally would require centuries to develop, will be able to jump the gap between the horse-drawn stage and Twentieth Century industrialization with absurd ease. Two thousand big air-carriers and a network of modern ports would convert China overnight into a serious competitor to any of the existing Powers.

If the promised new plateau of transportation is achieved, the agricultural products of India, China and South America could enter competition for the internal markets of the United States with no greater relative handicaps than those imposed on California in its quest for eastern outlets.

V

Any marked advance in the method by which goods or men are hauled over the surface of the earth establishes at one and the same time a set of interlocked economic, political and military realities, creating not only a new concept of the nature of markets, but an accompanying alteration in the design of power. The German *Drang nach Osten* which kept Britain and the United States on edge for two and a half decades, revolved around the German scheme to build a railway from Berlin to Bagdad. The consequence would have been the economic subjugation of the Turkish Empire and a wide military pathway pointing directly at the gates of India.

Any major modification of the means of conveying goods is decisive in the security of nations. Rapid and efficient communications are not only the wellspring of the national prosperity—they are also the key to the mobilization of armies. This significant fact makes the question of the air-carrier a most pressing concern to all governments.

The comparative ease with which commercial flight can be transformed into military operation is not lost on any of the nations. In the case of sea traffic, it is possible to keep alien ships beyond the three-mile limit, or confine them to various ports of entry. Commercial flight necessarily involves the crossing of intervening territory and subjects the most important installations of the nation to the prying eyes of foreigners.

The possibility of having large peacetime fleets traversing the air above their territories must give small nations a nightmare and intimidate all but the largest and most isolated. Even the right to land at airports for the purpose of refueling, or to escape bad weather, is a concession fraught with serious implications; while the right to discharge or take on passengers and cargo, might be for some nations like the right which permitted Cortez to land in Mexico—the beginning of the end.

The line between military and commercial air power tends to become so fine as, for all practical purposes, to disappear. By controlling air commerce with its complexity of operation, its expensive ground installations, warehousing, feeder lines, weather and radio range signal systems, its specialized know-how and maze of manufacturing problems, a system of continuing dominance is set up which may not be easily shaken off.

In the flight paths of the commercial planes ultimately would follow powerful fighter squadrons. There has never been a great mercantile fleet in history which was not finally backed up by a powerful war fleet. The two have always coexisted since the days of the earliest trading powers.

It is obvious that the plight of the smaller countries would be severe. Even if they possessed the necessary industries with which to support a considerable carrying system, they would lack necessary bases. Due to its limited extent the operation would be so uneconomic as to be maintainable only as a sop to the national pride.

The greatest strength of the small State would be its bargaining position with reference to countries whose air fleets must pass through its air space in order to reach scheduled destinations. A battle would ensue among the giants for control of the inevitable neutrals, who would become pawns in a new kind of power game. Some inkling of this was given in pre-war South America, where the German and Italian groups finally were ousted in a struggle involving the United States as a principal actor.

The ultimate development of air traffic will result in a corollary revolution in industry, comparable to that which followed the transition from the horse and sailing vessel period to the steam and automobile age. Manufacture and commerce no longer will be containable in the old channels. Regions formerly separated by barriers of mountain, desert or water requiring weeks or months to traverse, will be speedily modernized. Trade will crisscross itself in every direction.

New countries will be able to avoid the labor and shipping bottlenecks which handicap manufacture and distribution in the older industrial nations. Factories can be located close to the sources of supply instead of following the conventional design of industrial cities piled up at the meeting places of inland waterways, and their companion railroad junctures.

New Chicagos and Stalingrads will take their places on the industrial map, as important rich areas once far distant and inaccessible are made available. The international balances which will follow are fated to destroy the entire equilibrium of trade and existing distribution of power, much as did the expansion of North America in the century preceding.

There will be a sharp decline in the significance of waterfront cities such as London, San Francisco and New York, and an increase in the importance of such inland ports as Fort Worth, Winnipeg, and Duluth, whose strategic position on the new air routes nominates them as teeming ports of call and great crossroads of future international trade.

Already in the first small swells of this wave, air carriers in Central and South America are moving heavy machinery and various manufactures as well as such agricultural products as coffee, rubber and tobacco. Tentative advance schedules issued by Pan American Airways show luxury express flights from New York of nineteen hours to Moscow and twenty hours to Honolulu, at a price of $144 and $151 respectively.

It is probable that in the predictable future our country will possess upwards of a half million planes of varying sizes and uses. Nations like China and the Soviet Union with illimitable distances, virgin resources and vigorous populations, are certain to make use of this instrument, moving mineral, agricultural and animal products as well as machines and manufactured goods throughout the length and breadth of their realms.

The vexatious riddle of the air lanes is in the present circumstances insoluble. Reciprocal agreements in a world broken into diverse and straining fragments are not apt to solve the question, but rather to become instruments of international power politics, with results for the weaker countries comparable to those which followed the reciprocal agreements between Poland and her neighbors, Russia and Germany.

The military implications alone will compel all nations to take the view that they possess exclusive rule over their air spaces. The proposed declaration of freedom of the air, as comparable to the principle of freedom of the seas, is not likely to be accepted by any of the important States. The comparison cannot be made, since beyond the usual three-mile limit the oceans always have been a no man's land in which the question of sovereignty did not enter.

VI

These circumstances place an entirely different light on the problem of security. They revise Mahan to the point of making a succession of atolls more important than magnificent harbors or great shore installations.

A generation ago, the geographer, Mackinder, observed that the age of colonial expansion was a maritime age. Since the world was seventy-two per cent water and only twenty-eight per cent land, any Power which aimed to dominate it was compelled to be a naval Power.

The interaction of global commerce was commanded by water transportation. It was along the great shorelines and in the adjoining river valleys where civilization flourished and the population densities were heaviest. In the coastal cities were concentrated the elegance, learning, arts, authority and material wealth of the world.

The past position of the great Imperial States has depended on the following circumstances: (1) Control of the sea lanes, conferring both immunity from attack and the capacity to blockade or assault any adversary whose territories fronted on the seas. (2) Industrial superiority, enabling the maintenance of a continuous exchange of raw materials for machined products at a high profit. (3) Control of the machinery of finance capital, erecting a parallel command over the resources of the exploited countries through the utilization of loans, mortgages, management functions, and "ownership" of basic enterprises and services.

These empires have played a decisive role in the affairs of mankind for almost three centuries. Island States like Britain, Japan and the no less insular Holland were able to seize immense colonial regions and to hold them against all comers. Such areas were looked on as legitimate national spoils, to be industrially exploited and kept in an undeveloped state, either for the sake of the raw materials they provided, or the markets furnished by their populations.

Under this system we find cotton hauled from Egypt and India halfway around the world, to be turned into cloth in Manchester and shipped back to Egypt and India for sale. This made necessary continuous military occupation to keep down the rebellious natives, and the retention of a chain of naval bases along the entire route to the Imperial home country, to protect the ships carrying the exchange of merchandise. Among nations having extensive holdings the performance of this operation involved a multiplex entanglement of foreign policy, endless stratagems and manipulations to keep the native populations at each other's throats, and the subsidizing of many minor rulers and chieftains. Proper management also made mandatory gigantic armaments to intimidate would-be poacher nations interested in securing these colonial spaces for themselves.

The supreme exemplar of the modern Imperial Order was Great

Britain. The little island kingdom patrolled the seven seas with a long thin line of battle wagons by which she was able to intimidate a great part of the world and to play croupier to the rest.

Britain together with a compliant United States whose policy followed in line, commanded almost every major gateway in the world, including such strongholds as Gibraltar, Suez, Singapore and the Panama Canal. These became virtual police stations by which the entire shipping of the globe was placed under surveillance.

This fabulous mastery of the seas no longer exists except in name. The position of island empires today has changed from one of invincible strength to one of great potential weakness. Rule of the oceans no longer can be maintained from some faraway island fortress. Command of the seas is now entirely local. It depends primarily on air power, superiority of transport conditions, and possession of a powerful industrial hinterland. The Yellow Sea is patrolled by the Japanese, and even the Germans with their limited naval establishment have managed to keep the Skagerrak, the Baltic, and the eastern reaches of the North Sea free of enemy ships.

It is no longer militarily possible to hold the fringes of a continent without also possessing the interior. The rapid development of the railway, airplane and motor vehicle has made it possible for the centers of population to shift from the seacoasts and well-watered valleys into the deep inland areas. Tides of population began flowing into prairies and veldts which previously had been inhabited only by grazing creatures and herdsmen. The coincident growth of huge landlocked manufacturing and trading metropolises began to redress the balance of power between the inland regions and the great shore and river communities.

The nerve ganglia of nations no longer can be paralyzed by capture of a few principal shore or river points, nor can their commerce be decisively strangled by forbidding it access to the sea roads.

The movement of industry and population into the deep recesses of the continents, both renders them safe from sea attack and enables armies to push out from interior lines to seize the very harbors and bases on which enemy naval power depends. The capacity of a well-armed, puissant industrial State to mass men and machines against isolated military outposts becomes so great as to make it impossible to hold these places at all. If they are fairly distant from the maritime Power which controls them, the problems of supply become acute and hopeless.

It remained for the airplane to bring this process to conclusion in the military sense by destroying the former dominant role of the surface vessel. In the days to come battleships will be as vulnerable as so many sitting partridges on a limb, to heavy land based air power. They will not be able to approach the shores of any competent industrial nation capable of modern mechanized operation, except at great risk and under a powerful air cover of their own. Even here, the very nature of air power pyramids its striking strength in proportion to the nearness of its supply centers, service stations and bases.

The day when an Admiral Nelson could enter Copenhagen Harbor under fire and bombard the city, or a Dewey could catch the Spanish fleet napping in its nest at Manila Bay, has become part of the obscuring haze of the heroic age. In the future nothing but open sea will be safe for battleships, and here they will play their part out. It is certain that partially landlocked waterways, such as the Mediterranean, Caribbean, and Yellow seas, will be utterly impossible to patrol from distant points if some nearby industrial Power, equipped with strong air forces, is the adversary.

Against such an opponent a power system which depends on a scattered network of far-flung bases has not the remotest possibility of success.

If the mother country depends on the raw material resources these territories provide, its economy is saddled with an impossible problem of logistics in war and an unsound table of hauling costs in peace.

As soon as the present cycle is completed and the ability to police the waterways ceases to be the central condition of world power, distant holdings will lose all military significance except where they consist of loyal and populous regions which lend themselves by possession of both industry and space, to modern methods of defense.

These conditions do not apply in Asia as far as the Western Powers are concerned.

Under modern conditions colonies are a liability unless they represent a contiguous extension of the space occupied by the mother country or are near enough to lend themselves easily to armed defense.

The successful adjustment to modern power methods may be seen in the Chinese occupation of Tibet, Mongolia and Sinkiang, and the Russian colonization of Siberia, as well as in the attempted German settlement of Poland and Czechia. Thus, imperialism of the coming generations will be directly concerned with an expansion process which will demand a rapid industrialization and settlement of the occupied territories rather than their repression. The Mongol majority of Mongolia, and the Turkish majority in the huge province of Sinkiang, will find their countries inundated by Chinese, serviced by railroads and airports, and the once empty silences of their plains, valleys and mountains reverberating to the pounding of industrial machinery, and gleaming under the silver ribbons of irrigation ditches.

Outlying possessions which flank the borders of the possessing Power like so many layers of stiff hedge, represent still another set of appraisals. They constitute buffer outposts which exist for their strategic value, irrespective of such secondary considerations as might apply.

The needs of intercontinental defense critically demand possession of any outlying island bases from which big bombers can operate. If these lie close to the enemy's heart, his cities are in the most immediate and deadly peril. It is ownership of the thick cushion of island outposts in the Pacific which has kept Japan immune from effective attack for so long. It is the nearness of Great Britain to the heart of German industry which has allowed the American bombers to deliver those terrible overhead bombardments with which we are familiar.

Every piece of ground from which a foreign airplane can take off, is a gun pointed directly at the vitals of nearby nations. Warfare of the future as we have noted will be declared by the opening bomb bays of warplanes. The attacked nation will have no time to get itself ready. It will find its airports and rail centers smashed, its cities in ruins, and limitless tons of flaming steel pouring down on all strategic points from overhead.

In the next military age it will be essential to proper defense to possess a mat of island outposts which can be organized in depth like a series of impenetrable wire barricades defending the continental mainland.

Areas which have been scarcely of passing interest will assume determinative importance. One of these will be the Arctic Ocean. The Arctic is not only the weather kitchen of the world, and hence the key to vital weather information critical to the air age—it is also the magnetic center of the great populated land masses.

In the common flat map this region is presented as an out-of-the-way place distorted to three times its real size, and apparently of little commercial or military consequence. Under the new air geography our views toward the earth we inhabit must be revised to reorder the great land agglomerations into their true global relationship.

Geographically the United States will be seen to occupy the center of a roughly pyramidal land-mass cushioned on both sides by limitless expanses of ocean, and holding appended to its body like a ripe fruit on a stem, the smaller continent of South America.

Except for the narrow isthmus which links it to the northern land pile, South America will be descried as a giant island, actually more accessible to the Power occupying West Africa than to the United States.

Europe, Africa and Asia will be observed to consist of a single land mass enclosing six great inland seas.

Europe will be noted as a great peninsular projection of this mass, separated from Asia by the low foothills of the Urals and from mysterious Africa by the almost totally enclosed Mediterranean.

Asia will be found to consist of a huge inverted bowl of wind-swept plateaus, impassable deserts and lofty mountains, resting on a jagged plate of rich, populous coastal regions, and in the north, interminable reaches of prairies and forest lands, largely uninhabited and comparable both in size and attributes to that of the continental United States. This tremendous area which is already the site of much of the Soviet Union's remarkable industrial development, is destined, like the United States, to fill up with people. As Europe pushes eastward and China westward to populate these spaces, an entirely different picture presents itself of the relationship of Asia to North America. It becomes strikingly clear that America instead of being separated from the larger continent by a wide ocean, is actually less than thirty-six miles from its final northeastern finger.

The continent of Australia will be observed as a pendant suspended by a chain of massive islands to the throat of Asia. The connection of the Australasian group with Europe has no physical reality. The only stepping-stones which connect them directly with the white world are a group of widely separated islands in the Pacific by which conjunction is made with the United States.

Under examination the areas south of the Equator though blessed with all the potentials of great natural opulence, are relatively uninhabited and poorly situated for easy commercial intercourse. They consist for the most part of a few coastal cities bordered by vast rain-forest regions, potentially rich farmlands, and majestic, grassy savannahs.

As far as power is concerned, this is a Northern Hemisphere world. The areas above the Equator contain 93 per cent of the earth's people and by far the greatest portion of its riches. Without exception, all of the great power centers are contained in the North Temperate Zone.

Seen from the view of the crowline flight of the air age, these cities are seen to be joined like a sparse bunch of grapes by a stem situated in the North Polar region. This area in consequence is due to become the actual center of world military gravity.

Under the new global air projections it will be seen that the great circle routes which lie directly across the Pole are the inevitable trade routes of the future since they are the shortest lines between the great populated spaces of the globe. The German-held base at North Cape, Norway, is almost equidistant from Portland, Oregon, Denver, Colorado, and Washington, D. C. Montreal, though a thousand miles from the ocean, is three hundred miles nearer Liverpool than is New York. Flying west from Washington to Chungking the distance is 11,718 miles. Straight across the Pole it is barely 7,500 miles. Even from the Canal Zone it is a shorter course to Tokyo heading straight north and following along the Aleutian Islands than it is by flying straight west.

The other natural arc over which world trade will flow, connects the western projection of South America, over a 1,700-mile water gap, with Africa.

The keystone to the entire strategy of the Pacific is seen obviously to be the remote outpost of Alaska. The eastern hump of South America is beheld as being dangerously far away in terms of relative accessibility. Greenland, Iceland, Ireland and England are perceived as a single field of reference, capable together of outflanking either a totally-held Europe or America, if in possession of either.

To the United States the significance of these circumstances lies in the overwhelming weight of the Eurasian land pile, a universe in itself which so impressed Mackinder that he referred to it as the World Island.[1] It contains seven-eighths of the earth's population and probably raw resources in about the same proportion. On the global chart its arms will be seen to surround the Americas completely.

1 Sir Halford J. Mackinder. *The Geographical Pivot of History.*

VII

The result of the sweeping rearrangements of human affairs which have been occurring has been not only to make machine production synonymous with military readiness, but to introduce still another power factor into organized life, that of the anonymous mass-man.

The most important political fact of this century has been the emergence of the great working masses as the new political world power. In the past, ultimate authority has resided in the clergy, the nobility, the entourage of kings, in military dictatorships, financial and commercial oligarchies, and in some States, in an influential middle class of bondholders and white-collar workers.

It was inescapable that as our civilization became increasingly one of mines, factory towns, power-driven machinery and huge industrial settlements, the participation of the proletarian mass should possess a determining effect on events. It is only by the integration of workers into great interlocking bodies that modern industrial advances have been sustained and made possible. The organization of modern life has made them the very fluid substance of life itself. They man the machines, work the farms and are at the same time almost the total market for the products they themselves produce.

Modern total war cannot be conducted without their consent. A general strike alone can be an unreserved catastrophe. With or without the right of suffrage a general conviction on the part of the mass, if sufficiently intense, becomes a point of political urgency capable of overturning any government.

In its blind magnetic surge toward total power, this body is just beginning to feel its oats and to sense with frightening awareness the all-powerful strength of its position.

This unwieldy hermaphrodite structure to whom the scepter of rule is passing has long since abandoned the cultural idealism of the ruling elite which preceded it in power. It combines with great vigor a blind obstinacy and a disinclination to follow any other course than that dictated by its own inner urgings. As an organism it is truly amoral, and like Nietzsche's creature, Zarathustra, beyond good and evil.

It is by the power of this rising mass-man that the present large-scale social revolution is being conducted. All other revolutions, even that of France in 1789, or the Red October Revolution of the Russias in 1917, were the result of the impact of a small group of intellectuals against an opposition rendered powerless by its own internal decay. Lenin and Trotsky, as Murat and Robespierre, held power by seizure of a few strategic strongholds, and were able to impose a new mastery upon the nation which its people accepted finally and made their own. Whether it is with Garibaldi and Mazzini, or with that most noble of figures, Simon Bolivar, that history is concerned, it will be found that their followers came almost altogether from the upper and middle classes. The masses remained apathetic and indifferent. Even in America it was a handful of determined men who created the Revolution. The vast majority of the colonists, if they had any political opinion at all, were Tories.

The rise of the anonymous collective as the real center of political gravity, means that whoever manages to seize the imagination of the crowd possesses illimitable power. The leader simply plays on the moods and prejudices of the mass, using it as the sounding board for its own innate opinions.

Usually the leader gives his followers nothing new beyond what they have already intrinsically conceived, and acts on behalf of no ideas not already rooted in the mass mind. He is thus the incarnation of causes popular with the general populace, as well as the true reflection of their beliefs. In the dictator countries he is aided by the simultaneous pressures of State-controlled radio and press, and the circle is made complete.

All of this may be seen in the case of Germany, or in any of the other European countries where a popular despot has risen to power on the shoulders of such considerations as anti-Semitism, State ownership of property, race exclusiveness and the like.

Idealists are always shocked to see the masses captured by mendacious but realist politicians who add to every question old age security, job insurance, State protection against want and the general panacea of economic socialism. These are as easily added to the formula of anti-Semitism and national chauvinism as they are to the beautiful dreams of the humanitarians.

It may be seen by any careful observer that what the masses of men yearn for today is not a system of political purity, justice or freedom, but security. The whole view of modern man is bound up in this single word.

Political situations in this generation derive from a different set of material facts than those which applied when Zola wrote, or when Shelley and Byron expressed in their songs the noble aspirations of free-born men. In the age of early industrial society, freedom and democracy were the normal and expected desires of men, and were accompanied by a measurable increase in the well-being of mankind, as well as remarkable opportunities for riches and advancement. It was an era of dazzling inspiration which captured the mind and imagination of Western man, then rising to world leadership.

In the present epoch the philosophy of free competition and the sovereign individual, has yielded to the witchery of the planned economy and the sovereign State. Independent free enterprise has lost its grip on the minds of men. As a social ideal it has been assaulted from every side, both by organized group philosophies seeking to implement new orders, and by the inexorable force of events themselves.

The desire for discipline, for regulation and order, has grown in proportion to the tensions developed by civilization. Modern life has grown so complex and difficult as to make it almost impossible for the individual to bring general problems into focus.

Urbanization itself has acted to estrange men from the organic sources of a balanced physical existence and to develop in them all of the trauma of serious neurasthenia. They have been re-formed into social fragments whose daily function is limited to the role organized machine society assigns them. These collective millions of human crises create an abnormal attitude in society, in which the nobility, prudence, logic and moral courage of individual men is lost in the common forces which affect the mood of the mass.

It is from this psychological breakdown as well as by the mechanical failures of our economy that there has occurred the collapse of the social machinery which characterizes the age. This is a situation which places a premium on coordinated method, authoritative administration, and minute surveillance of the unregulated individual. The very nature of the managerial revolution involves executive direction rather than collaborative agreement, and gives rule by decree a functional advantage over government by law. The mere fact of membership in large regulatory bodies such as labor unions and business societies becomes antithetical to the profession of liberty.

The affairs of government thus fall naturally into administration by bureau. It is not an accident that we see the rise of a central bureaucracy everywhere, and that this rise is accompanied by a violent rejection of ideals which a short time before constituted the very essence of all that was desirable to man.

Wherever one looks, the demand for highly socialized forms of administration becomes increasingly articulate. The reasoning apparently is that the present system has demonstrated itself to be ridden with incurable weaknesses and inequities, and hence must be replaced by a more efficient type of regulation which operates for the many instead of the few. "Economic democracy" is to be substituted for capitalist freedom to form what is expected to be a more rational and responsible social order.

This process is going forward under cover of constitutionality everywhere, much as it did in Germany, and represents a revolution in the internal economies of all civilized States. What is taking the place of the old social relationships is the machine State dominated by the mass-man, who thus, with or without benefit of franchise, becomes assertive in a more or less primitive social horde.

There are two distinct trends. One is the revived concept of the universal man, rooted in a purely mechanistic interpretation of society. The other is the vision of the tribal swarm, operating as an exploiting elite over constantly extending areas. In the case of each, the ultimate goal is world control, and in each, personal "rights" has receded under the smashing impact of the Socialist ideal of "duty."

The conscious backing of the masses, whether it proceeds from possession of the ballot or from smoothly interlocking party organization, has been the backbone of the modern dictator State.

The predilection toward authoritarian rule, in which the citizen voluntarily becomes a subject, is part of the ineffable quality of the times. In making an adjustment to a managerial society the crowd, though compelled to give up the right to free expression, conceives that in reality it gives up little, since the dictator government together with its premises and its policies is already an intrinsic statement of the national opinion. In effect, the directorial leadership has been given an executive mandate to express that policy in the interests of the commonalty as it finds necessary.

The conditions of Twentieth Century industry and politics have demonstrated amply the great superiority of centrally controlled hordes over States burdened with the problems of internal competition and parliamentary wrangling. While democracies have shown that they are capable of conducting a successful war in modern terms, this is only done at the sacrifice of their own basic principles. Either in war or in peace, totalitarians who can neither be cajoled nor frightened if there are large stakes in the offing, and who need never revise their programs due to internal political considerations, are able to function on a more efficient plane. The totalitarian system lends itself perfectly to predatory operations, especially where timing and swiftness of action are prerequisites.

The existence of the mass-man and the totalitarian structure he inhabits, presents Western society with one of the most baffling of its problems. The entire technique of democracy and the theories under which it exists, render it unfitted to engage in the conduct of modern power politics. In the United States the system of checks and balances, and the free manifestations of public opinion, unfit it to play the balance of power game efficiently. An effective contest with the authoritarian governments in any of the power arenas, cannot be conducted except under such emergency decrees as those by which the United States carries on the present business of war.

An important consequence of the rise to power of crowds has been another significant revision in the nature of military struggle. The methods by which alien masses are attacked and conquered are known collectively as psychological warfare, and their heavy detonation charges, as propaganda. The assault does not consist of a species of arguments in the intellectual sense, but of a perfectly conscienceless and dispassionate strategical maneuver designed to outflank an enemy, disintegrate his position or secure his capitulation.

The aims are frankly those of pragmatism, expedience, corruption and control. The formulae used are infinite. The entire operation is essentially a study of revolutionary and disintegrative processes which seek to breach all previously held respect for tradition, authority and government, and to promote a condition from which lawlessness, disorder and chaos can ensue.

The Nineteenth Century French psychologist, Gustave Le Bon, whose writings remain the keystone to the arch of modern psychological warfare, discerned that the unconscious action of crowds may be exactly contrary to the character of the individuals composing them. Thus a crowd may be hysterically brutal, whereas the individuals out of which it is formed may be actually slow to violence. Le Bon noted that ideas which would be unsuccessful in disputation with single individuals are hypnotic with crowds. He observed further that the crowd is little adapted to reasoning but reacts quickly to an emotional stimulus. His monumental discovery was the fact that it was the unconscious action of crowds which had substituted for the conscious activity of individuals in determining the political characteristics of the present age.

Whether in connection with the initial seizure of power or the destruction of an enemy, it is on the control of the mass mind that modern psychological warfare rests, and not on the conversion of the individual. The plan of attack is exactly that in use against an army. The individual is ignored except as he is part of a larger unit.

Universal media such as the radio, newspapers and moving pictures have placed the minds of men within range of a terrific bombardment of carefully calculated material by which the masses can be influenced and controlled. If the propaganda is directed inwardly to the supporting horde itself, the national fears, ambitions and hatreds are turned to account in an effort which is almost one of religious exaltation. Its primary purpose however is the quite practical one of forming the State into a smooth working, functional mechanism from which all disturbing outside currents have been relentlessly excluded.

If directed against the social fabric of an opposing State the propaganda apparatus becomes a true striking arm capable of conducting the most ruinous types of warfare. The opposing nation is carefully studied with the purpose of breaking down its entire social structure. Religion is set on religion, race on race, social class against social class, the object being the overthrow of the State through the disintegration of its national unity.

The methods used are simple in conception though highly scientific in organization. "All propaganda," explained Hitler, "must be popular in tone and must keep its intellectual level to the capacity of the least intelligent among those at whom it is directed." This follows after Le Bon's assertion that "affirmation, pure and simple, kept free of all reasoning and all proof, is one of the surest means of making an idea enter the mind of crowds." A simple statement constantly reiterated, such as "the Jews and English are responsible for the war," can be more influential than the most careful compendia of facts.

This technique was first applied by the Communists to facilitate the world revolution which they then were certain was on its way.

It was explored, adapted and improved on by the Germans, and has since become a standard part of the arsenal of all nations.

The authoritarian countries, especially, have made it a deep study. It is a method of hostilities which will go forward in a rising crescendo of action after the guns officially have stopped firing.

VI

THE INDUSTRIAL ENIGMA

POWER methods similar in design to those employed in war also have been used by industrial States against their unprepared or weaker neighbors. In acquiring the aspect of complete totality, warfare thus took on still another and new dimension.

Economic warfare has taken the form of import restrictions, subsidies, trade barriers, monetary controls and tariffs, in addition to applied sanctions by which States openly attempted to destroy the basis of each other's prosperity.

In the more highly socialized countries, banks, cartels and trade organizations found themselves removed from the normal arenas of competition for profit, to become agencies of the State in the furtherance of its political policy. The picture of international trade changed from one of free competition to one of restraint, and from one couched in terms of fair trade methods to one of government backing, force and monopoly. In the Reich which was the most extreme example of this tendency, all commercial methods became in their purposes predatory. Exports and imports reflected the foreign policy of the nation rather than private commercial interests. Trade became an important tool of aggression.

Covert hostilities based on the struggle for markets, and on the need for such strategic materials as oil, chromium, mercury, nickel and rubber, brought into existence a whole set of new drives and objectives. They involved the use of exclusive agreements comparable to military treaties, dumping practices, currency manipulations and a complicated strategy of attack in which the State itself was the principal actor.

These new weapons proved to be of a highly destructive type. They showed themselves cruelly effective in weakening the economies of opposing nations and preparing them for the final rapier thrust of military shock by which the matador-State executed the *suerte de matar*.

The opportunities for dangerous dislocations of external commerce have grown in proportion to the expansion of the industrial machine. This might be seen in the extraordinary progression of international foreign trade figures which leaped by almost 2500 per cent in a century, stepping from $2,800,000,000 in 1840 to $67,700,000,000 in 1940.

Despite this remarkable increase, the growth of mercantile power among the nations has been spotty and uneven. This circumstance combined with the existence of fossilized and uneconomic political frontiers made it impossible to maintain an equilibrium between markets, centers of manufacture and sources of raw materials. The differences in levels of opportunity, power, training, knowledge, wealth and material possessions between the nations gave rise to a labyrinth of problems, frictions and issues of a difficult and often acute nature. The complex interdependence of industry placed a premium on large-scale operation, a wide variety of machine production, resources, and a numerous, energetic and instructed population.

As mechanical science increased its scope, the range of needed materials broadened with it. Metals whose very names had a strange and exotic sound but a few years back, such as molybdenum, beryllium, cobalt, manganese and vanadium, became essential to industry.

Once a large balanced commonwealth like the United States or the Soviet Union was set up, the concentrations of industrial power it was able to employ rendered all other national economies unsound.

The position of such countries as those of Western Europe, who were not self-contained and whose entire prosperity depended on a capacity to sell an exportable surplus at a profit, is obvious. Confronted with rising internal costs and diminishing markets, these States were faced continually with the threat of economic derangement, and ultimate political death. This could not fail to have an effect both on their inner psychological reactions and foreign policies.

While small industrial States also were to find themselves parlously situated, the more fundamental trend was for States producing raw materials to lose their purchasing power in comparison to industrial nations. A continuous fluctuation in raw material prices existed, whereas the prices of finished goods were maintained by fixed factors such as rent, taxes and rigid wages which could decline only fractionally. Such essential materials as rubber, tin and copper ran through a ruinous gamut of values, fluctuating as much as 2600 per cent in a single decade. As a result, the normal exchange of purchases came to a dead stop periodically. Great surpluses piled up which choked the entire economic system with their debris.

In general it is the small agrarian State which has suffered from tragic incompleteness. These must become increasingly subject to the will of countries occupying a superior economic position. As the larger and better organized nations quietly began to assume the position of *padrones* to the smaller, the relation of economic aggression to military exploitation became more and more obvious and direct.

Since the foreign trade of the dictator country is an extension of the State, price levels can be artificially created, completely detached from any cost accounting system. The hours and conditions of work are set by the State, which need not be concerned with any considerations save those of power. The consequence has been the evolvement of the special combat technique known as economic warfare, a tactic influenced and affected by the identical drives for world power which govern its counterpart in aggression, the military machine.

This type of warfare was brought to its highest point of perfection by the Germans. The States in the pathway of Germany's war chariot found not only their economic life under siege but their cultural and political institutions as well. Germany's commercial blitz tactics resulted not only in the industrial dependence of the victim State, but in its actual political capitulation.

The principle under which the Reich's trade policy operated was one of threats, cajolements and covert piracy. The lure which attracted the prey was embodied in long term credits whose purpose was purely predacious. The seller, once entangled, was confronted with a variety of manipulations of accumulated clearing balances which had the effect of coercing him by the alternative threat of ruin.

Under the Nazi practice, German firms no longer could make remittance to foreign creditors direct, but were forced to pay these amounts into a "conversion office for foreign debts." This office could at its discretion make payment to foreign creditors.

In theory, the clearing house agreements were to result in a precise balance to be struck between purchases and sales. Actually, the more powerful party could operate the agreement to its own advantage.

Funds would be placed by German importers in the exchange in Germany, but foreign importers would buy on long term credits, not placing any money into clearing exchanges in their own countries. Hence, they would have to wait until the money came in or until the credits fell due. In the case of Rumania, for example, the long term credits extended by Germany were paid for by the Rumanian exporter. Since he did not have financial resources to wait, the National Bank of Rumania had to help him. "Thus, in the end, the long term credits granted by Germany to Rumanian buyers of her goods, were financed by the Rumanian Central Bank by means of currency and credit inflation." [1]

These accumulated clearing balances enabled the Reich to coerce her trade partners into expanding their commerce with her

[1] Einzig, *Nazi Business Methods*, p. 5.

at the expense of trade with free exchange countries. The costs of German goods, at first offered at attractively low prices, then would be forced up by a system of currency juggling which will be discussed shortly. A deterioration in the quality of the merchandise delivered would accompany this procedure.

Caught with tremendous frozen trade balances, sufficient to ruin their producers if they were to remain unpaid, the countries party to these exclusive agreements had little choice but to continue.

The Reich found herself able to export according to her own circumstances, rather than those of her trade partners. Yugoslavia, for example, instead of receiving for her grain, money which could be used in the international markets to buy goods she really required, had to accept large quantities of unneeded items such as a ten-year supply of aspirin.[1]

Where creditor nations rebelled against this method of enslavement, Berlin found other means to whip them into line. One was to buy as much as possible from an individual country, acquiring the total product if possible, with the purpose of destroying the habit of purchase by other buyers. The surplus acquired would be re-exported at a loss, thus spoiling the market for the countries of origin. Markets for such commodities as Hungarian and Rumanian wheat, Greek tobacco, and Yugoslav timber appeared to dissolve in thin air.

German re-exporters of Turkish raisins or Bulgarian tobacco undersold Turkish and Bulgarian exporters. The disruption of other habits of purchase compelled the captured countries to continue selling to Germany since no other nation would buy from them. The existence of all their foreign exchange in the German clearing account made these States dependent on Germany for all their non-European imports, enabling Berlin to utilize their foreign trade for her own benefit.

Something of a like condition began to apply in Latin America just before the war. By bilateral trade agreements Germany began to accept large quantities of Brazilian coffee, and then sold the

[1] Staley, *World Economy in Transition*, p. 40.

same coffee on world markets at ruinously low prices, cutting down the amount of foreign exchange received by Brazil and making that country increasingly dependent on the Reich. The investments required by this long-range operation were also utilized in an effort to corner the entire Brazilian cotton output. For this purpose, higher than market prices were paid, amounting in effect to a German subsidy of Brazilian production. The political presumption behind these acts was that the producers of the seller State would force a policy of amenability, or even vassalage to the Reich, rather than risk the serious dislocations which would follow a sudden cancellation of orders.

The system worked to perfection in the agrarian Danube basin, which passed by degrees into a type of servitude dominated by the sheer economic terrorism of Berlin.

These trade activities were tied to conspiratorial political depredations and sinister forms of propaganda designed to destroy the political lives of the countries with whom Germany dealt. The downfall of the Austrian State, due to instigated political troubles, is a well-known instance.

The process also is evident in the capitulation of Hungary and Rumania. In both nations Germany was able to prevent the development of certain industries, such as canning. Since the German clearing account held virtually all of their credits, the only place where these nations could buy this equipment was Germany. To make the installation of these plants unprofitable, Germany raised the price of the necessary machinery several hundred per cent.[1] By keeping these countries agricultural the Reich kept intact her economic and political power over them.

By 1939, Germany had transformed both countries into satraps of the Reich. The economic treaty of March 23, 1939, gave Berlin priority on all Rumania's natural resources. Germany gained a position which in many respects could be described as extraterritorial. The resultant political effect was felt in the deadly impact

1 Einzig, *Nazi Business Methods,* p. 11.

of the Fascist Iron Guard on the frightened government at Bucharest, which had no choice but to abdicate.

Another aspect of this buccaneering operation is seen in the relationship with Switzerland. By threatening to withdraw the iron and coal required by Swiss industry, the Reich was able to force the Swiss State to supply the German war machine according to specifications laid down by Berlin. To exact the last possible benefit from the position, Berlin arbitrarily expanded the prices of her exports. These increases, against which the Swiss were helpless to defend themselves, ranged as high as 540 per cent for heating oil and 170 per cent for coal.

II

The Nazi Reich proved that by the use of proper stratagems a strong industrial nation could secure powers of life and death over its agricultural neighbors and could pre-empt a monopoly position either in reference to the purchase of raw materials or the supply of processed goods.

It was, however, by no means against the agrarian State alone that economic warfare proved efficacious. As ingenious and brutal tactics were used to sandbag the business economies of Germany's industrial competitors. A common routine was wholesale dumping with losses made up to exporters by special rebates and subsidies.

Dumping may be said to represent the same investment in money and goods which a great and critical battle represents in matériel and men. A decisive victory for the invading country succeeds in ruining the native industry, eliminating it as a rival for its own markets, and impairing the national military potential. Once the struggle has been successfully terminated, the invader may readjust his prices so as quickly to take up previous losses.

An illustration of the mechanics of this piratical assault on the economy of a friendly State is observable in the German trade war with Czechoslovakia. Coke was sold to Bohemia at eight marks per ton though the identical stuff sold in Germany for seventeen marks per ton. Alcohol priced in the Reich at sixty marks per ton nevertheless was sold abroad for twenty marks per ton.

The dictator country handles this operation as a bookkeeping performance. The loss to exporters is made up by various special rebates as well as by direct subsidy.

This type of strategy under the simulation of free trade, has shown itself quite capable of causing irretrievable harm to the military economy of the parliamentary States, wherever it has been tenaciously pursued by totalitarian dynasts. To push French manufacturers of phenic acid (an essential ingredient of high explosives) out of business, German firms sold this material to the French Ministry of War at ruinously low prices. By similar methods, German concerns even were able to usurp for themselves the manufacture of the diesel engines used in French submarines.

Another means by which the total State was able to prey with impunity on its neighbors, involved the use of private trade agreements for the division of markets, between business concerns of the free capitalist States on the one hand and the shadow trading agencies of the totalitarian body on the other.

These agreements were usually the result of an effort to halt cutthroat price-cutting wars which had been instituted by the Germans themselves, after which areas of jurisdiction would be allocated by agreement, the German portion always being dictated by ultimate political considerations.

In the name of business the German monopolies were able to occupy strategic points in the economic structures of the free trade States, and in the Western countries to restrict the manufacture of materials critical to wartime enterprise. In return the Reich yielded concessions profitable in the money sense, and markets which possessed no military significance to Berlin.

Through these restrictive agreements the Wilhelmstrasse sought deliberately to deal our war potential a fatal blow, barring our access to our own technology, and obstructing the development of nearby sources of critical raw materials. Because of these compacts, our nation was prevented from large-scale experimentation with many of the important alloys and synthetic substances, and did not venture into these operations until after war was declared. The result was to confront the United States with an acute wartime shortage in military optical goods, magnesium, pharmaceuticals, tungsten, carbide, rubber and other strategic materials.[1]

Germany also was able to secure exclusive control of the South American market for certain of her products, enabling her to utilize the resulting exchange of trade to establish an uncomfortably close relationship with the countries of our sister continent.

In this power competition the dictatorial State possesses an immeasurable advantage. Its mere presence as a competitor is certain to involve manipulations, subsidies, and concealed discriminations which are completely destructive to Adam Smith's law of free enterprise under which it purports to operate.

This situation can hardly be altered by some international code which all parties are bound to respect. Any theory of industrial equalization, or guaranteed access to markets and raw materials by all countries, is compelled to assume a limitation of sovereignty on the part of each State over its own territories. This would mean the end of the State itself, and a new social order. As long as the present political divisions exist there are no controls which can be instituted which would have the slightest real effect.

This fact faces our peacemakers with a series of vexatious questions. One of these is that of a stabilized currency which could act as a fixed point from which the universe of trade could set its compass.

The entire mechanism of exchange now finds itself an antiquated remnant in a world in which it no longer possesses authority.

The present currency system was the product of a fluid world responding to a single stable point in suspension. The stable point formerly had been Lombard Street in London. Later it became Wall Street in New York. The fluid situation by which money

[1] A graphic account is given by Borkin and Welsh, *Germany's Master Plan*.

gyroscopically maintained itself was capitalist incentive and the opportunity for exploitation provided by a socially undeveloped world.

A standard money backed by a gold reserve and the classic integrity of the subscribing banks, allowed for a free flow of raw materials and for the exchange of all types of goods. It gave flexibility to a system which would be otherwise one of inflexible barter attended by suspicion and limitless difficulties.

During the height of its power the authority of money was as absolute as that of sovereigns, and was as subject to maneuver, power strategy and shock tactics as were the movements of armies and navies. Until its ascendancy began to wane, the influence of money was great enough to sway the course of international events, and even to wage bloodless and undeclared wars of its own.

Under the national State sound money is no longer objective and a reflection of its own laws but has been yoked to the political needs of the nation. The disastrous depredations this encouraged is evident in the dealings of Germany with her neighbors. The Reich used a deliberately depreciated currency as a whip whenever she found it desirable. The Nazi Government instituted a large number of currencies whose monthly range fluctuated widely. These included more than twenty kinds of marks, each with its separate purchasing power. Utilizing the bewildering complexities of this system of devaluated money, the Reich would export on the basis of one type of mark and invoice her sales on that of still another.

This mechanism of exchange included the so-called blocked mark by which a period of moratorium was caused to exist on certain debts. The manipulation of the various types of money became so complex as to be barely understandable, and varied as much as 150 per cent in the course of a year. The object was that of extracting an added percentage of profit from all transactions, evading the fulfilment of Germany's international business obligations.

The harnessing of money to the planned economy destroyed not only its freedom and integrity but its ability to make its own necessary self-adjustments. The death of the classic finance and banking system and the destruction of the authority of international money, threw a large sabot into the machinery of international dealings. As soon as trade became the function of the State rather than of private individuals, and the monied oligarchy began to disintegrate as a form of power, the surviving currency system became a menace to the peace of the world. Money no longer is free and subject to market influences. Its relation to foreign exchange can be arbitrarily controlled by decree, rendering the use of sanctions by the State against its neighbors an ever-imminent possibility.

That peculiar product of logical contraries known as inflation, now is operating in widely separated countries, with fantastic results. The disrelation of money to any real economy is graphically illustrated by the currency chaos at present existing in China. The Chinese *sien* is pegged at the artificial rate of twenty to one in an effort to fix its value in relation to the dollar.

Since under present conditions the Chinese State is unable to enforce its will, the *sien* can be purchased on the black market at the rate of five hundred to one. A bicycle now costs as much as 50,000 *siens,* an incidence which turns the entire money situation of China into a burlesque.

The world-wide currency system now is anchored virtually in nothing—neither in gold nor in the command of some awesome authoritarian center such as was formerly provided by the money marts of London and New York. Russia and Germany have demonstrated that it was possible to substitute a working economy based on energy hours and raw materials for the classic money economy, and that the absence of money in the exchange sense was not fatal to the erection of powerful industrial and military establishments.

This discovery had a shattering effect on the last strongholds of money, without substituting some other operable mechanism by which modern international trade could be conducted. Its ability to meet this challenge will be a sensitive barometer of the world's capacity to solve other difficult questions now pressing hard on its cushion of tolerances.

The problem will be seen to be not a simple one, but one which descends to the bedrock of the various national, political and economic setups. It cannot be settled unless these, too, are redesigned to fit the needs of the current century.

The variable quality of exchange rates can at any point upset the whole international economic balance, altering the value of currencies as if these themselves were commodities of trade. In China, where the economics are based on silver, the decline in price of that metal a few years ago, from seventy to thirty-four cents an ounce, had the effect of cutting the country's buying power on world markets in half.

The United States has attempted to stabilize money by creating a perpetual market for silver at seventy-one cents an ounce and gold at thirty-five dollars an ounce irrespective of any natural price level affecting these commodities elsewhere. $22,743,000,000 of gold attracted to these shores by such unnatural price levels now are buried in a special vault at Fort Knox, Kentucky. They represent an exchange for substantial assets whose production involved the energy and sweat of men. If the remaining nations decided to ignore gold as a measurement of value, the United States would be left with four-fifths of the world's monetary gold stocks, and the choice of either going to war to enforce the old equivalences or of using this material for jewelry.

The fantastic instability which affects money can be seen clearly by reference to some fixed value such as the international public debt. To debtor States this represents a bookkeeping transaction only remotely related to current and real values. If it were demanded of debtor States that these mortgages on their national wealth be redeemed, they certainly would resist by force of arms. If this recourse were impractical, the amounts owed immediately would be reduced to zero by a runaway inflation, which to the State would be the same type of defense mechanism that a neurosis is to a human being.

III

Irrespective of the exchange symbol by which it is represented, the final measuring stick of all human effort in a working world must be energy-hours. These as a commodity have a definite value based on their cost as well as the efficiency with which they are utilized. Wherever human labor enters into the basic cost of production the conditions affecting it are bound to become decisive in the commercial relationship of nations.

Any marked difference between the wage and labor conditions of countries otherwise equal, will show itself in unequal competitive capacities, irritations, protective bilateral arrangements and high tariff walls.

As long as there are any important differences in the labor production costs of the various countries there can never be a world community in which the causes of international friction will be outlawed. It is not to be expected that a manufacturing State with a high level of costs will stand supinely by and see the entire basis for its prosperity challenged by nations able to combine efficient operation with a low standard of living.

We experienced something of this circumstance in our encounter with highly industrialized Japan. The competition offered by this small nation, suffering from a forced reliance on outside sources of raw materials, was so severe as to breed endless ill will.

The underlying situation was epitomized by the fact that Japanese women cotton spinners received twenty-five cents per day, compared to the $2.75 paid American women doing the same kind of work.

The revolution in communications has made it far more pertinent to our economy than it was in the last decade, and will cause it to become violently more so in the future, that the average monthly wage of Brazilian workers is $11.80; that the Assam tea plantations pay less than $5.00 per month; or that Javanese labor is worth eight cents a day for a working period which ranges from dawn to dusk.

As cheap transportation annihilates the distances which lay between us, the use of forced labor on railway projects in Africa or of indentured Chinese workers in the mines of Malaya, becomes of increasing significance to our own trade.

Unless some method can be found to span the deep gulf which separates these widely varying labor conditions, the result can be only a permanent large-scale economic instability and impairment of international friendships.

To escape its baleful effects on our own undertakings we should have to withdraw from all intercourse with the world. While this maneuver might be possible for an authoritarian enterprise such as the U.S.S.R., it is impractical from any view, and would be catastrophic for any State functioning on free trade principles.

We may regard it as certain that all countries will make a determined effort to adjust themselves to the machine era. If the firm factors are man-hours and useful materials rather than money, this outcome cannot be prevented, any more than it could in Soviet Russia.

What can be done in the way of industrial efficiency by regimented nations willing to accept a comparatively depressed standard of living can be seen in the success of Russia's Five-Year Plan, or in Germany's determination to give her citizens "guns rather than butter."

Even Latin America, which we look on as an agricultural hinterland, is making a supreme effort to modernize and streamline its manufacturing procedures. In Chile, the Argentine and Brazil, hydroelectric plants, steel mills and machine building plants are being erected. In Mexico, industrialization is the number one goal. The industrial competition of what were once submerged agrarian States is sure to reflect itself in salient alterations in the effective power balance. At present the United States with six per cent of the world's population, possesses fifty-seven per cent of its telephones, consumes sixty-six per cent of its petroleum, seventy-seven per cent of its copper, seventy per cent of its silks, and fifty-nine per cent of its rubber. This is a situation so one-sided that it can be accepted almost as axiomatic that it will not remain. It is certain to be challenged violently by newly industrialized States of the next few decades. These will attempt to compete with our mass production methods by the introduction of similar methods. They will possess the additional advantage of low wage scales and long working hours. They will make use of discriminatory tariffs, levies, and exclusive agreements with commercially allied countries.

The fierce impact of the ensuing trade rivalry would result in the gravest consequences.

VII

POWER CENTERS OF TOMORROW

THE organizing principles on which the social order of the future will be based are rooted in the cold realities of relative resources, populations, and geographic space. Power will take the form of an ability to dominate a number of converging economies, the productive and industrial as well as the purely military.

The result has been to increase the effectiveness of pure size, of weight of mineral assets, geographical holdings, population numbers and growth ratios.

The question of national philoprogenitiveness is more than a curious and interesting set of statistics on the demographic charts. Where the other balances are equal, it determines who among a given group of competitive States are finally to be supreme.

Any extraordinary rate of population increase possesses a direct power significance. Its precise nature will be determined by the energy of the races concerned, the circumstances reacting upon them and the nature of the fixed geographic boundaries with which they must contend. Thus a great increase in the population of the Soviet Union would offer quite different implications for the future from that which might occur in overcrowded and socially restless China and India.

When the demographers tells us that the population of the world has increased by two hundred million in the decade between 1930 and 1940, and that Asia alone has doubled its people in less than half a century, we must accept these facts as having a strategic bearing on the future peace. What it means in reference to the Asiatic millions who are destined to step from drowsy feudal particularism into the dazzling world of power-driven machinery and mass production, we shall examine shortly.

In the special sense of being activated by kinetic forces peculiarly their own, populations appear to possess an age cycle. At one point the forces involved are youthful, expanding and irresistible. At another they subside, taking on all the appearance of senescence.

What this means translated into the competitive facts of national existence may be seen in the relative positions occupied by France, Germany, Russia and Italy on the European Continent.

At the end of the Eighteenth Century the population of France was twenty-seven million. That of Germany was twenty-five million, Russia thirty-six million, and Italy, sixteen million. This was the numerical balance which existed in the days of Napoleon Bonaparte and which permitted France to dominate the Continent.

By the end of the Nineteenth Century, the Reich had far overtaken its French neighbor, and Italy was emerging as a respectable population competitor. Together with Russia these States continued to gain rapidly in population.

The result of these increased manpower reserves was partially shown in the heightened effectiveness of the Reich's industrial position, as well as her military strength. It bequeathed a sense of power which added to the already existing national arrogance and restlessness.

By 1940 the population of France had dropped below that of Italy and was only half of that of Germany, and a fifth of that of Russia. The demographic chart now showed France with 38,000,000 people, Germany as 80,000,000, Italy 46,000,000, and the U.S.S.R. as 193,000,000. For each ten French births there were now eighteen Italian, twenty-eight German and eighty Russian. The Gallic Republic which once had been the proud mistress of Europe had become symbolized by the aging Petain, and rapidly assumed the position of a second-class Power.

II

The corollary of mass numbers is compelled to be mass space, the one representing the element of organizing energy, and the other the raw resources to which it is applied.

A backward economy as has been noted in the case of the Soviet Union, can be refashioned and modernized. A booming industry, and bustling cities, may rise quickly in territories occupied formerly by herdsmen and plodding agriculturists. Where once was only swamp and desert, intelligence, drainage and irrigation can create a modern, intensified agriculture. Even paucity in numbers, while gravely limiting, is not necessarily fatal, given a wise immigration policy and a high rate of natural fertility.

A limitation of resources or space, however, such as would apply to a nation like Belgium, or even Italy and France, cannot be rectified. In an era which offers its highest rewards to diversity of resources, and bigness alone, these States are deficient in the entire balance of assets required to compete for survival with such political organisms as the United States of America, or the U.S.S.R.

If a modern State is to be a going concern, it must possess in addition to large space and a vigorous, multitudinous population, oil, coal, a wide assortment of minerals, access to the products of all the principal climes—tropical, subtropical and temperate—and outlets to the major seas.

It must present within its own national apparatus a balanced market capable of absorbing its entire production if needed.

If all of these factors are not present in equilibrium the State is subject to grave peril which by its very nature cannot be relieved. Without these prerequisites a secure and independent modern economy cannot exist either in the military or industrial sense.

It is no longer West Point, Moscow and Washington which determine the issues of prosperity, war and peace. It is Pittsburgh and Gary, and Magnitogorsk and Dnieprostroy. It is vast space such as that which compelled even so magnificent an instrument as the German army to wear itself out in fruitless and indecisive waves of assault. It is mines and oil, agriculture, fisheries, and a catalogue of multiform raw materials from which wealth is compounded.

It is the capacity to put these things under the control of central authority which makes for superiority of industrial plant and military installation, and which has created the sharply increasing disparity of power among the world States.

To be militarily solvent, the modern State requires manpower and space resources adequate to meet the type of massive shock assault which now may be made upon it. This implies space sufficient to contain a galaxy of nerve centers forming a loosely related pattern, rather than a single vulnerable concentration of industry in some central urban area.

A sudden concentrated attack on a small nation like Holland is sufficient to end its existence within a matter of days or hours. The smashing of its principal nerve ganglia would instantly disrupt its economic life and might make it impossible even to mobilize its armies.

It is only possession of extensive elbow room which can prevent from immediately being decisive a mechanized military assault to which overwhelming power has been applied. This is especially true as it relates to the increasing deadliness of an envelopment movement operated from overhead and paced by the terrible demolition machinery military aviation now has at its disposal.

It is only by retreating into space that the recuperative powers of the attacked economy can have the slightest possibility of functioning. This was proved in the case of both China and the U.S.S.R. during the early days of the present war.

Had the Russians not been able to retreat to the Leningrad, Moscow, Stalingrad line they would have suffered the quick garroting which was the fate of the Western States. If behind the Kremlin there had not been the thriving industry of the Urals with its vast sandbags of space neatly piled around it, the Soviet Union would have disappeared from the map.

In China the extensions of pure space, and the determination of inexhaustible human masses in themselves were sufficient to dissipate the enormous mechanical power of the Japanese attack. Though the Japanese won innumerable victories, at no time have these been decisive.

The areas have been so vast, and their inhabitants so numerous that it became a physical impossibility to police them. The conqueror was compelled to isolate himself to certain strategic cities and strongholds, each of which remained surrounded by an obstinate and recalcitrant population capable of putting millions of disciplined guerilla fighters in the field and of conducting a counter terror, in some ways comparable to that exercised by the invader himself.

The result was that China, which had no army, still maintained a government which operated unmolested in the unreachable back parts of the country. Even in the regions occupied by the Japanese, a guerilla government has managed to function, with every village a latent seat of resistance and source of serious disturbance to the Japanese war machine.

Thus we witness that terminal conclusion of all military invention—the ability of counteracting forces to nullify it. For all the immense superiority of modern arms this is exactly what has happened in Russia and the Far East. Here it has become plain that the properties of strategic defense depend not only on the weapons and industrial organization of the struggling peoples but on their relative numbers, the quality of their will, and the size of the space which must be occupied and policed.

III

One is drawn irresistibly to the conclusion that the small modern State no longer is economic and that the world we have known in the past, of small closed political corporations, can never exist again. The little nation of today is an anachronism, an element of society which has outlived its function and which by its mere existence throws the sabot of incoherency into the humming machinery of international life.

Today there are sixty-three States which can claim to be independent and whose actions are governed only by their own authority and will. There are in addition a number of others which are in transition to independence, such as the Philippine Islands, Syria, Palestine, Burma, Croatia and Slovakia.

Yet of all these States there is only a tiny handful which are able to discharge the obligations of a modern manufacturing, trading and military Power. The rest, by virtue of their separate political organizations are always on the border of trouble and will be increasingly so. There is no way, for example, by which an independent fragment like Lithuania can be compared in terms of organized social strength with the vital and self-contained U.S.S.R. The former must be, as events since have proved, completely at the mercy of her big neighbor.

The fact is that national "independence" no longer makes sense in terms of economic production, trade or military relations. A nation of ignorant, ill-fed peasants, living under feudal princes, like Hungary or Rumania, is not a force in the modern world. It is merely a vestigial survival.

By no stretch of the imagination can countries like Guatemala and Nicaragua which depend for their prosperity on single products such as coffee and bananas, be considered as valid universes capable of maintaining separate existences. Such organisms as Bulgaria, Afghanistan and Thailand are equally unsuited to modern conditions. They are subject to the irresistible economic power, political pressures and ideological penetration of their giant neighbors. Their productive enterprise is feeble and unbalanced. Their markets depend on the favor of others. Above all, they possess the heinous weakness of being militarily insolvent. Where in the past they could hold off armies for many long months until aid could reach them, in the morrow of death-dealing bomber planes, rocket guns and lightning transport, they can be taken almost instantaneously. Their psychology, as one may see from a review of German penetration of the Balkans, is increasingly one of cowed acquiescence.

For no other reason than that it exists, the small nation offers a constant invitation to aggression. It possesses assets of geographic position, raw materials or purchasing power for which the larger States must compete, together with insistent opportunities for a derangement of the vital power balance with which all nations must be concerned. Inevitably the little nation must become a bone of contention among the larger, unleashing animosities, fears and suspicious antagonisms as the great States maneuver for position.

Today the need is self-evident, not only for larger corporate structures, but for social bodies whose interests no longer will be in clashing opposition to each other, and whose antagonisms can be moderated by evident circumstances of self-interest. In the universe of tomorrow even the fiction of complete independence of small national States will disappear since no nation actually can be independent of its markets or the sources of its raw materials.

Total sovereignty only can exist where it represents a more or less completely self-contained economy capable of maintaining itself against all comers, or where it possesses no vital bearing upon the affairs of others. The moment the sovereignty of one State impinges on the welfare of others the internal affairs of the one automatically become the concern of all. Irrespective of platitudinous theory, it will be so acted on in practice.

The pure weight of their own functional demands will force the consolidation of small States into new political orders in which nationalism as we know it will be only incidental. To the extent that man is dominated by the science and machinery he has discovered, built and organized, this new type of human society must finally take shape. Today we see only the bare outlines of this transitory passage. Tomorrow they will assume better form and the definitions will be clearer.

That relic of a disjointed, unrelated universe, the "neutral" is due to disappear for exactly the reasons which are affecting the issue of sovereignty. The question of "neutrality" rapidly is becoming one of hypothetical assumption not altogether applicable in practice. It is obvious that the economic and military situation of Iceland, as of Cuba, limits the sovereignty of these States to issues not in opposition to fundamental considerations affecting the well-being of the Continent. A Latin American state, for example, could not become a non-belligerent supplier to Germany, as was Spain in Europe, without inviting from the United States vigorously applied sanctions which would amount to a state of intervention.

The true policies of the United States are reflected in our power relations with Cuba, Nicaragua, Haiti and other areas of strategic importance to this country. We have not hesitated to move expeditiously where our interests seemed to require it. When Colombia refused to agree to our request to build a canal across the Isthmus, our nation took a quiet interest in a movement for secession of the Isthmian provinces, and recognized these overnight as the Republic of Panama.

An analagous condition may be observed in our occupation of Greenland and Iceland, possessions of the Crown of Denmark, a nation not at war with us and presumably friendly to our interests despite its present investure by the Germans. As a result, Iceland severed its ancient connection with the Danish Crown and declared its independence as a free republic.

Similar compulsions affect such ostensibly neutral States as Liberia, Egypt and Iran, all of which are now garrisoned with troops of the United Nations.

The world will have to get itself used to new realities in relation to the question of jurisdiction. The whole concept of unrestricted rule which accompanied the old principle of sovereignty, is succumbing to the new power facts of the machine age. It is crumbling under the battering onrush of the internal combustion engine, the vacuum tube, the chemical laboratory, and the power-driven apparatus of mass manufacture. The State has begun to lose its identification as a complete and fundamental universe existing as a law unto itself. It is no longer bolstered in men's minds by the impregnable morality of divine sanction.

Even the handful of great Powers whose physical means and geographic space now give them determinative weight in international affairs, may find tomorrow that they have grown too small to remain as self-constituted, independent universes. They are constantly shrinking as new discovery continues to annihilate distance and spurs the formation of still larger political structures, more efficiently related to the revised transportation, production and military needs of organized society.

The small States already are in an impossible dilemma from which they can escape only by a voluntary act of good sense and courage hitherto unknown in the political dealing of nations. This would require them to yield their decaying prerogatives as individual entities, in favor of participation in a deliberately reorganized world while the opportunity still exists to do so.

It is natural that any attempt at bald readjustment to the new circumstances which govern our times would be resisted violently, and denounced as a dastardly violation of the most sacred elemental rights. Indeed, much that is strange passes under the holy name of patriotism. We still have Otto of Habsburg seeking desperately to seat himself on the throne of an all but defunct Austria. Even the ghostlike Bourbons and Bonapartes, who are little more than bizarre specters out of a long-since buried past, still aspire to a renewal of their rule. There remain millions of White Russians who dream of the day when the Soviets will mysteriously disappear and the Little White Czar will return together with the big estates, the banquet halls and the gaiety which attended the life of St. Petersburg and Moscow.

To any student of history it is obvious that absolute title, vested rights and enshrined legitimacies are impermanent. They are the momentary attributes of a chameleon-like reality. They constitute evolutionary forms which in their own place and age are of true functional worth. When their time is past they must give way, as have those social institutions which sanctioned the ownership of slaves, or of wives.

The pattern of human view changes from time to time as the circumstances which support human life on this planet alter. Nothing is absolute which does not conform to an intelligent grouping of power elements, or does not invoke a devoted acceptance by the masses of mankind, who alone are capable of endowing a regime with the aura of inviolability.

It seems clear that the world can no longer view its destiny in terms of the existing political boundaries. This need involve no violation of essential rights. An orderly rearrangement of the globe, based on the changing interests of mankind, must be envisaged in prospect by our peacemakers who may be sure that a new morality will rise to cover the operation once it has been undertaken. This occurred after the French Revolution in justifying the dispossession of the aristocrats. It was true after the Red Revolt in Russia, vindicating the most relentless reshuffling of human institutions ever to take place.

When forms of government no longer serve the welfare of men, they lose all essential meaning. Hence the world need concern itself no longer with the geographical boundaries of Austria any more than it need trouble with the divine right to rule, once considered the inalienable property of the Bourbon kings. We need only be concerned with those real problems created by the relationship of men with each other, and by an equal distribution of wealth, resources and opportunities so that the inequality of men and nations is not so obvious and flagrant as to throw life into imbalance and chaos.

To attempt to reconstruct the *status quo ante* and to combine with the managerial revolution of the Twentieth Century the archaic political standards of the Nineteenth, would be simply to fall into a political vacuum. It will be seen that there are only four Powers in the world whose position in space could possibly enable them to meet the problems of the present century. These are the

United·States of America, the Union of Socialist Soviet Republics, the Republic of China and the United States of Brazil.

By reason of their limited space economies, all other States are more or less fatally handicapped. To these the conquest of science and the further advance of technology can bring little more than disaster.

IV

Of the four potential masters of the globe, by far the weakest is Brazil. The enigma of this enormous Portuguese-speaking Republic easily could dominate the events of the coming twenty-five years.

Brazil is 248,739 square miles larger than the continental United States, and is ideally situated to rule both the military and trade geography of South America. Once industrialized and under aggressive leadership, Brazil would be able to pick off her neighbors in detail with something of the same ease as did Nazi Germany in Europe.

Although the Argentine is commonly described as the strongest of the South American States, it will be seen by reference to the atlas that this is a misnomer. The Argentine is contained almost wholly in the temperate zone and is less than one-third of Brazil in area. It possesses little of the latter country's balanced natural riches. The interior of Argentina consists of a magnificent plain which merges into a ring of swamps, jungles, arid plateaus, prairies, and impassable mountain ranges, as it moves toward the frontiers. These central plains, or pampas, providing illimitable grazing grounds for Argentina's fine cattle, have been responsible for the country's quick wealth. Its possession of these valuable exports, together with a proud, able and disputatious citizenry, has raised the illusion of great strength.

Actually, the Argentine except for its specialty of animal husbandry, is the most ill-favored of all modern States, both from the view of international trade and military adventure. It is the farthest of all States away from the main trade routes of the new air age.

It is separated from its neighbors by a wild, difficult terrain, and can invade successfully only from the Atlantic side. The Argentine's own nerve ganglia are grouped in a solid knot at the very mouth of the Rio de la Plata, and could conceivably be taken overnight by a determined enemy, thus putting a sudden end to the Republic.

Brazil, on the other hand, is the natural jumping-off place to Africa from which it is separated by a band of ocean only fifteen hundred miles wide. The commercial and industrial development of the Dark Continent will see a parallel development in Brazil, through whose eastern hump is destined to flow much of the commerce between the Americas and the Old World.

If Brazil were to become possessed with the vision of martial glory, its location would enable it to strike from any point of the periphery with crushing force against comparatively weak neighbors. None of these can hope to attain the decisive industrial strength which will feature the Brazilian picture of the future.

Within the confines of the Brazilian State is almost every known resource necessary to achieve national greatness. Her soil is fertile and capable of growing any crop within the tropical, subtropical and temperate zones. Though her country is undeveloped and grotesquely underpopulated it already is one of the major grain, meat and cotton producers of the world. Brazil's mineral assets have only been partially explored but they are known to exist in breath-taking abundance. Her iron reserves are said to be nearly twenty-five per cent of the world's total. She possesses unlimited deposits of bauxite and, it is believed by American geologists, tremendous quantities of oil and oil-bearing shale.

The Amazon basin is a region of fabulous tropical fertility, containing one of the three largest primitive forest areas in the world. This almost unknown territory is drained by the greatest of all river systems, its main waterways navigable by large vessels more than two thousand miles into the interior.

The only observable weakness of any dimension in the potential industrial capacity of Brazil is a partial deficiency in coal. This defect may be corrected by later discovery, or by utilizing the lavish natural resources in hydroelectric power. The conspicuous short-coming of present-day Brazil lies in the character and sparsity of her population. It is estimated that this fabulous land empire is capable of supporting in comfort over four hundred million people. At present it holds forty-five million. Of these, pure Caucasians are about half. The rest consist of Negroes, Indians and the various Mestizo, and Caboclo, or mulatto, mixtures. Less than twenty-five per cent of Brazil's inhabitants can read and write.

There is some question as to whether this indolent and easy-going combination of racial stocks possesses the capacity for high speed competitive organization; or whether it could give rise to a leadership possessing the will to power which characterizes military conquerors. In the past no irresistible conqueror has ever risen from tropical regions. The path of conquest has been from the North to the South. Regions of tropical heat and lush vegetation have appeared always to be inimical to the growth of the martial spirit.

For these reasons, Brazil is a giant question mark. Nevertheless, because of its position and natural resources it must be given a place in any estimate of the future. It requires only an extensive immigration of modern European or Asiatic peoples to give it the strength to dominate the Southern half of the Americas and place it on a basis of parity with the *Yanqui* Titan to the North.

Like China, Brazil desperately requires roads, railroads and air-ports. She needs engineers, construction experts and machinery of all kinds. Much of her problem will be answered by the trans-port plane, which will provide the means by which her majestic distances can be controlled and exploited.

Though Brazil's industrial enterprise is of minor consequence, it is growing steadily. Manufactured exports rose sixty-nine per cent by volume and 184.3 per cent by value, in the single year of 1941.

Since 1914 Brazil's industrial production has increased by three thousand per cent. Factories, mills, airports, roads, railway lines, mines, agricultural projects, dams and hydroelectric power plants have been undertaken, with the assistance of American money. The most ambitious of these is the Volta Redonda Steel Mill in the State of Rio de Janeiro which is expected to produce three hundred thousand tons of steel annually, in addition to pig iron and the various chemical by-products.

The immediate danger this magnificent country faces is that during its defenseless growing period it will become the prey of some imperial ruler rising out of the chaos of Europe, who will utilize it as his bridge to conquest of the Western World.

VIII

THE RUSSIAS

THE State occupying the strongest potential position of all is the Union of Soviet Socialist Republics.

Within the confines of the Soviet Union is almost every resource needed for a self-sufficient balanced civilization. By its control of the North Polar routes the U.S.S.R. dominates the system of flight paths over which the larger share of global commerce some day must pass. It possesses highly developed chemical and metallurgical industries capable of fabricating every type of machinery used in peace or war. These are distributed over a number of autonomous districts so as to provide that decentralization indispensable to modern military dispositions.

The tremendous extent of the land area in possession of the U.S.S.R. is difficult to grasp. Without Bessarabia, Eastern Poland, the three Baltic nations, and the Sovietized Asiatic regions of Outer Mongolia and Tannu Tuva, the U.S.S.R. measures 8,175,500 square miles. This enormous territory, which may be compared with the 2,973,776 square miles of the continental United States, stretches in one solid piece from the Black Sea to the frozen North, from the Baltic to the Bering Strait, and from the cotton-growing regions bordering on Turkey and Iran to the timeless tundras on the roof of the world.

The European section consists for the most part of an endless rolling prairie watered by three gigantic river systems, its separation from the awesome steppes and forest reaches of Asia marked only by the minor foothills of the Urals.

160

The northern frontier of this colossal space fortress is protected by the eternal snows of the Polar regions. Guarding the entire length of the southern border is a breastwork of weird deserts, towering plateaus and mountain ranges. Not until it strikes the extreme Asiatic East in the Amur River region does Soviet territory meet an adjoining terrain over which easy communications can be established.

It is only on the European side that the Soviet Union is dangerously exposed to enemy attack. Here it flows uninterruptedly into the unbroken plain of Northern Europe. This is the only existing door to a successful attack on the Russias, and opening it merely exposes to the would-be conqueror a dreary prospect of exhaustion and suffocation in the interminable spaces to the East.

Inhabiting this vast domain is a mixture of races, overwhelmingly dominated by Eastern Slavs, who are increasing at twice the rate shown for the peoples of Northwestern and Central Europe. It may be safely assumed that the population of the U.S.S.R. will reach the 300,000,000 mark by 1975. The estimate of the eminent statistician, Dr. Dublin, is 340,000,000,[1] a figure which undoubtedly will require revision downward due to wartime losses.

By way of interesting comparison, the demographic projection for the United States for 1975 is computed at around 152,000,000; the populations of England and France are expected to show a decline from their present peaks; Germany's will become stationary. Only Italy, the Balkans and the ever mysterious East will exhibit population gains comparable to those of the Russias.

The Soviet Union is actually a world government in miniature, a great power center around which is grouped a melange of cultures, religions and races which cover the entire range of the Caucasian-Mongolian arc. There are all told seventy-four recognized autonomous units who speak more than eighty different languages. Sixteen of these regions have the name of independent republics

1 Bruce Hopper in *Limits of Land Settlement,* prepared under the direction of Isaiah Bowman.

within the Soviet framework. All maintain complete cultural freedom, but have yielded all authority, economic as well as political,
to the central government.

Under the Romanoff Czars this patchwork of peoples had been
eternally restive and rebellious. The forging of these antagonistic
multilingual groups into a loyal, solidly knit community is one of
the miracles of the present age. It was Hitler's miscalculation concerning these facts which doomed his adventure in Western Russia
to disaster. The Nazi leader believed that the Union would not be
able to survive the first shock of defeat. He looked for dissident
minority groups to take over the government of their provinces
as was done in Slovakia and Croatia. The extent of his miscalculation was to measure the extent of the German failure in this bitterly fought campaign.

The U.S.S.R. is an hermetically sealed area which maintains
at the moment pleasant relations with all non-Axis nations but
which otherwise has closed its economy off from intercourse with
the world.

Up until the very outbreak of war, it was an outlaw State shunned
and feared by the entire community of nations, though the proper
civilities were exchanged and diplomatic amenities observed.

Even at the present time there is little evidence which joins the
Russians into the common design of the United Nations. The lack
of contact is so complete that even in the midst of a war in which
we are mutually engaged, the Anglo-Americans have little real
knowledge of the Soviet equipment, numbers, or disposition of
their armies. We know little of the Russian industrial plant, its
location or its output. There is no detailed exchange of military
or espionage information.

Despite the parallel struggles now conducted by the Red armies
and those of the Western States, the dynamics of the Soviet Union
are so fundamentally opposed to our own that the U.S.S.R. must be
considered as a gigantic island occupying space adjacent to the
conventional nations, but floating in another and alien dimension.

The totalitarian structure of the Soviet Union makes normal

competitive intercourse with the free trade States a virtual impossibility. The central fact which cannot be relieved by diplomatic pleasantry is that the great economic trusts of the Soviets are not only subsidized by the State—they and the State are identical. Foreign commerce in the Soviet Union is a governmental monopoly directed by the Commissariat of Foreign Trade. Imports and exports are regulated in accordance with the country's political as well as economic needs. Competition for markets from the view of the central authority dominating the Soviet machine, could hardly be a competition for profit but a struggle for ascendancy in which questions of profit and loss hardly enter.

A somewhat analogous condition obtains on the political side, where the parliamentary States are handicapped by the inability of their governments to act decisively at the moment when action is most effective—or even to take action at all.

The ability of the huge Soviet enterprise to wheel as a single relentless unit was demonstrated to the point of absurdity during the recently announced change in Soviet constitutional form. Here the sixteen associated Soviet Republics were declared to be independent States, empowered with the right to raise their own armies and conduct their own separate diplomatic dealings with other countries. This step, apparently of the most momentous significance to history, took place perfectly timed to meet the complicated circumstances resulting from the German retreat from Russia. Without preliminary discussion the Soviet Congress met, listened to Premier Molotov outline the plan in a forty-five minute talk, and approved it without debate by an unanimous show of hands.[1]

It is not necessary for the Soviet Union to placate minority parties or to submit its acts for ratification to a Congress whose members in turn must satisfy the infinite diversity of interests existing in their constituencies. The overnight reversal of policy

[1] In our own Republic, points out Walter Fitzmaurice (*Washington Post*, February 2, 1944), repeal of the relatively unimportant Prohibition Amendment was preceded by years of debate, evoking the fullest expression of opinion, with the issue finally decided in a presidential campaign.

executed by the Soviet Union in the non-aggression agreement of August 24, 1939 with Nazi Germany, symbolizes the immeasurable difference between the spirit of the two economies, and the inevitable tension to which this must give rise.

II

The U.S.S.R. is an absolute dictatorship in the hands of hard-fisted, capable men who did not hesitate to place before firing squads almost all of the heroes of the original Revolution, or to liquidate by starvation the three million *Kulaks,* or landowning peasants, whose recalcitrance had threatened the success of the national agricultural policy.

The men who rule the Soviet Union have survived persecution, adversity and danger. They have been hardened by years of underground struggle and conspiracy. They have known what it is like to operate against savage odds and remorseless opponents. They are probably the toughest and ablest group of administrators at the helm of any government today.

The supreme authority of the country is the All Union Congress of Soviets, which meets however only for a few weeks every two years. The actual responsibilities of government are wielded by the Central Executive Committee and the Council of People's Commissars. Below these, and composed of the heads of the gigantic bureaus, is the omnipotent Gosplan, or State Planning Commission.

This imposing structure which reaches like a colorless web into all spheres of Soviet life, extends in a constantly widening system of lesser bureaus from Moscow to the least village of the Union. No portion of Soviet existence manages to escape these clutching filaments which integrate all with the purposes of the State.

A democratic constitution was adopted in 1936 providing for a popular legislative body, direct elections, universal suffrage, a secret ballot and guarantees of freedom of speech, assembly, press, worship and personal liberty. This constitution for reasons which may or may not be connected with the constant duress under which the Soviet Union has found itself during these years, has never been given effect. It is moreover reasonable to believe that its basic premises are antithetical to the regimentation required by a totally organized, managerial society. The very concentrations of authority made mandatory by the Soviet system would seem to nullify all free processes and make them unworkable. So far, the country is under a benevolent, but harsh and unyielding dictatorship in the hands of a few outstanding individuals who could easily say, with Louis XIV: *"L'état? C'est moi!"*

The real ruler of the Soviet Union is the highly disciplined Communist Party. The Party is variously estimated to contain a membership of two to four million, with another two million probationers on the waiting list. The actual power in the Party itself is held by an elite of about one hundred and fifty thousand stalwarts, who combine cold-blooded practicality with the visionary determination of the zealot. As a collective body the Party is the most flawlessly coordinated apparatus ever to appear in political life. To the military precision of the Prussian army it adds the unswerving devotion of the medieval monastic society; and to the rigorous repression of the tyrant State, it unites the pledged brotherhood of the secret and exclusive order. It is at the one time knightly in its professed aims, and brutally barbarian in its acceptance of the means by which these are to be achieved.

The organic structure of the Party runs almost directly parallel to the political system which is subordinate to it. "No Soviet official, however highly placed," comments Chamberlin tersely, "no Prime Minister, no general, no diplomat, would hold his post for twenty-four hours after the Party's Political Bureau had decided on his removal." [1]

Until the German attack, the supreme dictator of the Russias, Comrade Stalin, had never held a political position of any kind within the regular framework of government. It has been from his strategic post as secretary of the Party that his power was derived.

[1] William Henry Chamberlin, *New York Times Magazine*, April 9, 1944.

The Party has been the traditional spearhead for the goal of world revolution, operating through the Executive Committee of the Communist Internationale. The Bureau to whom this invidious task was committed was the *Comintern*. When the Communist Internationale suddenly acted in 1940 to dissolve the latter body the event was taken in many quarters to mean that the Soviet Union had gone nationalist and had abandoned the international Marxist ideals which had dominated her policy for a quarter of a century.

The improved relations with the other national governments of the world coincided with what appeared at first to be a violent return to primitive nationalism.

Precipitated by the catalyst of invasion, the Soviet view now seemed to be strongly magnetized by the ancient patriotism, surging emotions and eternal problems which had engrossed Russian policy in the antiquated past. Buccaneering figures such as Ivan the Terrible and Peter the Great, became the heroes of Russian textbooks again after having been excommunicated during a hardbitten generation of Marxist teachings. The sacredness of marriage, of chastity and of large-scale motherhood were widely stressed. The easy sex life and State abortion clinics disappeared. The mystic phrase "Mother Russia" took on its old sacred glow.

Recently, the Holy Synod of the Greek Catholic Church ceremoniously was re-established in Moscow. The Church was allowed to open a seminary for the training of priests though previously this activity had been considered counter-revolutionary. The League of the Militant Godless which once possessed a membership of six million, found itself abruptly liquidated.

The result of the installation at Moscow of the venerable Metropolitan Sergius, meant an accommodation on the part of the Church to Communist economic ideology, and the fashioning of that august body into an ornament of the State.

It is indicative, too, of a renewal of the old political line directed at the Balkan peoples whom Czarist Russia always had considered her wards. Moscow has become once more the religious capital of the devoted Greek Orthodox population of the peninsula, as well as the traditional headquarters of Pan-Slavic prestige and power.

There is no incongruity in the dual position occupied by the Soviets in reincarnating the ancient essence of the Russias while at the same time basing their economy on Marxian principles. Modern demagogy has learned from Hitler that academic contradictions may be recited with impunity if they involve propositions which, though mutually irreconcilable, are separately attractive to the masses. The Soviets may quite advantageously appeal in the one breath for the emancipation of all peoples on a Socialist basis, while in the other be the power front for the "higher destiny of the Slavonians."

No part of these circumstances is sufficient to congeal the tremendous political tides which have swung the Soviets onward to dazzling success and unbounded assurance. The original retreat from militant Communism followed on the conviction of Stalin, Zinoviev and Kamenev that the Soviet experiment would fail unless the Red government managed to bridge its troubles by a policy of shrewd expediency. The opposing wing led by the brilliant Trotsky, vigorously opposed this course as one which ultimately would prove fatal to the purposes of the revolution.

It cannot be doubted, notwithstanding, that all factions believed world revolution to be the only possible goal. This consequence is intrinsic to the Soviet system itself, despite the reasoned and pragmatic course the rulers of the U.S.S.R. have attempted to follow. These men are realists who believe with Lenin that "facts are stubborn things." While endeavoring to keep to the long view, they are attempting also to follow the path of least resistance.

The Soviets possess none of the extravagant truculence which distinguished the German bid for world power. Nevertheless, this bid must be made since it is inherent in the Marxian concept of the world. The Communists see capitalist society in the act of dissolving itself and of reformulating the terms in which it is couched. These, from the Marxian view, inevitably must be Socialist.

There is also the quite practical question of the local Communist organizations of the divers countries. Though not the only friends possessed by the Soviets, these groups are the only ones of organized importance whose strength might be relied on in crisis. They represent essential elements in the game of modern power politics. They are a counterpart of the remarkably efficient networks established abroad by the Germans, and provide a pipe-line to the universal mass-man whose support is now the first objective of all national contestants.

The question is not whether the dynamisms of the Soviet system are opposed to ours. The fact is obvious that they are. With the best of good will in the world, the two views have no common ground on which to stand. There is no community of aims or interests between the Soviet world and the failing system which the West is so desperately attempting to prop. If the two are not antithetical they are at least alien to each other, which is perhaps another expression of the same thing. They unavoidably must clash if the present construction of disorderly, jumbled and unequal political power forms continues into the postwar world.

The real issue is this: Does the Russian enterprise hold the future answer to those discordancies which have all but wrecked Western society? If it does, no amount of struggle will avail against it; it will come with the ruthless certainty of death itself. This is the only question—whether the Russian system can unravel the riddle which has been throwing Western society into continually greater convulsions of war; and whether it can relieve the social strains which have resulted from the incessant pounding of a constantly rising wave of scientific discovery, invention, and production skill.

The question is also whether this technique of government can satisfy the spiritual needs of man, or whether its automatic destiny would slate it to become the bloodiest and most oppressive of all the devices originated by man to meet his problems.

It is impossible to tell how much of the Soviet's industrial success has been due to the hostility of the outside world. In surrounding the Soviet Union for two long decades with a ring of steel the Western Powers succeeded in evoking all of the resistance, patriotism, pride and spirit in the Russian peoples.

The magnificent economic victories attained, have been achieved on the basis of total sacrifice by the entire nation, and at almost insuperable cost.

As long as Communism remained an object of religious fervor rather than normal material performance, the bureaus could continue to operate smoothly.

In a normal world where the pressures of belligerent function have been withdrawn, the gigantic and complex departments might bog down and prove inoperable. It is these bureaus which are the heel of Achilles of the Soviet system. What they are able to accomplish in the brave fervor of defense against outside aggressors they might be quite unable to handle under normal stresses which have collapsed far less top-heavy and involved government structures in the past.

III

The Soviet leaders believe that it is only within the frame of a highly industrialized society that the ultimate aims of the Socialist commonwealth can be achieved. They are certain that given time the U.S.S.R. will out-produce and out-operate the capitalist States in every department.

These men have turned the pursuit of material science into a cult, and the glorification of the machine into a form of adoration. They place an extreme premium on scientific know-how of every description, and have left no stone unturned to prepare their people for the destined leadership of world affairs which they believe is soon to come. Millions of accomplished technicians are being ground out of the Soviet educational system and fitted like so many nicely machined parts into the new mechanized State which is to prove the worth of universal state socialism.

On the record, the Soviets have plenty of reason to justify their great optimism. Rising by its own bootstraps in the face of universal hostility, the U.S.S.R. has succeeded in forming itself into both a great European and Asiatic Power. Where the armies of Western Europe crumbled almost overnight under the concussive shock of the seemingly irresistible German war machine, the Soviet armies stiffened and held, and finally after the epic stand at Stalingrad, rolled the Germans back and with them the course of human history.

The seasoned Russian armies are probably the most numerous and also the best disciplined in the world. Their staff work is said to be unsurpassed. Their fortitude and courage have been proven in the fiercest battles of modern times. In their rear is almost illimitable strategic space. Their flanks are protected by the frozen North and the unbreachable deserts and mountains of the South. Distance everywhere is their ally.

Behind the crushing power of these armies is not only a matchless position in space but an efficient and rapidly expanding industry, and a unity seldom achieved before in peoples, and never in empires.

It is evident that Russia could not be conquered except by a total combination of the great Powers. This would have to include a highly industrialized China capable of outflanking the Soviet eastern borders. Any struggle between the Soviet Union and the West alone would result in a long continued, costly stalemate in which the Russians probably would exhibit the greater staying powers.

The Soviet triumph has been as great on the production end as on the battlefields. The country obviously is on the path of a pyramiding industrial expansion whose limit cannot be foreseen.

The mining of coal has increased by seven hundred per cent in a decade, and the industrial output by almost as much. The Soviet Union is now first in Europe in machine building, tractors, combines, motor cars and trucks. The most extensive tractor plant on the globe is at Chelyabinsk. At Kuznetsk are the world's largest steel foundries.

The Russians are developing tremendous manufacturing combines in Central Asia behind the impenetrable wall of the Hindu Kush Mountains and the vast deserts of Turkestan and Tibet. Out of the barren steppes behind the Urals are emerging great cities and huge industrial complexes planned on a Brobdingnagian scale. The furnaces, mills and machine shops of Magnitogorsk cover twenty-seven square miles. Even in the Arctic Circle important electric power stations have been built, timber combines set up and seaports created.

Everywhere the tempo of construction is driving relentlessly forward. Whole industries rise where yesterday was little more than wilderness. It is said that over a hundred cities of more than one hundred thousand population each, have been brought into existence during a generation.

Siberia which twenty-five years ago was a dread name that sent shivers down the backs of European Russians, has changed from a dreary wasteland with less than fifteen million people to a pioneer territory throbbing with the sound of industrial hammers, the whir of agricultural machinery, and belching flame and sooty smoke from thousands of blast furnaces, plants, factories and assembling works.

Soviet industry has long since outstripped that of England and France, and in the past two years outraced that of Germany. It is now second in world production to the United States.

Soviet manufacture has been carefully planned so as to be adjacent to its sources of supply. It also, apparently, has been located with a frank view toward its military potential.

Behind this vaulting effort are resources so lavish as almost to take one's breath away. The known coal is said to total 1,263,000,-000,000 tons. The Kuznetsk Field alone is said to have over 400,-000,000,000 tons, or enough to supply the entire needs of the world for the next two hundred and fifty years.

The resources in oil, iron, timber, agricultural and animal products are on a similar grand scale. The Soviet Union contains sixty per cent of the world's store of phosphate rock and more than half of its manganese. She has an inexhaustible supply of copper, zinc, asbestos, chrome and silver. Her timber wealth must be close to thirty per cent of the world's total, and her known oil reserves as proportionately great. She is said to possess more than half of the world's iron, and is richly endowed with regard to both ferrous and non-ferrous metals.

The Union has a marked deficiency only in tin and tungsten, and if forced to become entirely self-sufficient would suffer for lack of certain tropical products such as quinine, kapok, natural rubber and copra. Substitutes for these, however, could be synthetized by her scientists, who are among the best in the world.

In the development of this stupendous enterprise, the Soviet Union has been handicapped by an inferior transportation setup inherited from the Czars. The railroad system has been entirely insufficient for these tremendous spaces and has creaked badly under the load. On the other hand, the development of river traffic has been impressive. The navigable river and canal system is said to be the most extensive in existence. Waterways now under construction are planned to connect the entire country with a unified network of water routes reaching from the Black Sea to the Sea of Azov, and from the Caspian and Baltic to the Arctic Ocean.

It is in the realm of air transportation that the most noteworthy progress has been made. The airplane is expected to be the binding agent which will tie the immense Russian distances together and give them unity. A complete network of airlines feeds almost every portion of the Union. The Soviet Arctic is served by more than two thousand planes which connect the settlements in the Polar Basin with the rest of the country.

In post-war years the Soviet Union's airways will become an important feature of the world's transportation economy. Their position at the very top of the globe will make them indispensable to air commerce between Asia and the New World.

While the Russians are still far behind the United States in factory output, they are in a distinctly superior position in industrial potential. Since the present achievements have been carved out of the stagnating rural economy left by the feudal nobility, it may be assumed that the Kremlin finally will make this potential good.

The major weakness of the Union's setup was the failing of the old Imperial Russia—the need for assured access to tropical products, and for ports on ice-free waters. The greater part of the history of the balance of power system in Europe has been concerned with preventing Russia from attaining this final goal of all its policies.

IV

As history repeats itself, the Russians will seek to emerge on warm water everywhere. As the Soviet Union moves from the grim dynamics of a revolutionary and outlaw State to the older motivations of State imperialism, these needs will become more and more pressing. The desire for a warm-water window on the Atlantic has been traditionally directed to the ports of the northern Scandinavian peninsula, which are bathed by the Gulf Stream.

The opportunity to acquire them will come with the collapse of Finland and of German rule in Norway.

Soviet occupation of a portion of Iran, leading to an outlet on the Persian Gulf, is likely to be permanent. The Russians also are unlikely to allow themselves to be locked out of the Mediterranean. Their minimum insistence is almost certain to be the internalization of the great fortress city of Istanbul. Moscow is not likely to forget that a secret treaty with the Allies ceded this key position to the Czars in 1915, though this agreement was disregarded after the Russias had chosen their present form of government.

The U.S.S.R. is certain to re-annex Eastern Poland and the Baltic States of Latvia, Lithuania and Esthonia. She will undoubtedly reacquire Bessarabia, and perhaps Finland, and may swallow up Moldavia to the Carpathian Mountains, thus taking another step forward toward the Straits.

In these visions are ample grounds for conflict between the Soviet Union and the Western States, who are bound to look with fear at the further expansion of this inscrutable giant.

Stalin cannot forget that after the Red Revolution it was the British and the Americans who financed Denikin, Semenoff, and Wrangel and who almost succeeded in wrecking the infant Red enterprise and turning the Russias into a colonial preserve. The stratagems employed by European statesmen in the hope of isolating the Soviets, had the effect of increasing immeasurably the Kremlin's suspicions of the capitalist Powers.

The Russians moreover feel that it was they who fought most of the war and who determined by their bravery and sacrifice the final outcome. It is almost certain that Stalin will not enter any condominium for the purpose of governing the defeated Axis States, or agree to any projects which look to the permanent retention of the existing order. While it is certain that he is at present friendly to the United Nations and is expected to remain so, he has made it substantially clear that the U.S.S.R. is not fighting for the common purposes of the Anglo-American bloc. Stalin has acted with disquieting suddenness, without consultation with his allies, as when he recognized the Italian general, Badoglio, with whom the Anglo-Americans had been dealing but had accorded no official standing. This precipitous shift from what had been a previous anti-Badoglio position involved the acceptance by the Italian general of a coalition government to contain Communist elements whom he had been heartily denouncing but a few short weeks before.

As in all governments, two sets of views, radical and conservative, moderate and extreme, exist among the men who guide the destinies of the State. Such figures as Litvinov and Kaganovich who have been the champions of inter-Allied post-war cooperation, have lost ground in the inner councils of the Kremlin, to those who urge the full utilization of the Soviet Union's independent position with its unparalleled opportunities for unhampered political action.

It is hopefully held in some quarters of Washington and London that the Russians can be bought off by the use of badly needed economic assistance. Though the Soviet machine requires peace to achieve its ends, it is not likely to give over the basic objectives of its foreign policy at the very moment when it feels it has the power to achieve them.

When the United Nations occupy Germany and the other European partners of the Nazi New Order, the purpose of the Western Allies will be to suppress all Left Wing enterprise or revolutionary terror. There can be no doubt that the intention of the Soviets will be the contrary one of suppressing all Right Wing enterprise and terror.

The tacit struggle between the two forms of social organization will take on new impetus, watering out the fine pledges of collaboration which will be exchanged vocally by the three big Allies. When the British Communist newspaper, *The Daily Worker,* sought to have an accredited correspondent attached to the armed forces, the request was refused. The frank reason given by the government was that accredited correspondents had access to important military information and that "in recent times some of its [the Communist Party's] members or adherents have shown they are ready to subordinate the security of the State to the purposes of the organization."

The attitude toward Germany will spring from two differing sets of causes. The Anglo-Americans will be influenced by a whole hodgepodge of conflicting currents. These will range from the desire to crush Germany permanently by demolishing its industry, to the hope of resurrecting the Reich as a willing partner in the task of keeping the Soviet giant encircled and within bounds.

The view of the Russians will be exactly the converse. The Kremlin would regard the razing of heavy German industry as a genuine disaster to the Soviet Union, destroying the industrial and military balance of world power and exposing the U.S.S.R. to the possibility of a mass attack by the capitalist countries before she will be able to recover from her present catastrophic losses.

A Soviet Russia which regarded itself as menaced by the Western Powers must consider Germany as the very key to Europe. In addition to its industrial strength, it controls the important rivers which drain the Central European basin. If German industry were in Soviet possession or in close alliance, the Soviets might remain within the fortress of Eurasia, beleaguered for a generation without fear. It would be the cutting edge of the Soviet phalanx, more than balancing off the overwhelming superiority in military manufacture enjoyed by the Anglo-American partners.

The view has been made clear numberless times in the utterances of Soviet statesmen. At the very height of the battle for Stalingrad, Stalin declared flatly: "It is not our aim to destroy all military force in Germany. Every literate person will understand that this is not only impossible in regard to Germany, as it is in regard to Russia, but it is also inadvisable from the viewpoint of the future."

The cool and dispassionate thinkers of the Kremlin realize that the friend of today may be the enemy of tomorrow. They remember that a strong undercurrent of realism has always operated to draw Germany and Russia together into a common orbit. Within the tangled skein of political action which antedated Hitler, Russia had been a tacit supporter of German military rearmament. It was in the Soviet Union that German military planes were built and where German flying officers received their training. The geopolitician, Haushofer, together with the great bulk of German generals wanted alliance with Russia rather than war, as the necessary prerequisite to military decision in the West. It may be deemed certain that the German military mind will regard the abandonment of this view as having been the tragic mistake of German policy in World War II.

Marxist doctrine does not recognize either race or nation as basic elements in history, which it considers is determined solely by the struggle of social classes. The Soviets regard Hitlerian aggression as the final stage in the decay of the capitalist economy, and the necessary prelude to revolutionary change.

The Kremlin has caused a manifesto to be issued by a group of political exiles and war prisoners, known as the German National Committee in Moscow. Omitting all reference to the "unconditional surrender" demanded by the Anglo-Americans, this document calls on the German people to revolt and prepare to negotiate an immediate and honorable peace.

The new circumstances will compel a cleavage between the European policies to be pursued by the United States and Great Britain. London is faced with the bleak prospect of living next door to a Europe dominated for the first time by a single Power, and must make an adjustment to this fact. The United States may be expected to follow a policy of stiffening resistance to the new dispensation proposed by these developments.

London, gravely alarmed, is making a desperate effort to find some *modus vivendi* by which she can go along with the Russians without future friction. This may be observed in Britain's change of front on the Yugoslav imbroglio. London which formerly supported the Chetnik leader, Mikhailovich, now has abandoned him in favor of the Communist Marshal, Josip Broz.

The future political complexion of the Balkans is already intertwined with ancient strategic views, as well as bitter ideological contentions which can be settled only by internal violence. The situation in the big peninsula gives a preview of a struggle likely to take place finally all over Europe. The U.S.S.R. has openly backed the Partisan forces under Marshal Broz, who has repudiated the Yugoslav Government in exile and has engaged in a bloody internal war against the titular war minister, Mikhailovich.

Mikhailovich who enjoyed American support and has been supplied by Lend-Lease aid, is accused by Moscow of actual collaboration with the Axis. His opponent, Marshal Broz has ignored national lines and incorporated in his forces contingents of Bulgarian troops as well as Italians. Broz now asks for a united Southern Slav State which would include the Bulgarians and the various units of Yugoslavia, bringing back to life the Great Bulgaria of Czar Alexander II, whose brief existence was terminated in 1878 by the armed intervention of the Powers.

In Greece where the Soviet Union again ignores the British supported government in exile, castigating it through the Soviet controlled press as Fascist, the Russians are espousing the Greek group known as E. A. M., against the more conservative faction known as E. D. E. S. The latter under Colonel Napoleon Zervas, is charged by Soviet writers with being an accomplice of Mikhailovich and thus, despite his guerilla activities, in league with the Germans.

The American Government has steadfastly refused to recognize the annexation of the three Baltic nations to the territory of the Soviet Union and continues to accept diplomatic representatives from the deposed regimes. In Poland the Soviets and Anglo-Americans are committed to widely divergent programs. The Anglo-Americans are pledged to return Poland to its pre-war frontiers, and recognize a Polish Government in exile. This government the Moscow radio has unreservedly denounced as being largely comprised of Fascists who "live in a visionary world of Hitlerite mirages." The Soviets sponsor a Union of Polish Patriots whose purpose it is to take over the government when the moment of decision arrives. The head of this Union is a woman, Wanda Vassilevskaya, whose husband, Alexander Korneichuk, is the present Foreign Commissar of the Soviet Ukraine.

The U.S.S.R. already includes within its borders autonomous republics of Finns, Armenians, Poles, Turkomans, Mongols and Rumanians, all of whom are allegedly now free governments capable of ordering their own foreign policies. Since the Soviets are not likely to disgorge these lands, there is no particular reason why the so-called national "republics" should not be held by the Soviets in whole as well as in part. Thus, Soviet Poland could aspire to the balance of the Polish dominions as *irredenta* territory, as could Armenia to territory in Turkey, and Moldavia to the whole of Rumania.

It is possible that Moscow visualizes her post-war boundaries as including all of Poland and Eastern Prussia to the Oder. The important mines and heavy industry of Silesia would fall to the Soviets, and the Baltic would become a Russian sea. Soviet policy conceivably may visualize a destiny in the Balkans which carries the Red flag as far as the borders of the Adriatic. In the event of successful Communist upheavals in these regions, it is difficult to see how the newly formed Red States could be prevented from joining themselves to the parent Union of Soviet Socialist Republics. Whether this occurs, or whether these lands are ruled by the "friendly governments" on which Moscow is certain to insist, they will fall completely under the shadow of the Kremlin.

In the Far East, the Soviet policies have long been a source of unrelieved anxiety to the Western nations. Communist philosophy has proved hypnotic to the submerged peoples of Asia though it has taken a latent nationalist, or national socialist turn. The stand taken by the Soviets demanding the liberation of enslaved nations and the "abolition of racial exclusiveness" has proven as seductive as the promise of a socialized economy. Only the slogan of the Japanese, "Asia for the Asiatics," has had anything of a like hypnotic effect.

The Russian willingness to accept the yellow and dark races on a basis of equality has strengthened the Soviet hand in Asia immeasurably. It was among the great toiling, underprivileged masses of the East that the Soviets hoped to touch a responsive chord. It was here they sought to deal an early and fatal blow to the capitalist enemy whose unexpected vitality was holding up the advent of the cherished World Socialist State.

Among these masses the Soviets did not find the success they had anticipated. Running parallel with the dynamics of social revolution had come an unexpected nationalist ferment which proved the more powerful of the two. Nevertheless, there are still strong Communist sections in all of the Eastern countries, principally in China, where the Communist armies are in control of entire sectors in the northwest.

The minor republics and kingdoms which border Soviet Asia

live in continuous fear of an overnight coup. They gaze with stark terror at the prospective destruction of the European balance of power as being of evil omen to themselves.

The zones of incipient conflict between the Soviets and the Chinese are considerable, though the two possess common strategic interests which may throw them into each other's arms in the future. After a series of incidents which arose from Chiang Kai-shek's expulsion of Soviet agents in 1927, China and the U.S.S.R. severed relations with each other. A number of border battles were fought over the question of the Chinese Eastern Railway.

The animosities between Nationalist China and the Communist-held sections are far from settled. The Soviets moreover hold in all but name the Chinese provinces of Tannu Tuva and Outer Mongolia. The latter, known as the Mongolian People's Republic, is factually under Soviet administration but is officially claimed by China.

In this sector the Russians have held their ground over strong Chinese protest, though Moscow has withdrawn from the big interior province of Chinese Turkestan, or Sinkiang, after having occupied it for a period of years. In the confused politics of Asia this may be regarded as a remarkable exhibition of farsighted statesmanship, or may be due to some other aspect of the power game, not yet clear.

No one quite knows whether the Russians still have eyes on Manchukuo, with its inexhaustible mineral and agricultural riches and its outflanking position on the rim of the Soviet maritime provinces. It is not known whether the historic ambitions of the Czars for possession of Korea remain a factor in inner Russian policies— or, for that matter, whether these now have extended to include the islands of Japan themselves. These are an attractive prize of whose worth the Soviets are well aware. Possession of Nippon would give the Soviets the most important workshop in Asia, and an entirely new position in regard to the warm waters and great tropical treasures of the South Seas.

Whatever the answer to these mysteries, the Kremlin is in a

privileged bargaining position in the Far East. It is Soviet Siberia which dominates the approaches to the vulnerable Japanese rear. After the collapse of the European war theater it will be seen that no easy reduction of Nippon's fortress islands can be contemplated without the cooperation of the Russias.

IX

THE ORIENTAL COLOSSUS

THE most important Asiatic State of the future is China.

This ancient nation encloses within the spread of her wide spaces substantially every resource needed for greatness. She sits like some ageless phoenix brooding over mysteries which men have long since forgot. She, and the nature of her destiny, are paramount among the ruling enigmas of this century.

Together with the contested regions on her periphery [1] the Chinese Republic covers approximately 4,444,000 square miles of territory, peopled by a gifted and industrious race which has never been counted, but which numbers anywhere from 425 to 560 million.

A peculiar character of this oldest of States lies in the almost terrifying emptiness of its inner territories. The overwhelming bulk of China's people are concentrated on the big alluvial plain which fronts on the Yellow and China seas, and in the valleys of the three great eastern rivers, the Hwang Ho, Yangtze and Si Kiang.

Southern, western and central China are almost unknown and unexplored regions, separated from the rich coastal valleys by gigantic windswept plateaus and forbidding deserts and mountain ranges. The present wartime capital, Chungking, which is located well over in the southeast portion of the country, is to the Chinese the far west.

Except in the northeast where the rolling plains of Manchukuo merge with the dominions of the Soviets, the nation is insulated

1 Tibet, Sinkiang, Manchukuo and the two Mongolias.

from the balance of Asia on the north and west by uncharted desert, and on the south by the snowy fastnesses of the Himalayas and steaming jungle.

China is the military pivot of the Continent, possessing on a much enlarged scale the very organic qualities of position, resources and population which have been the source of Germany's military strength in Europe. With the industrial conquest and settlement of her central and western territories, China's strategic position for the eventual conquest first of Asia and then the globe, is in certain respects even better than that of the Soviet Union.

China would be the very heart of Asia-Oceania. Her already prodigal wealth in manpower would be pyramided by the control of central communications enabling her to strike in any direction. In an air age, thinly populated Siberia, or even the big sub-continent of India, would be vulnerable appendages, precariously cemented on the periphery of the teeming Chinese center. Unless they were defended in depth by a single Power, the islands of the South Seas could not be defended at all. They would fall like rich, ripe plums whenever the Chinese Cyclops decided that the moment had come to take them.

The conditions required to make such a result possible would be a united will on the part of her people, plus a continued division of the world on the present broken political lines. As was the case with Germany, China's central position would enable her to crumple her small neighbors of southern Asia by the sheer mass weight of the troops, machinery and high explosives she would be able to hurl against them.

If China succeeds in overcoming the medieval backwardness of her economy, she will occupy the identical position on the Continent which Japan vainly has spent half a century of desperate military effort to achieve.

The present industrial weakness of the Chinese nation may not be regarded as a permanent defect in her power picture. It undoubtedly will be rectified as the force of events magnetizes future pieces of the Chinese jigsaw puzzle into place. What is of infinitely more significance is the fact that China increases its population by forty million souls every ten years. Thus, a weight of potential man-hours equal to that of European France is added to the already massive human assets of this giant every decade.

China may not require even the brief period taken by the Soviets to emerge into the sun of industrial and military competence. She will have at her behest methods and techniques which have shortened all historical processes. Within the gnarled hands of the rising Chinese Republic is every property which should enable it to leap the tedious intervening phases through which older industrial nations have been compelled to pass.

Much like the Soviet Union she will come forward with dazzling speed into complete modernity. As puny as China's industry is, it has grown at a much faster rate than that which marked the rise of Japan from an impotent little Asiatic kingdom to one of the first Powers of the age. The development of the Chinese cooperatives, for all the dirt and squalor which obscures it, compares favorably even to that of the Russians in a similar stage.

The military possibilities this contemplation conjures up are awesome. Operating within the paralysis of a medieval void, with all his major industrial centers in the hands of the enemy, the Chinese Generalissimo Chiang Kai-shek has in the neighborhood of five million soldiers in the field. Were he able to equip them he undoubtedly could raise fifty million without trouble.

These troops, provided only with small arms and light artillery, without any of the equipment of a modern army and painfully short on gunpowder and shells, have been able to keep half of the forces at Japanese disposal tied up over a shifting front twenty-eight hundred miles long. The Chinese, it is true, have been aided decisively by their magnificent sweeps of country; but like the Russians, they did not collapse under the pressure of what appeared to be irresistible military shock. Like the Russians, too, they showed intrepid foresight, moving entire industries from the coast into the protecting wilderness of the rear.

This record alone is convincing evidence of the ingenuity, valor and stamina of a people whom we fatuously still regard as decadent, stagnant and living in the past. If our policy is to be ruled by this gross misconception, it is likely to be shown once again, as it was in regard to the Japanese, that it is we who have been asleep and living in the past.

The Chinese should not be judged by the social degeneration, palsied infirmity and general dilapidation which has for the moment enshrouded the ancient body of their culture. The period of effete physique, of pigtails, of enervation and flaccid powerlessness is the trough of one of those great cycles which at intermittent intervals engulf all great States. It is a period of tempest, of toxic convulsion, in which the old dissolves itself, is swept away, and the new is born.

China is a nation in the vegetable phase of civilization. It is a country of men little above the stage of draft animals, painfully grubbing in the soil for their limited sustenance and patiently prostrating themselves before the priestlike superiority of the literary Mandarins and feudal lords. It is a nation which has passed through an extended period of conscienceless foreign aggression and even more disfiguring civil war.

Thus, the visitor may be fooled by the venality, rapacity, dirt, degradation, opportunism and face-saving skulduggery which exist side by side with a feverish national pride and determination to enthrone the dynasty of science in Chinese life.

The hope for modernity bites like an irresistible infection into the very soul of China. As reorganized central authority gradually compels the divergent forces of the nation to its command, China's rich resources of character, ability and wealth are being brought to bear on the problem of modern technical organization.

This hope permeates every class—workers, farmers, managers, executives and scholars. It dominates stolid peasants who do not even know what it means. It received its first stimulus from resentment against the arrogance of the encroaching white man. It was fed by hatred for the Japanese invader and reacted on by Japanese propaganda for a new and self-sufficient Asia. Through the younger

Chinese intellectuals it has been profoundly imbued with the Socialist beliefs of Marx.

The philosophy of the cooperative society has found easy acceptance in China. The Chinese have never been rugged hard-shelled individualists in the sense which has distinguished the love for personal independence in the West. Throughout their long history they have had to labor and build together with infinite patience and resignation, sometimes imposed by their own emperors and sometimes by outside agencies. They can be formed into a tightly-geared social apparatus, functioning with a minimum of abrasive friction, and well capable of all the glittering material accomplishments of the West.

The Chinese have lingered longer than any of the Caucasian races in the hallway of antique feudalism. China possesses, on the other hand, a longer history of social development than any other nation, with the possible exception of India.

The Chinese people were already old when Sargon of Assyria was making war on great States whose very names are now forgotten. It had its scholars, scientists, savants and statesmen long before Greece or Rome appeared on the map of the world.

The Hsia dynasty with its already great civil service, is generally credited with beginning in 2205 B.C. Three centuries before Jesus, the Emperor Shih Huang Ti had welded together an empire which embraced all of populated Asia east of the Great Desert and north of the Himalayas. This notable administrator adopted a uniform system of law and coinage for his dominions, encouraged commerce, regulated the calendar, adopted the decimal system of division and built extensive irrigation works. It was he who erected the Great Wall, still one of the engineering marvels of all time.

The periods of civil war, weakness and social failure which have sprinkled Chinese history, have alternated with strong, able governments comparable to any which have ruled Europe. The fall of the Chous in 256 B.C., after nine centuries of classical magnificence, saw the accession of the powerful Shih Huang dynasty. A period of typical disorganization was followed by the firm rule of the Hans, which in turn was succeeded by four centuries of civil war after which came the golden age of the Tangs (618-907) when China reached the peak of its power and culture. Under Tai Tsung, the sway of the Celestial Emperor reached all the way from what is now Iran to the Sea of Japan. It included all of central Asia and part of Indo-China and Thailand.

After an interregnum which marked the final failure of the Tangs, came the regime of the warlike Khans. The empire of the fourth of this line, the fabled Kublai, reached from the Black Sea to the Yellow Sea, and from Northern Mongolia to the jungles of Annam. After another period of shattering enervation came the glorious era of the Ming Emperors (1368-1644), then recession once more, and then the fierce Manchus who ruled from the bleak, unpeopled forests of Siberia to the luxuriant deltas of the Bay of Bengal. It was on the long slope of Manchu decline that European imperialists found the already flaccid and crumbling Chinese State and drew from this fact a fixed estimate of Chinese character.

The Caucasian is apt to believe that because these people have yellow skins and slant eyes they are removed from the realm of ordinary emotions. Actually, of course, they possess all of the feelings which intelligence and the five senses grant to human beings, and are quite as well equipped psychologically as well as mentally to compete for the good things of the world.

Studies by modern social scientists indicate no perceptible inferiority on the part of Orientals as against Occidentals generally. The works of Porteus and Babcock, Livesay, Pinter and others show that for pure intelligence Chinese and Japanese children are quite equal to the average European.[1] These studies indicate that Orientals lack neither prudence nor shrewdness, and are capable of analytical reason, foresight, endurance, resolution and creative action. They moreover are subject to much the same restlessness, suspicions and psychoses which have affected the white races.

---

[1] R. Pinter, *Intelligence Testing;* Porteus and Babcock, *Temperament and Race;* T. M. Livesay, R. Adams, E. H. Van Winkle, *The Peoples of Hawaii, A Statistical Study.*

Wherever Chinese have met white business men on equal terms, they have demonstrated a capacity to more than hold their own. This has been shown to be amply true in the Hawaiian Islands and the South Pacific.

In printed cotton goods, the only considerable Chinese business in native control before the war, the Chinese were demonstrating a capacity to undersell Japanese cottons on markets from which the latter had already driven the American and British exporter.

The high utility sense of the Chinese is nowhere better shown than in their management of the soil. We who have been depleting this source of all wealth at a fantastic rate must be amazed that China's earth has been farmed intensively since long before the first days of the Christian era, yet its tilth and fertility have been carefully maintained. For all their primitive agricultural equipment, the Chinese manage a yield per acre of sixty per cent over the world average in rice, forty per cent in barley and twenty-six per cent in cotton.

The Chinese peasantry is unskilled and for the most part pathetically ignorant; but this is an alert, tenacious people, and it is being moved by something of the same contagious spirit of fanaticism and adventure which has turned the ox-like Russian peasant into the skilled worker of Magnitogorsk and the hero of Stalingrad.

In addition to these qualities and an unfailing gentility and good humor, the Chinese possess another character which the Western world could well note. Throughout the long, variegated history of this country, its people have had little feeling for the sanctity of life as it is known to the West. Although Chinese governments have with few exceptions encouraged learning, philosophy and the arts, they have been inflexible and unsparing in the execution of their will. Conquests have been accompanied by a grinding terror and ruthlessness from which no means of torture or extortion was excluded. The ears and noses of defalcating ministers were cut off, or these worthies were sawed in two in the market place. When one of the Ch'ins found his palace too small, seven hundred thousand castrated prisoners were set to work to build a new one.

II

In determining to exchange Western know-how and industrial techniques for the Manchu pigtail and unworldly scholarship of the Mandarins, China will not abandon the past. The tricks of modern craftsmanship will be placidly absorbed by the old civilization, which will remain stronger than ever. A culture which has lasted over four thousand years may not be set aside, even in such revolutionary scenes as this. It may be deemed certain that modern technology will be molded, hammered and pounded by the Chinese until it fits into their own peculiar pattern. These people are too old, too resistant and too intent, to become a bad carbon copy of a white man's world.

Before the war Chinese industry was microscopic by comparison to the giant size of the country. It consisted for the most part of a few consumer undertakings such as those producing cotton goods and kitchen utensils. With the exception of some minor blast furnaces there was little in the way of a heavy production industry. The whole merchant marine consisted of some fifty thousand tons. Highway communications scarcely existed. Altogether there were twelve thousand miles of railroad, most of which was under foreign control.

With the exception of about two million spindles in the cotton mills, China's basic services, utilities and general commerce all were dominated by foreigners. The greatest number of Chinese factories were in Shanghai and the valley of the Yangtze, and were owned and operated by the colonial and investment Powers.

What is today free China possessed no industry at all.

The existence of any kind of modern manufacturing facilities in China is a miracle. The factories of Shanghai and Canton were almost totally wrecked by the Japanese invaders or transferred bodily to Japan. In their trek westward, the stream of Chinese patriots who receded from the first lethal blow of Japanese aggression, brought with them the machinery of some four hundred modern plants. This precious apparatus, weighing over seventy-five thousand tons, was carried on the backs of men under the most unbelievable conditions across mountains and rivers while subject to almost continual aerial attack.

It included the equipment of machine shops, textile mills, metallurgical and electrical works. All these were set up again in the north, central and western wilderness. The significance of this unparalleled feat is difficult to visualize. It leaves no doubt at least that no one may with safety underrate such a people as this.

Though only a small portion of China's meager machine equipment was successfully evacuated, it has been added to by imports from Russia, as well as local manufacture. Within Free China, scores of small industries have sprung up, roads have been built and rivers dredged. Hundreds of new factories have been erected. These have the advantage of being located close to coal deposits or newly discovered mineral sources. By pure force of circumstance China's infant industry is already widespread and decentralized. When it attains maturity it will not be bound to the congested cities of the coast or to river and rail bottlenecks, as will be the case with the older manufacturing States.

The textile industry especially, has moved forward on a substantial scale. During the past few years, metallurgical factories are said to have increased from four to eighty-seven, machine shops from thirty-seven to 376, electrical appliance factories from one to forty-four, chemical works from seventy-eight to 380, and modern paper mills from three to seventeen. There are now twenty-two refineries producing synthetic gasoline, and fifteen making diesel oil. It is doubtless true that these numbers may possess no real relevancy to actual production quantities. But in a country just emerging from monastic medievalism, beset by civil disturbances, experiencing floods, famine, a disastrous currency inflation, and cut off from the rest of the world by what is almost an airtight blockade, it is an achievement which must be regarded with admiration.

The Chinese are laying out ambitious plans for a gigantic post-war construction, to be operated on a socialized basis. A National Resources Commission composed of engineers and industrial planners is preparing a five year plan of industrialization which is to be gone at hammer and tongs when the war ends.

The day of the illiterate, trotting coolie, of all-powerful mercenary mandarins, of foreign leaseholds on seaports, and alien-owned railway grants and mining franchises is gone, together with the system of spheres of influence and extraterritorial rights.

The old method of imperialist finance conquest will no longer obtain, though this land is without capital and largely without technical means. Foreign investments of money, machinery and experience made here inevitably will fall under the ax and be commandeered in the name of the Chinese people.

China's only machine building industry already is nationalized. So are such critical materials as tungsten and iron. The monopoly type industries and utilities are to be State controlled. Still others are being built along the lines of industrial cooperatives. It is clear that in the Chinese view, industry is considered a function of the State and will be rigidly controlled with at least one eye cocked to the needs of future Chinese military forces.

The Chinese intend to build more than a million miles of hard-surfaced highway and over one hundred thousand miles of railroad. A few filaments of this construction program already have been completed. One of these is the great road from Chungking northwest into Siberia. Other highways are planned to stretch through the far west and into India via Burma and Tibet.

Connections with India and Russia are to be furnished by an interwoven reticulation of railways, motor roads, harbor projects, canals and airports. There are to be great mills, factories and mines. The development of a hydroelectric power potential of twenty million kilowatts is high on the list of objectives.

The five year plan visualizes a radio industry capable of turning out five million receiving units a year, complete with a network which will ultimately require a thousand broadcast stations. The chart calls for 25,000 locomotives, 300,000 freight cars, 30,000 passenger cars and 500,000 new automobiles each year for ten years. It contemplates an annual output of five million tons of steel, precision machinery of all types and the use of 450,000 textile looms. There are to be eighty million telephones, ten million tons of nationally owned merchant marine, many millions of new homes and thousands of up-to-date factories and plants.

This outline has been reduced to meticulous detail by Chinese engineers. The entire country has been made into a single unified project and mapped and blueprinted as if for a military campaign.

The Chinese will seek foreign credits of five to ten billion dollars to facilitate the handling of this enormous operation. It is estimated that China will need 160,000 engineers of various types, together with many hundred thousands of other skilled specialists and professional men.

If China does not get help from the West, she will go ahead defiantly to reach her goal the hard way, as Russia did. "If we shall have to build without outside help," declared Dr. T. V. Soong, China's Foreign Minister, "we shall not shrink from denying to our people consumer goods in order that we may have our industries." [1]

What may be done industrially in this huge, unkempt land is indicated in the Japanese-Manchukuo development which China probably will inherit. Under the impetus of Japanese wartime needs Manchukuo has acquired an important heavy industry. The production of pig iron and steel is comparable to that of some of the larger European countries. There are now extensive chemical plants, mining operations, blast furnaces, machine industries, oil refineries, hydroelectric stations and many miles of efficient, new railways. There are factories for building every type of vehicle,

[1] *International Postwar Service*, September, 1943.

tools, electrical appliances, machinery, aircraft, tanks, munitions and agricultural equipment.

III

Critical studies of Chinese industrialization in the past have resulted in pessimistic estimates. These were based on the twin assumptions that (1) Chinese social institutions were different from those of the mercantile States and did not posses the powers of revolutionary adjustment, and (2) that China had few mineral resources. She was said to lack all the leading metals, including iron, zinc, lead and copper.

The forepart of this estimate may be categorically rejected. The second is only in part true, a fact which must be noted for its bearing on Chinese external policy for the future.

The trinity of raw materials required for a thriving industry is coal, iron and oil. In her stores of the first, China is particularly fortunate. She possesses the only coal of coking quality in the Far East. There are deposits in almost every province, with a total running up beyond 500,000,000,000 tons. Her iron reserves are said to be around four billion tons. In the Tungpientao region of Manchukuo alone, the high grade ores are said to total 1,500,000,000 tons. Manchukuo is also known to possess astronomical amounts of bauxite, magnesite and oil shale.

In 1932 China's only known oil was contained in the minor wells of Szechuan and the North Shensi Basin. Since then, the list of possible oil sources has advanced steadily. Oil has been found in western Kansu and is believed to exist in Inner Mongolia and the hinterland province of Sinkiang. The deposits of oil shale in Manchukuo are estimated roughly at 5,400,000,000 metric tons.

When surveys are completed in the practically unexplored south and southwest, it is certain that there will be a considerable expansion in the known inventory of raw materials. Sulphur, in which China seemed to have been seriously deficient, is now found in some quantity in Inner Mongolia. Copper, once on the list of scarce minerals, has been discovered in Yunnan, Inner Mongolia and Manchukuo. China had been believed wanting in lead, antimony, mercury and zinc, but is now known to be richly endowed in regard to all of these. She has abundant quantities of such ores as bauxite, tungsten, tin, mercury, antimony and gold.

China's stores of phosphates, required in agriculture, are meager, as are her forests. More than half of China's available timber supply is in Manchukuo, with other wood resources in areas difficult of access, such as the mountains of Yunnan and the gorge country of Tibet.

There are ample sources of hydroelectric power. Many sites are available, principally in the Yangtze basin. The Yangtze will be one of the great transportation arteries of the world. It flows thirty-two hundred miles from the Tibetan wilderness to the sea, and is navigable for six hundred miles from the coast. At its mouth, the city of Shanghai, already fifth among the earth's cities, in another generation will vie with such international capitals as New York and London.

China's most pressing problems are those of food and overpopulation. In the heavily populated section every inch of available country is intensively cultivated. Even the hill areas are nicely terraced to utilize the last possible bit of growing space.

The big Oriental Republic leads the world in total agricultural output, almost all of it devoted to the grain and vegetable crops. There is little animal husbandry since precious acres must be devoted to crops which go directly for human consumption. Few pasturelands or hayfields can be supported except in the far north and northwest. Meat is a rare luxury for most. Milk and butter are only for the privileged few.

Even under her present poor living standards, China is forced to import food.

This problem will become more and more acute as China's already massive population continues to increase. In the past, unsanitary living conditions, poor diet and endemic disease tended to balance the high birth rate by an equally high rate of mortality.

As China moves forward into the warmth of technical achievement she will duplicate the population gains experienced by other freshly industrialized States until adjustment to the new dispensation has been completed.

This phase occurred simultaneously with the industrialization of Europe which increased from 185,000,000 in 1810, to 550,000,-000 in 1935, and is now at the point where births only slightly exceed deaths. A striking example of a country in the midst of this process, though past its peak, is Japan, which grew from 26,907,000 inhabitants in 1846 to seventy-eight million in 1940, and is increasing still at the rate of one million a year.

With the better medical care and higher state of nutrition which follows in the path of higher standards of living, China can be expected to follow an identical cycle before she, too, begins to level off.

Under any condition China's population will grow. If she is able to make the transition to the machine age, her numbers by 1975 will increase to somewhere near the astonishing figure of eight hundred millions.

IV

The Government of China is a dictatorship in the control of a single party apparatus, the *Kuomintang*. This body originally was formed by the federation of the old revolutionary anti-Manchu secret societies. After the terrible days of China's civil war, the *Kuomintang* turned to cooperation with Russia under Communist tutelage. A decade later the Communists were expelled bodily in a sanguinary renewal of civil conflict.

As in the case of the Soviet dictatorship, the announced intention is to prepare the way for ultimate constitutional rule. Whether this "intention" ever will be realized short of revolution, only the future can tell. For the present it must be accepted that vested powers, once grooved in the habits and machinery of operation, never are voluntarily relinquished.

However this might be, no democratic processes of any kind are observable in present-day China. China is an authoritarian State and is likely to remain so. The "Party" pervades everything and it is only in the distant provinces that its influence is watered out.

The *Kuomintang* is sometimes represented as the party of the landlords and wealthy mandarins. This critical comparison with Western agencies leads to a totally inaccurate conception. While the *Kuomintang* represents, in part, the most conservative and reactionary elements, it also possesses volcanic dynamisms of the most revolutionary kind. Despite this spread of contradictory forces, to which the world has become accustomed in modern political movements, it is a true instrument of revolutionary social upheaval.

The *Kuomintang* has its political bureaus almost identical with those of the Communists, as well as the whole panoply of indoctrination agencies visible in Germany and Russia. It has its marching youth groups, its torchlight parades, and spectacular mass stagings characteristic of the Nazis. It even has had to subdue peasant revolts against forced grain collections much as did the Russians in the famous Kulak rebellions, a type of uprising the *Kuomintang* has put down with equal severity.

The attempt at detailed regulation of the country has involved its division into 1,905 districts. The ruler of each receives his appointment direct from Chungking, and is responsible to the party machine. This unwieldy mechanism imposed on the septic decay which already has laid China prostrate, has resulted in fantastic corruption and demoralization of community life. Strangely, to the long-suffering Chinese peasant and villager these are but surface evils which may be accepted philosophically as minor aspects of the luminous tableau in which Chinese destiny is being acted out.

The reigning clique of the *Kuomintang* has set itself completely to rule Chinese thought. Native Chinese newspapers are carefully regulated by the Ministry of Education and are allowed to express no independent opinions. Every Chinese news correspondent abroad must be a Party member. Students abroad must have Party approval and must submit to the supervision of Party representatives appointed for this purpose. The ubiquitous Japanese program of "thought control" has become an integral part of reorganized Chinese life. The Chinese even have their own version of Goebbels, a powerful and perhaps sinister figure named Ch'en Li-fu, who combines, it is reported, an acute scholarly intelligence and clerical mysticism with a vigorous chauvinism.

The methods of control exercised by the *Kuomintang* closely parallel those of the Communist Party in Russia and the National Socialist Party in Germany. Contrary to the policies of these States, however, other parties may exist, though merely within the intellectual cadres. Except for the Communists who control a considerable portion of the North, no party but the *Kuomintang* has legal standing. Lip service is paid to democracy in the shape of a weak advisory body called the People's Political Council which possesses no actual powers. On this Council sit representatives of the "minority" parties.

All politics are dominated by the Generalissimo Chiang K'ai shek, and the allied Soong family.[1] Until recently, Chiang took power as chief of the *Kuomintang* rather than as the highest officer of the Republic. With the death in 1943 of the almost unknown Lin Sen, who had been President of China for eleven years, the Generalissimo had himself named President. With this office he combines in his own name all top party and governmental executive posts, including that of Grand Marshal of China's armed forces.

Chiang is a master of intrigue who does not hesitate to use power methods whenever he feels them necessary. He heads an airtight dictatorship operated by an alert and ruthless secret police. He governs by parcelling out power to friends, relatives and associates whom he can trust. Where any question arises, he takes over the

[1] Me'ling Soong is the Generalissimo's wife. One sister married China's national hero, Sun Yat-sen; another married Dr. H. H. Kung, descendant of Confucius and one of the great names of the revolution. Three brothers, T. V., T. L., and T. A. Soong sit high in the Party hierarchy.

post for himself. Chiang refers to individual liberty as "like a sheet of loose sand which cannot exist either now or during the postwar period."

In his political testament, *China's Destiny,* issued last year in Chungking but forbidden publication outside of China, Chiang speaks with blunt frankness. His expressed dislike for foreign Powers, whom he holds responsible for all of the evils which have befallen China, is unequivocal. "The territory of China up to a hundred years ago," he writes, "comprised more than 6,250,000 square miles. It included no area which was not essential to China's existence and no area that was not deeply influenced by Chinese civilization. Until the whole country has been recovered, we cannot relax our efforts to wipe out this humiliation . . ."

The Generalissimo has a pious belief in the absolute superiority of Chinese culture. He envisages a military nation in which "the State comes above everything," and in which "the grand old spirit of our race, handed down for fifty centuries, will be revived" and the "existing weakness, servility, and decay will be totally erased. Every young man," states Chiang grimly, "must make up his mind either to be a mechanized foot soldier or an airman."

Like many strong men the Generalissimo is reputed to be merciless and a respecter only of his own will. His purges of dissident politicos have been relentless and bloody. In the old struggles between the Communists and the *Kuomintang,* Communists invariably were shot on sight, the object being to exterminate rather than reform them.

Chiang is a realist who must be taken seriously. He combines a disarming charm of manner and great personal simplicity with an iron will, tremendous patience, tact, determination and an evangelical faith in the future of China. Chiang possesses also the intense singleness of purpose of the revolutionary reformer, and is undoubtedly one of the great men of Chinese history.

The folds of the dictatorship drape loosely in many spots, but the Generalissimo is rapidly extending an airtight control. In addition to the areas under Red rule, there are other autonomous regions which Chiang has not yet succeeded in bringing under his authority. The Generalissimo has only a nominal control over the so-called Kwangsi generals, Chung-shi and Li Tsung-yen. Yunnan is governed by a warlord, Lung Yun who, however, is closely identified with Chungking. Chiang's most potent weapon among this nation of realists, despite the limited extent to which it has been applied, is American Lend-Lease which provides him with the finest armory of weapons in China.

The most intractable of the Generalissimo's internal problems is the separate existence of Communist China. Practical politics forces Chiang to recognize the existing Communist control of a large section of the critical Northwest, where the Reds are said to possess eight hundred thousand active combatants. The Communist armies are virtually independent, but cooperate with Chiang through a peasant leader named Chou En-lai, a figure of stirring proportions whose name has already become a tradition in the Orient.

Chiang maintains a rigid blockade around the Communist regions, immobilizing troops sadly needed in the mutual struggle against the invader. Bloody clashes often occur, with the *Kuomintang* usually the aggressor.

It is difficult to tell how much control Moscow holds over the Chinese Communists. The Chinese Communists possess a distinctly National Socialist tinge, though it is worth noting that after the Nazi-Soviet pact, the Chinese Communist Party concentrated on anti-British and anti-American slogans in much the same way as did the French Communists and others throughout the world. The Communists are active and assertive, and gaining in influence. The guerilla warfare they conduct against the Japanese is the most effective in China. They possess their own inspired Trotsky in an able military leader named Mao Tse-tung. The possible support the Kremlin may give these elements at an awkward moment in the future, is a source of perpetual anxiety to Chiang and his supporters.

In assessing the final political course to be taken by the Chinese

Republic it is useful to note that every one of the tolerated political groups represented on the People's Political Council has a strong Marxist tinge.

These parties are: (1) the National Socialist group who seek to combine nationalism with a planned economy; (2) the Social Democratic Party which fathers a Marxist economy to be achieved by evolution rather than by revolution; (3) the Young China Party which combines antialienism with a demand for State ownership of industry and land; and (4) the so-called Third Party, which seeks to reunite the Communists and the *Kuomintang* into a single party under the name of Unity. This party also is anti-imperialist, if not antiforeign, and incorporates the land reforms and anticapitalist policies of Marx and Lenin.

It seems inevitable that no matter what might be the fortunes of the little coterie which rules the *Kuomintang*, China is fated to possess a tightly closed economy. The present Draft Constitution lays claim to all subterranean resources for the nation. It proclaims the ultimate intention of operating all large-scale enterprise as a government monopoly. Wealth of every kind is to be rigidly supervised and controlled.

V

We should recognize that the policies of States are never constant but change with their circumstances. The identical course a State will pursue when it is weak and disorganized, it will disown after it is sufficiently strong to assert itself. In a year where five or six million people die of famine on the Yellow River alone, a politically weak China will receive with fervent thanks the relief offered by a charitable Western World. A strong China, impelled by the power of its own needs, must move like a magnetized automaton in the direction of the rich rice growing regions of the Southeast, where the country's food troubles would have promise of being permanently relieved. If the marginal land available to absorb the swelling population growth is insufficient, China will burst its boundaries in all directions, bubbling over like a boiling pot into the territories on its periphery.

A considerable part of this giant question mark is concerned with vacant and almost unmapped Central Asia. To what extent these literally unknown regions may be exploited is difficult to determine.

On the surface such virgin domains as Tibet and Sinkiang appear to represent unlimited outlets for colonization. The Chinese themselves are not optimistic, having in mind not only their present needs but the accelerating rate of population increase. The Chinese authority, Dr. Wong Wen-hao, asserts "that with the utmost optimism we cannot possibly hope to find room for more than ten million new settlers in all of the great Northwest." [1]

The American expert, George B. Cressey, estimates that only eleven per cent of provincial China is suitable for cultivation. Beyond the alluvial plains, he describes the geographical aspect of the country as being one of wild, barren mountains, poisonous jungle and incalculable depths of parched, infecund desert.[2]

In the far Northwest lies the mysterious province of Sinkiang, or Chinese Turkestan. Little is known of the territory, which is estimated by the *Encyclopedia Britannica* to contain 550,340 square miles and by the *Chinese Year Book* (1940-41) as 1,142,750 square miles. Adjoining Sinkiang to the northeast is Outer Mongolia which the Chinese estimate at 1,013,250 square miles, a figure almost double that of the *Encyclopedia Britannica*. Sinkiang itself is probably the size of all the United States east of the Mississippi River.

In the south is another empty expanse of great dimensions, of which even less is known, Tibet. The *Chinese Year Book* estimates this region to measure 759,950 square miles; the *Encyclopedia Britannica*, 503,121.

1 Wong Wen-hao, *The Distribution of Population and Land Utilization in China*, Shanghai, China, Institute of Pacific Relations, 1933.
2 George B. Cressey, "Agricultural Regions of Asia," *China Economic Geography*, Vol. X, No. 2, 1934, pp. 109-142.

In all of these incredible empires of space together there are not more than 5,500,000 inhabitants. These are quiet, pastoral people, far removed from their warlike nomad ancestors whose fitful restlessness once had made Central Asia the nursing grounds of roaring international lawlessness and piracy.

Each of these frontier lands is peopled by alien races who speak non-Chinese languages and possess their own religions and cultures. Two-thirds of the inhabitants of Sinkiang are Turanian Urgurs, a Turkish tribe subscribing to the Manichaist religion. The balance is a mixture of more or less related peoples, Tatars, Uzbeks, Kazaks and Kirghiz. There are only 180,000 Chinese, who are for the most part newcomers. Similar situations apply in Mongolia and Tibet.

These territories certainly will be settled by great inundating waves of Chinese who will seek to exploit them to the last degree, perhaps dispossessing the present tribal owners altogether. Hence we see the rather naive phenomenon of Chinese imperialist aggression at a moment when the Chinese themselves are disposing of that of the white man.

There is little tangible knowledge on which to base a judgment of the possibilities of these regions. There is almost as little known about them as there is about the other side of the moon. They constitute a world set apart, a timeless creation of almost absurd fantasy, yet they may require only roads, airports and the ubiquitous irrigation ditch to enter the throbbing stream of civilization.

Despite the pessimism expressed in reference to China's frontier lands, they may provide a large part of the answer to the food and excess population problems. The Chinese are expert colonizers. This may be seen in Manchukuo which has had an influx of more than forty million Chinese settlers within the past thirty years, and might have swallowed seventy million more had the Japanese permitted it.

So far, all estimates must be counted as pure guesswork. Most of Tibet seems unalterably hopeless. The main plateau, the Chang Tang, lies between 15,000 and 17,500 feet above sea level. "Hardly anywhere does the surface sink below the level of the highest point of the Alps." [1] 250,000 square miles are said to be "uninhabited and uninhabitable." [2] What little agriculture exists is mainly of a pastoral variety, though intensive farming may be possible in some of the valleys which flow from the main plateau to the plains of Assam.

Parts of Sinkiang where irrigation is practised are said to yield the finest melons and tree fruits in Asia. Other portions are well suitable to grazing. Exploration to locate subterranean water tables as well as oil and mineral deposits may render all current assessments inane and valueless. The waterless plain of Mongolia is said to have been once fertile and to have suffered its present fate because of savage deforestation.

East of Tibet is another bizarre country which is largely *terra incognita*, the province of Yunnan. About twice the size of France, Yunnan contains a population of less than eleven million. It also consists of a high plateau, but is deeply notched with pleasant valleys and rich bottom lands. The rivers which tumble through Yunnan's weird gorges are said to provide ample opportunities for water power.

If these territories are not capable of absorbing the titanic energies of the new China, Chinese policy must gravitate like a huge landslide in the direction of Thailand, French Indo-China, the Malay States and perhaps Burma and the Indies. As we have observed in Central Asia, an active Chinese imperialism already exists and would be easy to extend by the simplest measures of rationalization. If China is to remain within her own borders she may be able to do so only by reliance on a constantly expanding economy. She will have to export processed goods and import food, a contingency which would lead to trade warfare with her Caucasian competitors on a scale never before visualized.

If it should come about that China's need for potash, phosphates,

---

[1] H. Lee Shuttleworth, *Geographical Review of the American Geographical Society of New York*, Vol. XIII, 1923, pp. 552-558.
[2] F. Kingdon Ward, *The Riddle of the Tsangpo Gorges*.

oil and sulphur cannot be satisfied within her own frontiers, or if she is restricted from free participation in the tropical wealth of the Indies, her policy will be oriented exactly as was that of Japan, toward final possession of these regions.

The greater part of the hidden pressures which actuated military Japan would be inherited by the growing Chinese economy and given a vigor, force and power which the geopolitical position of Japan has never permitted.

It would not be lost on the realistic rulers of China as their country became a busy center of mercantile activity, that its entire prosperity was more and more dependent on the good will of far-away colonial Powers who would not fail to be regarded as inter-lopers in the Far East.

If the bauxite deposits of Manchukuo and Sinkiang should prove insufficient, Chinese eyes would turn in the direction of the inex-haustible aluminum-bearing clay fields of the Netherlands Indies. The tropical resources of these islands, their spices, copra, sugar, quinine and mineral products would prove an attractive bait for a nearby authoritarian economy seeking an easy solution to its troubles. The copper deposits of Japan, or the great petroleum fields of Borneo, Sumatra and Java would act as lodestones to hungry Chinese ambitions. These places would fall within the natural precincts of the Chinese trade bloc. From the military view they could be invested and taken almost at will.

The principal prize, the Malay Archipelago, contains close to two million Chinese, in addition to a great many East Indians. Outside of Australia, Tasmania, and New Zealand, Europeans are scarce.

The Indonesian inhabitants of these Islands deeply resent the discriminations practised by Europeans who look down on them as inept and inferior. Young Chinese and Japanese firebrands, moreover, have been preaching Asiatic self-sufficiency in the in-terior villages of the Islands for a generation. The Indonesians now are cooperating with Japan and would look on an association with a revived China with enthusiasm. They would see here an outlet for their products, increased wealth for their Islands, and the complete social acceptance which European rule denies them.

With the Philippines and New Guinea, the Malay Archipelago has a land area of 1,094,863 square miles, or almost identically the size of Europe west of Poland and Bulgaria. Together with Australia and New Zealand, this tropical empire is three hundred thousand miles larger than all Europe to the Urals.

This tremendous estate situated right next door to the teeming East, has a population of around ninety-five million. Slightly more than half of these live in the comparatively small island of Java. The Orient sees this rich domain a land of milk and honey, capable of holding a population equal to that of India and China together. The white Colonial is regarded as a usurper and exploiter whose sole purpose in remaining is to drain off the wealth of the Islands to faraway metropolises.

Southeast Asia and the Archipelago are tremendous prizes whose value a renascent China could hardly ignore. The Chinese are not likely to feel it incumbent upon themselves to recognize in perpetuity the ownership "rights" of far-off European proprietors.

Strong revolutionary tides exist throughout these regions which will have been quickened by Japanese occupation. Whatever their cause, it is certain that the spiritual home of future movements for Asiatic liberation will be China, and that this interest will be coequal with Chinese economic needs and resentment against the racial practices of the white foreigners.

The consequence of any successful revolt will be eventual Chinese control. China will be the natural market for any segment of free Malaya as well as its principal supplier of cheap manufactures. Much of the trade and commerce of the Islands even now is conducted by Chinese. The role of these numerous groups in Southeast Asia yet may be analogous to that of the Germans in Czechoslovakia and the other countries.

Much of the reason which has driven Russia blindly forward in a quest for warm water outlets will cause the Chinese Republic to seek access to the Indian Ocean and the short route to Europe. Burma which rests on the east shoulder of the Bay of Bengal undoubtedly will be considered Chinese *irredenta* territory. It once belonged to China and is almost altogether Chinese by race though its civilization has been heavily modified by Hindu influences.

Burma is a natural granary, exporting three million tons of rice annually even under present desultory conditions. The magnificent delta of the Irrawaddy as well as other river basins are miraculously fertile. By proper exploitation they could be made to produce crop yields far beyond the present. Burma possesses many valuable minerals, endless timber and a limited amount of oil.

French Indo-China also had been part of the Chinese Empire. It was not seized by the French until the latter part of the Nineteenth Century. Within its 286,000 square miles are the fecund Cochin-China and Tonkin deltas, which produce in lush abundance such products as rice, corn, cotton, rubber, sugar, tobacco and spice. Among Indo-China's other assets are extensive phosphate deposits, coal, and a variety of minerals.

In the middle of the big Malay Peninsula is the country of the Thais. This State is about the size of France, and consists largely of a rich alluvial plain. There is no area in the world better suited for the raising of fine rice, or for intensive truck gardening and fruit growing.

The Thailanders are racially related to the Chinese, emigrating from Central China during the Eleventh and Twelfth Centuries. The languages of the two nations are very nearly alike. There is in fact a closer kinship between the Thais and the residents of Southern China than there is between the latter and the men of Hopeh, Shantung or Yunnan. Four million of Thailand's thirteen million population are immigrant Chinese who constitute the middle class and merchants of the country.

At the extreme end of the long peninsula, shaped roughly like the head of an ax, are the collection of principalities known as the Malay States. Malaya is one of the finest pieces of booty in Asia. Previous to the war it accounted for forty per cent of the world's rubber and an equal amount of the world's tin. It has in addition a vast store of strategic metals, such as iron, manganese and bauxite. Of the total of five million inhabitants, Malays actually are in the minority, numbering 37½ per cent, compared to 39 per cent for the Chinese, with the balance Hindus, Eurasians and others. This spot in consequence is due to become early the hot corner of Asia. It was in Penang, in fact, that Sun Yat-sen began his agitation for Chinese independence, and where the powerful Chinese nationalist movement developed its first, tough, inner core of leaders.

This entire corner of the Orient is the natural pantry for a hungry China. It has been endowed lavishly by a generous nature as if to prepare it for its manifest destiny as the food storehouse of Asia. Much of the peninsula has never felt the heel of the plow or heard the sharp clang of the ax in its dense woodlands. One hundred million Chinese undoubtedly could move into these thinly populated reaches and thrive there.

For the future it will be unthinkable that a powerful industrialized China would consent to European control and exploitation of regions such as the British Malay States where the Chinese constitute the largest single population bloc. In the British stronghold of Singapore itself, the Chinese are 74.3 per cent of the population. In the strategic Portuguese island of Macao they constitute almost the entire population. The very effort at retaining these places will be construed by the Eastern masses as an act of moral aggression.

It is probable that in the post-war period, the economy of Southeast Asia will suffer a disastrous depression. Bolivian ores will take the place of Malayan tin. The natural rubber of Latin America, and the synthetic North American product will take over the important American markets. As an aftermath of war, the West will find itself largely independent of Asia even in such crops as tea, sugar, kapok, quinine and the spices.

The European owners of these territories simply will admit the dilemma but will not seek to create a balanced industrial economy in compensation for these catastrophic losses. Hence, the situation which is bad now, is likely to become an impossible one. A Chinese campaign claiming these lands as sectors to be rewon for the Chinese nation, would find many willing friends throughout the peninsula.

VI

The major obstacle to practical world organization is not political or economic, but social. It derives from the immovable barriers erected by the Caucasian between himself and the non-white masses. It is dominated by the overmastering fear as to what will happen when these masses make their weight felt and begin to move freely over the surface of the earth. Every question of international trade and political organization is hopelessly complicated by this problem.

The political fact we must face is that the main challenge to the present world equilibrium is coming from Eastern Asia. We note Chiang K'ai-shek expressing in a letter to Nehru the ominous conviction "that the question whether the future world order will be worked out of the present chaotic state of affairs depends upon the outcome of a united struggle of our Asiatic peoples." [1]

The Chinese, together with the peoples to the Southeast number close to seven hundred million people. Four hundred million more dwell in India, together with the millions of the Indies, southwestern Asia and Arabia who easily might be expected to fall within the sphere of China's influence and be attracted to her orbit as the central sun of their existence.

The Chinese Republic even now has indicated an unyielding resolve to stand as an equal among the nations. Much like the U.S.S.R., she gazes with alert suspicion at every move made by the Anglo-American allies. If Chungking is able to play a lone hand, guided solely by the interests of China, it will do so.

China is quietly but bitterly distrustful. We find as cool a mind

[1] Krishnalal J. Shridharani, *Warning to the West*, p. 165.

as the brilliant Lin Yutang voicing the exasperated opinion that "the blockade of supplies for China is political and not military" [1] and describing the Chinese as "getting the impression that their allies are wholly selfish and insincere." [2] China even suspects that Britain and America may attempt to deprive her of her air force, and that when her role as cat's-paw in the struggle against Japan is done, may seek to reduce her to peonage again.

The Chinese have not forgotten the series of tragic steps by which their nation virtually was partitioned among the Caucasian Powers. The fierce Boxer Rebellion in which culminated the acts of rape and degradation to which China had been forced to submit, will be remembered in that country as an occurrence of great patriotic significance, preliminary to the Chinese revolution itself. In the Western countries, it will continue to be regarded as a homicidal assault by an aroused and murderous rabble.

Foreigners are not liked in China despite the common courtesy with which they are greeted. The system of extraterritoriality and special privilege by which resident foreigners were granted independence of Chinese courts of law, and allowed to appropriate mines, concessions and special spheres of interest, and to treat the Chinese people as menials in their own land, left China with a deep-seated anger which in the years of the Republic have subsided into an icy antipathy.

It would be a mistake to assume that the people of free China have been unaffected by these humiliating events though these privileges have now been renounced in special treaties by both Britain and the United States.

Similar pressures have forced the abandonment of the old Chinese Exclusion Act, of which Japanese propaganda had made so much capital. The Chinese do not regard these measures as the end but only as a beginning. They are aware that the Western States mean still to keep them cooped up within the confines of their suffocating Oriental ghetto.

1 Lin Yutang, *Between Tears and Laughter*, p. 112.
2 *Ibid.*, p. 86.

The Chinese have not been backward about making their point of view clear. The West simply does not listen.

What the West also fails to understand is that these people are totally unawed by the white man. The writer will never forget the reply a Chinese woman made to him when he asked what her impression had been of American missionaries when she met them for the first time, in her North China village. She replied, frankly, "I was struck by their eyes. They were blue and green—just like wild animals'."

The dislike for Britain in particular is intense and unbending. London has given no indication that it intends to return the island of Hong Kong, or does not propose to retake Burma for the Empire. In Tibet, Chinese imperialism has run head-on into British imperialism.

The British are determined to maintain the Tibetan frontier against Chinese encroachment. Today, Tibet is for all practical purposes a British protectorate with Chinese troops forbidden to cross the frontier though the country is under nominal Chinese sovereignty. China surveys uneasily what it regards as a series of pernicious stratagems for isolating her and stultifying her future. She means to be the principal Power in the Far East, an ambition which unfailingly must bring her into conflict with the alarmed British.

China has an incipient quarrel with the Soviet Union centering around the activities of the Chinese Communists.

Since the abandonment of Sinkiang in 1943 by Soviet troops, the outstanding point of immediate friction is concerned with the fate of Outer Mongolia. This is now organized under Russian tutelage as the Mongolian People's Republic, though by meticulous legal nicety it still remains as part of the territory of the Chinese Republic. Still other bones of contention may be Manchukuo and possibly the Japanese Islands themselves.

It is believed that both China and the U.S.S.R. would consent to the "independence" of Korea, though such an act would be fatal to the economic existence of that peninsular State. It also is assumed that China would yield all rights to the Soviet Amur region, stolen from her by the Czars, but now the most important part of East Siberia.

The Chinese are good politicians and have learned a great deal quickly about the modern art of diplomacy. They undoubtedly will recognize with shrewdness the centrality of their position, utilizing this as a make-weight in future dissensions between the U.S.S.R. and the West, attempting to exact for themselves the largest advantage possible. In the last analysis the Chinese attitude toward the U.S.S.R. will depend on the type of relations Chungking is at the moment able to maintain with the Western Powers.

These are China's trump cards. Punitive measures attempted by the West in an effort to meet a succession of Chinese demands, would throw the big Asiatic Republic directly into the lap of Russia. To the West such an outcome would be unthinkable and would have to be forestalled at all costs. The Soviets with China together would form an utterly invincible bloc capable of laying hands on India and the entire residue of Asia.

In the threat to slam shut the "Open Door" to the greatest potential market in the world, China has another powerful instrument with which to strengthen her bargaining position. From any view, she seems to hold in prospect the actual balance of power in Asia—and perhaps in the world.

When the hostilities are over, China will tender a demand for Japanese industry and machinery as reparations. She will want the Japanese merchant fleet and heavy mill equipment. She may seek to become the mandatory over Japan itself, utilizing the Nipponese productive plant as the building agency for Chinese heavy industry, relieving China of a dangerous reliance on the West while she is undergoing her vulnerable growing period.

China will make many claims in many directions; but while she is weak there will be no show-down, unless she is driven into a corner and no longer can avoid the issue.

VII

It is almost a certainty that the West, secure in an overmastering sense of its own military, economic and racial superiority, will make no effort to settle its differences with the Orient on a broad and peaceful base while it yet may. The policy of the West will be one of manipulated checks and balances in an effort to hold these people within limited boundaries and to prevent them from becoming a military Power.

The struggle from our side will go forward without plan, based on the premise of the permanent inferiority of the East. While we are following this irrational course, it is inconceivable that we will omit selling the Chinese the heavy machinery and other materials they require to set up a powerful industry with which finally to enforce their will.

We will be unable to reconcile into a single pattern the three fixed factors which can be expected to dictate our future course in Asia—our prejudices, our commercial instincts and our, by now, traditionally purblind conservatism. Our very democratic institutions will cause us to operate at cross purposes with ourselves, affronting the yellow man and walling him off into a huge Oriental ghetto, and at the same time providing him with the machinery to tear through these barriers with brutally efficient force.

There are three firmly rooted influences at work within the greater Asiatic economy, all of them driven by an unalterable inner automatism. These are the stubborn native cultures, a vigorous new nationalism, and the explosive dynamics of revolutionary faith. They will provide enough dynamite to blow the roof completely off the world within the next twenty-five years.

The paramouncy of Western man may not be accepted as a permanent feature of human existence. It must be assumed his advantage in the race for global power has been only that of time. The North European emerged on the scene of social development late, but like many newcomers was quick to seize his opportunities, and hence was foremost in the development of those sciences which led to military and economic pre-eminence. The basic equilibrium the Caucasian has succeeded in establishing is certain to be rudely shaken by the entrance of the great Asiatic masses into the international arena as outright competitors.

The belief that non-military nations are perpetually incapable of bearing arms is an illusion. Napoleon once referred contemptuously to the British as "a nation of shopkeepers." The Germans had a similar disregard for the United States in World War I, and the Japanese in this one.

Western domination of Asia is an occasional, not a conventional phase of history. In its present form it has been in existence less than two hundred years. Anyone who has studied the history of the Mongols under the great Khans knows that the yellow peoples are capable of producing strategists and warriors of a most gifted and soldierlike quality. Asia has produced some of the most ruthless, brutal conquerors in history, men capable of every exercise of courage, daring, organization and skill. It was Asia which cradled the Mongoloid Turks who up until comparatively recent times held all of Europe to the Danube. Asia produced that great scourge, Timur the Lame, the Tatars, and that fierce warlike people whose very name is a synonym for reckless destruction, the Huns.

During the Mongol invasion of Europe, the soldiers of Chèpè and Sabutai were not Mongols proper, but Chinese.[1] These troops, almost always inferior in numbers, defeated the best armies Europe could bring against them. Before returning unbeaten to Central Asia they had subdued Europe in a single lightning campaign up to the borders of Saxony, defeating in order the forces of Germany, Bohemia, Poland, Russia, Austria and Hungary. When this flood receded all Europe breathed a prayer of thanks.

Chinese pilots have been described by American officers who have worked with them, as skillful and brave, and supplied with proper equipment, the equal of any in the world. The celebrated

1 The Mongol horsemen were busy in occupying the Kharesmian Empire. Captain B. H. Liddell Hart, *Great Captains Unveiled*, p. 21.

Siberian division under Gurtiev against which the waves of German attack at Stalingrad broke futilely, as if upon a rock, were Mongolians from Siberia.

To those acquainted with the rigid discipline and machine efficiency of the West, the ragged Chinese army is not imposing. It is more of a horde than a military force, yet to so write it off would be the most costly misjudgment of our times.

These soldiers have been hardened as have no others. During six years of pitiful marching without shoes, food, medicines, tanks, flame throwers, airplanes, munitions or even elementary comforts, they have hung on against a superbly equipped host who still is as far from final victory as he ever was. Like Napoleon's ragged soldiers when they first swarmed over the passes of the Alps into Italy, they are youthful, eager and tough.

The Chinese soldier is inured to rough going. If he is fighting for the good things of the world, he will be a terrible antagonist. Behind his ranks will be still other ranks of poverty-stricken, blindly pushing Orientals from the Asiatic deep south.

X

THE FABLED LAND OF IND

SEPARATED from China by the Himalaya Mountains and wilderness plateau of Tibet is India. Although the two nations are next door neighbors, their historic intercourse has been veritably nil. Ice-clad mountains, hot stagnant jungle and untraversable mesas have stood between the two States as if nature itself had erected perpetual walls to shut them off from each other forever.

In the days of Marco Polo, when legendary India and golden Cathay fascinated the dreams of all Europe, India could be reached only by long, hazardous journey from the mysterious realm of Mangi (South China) which bordered on the great Southern Sea of Ch'in.

In the age of railroad tunnels and air navigation, the terrifying desolation of this impervious wasteland barricade no longer is of major importance. The decisive influences will be rather the needs of the more than one billion people of this area, the things they have to buy and sell, and the political view they take toward their neighbors.

The major consequence of these facts, plus the inevitable industrialization of China, will be to turn Chinese eyes longingly in the direction of the Indian market.

The advantage Chinese production will hold over British manufactures is obvious. China's central position, cheap labor, nearness to markets, and perhaps even the modernity of her machinery, will make it impossible for Britain to compete on most categories of goods.

Indian cotton which has to be hauled halfway around the world to Manchester and Birmingham, and then hauled back to be sold in the shape of printed cotton cloth in Calcutta and Madras, cannot possibly contend with the products of Shanghai or Canton. As the Chinese become more powerful they are not likely to allow themselves to be closed out of this market, nor will the Indians readily forego the privilege of buying cheaper in order to fulfill their duties to the Empire.

In examining the spatial position, resources and character of the two peoples it is difficult to avoid the conclusion that the industrial maturity of China will force India into a position of subordination to her larger neighbor.

India occupies a total area of 1,575,000 square miles, almost two-thirds the size of non-Soviet Europe. Its massive population of four hundred million crowds close on the heels of that of China itself. Nevertheless it will be seen by recourse to the map, that when the relativities are considered on a grand scale, this great subcontinent possesses the physical weakness of dangling in space as an appendage to a central body. Hence, she is likely to be to China what Italy has been to the German Empire.

Of the two races, the Chinese possess the superior energy and productive capacity, as is indicated in the labor market of Malaya where Chinese workmen receive twenty-five per cent more per day than Indian laborers doing the same type of work.

Like all peoples of the warm weather zones, they appear to be wanting in the efficiency, endurance, robustness and force which enable modern peoples to take control of their environment. Indians suffer from poor physique and limited energy, which may be due in part to the hot, moist climate of the country which favors a natural debility, or to poor food, disease, and unhygienic surroundings.

When put to the test in wartime industry Indians have proved themselves capable of the most skilled craftsmanship. Indian soldiers have performed well on the battlefields, wherever they have been tried. Hence, in any reasoned appraisal, India must be written down as an unknown quantity, capable perhaps under inspired leadership and revised political conditions of altering her now deficient space economy and becoming one of the pre-eminent Powers.

The Peninsula possesses superb natural advantages and resources comparable to those of almost any State. It contains an amount of coal estimated to be in the neighborhood of sixty billion tons. India is poor, however, in coking coal, with which China is well supplied. Her reserves of high grade iron ore are among the largest in the world, and may be said to be inexhaustible. She possesses half of the world's known bauxite, and is rich in manganese, mica, and chromite. She is poor, however, in zinc, lead, tin, copper and other essential industrial materials, which easily could be supplied from Burma and China.

The industrial future of India undoubtedly will be a substantial one, though it does not appear that it ever will be comparable to that which destiny holds in store for her powerful neighbor to the north. The two countries would seem to be complementary to each other, balancing the pattern of natural assets and deficiencies existing in Southern and Eastern Asia and creating, whether by alliance or merger, a power aggregate capable of fulfilling to the hilt the ambitions of the Asiatic peoples.

The Indians, like the Chinese, would prefer to see a unified world order which allowed them to move around and partake freely of the good things of the earth. Wanting that, Nehru states, "We should like to be closely associated in a federation with our neighbors— China, Burma, Ceylon, Afghanistan, Persia." [1]

The sympathy of the Chinese leadership for the aims of the Indian *Swarj*, or independence movement, has been fully if decorously expressed. The published declarations of the Central Committee of the *Kuomintang* clearly envisage a political order more just to the peoples of Asia and beneficial to China. They indicate as well that China will fight to produce such an Order. The Generalissimo, Chiang K'ai-shek, did not hesitate boldly to publish his "hope" that Great Britain "without waiting for any demands on

[1] Jawaharlal Nehru, *Toward Freedom*, p. 387.

the part of India, will as speedily as possible give India real political power" so that this war will become the turning point in the Indian people's struggle for freedom.[1]

Just as the young Bonaparte, fired by the zeal of the Revolution stood on the last passes of the Alps and told his tattered troops, "Yonder lie the green fields of Italy," the voluptuous riches of India will beckon the veteran Chinese warrior like a woman's arms. All that will be required to create this situation will be an auspicious moment and continued political unrest in India. The growth of sympathy and the pressure of practical politics will act unfailingly to throw the two nations together. In the event of armed hostilities, the Chinese armies would enter India as liberators, able to offer literacy, economic benefits and full political equality.

II

The British are determined to hold India within the confines of the Empire by whatever artifice which becomes necessary. "The loss of India," wrote Mr. Churchill candidly, "however arising, would be final and fatal to us. It could not fail to be part of a process which would reduce us to the scale of a minor Power."[2]

The attempt to return to the old colonial status in Asia after the war is an utterly hopeless effort at reversing universal trends. There is no longer the possibility that England can retain its hold on India counter to the will and sympathies of the billion people inhabiting Eastern and Southern Asia. Whatever may be the moral position, the British can no longer physically defend their holdings in Asia, and at some point must be compelled to withdraw.

These are the facts and no amount of theoretical argument on the virtues of British rule can alter them. If the British are determined otherwise, the result is sure to lead directly to a racial war even more disastrous than today's global struggle. Since our own foreign policy is inseparably interlinked with that of the Anglo-

1 Chiang K'ai-shek, *All We Are and All We Have,* pp. 167, 168.
2 Winston Churchill's *Speeches on India.*

Saxon motherland, we must face the prospect of American involvement in World War III as an inevitable consequence.

The question of India is not one of justice and the determination of essential human rights alone. It is rather a matter involving a quite proper expediency, that of relieving a point of intense pressure certain to end otherwise in an explosion which will involve the world in the last and most terrible of its great wars. This most titanic of all slugfests would be for possession of the world. In it, the whites would occupy the poorer position geopolitically, numerically and perhaps, morally. Unless we are able to prevail on Britain to settle this situation with good sense and realistic judgment, we shall bring down on our heads within the next three decades that ultimate ruin which has been in the past the common fate of all great civilizations.

Whole libraries have been written around the question of British rule in India, and whole libraries could be written again in an effort to determine its pros and cons. Gigantic volumes could be composed around the argument that under the paternal hand of British administration the natives have received great civilizing benefits. The British can point to the building of more than forty thousand miles of modern railroads and the creation of many thousands of miles of irrigation system. They can point to the relative peace and tranquillity of the country under what has appeared to be the most difficult of conditions; to the huge British investments made in "developing" the nation's resources; to the substantial markets for Indian goods provided by the Empire itself; and to the favorable trade balance enjoyed by India.

Indicating an unreserved willingness to alter their system if the facts so warrant, the British will show that the struggles between the various religions, castes, principalities and races which make up the country, create fundamental chasms which may not be easily bridged, exposing India to anarchy unless they are reconciled by a strong hand. The British will say, finally, that they have no objection to giving India dominion status when in the normal evolutionary process this can be shown to be warranted and without danger to the security of the Empire.

An equally impressive argument can be made out for the charge of British exploitation, capital-finance slavery and tyrannical suppression of the most elementary human rights.

The Indian Nationalist will point to the fact that the British are interlopers and maintain themselves by force of arms. As for their beneficent works, he will mention that the worst slums in the world are those of Bombay and Madras, that children as young as five years, work twelve hour days for wages of less than five cents per day. He will quote the report of the Simon Commission of 1921-22 which estimated the average Indian's income at ten cents per day, and will prove that there has been a considerable drop from this level since. He will say that the wages in the mines of Mysore are so low that the entire amount available for a miner's family is twenty-five per cent below the minimum requirement for maintaining criminals in Indian prisons.

Disease, he will demonstrate, is widespread everywhere, including such chronic ailments as malaria, hookworm, syphilis and tuberculosis. He will assert that in most industrial centers, not less than two-thirds of the workers are so badly in debt as to render their eventual emergence from this condition hopeless; and that the common rate of interest runs anywhere from 75 to 325 per cent, so that a small loan becomes a permanent debt within a few years.[1]

The Indian will prove from official British statistics that the average length of life in his country is twenty-seven years as against sixty-three years in the United States, and that forty-five per cent of all children die before the age of five. He will prove that illiteracy in his country is close to ninety-two per cent, and that though there has been a spectacular growth in some industries, this has been due entirely to war needs and will be strangled after hostilities cease by those covert methods which are always available to unlimited central authority.

He will point to the recurring famines which have settled like a

[1] Joan Beauchamp, *British Imperialism in India*, p. 10.

blight over India, in the last of which, that of 1943, the price of rice rose from two to sixteen cents a pound, and more than 1,250,000 Indians died of starvation. He will claim that this is due not only to bad administration, but to a carefully preserved medieval agrarian structure, governmental indifference, and failure to compensate for the growing population by an adequate industrial development.

He will say with Nehru that "India has been ruined economically," [1] that village industries such as hand-spinning have been destroyed with nothing substituted to fill the gap as in other countries; and that British manufactured goods are forced on the peasantry by a system of brutal partiality which keeps the manufacturers of other countries out, and prevents Indian manufacturers from rising.

The Indian spokesman will say that native industry, once famous for its printed cottons and fine steel, has not only declined severely by percentage in comparison to the general world table, but actually has declined in its dollar value per capita. He will point out that in 1880 some fifty-eight per cent of India's population lived on agriculture. By 1929 this proportion had become seventy-four per cent, completely reversing the trend operative in all other countries.

The Indian will contend that all of this is due to the unsympathetic management of Britain and that this policy of colonial exploitation has been the only possible policy that could justify Britain's presence in India. He will make out a case for the deliberate hamstringing of Indian manufactures by high import duties on needed raw materials, oppressive taxes, and stiff tariffs on Indian goods sent to England itself.

He will assert further, that despite the claims of British publicists, England is not getting out of India—she is moving in. British capital investments in India are now over twenty-five per cent of the total of British investments abroad, as contrasted with a figure of eleven per cent for 1911.

The Indian will establish that some one hundred fifty million pounds goes to Britain each year in dividends and similar payments,

[1] Jawaharlal Nehru, *Toward Freedom*.

the profits of the tea plantations alone often running as high as forty pounds per acre, with dividends reaching the absurd level of two hundred fifty per cent. India, he will say, moves backward instead of forward, with a continually increasing number of plantations owned by European joint stock companies. He will prove that in only one province are Indian plantation owners in the majority, and that in some sections the ownership and management in European hands runs as high as ninety-five per cent. He will show that India contains over one hundred million landless laborers and tenant farmers.

All of this, he will say, is in the face of the fact that there is no white colony in India, and that no white man proposes to remain there and make it his home.

The Indian will assert that his country can do without the protection of the British army and navy and does not wish dominion status within the Empire under any circumstances. He will say that the whole conception of dominion status belongs to past history and cannot survive this war; but that whether it survives or not, "we do not want to be bound down to a group of nations which has dominated and exploited us; we will not be in an empire in some parts of which we are treated as helots and where racialism runs riot." [1]

Rejecting British tutelage as presumptuous, the Indian may declare that his countrymen possess a greater and richer civilization than does their British patron, that it reaches back into the oldest known antiquity, and that British "superiority" is not one of civilization and culture, but of rifles and cannon.

The Hindu will allege above all, that Britain cannot grant India equality within the Empire without allowing Indians to move freely into all of the Empire's empty spaces, a feature which would result in the Indianization of the King's entire realm, an issue which race-proud Anglo-Saxons could be counted on to resist to the last.

In rebuttal, the English will demonstrate that the problems of

[1] Jawaharlal Nehru, *Toward Freedom*. p. 387.

India are highly complex and cannot be reduced to the simple terms in which the Indian Nationalist couches his arguments.

They will maintain that the efficiency of the Indian worker is low, that, for example, the coal production per man in 1928 was 131 tons for India against 250 tons for England. They will show that India's agriculture, intrinsically one of the richest in the world, is badly worked, that the Indian rice yield for a typical year was 730 pounds per acre compared to three thousand in Italy. They will quote their own Royal Commission on Labour of 1931, to the effect that the Indian worker has neither the physical strength nor the stamina to handle the work of heavy industry in competition with other races, asserting that he produces "less per unit than the worker in any other country claiming to rank as a leading industrial nation."

The British will direct attention to the highly resistant caste system as an item which restricts the industrial growth of the country by rigidly fixing the supply of various kinds of labor. They will refer solemnly to the sixty million untouchables, the lowest rung on a ladder which has thousands of steps, and will say that even the shadow of one of these pariahs cast on the path of a high caste Hindu is considered to be defiling. They will demonstrate that India is not a country but a continent, made up of a hopeless maze of mutually hostile groups and enclaves who are always on the verge of cutting each other's throats. The British will represent themselves in the role of pacifiers and mediators. They will point out that there are 562 native States, or feudal principalities and that much of the country is administered only indirectly by Britain, the real power lying with the Indian princes.[1]

According to the British census returns, the native peoples will be shown to speak 225 recognizable languages and many more dialects. In addition to being divided by tribe, nation, opinion and race, they are partitioned off into numerous warring religions and

---

[1] This the Indian spokesman will vigorously contest, pointing out that while these rulers possess undoubted autonomy, the Government may at its option control or actually depose them.

sects, including Hindus, Mohammedans, Buddhists, Christians, Jains, Sikhs and a sprinkling of Zoroastrians and Jews.

In particular, the sixty-eight per cent who are Hindus find themselves in unbending opposition to the twenty-two per cent who are Mohammedans. To illustrate this grievous situation the English will quote Mohamed Ali Jinnah, head of the militant Moslem League, who defines the essential difference between his people and the Hindus as follows: "They worship cow. I eat cow. I defile a Hindu if my shadow falls across him. A Hindu would not take water from my hand. We are utterly different."

Burma, which is an integral part of economic India and inhabited by a race allied to the Chinese, is solidly Buddhist. The six million Sikhs from whom are recruited the best soldiers of the peninsula, detest both Moslems and Hindus.

The Hindus themselves, declare the British spokesmen, are sadly disunited. There are the Fascist followers of Subhas Chandra Bose, now a fugitive in Germany. Within the All India Congress Party is a wide divergence of opinion, ranging from Mahatma Gandhi's preachings of mass civil disobedience to the more vigorous doctrines of the stern intellectual, Nehru.

The British will aver that there is a large body of Communists among the limited but influential industrial proletariat of such factory cities as Bombay and Calcutta. They will show that the worst of the exploiters are the Indians themselves. They will point quietly to the great maharajahs and nabobs who live as in the days of the Arabian Nights and who still practise old-fashioned slavery, buying and selling human beings on established slavemarkets.

To indicate the gravity of the problem, the British quote the irrepressible Jinnah to the effect that "Even the combined forces of China and America cannot impose on us a constitution which will sacrifice Moslem India." Citing the other horn of this dilemma, they refer to Mr. Savarkar, president of the equally militant Hindu Mahasabha, who has announced that Mahasabha will suppress with rifles any revolt on the part of Moslems against a predominantly Hindu India.

Here, say the British, is the quandary. They have given the Indians as much power as is possible in view of the mutual antagonisms; and they are attempting to prepare by a careful evolutionary process for the day when India can attain "full self government with a constitution as free in every respect as that of Great Britain or any of the great dominion members of the British Commonwealth of Nations."

As contrasted with these benevolent plans, the British can show that the normal government of an Indian principality is one of unrelieved despotism, without any electoral rights whatsoever. With paradoxical virtue they, nevertheless, assert that they are bound by treaty obligations to these 562 nabobs, rajahs and maharajahs which absolutely preclude the establishment of an independent Indian State such as is demanded by the All Indian Congress.

To the Indians, all of this is just so much pious pap enunciated for the sole purpose of buying India off cheaply at a moment when Britain is in trouble and the weight of events is in India's favor. The Indian answer to this mass of argument is that most of it is untrue and imaginary, or has been badly distorted. They will tell you that the British operate on the old Roman system of *divide et impera,* and also that the greater part of the deplorable native conditions Britain points to are due to the presence of the British themselves, who are determined to keep the country divided and submerged in feudalism.

The Indians will remark drily on the fact that during the very decades when world industry was leaping forward in giant bounds, the number of Indian workers employed in industry and handicrafts continued to decline; that however, when the Empire was in mortal jeopardy from the Axis attack, India suddenly blossomed as the great arsenal of the Orient with factories and mills pouring out continuously increasing quantities of iron, steel, machine tools, textiles, machine guns, airplanes, engineering stores, truck bodies, seagoing vessels, munitions and supplies of all kinds. India is not only supplying a native army of more than two million men with all but the most specialized military essentials, but is exporting considerable quantities of war goods abroad.

This stimulated production, the Indians will show, places India eighth among the world's industrial giants. At the same time they will assert that the future is weighted against the retention of this temporary gain. They will refer for illustration to the British attitude toward India rubber growers, who would compete with the British-owned Malay plantations. Despite urgent wartime requirements, say the Indians, their producers are overcharged for supplies and underpaid for rubber. For such necessary materials as copper sulphate sprays, the Indian grower must pay through the nose to British exporters at approximately twice the American market rate.

The Hindus will detail further that it is Gandhi and the All India Congress which is conducting the fight against untouchability, and that if the British-protected feudal structure could be swept away, these remnants of medievalism would be swept out with them. They will also allege that the whole burden of argument on the diversity of race, religion and climate which has been applied to India, could with equal aptness apply to the United States under such a system as the British have introduced. They will say that the efficiency of Indian workers, while acknowledged to be low, is determined by actual starvation, ignorance, disease and unsanitary surroundings.

The All India Congress will assert that the Moslem-Hindu conflict is largely a synthetic one, and that it has been artfully instigated in order to keep India divided so that foreign rule might be perpetuated. The only test of this matter which the Government has permitted was the election of 1937. The All India Congress, which has been the moving spirit behind the demand for Indian independence, received an overwhelming mandate at that time. In six of the eleven provinces of British India, the Congress received an absolute majority. In three more, it received the largest single vote.

In the Northwest Frontier provinces, inhabited predominantly by Moslems, the Congress won an absolute majority. In Bengal, the home of thirty million Moslems, Mr. Jinnah's Moslem League won only forty out of a possible 171 seats.

Among the Mohammedans, apparently it is the Moslem League alone which takes a stand against a coalition government and is in favor of the proposed separate Moslem State of Pakistan.

This the Hindus and the remaining Moslems declare to be a British, not a Moslem project. They point to the fact that a Moslem is president of the Congress and that the orthodox Shi'as who constitute twenty per cent of Mohammedan India have given it their unqualified support. The forty-five million members of the Momin sect also repudiate the Moslem League and support Indian independence, as does the Jamiat-ul-Ulema, the powerful organization of Moslem religious leaders.

The Indian patriots contend that the project for an independent Moslem India is an absurdity which involves a still wider dream on the part of a handful of Indian Islamic visionaries. In a book published by the Moslem League with a foreword by Jinnah, the demand is made for an interlocking body of Moslem States to consist of a large section of India, Arabia, Palestine, Syria and Iraq, Persia, Afghanistan, and practically the whole of North Africa including Abyssinia, Somaliland and such colonial territories as Sierra Leone, Senegal and Nigeria. It includes Albania, Turkey, the Soviet provinces of Central Asia and Circassia, and the Chinese territories of Sinkiang, Kansu, Shensi and Yunnan.

They assert that Moslemism has spent most of the dynamics which once made it a potent force in political life, and that it is being cut across by modern social philosophies and material interests and is liquidating the fierce power it once exercised over the human mind in large areas of the globe. The Pakistan scheme poses a type of theocratic State which is completely at variance with the facts of this century and hence impossible to implement. The very use of the words Mohammedanism and nationalism in the same breath they declare to be a contradiction in terms. Racial pride is unknown to Islam. Everyone who confesses Allah is accepted as a brother and equal whether he be a Negro, Malay or European.

The Indians state that the picture of unmanageable Moslem intransigence has been badly overdrawn by being made the hand-maiden to British political manipulation wherever the divide and rule theory provided an easy answer to the question of continued domination. It is the British, they say, who are the world press agents for an Islamic political solidarity which their own Lawrence of Arabia once referred to as "a fiction."

Moslemism, say these critics, is broken into almost as many sects as Protestant Christianity. Whereas those of Protestantism are more or less friendly to each other, those of Islam are divided by vigorous enmities. The Sunnis and Shi'as are as often at each other's throats as they are at those of the infidel. The orthodox Ishmaelites of India regard other Moslems as shameless infidels.

The Indian Nationalist will point out that the Moslem League does not give any public figures as to its membership, and that in the 1937 election it was only able to muster 4.6 per cent of the total Moslem vote.

It is true, the Indian will admit, that out of the present clashing discords, Mr. Jinnah's League has managed to make considerable headway during the past year, and that it now is influential in several Provinces through the use of coercive methods against Moslem advocates of unity. These are stigmatized as traitors to the true faith and terrorized by propaganda tricks and tactics much like those utilized by Hitler against his opponents.

Nevertheless, in May of 1943, Jinnah invited Gandhi to discuss the possibility of putting an end to the disagreement between the All India Moslem League and the All India Congress. Gandhi, who together with the other leaders of the All India Congress was repos-ing under the lock and key of a British jail, was unable to reply to this invitation since "the Government of India denied him the facilities to communicate by letter with Jinnah." [1]

The Congress leaders had been seized under the Defence of

---

[1] DeWitt Mackenzie, *India's Problem Can Be Solved*, p. 219.

India Act which allows for the arrest and imprisonment without trial of all who disturb the tranquillity of the State. In the relentless actions taken to subdue the Congress, 1,028 had been killed, 3,500 wounded and 45,000 jailed.

Police rule applies throughout the country. Even in a normal year the cost of the armed forces maintained to keep order in India is well over forty per cent of the total budget.

The constitution granted India by Britain in 1935 provides for suffrage on a property basis. This provision excludes eighty per cent of those of voting age. The voting privileges, moreover, may be invoked only along religious lines—that is, a Hindu must vote as a Hindu, and a Moslem as a Moslem, for purely Hindu and Moslem tickets.

The actual power of government is wielded exclusively by the British Viceroy. In the superior grades of India's civil service, fifty per cent of all appointments must be held by Britons. Of the eleven provincial governors, all are British. The important portfolios in the Viceroy's Council are a British monopoly.

III

The phenomenon, of greatest importance to the world, which is eventuating from this troubled situation is this: India is turning its back on the West. Out of the inconceivable poverty, ignorance, degradation and festering rancor which has gripped this huge population, is rising an Oriental radicalism which gains in strength daily. The tide has turned away from such moderate men as Mr. Rajagopalachariar and Sir Tej Bahadur Satru, and even from the socialist intellectual, Jawaharlal Nehru, who but a few years ago was himself considered a firebrand.

This ground swell of ideas not only embraces extreme political and social views; among the young intellectuals it feeds on something close to chauvinism and a bitter uncompromising resentment against the continued presence of the Caucasian in Asia. Dislike for the white man is building rapidly, and runs in danger of becoming an incurable pathology.

The idea that India cannot be militant because she is not now, is apt to prove an erroneous one. The Indians have only to be fed with sufficient hatred for the white imperialists to embark enthusiastically on an imperialism of their own. They have proved themselves in this war to be good soldiers. India already has its military party, the Mahasabha, the faction of Hindu extremism which is dedicated to the establishment of a great Indian military State. In the Emperor Chandragupta, a Fourth Century Hindu leader who drove the invading Macedonians out of the Indus Basin after the death of Alexander, the Party has its enshrined champion, an effulgent figure who signifies the might of the Hindu people and their final victory over the invading European.[1]

This concentration on the ancient glories of the country is not shared by Mahasabha alone. There are large groups of leaderless men who are fascinated by this design for the future. Their natural leader is Subhas Chandra Bose, a disciple of Hitler who is now chief of Tokyo's Quisling Indian government, and commander of a pro-Axis Indian army claimed to be one hundred thousand strong. This man's status may be judged from Gandhi's unhesitating statement that he regarded Bose as a patriot, though a misguided one.

It is believed by many Indian leaders that if Bose were to return to India he would be able to rally forces to his command more powerful than those of any other Indian leader. Bose speaks the magnetic language of the new era toward which India is relentlessly being driven by the whip of British policy.

Apart from the struggle with Britain, India's major problems are very much like those of China: she has too many people and not enough land. Quite unlike China, India has no empty provinces which might offer a partial solution to her problem.

The population of the big peninsula increased by fifty-one mil-

1 Chandragupta's empire stretched from the Arabian Sea to the Bay of Bengal, including most of what is now Afghanistan.

lion in the decade between 1931 and 1941, a figure greater in itself than the total population of the British Isles. If plague and famine were done away with, the population would nearly double in two generations. Even under the present low living standards, India's population should approach six hundred million by 1975.

The Peninsula has utilized almost all of its potential farmlands, peasants often existing on holdings of no more than a fraction of an acre.

In the Punjab an extension of the already extensive irrigation system could make room for a few million additional settlers. The dry, desertlike territory of Baluchistan might offer similar opportunities, dependent on the possibilities for drilling hydraulic wells or of creating a system of storage tanks for gathering the winter rains. Some additional potentialities exist in the broad belt lying at the foot of the Himalayas. Here the difficulty is one of a deadly malaria which in some sections prevents all but the most hardened aborigines from subsisting.

A measurable part of this problem could be solved by the introduction of scientific machinery into Indian agriculture. This immediately poses the question of an advanced and heavily industrialized East, which the West is anxious to avoid, and offers no adequate answer to the ultimate question of population growth.

To relieve the continuously rising pressures generated by its central problem, India will require in addition to an intensive farming program under the direction of an interested Government, industrial competence and external areas of settlement capable of draining off a proportion of its human increase. If these provisions are not made, India's constantly growing misery will reach the point of general starvation. From this physical agony and the psychological hurt which goes with it, the natural longing for relief will be transmuted into a tempest of violent and illimitable appetite. Like the power hunger of the Germans it might reach far beyond the physical needs of the Orient to encompass such territories as Australia, New Zealand, Africa and South America.

The Orient observes with increasing exasperation and anger

that the nations possessing the greatest amount of arable land are those least able to make use of it. Wherever these people turn it is the recalcitrance of the white man which interferes with their relief. The sign is hung out over all of the empty and pioneer places of the world to which men will sojourn for the future, "Orientals Not Wanted."

Overcrowded Southern Asia cannot fail to note that a great part of these unused regions are in tropical rain forests acknowledged to be unsuitable for Caucasian settlement, such as the luxuriant tropical savannas and forests of the Congo. These areas, say the Indians, could quite readily be colonized by their people.

In Arabia they observe that the scattered natives have so much land as to be land poor. The peninsula south of Turkey covers an area almost as large as that of India itself; yet the total of people inhabiting it could not be more than eighteen million.

Despite the legend that Arabia is unfruitful, quite the contrary is the case. Even in the presence of this sparse and semi-barbaric population, one-fifth of the supposedly arid desert is under cultivation. The northern valley of the Euphrates has no peer on this planet for natural fertility. In the south the country of Yemen was known to the Romans as *Arabia Felix,* or the Happy Arabia, due to the excellence and abundance of its products.

On India's western borders are well-watered, productive and thinly inhabited lands which in olden times were great centers of civilization. The valleys of the Tigris and Euphrates were once the most populous centers of the earth. In Eastern Afghanistan was located the ancient Bactria, a pulsating, populated hive of human activity long before Alexander passed through it on his way to India. What now seems to be an arid, desolate Iran was before its paralyzing investiture by the Mongols the seat of the wealthy Kharismian Empire whose capital was the storied metropolis of Samarkand.

In Western Turkestan and the river valleys of Mesopotamia, Iran and Afghanistan are opportunities for the absorption of several hundred million people.

Excluding the sections controlled by Soviet Russia, these regions are in the possession of minor peoples, made up for the most part of fierce, wandering tribesmen still in the pastoral stage of existence. The single real obstacle to mass Indian colonization along lines made familiar by white settlement of the Americas, is the determination on the part of the Caucasian Powers never to allow it.

IV

As technical means become available and common to all the nations of the earth, it will be seen that the balance of power has shifted permanently as it did when it moved from the countries of the Mediterranean basin to Northern Europe. The gigantic shadows of these new power forms which are emerging to take possession of this planet, already are cast in bold, rough outline across the pages of destiny.

Since it holds the greatest resources, the most magnificent extensions of space, and by far the greatest population, it is to Asia that we must look for the emergence of the most powerful of these new empires. In particular, as China moves forward into the broad daylight of industrial power, India will seek to accompany her.

To the Western States the importance of this phenomenon is accentuated by a fact on which too much emphasis hardly can be placed: this area *has doubled its population in less than half a century, with new millions being added at the rate of one hundred million a decade.*

The Western nations are still so close to the peacock's throne from which they have held temporary suzerainty over the earth that they cannot see that their talismans and amulets have begun to lose their charm. They see Asia still as the servile and overborne creature of the last two centuries of disintegration and weakness. They are unable to visualize these ancient centers of civilization as rising like some terrible phoenix from the flaming ashes of their own ruined and tumbling house, destined to crush as if they were walls of tissue paper the carefully erected social and economic barriers which the white man has built to contain them.

When the gentlemen talk of a pact for the future, they visualize great India as a huge backwash of brown, little men immersed in philosophy and filth. They conceive of the inclusion of China in this group as a euphemism which will serve to point up the pride of the little yellow brother and make him more amenable to handling.

That the Western States may be playing the role of Mussolini to the newly appointed and still gaping Hitler, they cannot conceive. Yet, proteges do not remain weak amateurs forever. As in the case of Germany, the decision was made not by Mussolini's prior existence as a patron, but by Germany's fundamental position in space and her applying resources in men, character and materials, which alone decided who was to be master.

The situation must be faced squarely and measured for its true implications. Merely gratifying the pride of these people by gratuitous, kind references will not be sufficient. If the white man does not manage to solve this problem during the immediate post-war period, it will become insoluble altogether. When the earth reverberates beneath the feet of the marching Eastern hordes, a policy of appeasement will be worth little. By then the Asiatic masses will be ruled by eternal hatreds and fixed goals from which they can be turned only by military defeat.

If the West cannot protect itself against the dangerous beliefs which hold its judgment captive, it will rush on to suicidal conflict, blinded by the legends of "backwardness," "illiteracy," "debility," and "incapacity" of the erupting power centers in the East. We will see them as they were yesterday, as they still are in most part today, but as they will not be tomorrow—lax in discipline, thoroughly disorganized and untutored in the techniques of modern commerce and war. We will make no effort to analyze properly the questions which apply, or make a wise, statesmanlike and lasting settlement. Instead, we will allow them to fester and grow beneath a swathing of protocols, agreements, stipulations, promises, backstairs manipulations, and meaningless diplomatic jugglery, until they are literally beyond cure.

If the yellow and brown peoples must gain everything by threat and force, they will have learned the technique at an efficient and able school. They will not stop when they have achieved the equivalent of those modest demands which might satisfy them now. When once the successful application of force has been learned, its use does not cease until the end. There are no friendships then to restrain the hand, and no deep, common interests whose existence would give the lie to the heroic purposes of war.

As long as it is only the sword which guarantees access to the wealth, freedom and prosperity of the universe, the slightest material change in any aspect of the world power equilibrium must be gazed on with anxiety by those States fortunate enough to be in the exploiting position. What these nations must ask themselves is the simple, realistic question: as far as any long range view is concerned, are they in a position to protect their extensive global holdings and to enforce their pretensions to physiological superiority?

The gentlemen who will make the peace will be compelled to weigh in the balance two questions: How badly do we need peace in order to continue with an acceptable minimum of well-being, and what concessions are we willing to make, morally and materially, in order to assure it?

From any consideration it is hard to avoid the conclusion that no practical method of organized peace is possible under the existing system of social and material inequality—unless one wishes to grant a future adjustment to a world-wide slave economy in the hands of a purely Caucasian military order.

To most free men such a solution is both monstrous and unthinkable. It moreover presents difficulties of a nature far too grave to be undertaken except by a megalomaniac race to whom every conception of utility and good sense is lost in the overmastering dream of glory.

Under the circumstances, a working settlement with the Orient would seem to be of supreme importance to the West. If a substantial easement of the troubles agitating the East cannot be arrived at as part of a sensible world-wide settlement of problems, straining Asia will have recourse to that first precept of nature, that necessity makes its own law. Nothing then will be regarded as inalienable or sacred, certainly not the white man's concept of his own stewardship of world affairs, or his rule over such immense, thinly settled areas as Canada, South America, Africa, or our own far west.

XI

DECLINE OF EMPIRE

WHEN the lightning of the Japanese war machine struck finally in the Far East, the devastating ease with which the Japs were able to take over Singapore, the Malay States, Burma and the Indies proved beyond argument that the Pax-Britannica which had existed for two hundred and fifty years had become defunct. Britain no longer ruled the seas.

The startling disclosure that finance power had burned itself out as a decisive influence in the affairs of men, and that sea power had given way to the Fighting Team paced by air power, was brought home to thinking Americans with stupefying suddenness along with the reverses suffered by British arms in Asia.

The United States had relied on the British Navy in creating such sketchy foreign policy as it possessed. It was the invincible British line of seagoing battle wagons which enabled the United States to enforce its Monroe Doctrine, though it was the British themselves who from time to time violated it.[1]

During the full blossom of the reign of sea power the little green island could enforce its will against any nation with an exposed coastline by the simple expedient of parading its men-of-war in nearby waters. When the rights of a British citizen were violated in the banana republic of Honduras, a British gunboat pulled into harbor at La Ceiba, where its captain coolly promised to blow the city into kingdom come unless amends were made at once.

[1] They protected the landing of the Emperor Maximilian in Mexico, and seized various areas on the mainland of the Americas.

This act symbolized the magnificent might of British world power in its hey-day. The core of British policy was to make the world safe for English commerce, which traversed freely all of the oceans and sea gateways, a law unto itself, completely uncowed by the panoply of arms of the greatest States.

The revolutionary alterations in the power scheme we have already traced, have been fatal to continued British hegemony. The British Century no longer runs parallel to the stream of kinetic forces which dominates our expanding machine civilization.

Today the Empire is an unhappy anachronism. It belongs in the past together with the huge banking and investment apparatus which developed concurrently with it. The power scheme under which Britain exists is a relic of the day of adventurous seamen when control of the great sea routes conferred a functional command of the world.

Today the very ownership of the strategic land points by which these waterways traditionally have been controlled, becomes more and more a heavy liability. They are for the most part *irredenta* territories, objects of the passionate ambitions of adjacent States. Spain wants Gibraltar, and Italy, Malta. Aden and Singapore are sore spots in the Orient. Suez, located on the lid of a perpetually boiling Egypt, is an object of the cupidity of more than one Power.

The land routes which make conjunction with these seaways are just as precariously held. Turkey eyes British-held Iraq. India is recalcitrant and rebellious. Burma has had a taste of "independence" under Japanese domination. The controversy with France over Syria and Africa has just begun. The potential quarrel with Russia extends in every direction, as does that with China.

Under the exacting demands of modern warfare, the possessions under British jurisdiction present all of the deficiencies which make a successful defense impossible. They are far away from the home supply depots. They are adjacent to what are, or will be powerful industrial empires which can concentrate overwhelming strength on their destruction at any time. They are no longer sources of power but provocations to war whenever in the future a conflict of interests may arise.

It is safe to say that wherever British holdings represent a mere exploiting imperialism rather than a physical extension of the motherland as is true of Canada or Australia, they cannot be held at all. The Indies, Tibet and Singapore would prove easy prey to any nearby mainland Power. Neither Iraq, Persia, Aden, or Omen could be held against the Soviets. The islands of the Caribbean and the South Atlantic, together with British Honduras and Guiana would collapse immediately before an assault from the United States. Even the Falkland Islands could not be retained against the comparatively weak Argentine.

In the event of the destruction of the European power equilibrium, either by a single nation or concert of Powers, Gibraltar, Cyprus, Malta, Suez and the regions of the Near and Middle East would become untenable and would have to be abandoned.

The epic crash of the German war machine threatens to present Britain with this catastrophic issue, which three centuries of British policy has labored desperately to prevent—the assimilation of Europe into a power system dominated by a single State.

Such a Power once established, undoubtedly would close the economy of Europe off from all outside influences, and would attempt to seize the entire Mediterranean littoral, turning that sea into a European lake. From such a Colossus, Britain would be separated only by the twenty-one miles of the Strait of Dover, a minor obstacle to the attacking airplane.

The relation of production facilities to military power is such as to render Britain automatically helpless to any all-out air assault which might be launched from a united Continent. Despite the magnificent record British airmen have left in repelling the essentially inferior German *Luftwaffe,* the relative smallness of Britain's territory greatly increases the power of the offensive which may be directed against her. Nor can she hope in the future to maintain an industry comparable to that of the Continent, or to compete in terms of productive man-hours with the teeming masses of Europe.

Thus, England is perfectly set up as a target for future military blitzkrieg, just as the unified Continent would be protected from this eventuality by its superior distances and decentralized spheres of industrial power. Unable to retreat to inland power centers to gain respite, Britain might be compelled to capitulate in a matter of days.

It is most unlikely that a predominant Continental Power of the future will repeat the gigantic mistakes which in the Battle of Britain cost Germany the world. The attack would be made in force with powerful reserves. The initial thrust would be against Ireland in order to lock Britain in completely and cut her off from the rest of the world.

If the initial shock of concentrated assault failed to be decisive, the contest would be determined by the relative man power, space and raw material resources at the disposal of the rival commanders. This unequal encounter would find Britain with her main power center helplessly exposed, as would also be the lesser strongholds on the Empire's periphery. The scattered nature of British strength and its vital dependence on a set of power factors whose potency is swiftly declining, will make it increasingly difficult for Britain to operate effectively in military crisis.

Tomorrow the seas will be controlled from adjacent shores by transports and gun platforms on wings, whose effectiveness will be cubed by their proximity to supply bases, and will be backed by the great space reaches of tremendous industrial societies organized on a total scale.

Such control of the seas which exists has definitely passed to the United States, which now possesses in its two-ocean navy the greatest aggregation of naval power ever known. Since this enormous might is being transmuted more and more from the floating to the winged stage, and thus becomes largely an expression of heavy industry, it may be assumed that in the control of the waterways of the world such States as China and Russia will also far surpass Britain in the future.

These changes in power position will have a marked effect on the relationship historically borne between Great Britain and the United States. In the postwar period that relationship will be as of strong, rich and influential Carthage to the dying island fortress of Tyre. As in the case of the great Phoenician mother city, the physical position of England in the power universe must continue to deteriorate, so as to threaten her very existence as an independent state.

The bearing these altered circumstances will have on the political course of the United States will be large. Despite the fact that the United States fought two bitter wars with the mother country and almost engaged in two more, it is bound to Britain by sentimental ties, by a long tradition of concurring foreign policies, and by an indestructible kinship of language and inheritance. Great Britain is the land from which almost all of America's institutions have been derived. She is the foundation source of America's national culture. From her own indomitable character and the treasures she sieved from the cultures of Israel, Greece and Rome, the United States received its love of freedom, its scheme of constitutional govrnment, its system of jurisprudence, and the devotion to the arts and sciences which have made it great.

The luminous minds which grace England's scholarship, science, literature, wars and politics, America accepts as being interchangeably her own. The Darwins, Huxleys, Shakespeares, Keats, Carlyles and Dickenses, the Clives, Rhodes, Raleighs, Nelsons and Marlboroughs, are as alive to every American schoolboy as if they had lived and labored on the American continent itself. The whole long, peerless line of poets, dreamers, pedagogues, philosophers, scientists, administrators, soldiers, adventurers and statesmen possesses an unrivalled claim on the national imagination of America.

Nevertheless, it is perfectly clear that England is not liked in the United States. The extent of this feeling may be gauged from the suggestion offered American soldiers in an official guidebook that "People who have their own private reasons for not liking the British should remember that this is not their private war, and that even if it were, Britain is not the enemy."

With all this, Britain paradoxically enjoys the reverence due an estranged and oft-reconciled parent. The instant she is threatened, the degree of our inner attachment to her will become clear. Sentiment alone will cause our physical interests to seem identified with her ultimate fate. We will not stand by and see her destroyed, or sink into oblivion.

Our foreign policy, in any event, will be heavily magnetized by the consequences of Empire politics, whether in our own adjacent Caribbean or in the Far East. We could not ignore the intervention of some other Power on the British islands near our shores. The fate of England itself must be of primary interest to our statesmen. If she were broken by some powerful enemy in Europe, it would be as if our most important outpost in the jungle of Europe had disappeared, threatening not only our military position and mercantile prosperity, but the very character of our institutions as well.

If the attack on Britain came from Asia we would be bound by that other resistless summons to war, the struggle of the races. An affray resulting from a Chinese effort to recover Burma, or even Hong Kong, would have to be viewed with the gravest concern by our nation; and a blow struck at Australia or Canada would be considered as a blow struck at the United States itself. The problem of Britain and her Empire hence must be considered largely as our problem also.

Since the beginning of the Eighteenth Century, Britain has been in the middle of every major war in defense of her rich holdings. Now that she no longer is the balance wheel of world politics, her position, and ours, will be one of inevitable embroilment in a series of struggles dominated by the failing British situation in space.

The gravity of this situation as it applies to our own future commitments, lies in the widespread character of the trouble zone and the almost fatal diffusion of forces required to police it. The British are everywhere, and in potential conflict with the national interests of virtually every nation. Whether it be by the ownership of distant colonies and coaling stations, or by the far-flung invest- ment structure which is as powerful in Iran, Mexico and the Argen- tine as it is in India, Britain stands today destined to become world enemy number one. She possesses what a great many people want and is at the same time vulnerable—a fatal combination. The very existence of her system makes her the symbol of the *ancien régime* against which all the world now is in revolt.

II

The faraway Dominions, finding themselves imperilled in the real world of today will be compelled to gravitate to other political associations as it becomes clear that the Motherland no longer is capable of protecting them.

The Dominions are in a precarious situation. They possess enor- mous territories and great natural wealth, yet their total combined white population is not more than twenty-four million. As the possessors of immense means and vast estates which they are un- able to protect, the Dominions are in an unpleasant predicament. Australia and New Zealand, lying within striking distance of dense- ly crowded domains, inhabited by peoples scourged by hunger, hatred and overpopulation, are in genuine peril. Australia, with only seven million people possesses an area almost identical in size with that of the United States. The pleasant and fruitful sister islands of New Zealand hold 1,750,000 inhabitants in a territory about one-third larger than New England.

The Dominions are rapidly evolving into independent national bodies whose ties to the Empire grow increasingly more limp. The Irish Free State, though still claimed for the British Common- wealth, has remained neutral throughout World War II. When in 1939 the United Kingdom found itself engaged in hostilities against the Axis, Prime Minister King of Canada did not accept the matter as automatically involving his country but referred it to the Cana- dian Parliament where a separate declaration of war was issued.

A similar attitude was taken by Australia when she announced that a state of hostilities existed between herself and Japan.

By the Statute of Westminster of 1931 the Dominions crossed the Rubicon and were granted the right of independence whenever they chose to implement it. Their sovereignty over their internal affairs is absolute and unqualified; and their autonomy extends to the right of maintaining their own separate trade and other relations with foreign countries if they so desire.

The financial dependence of the Dominions on London has steadily declined. Wartime activities, so destructive to the mother country, have contributed to a husky industrial boom in the daughter States. After the war, native industry in all of the Dominions will compete with British manufactures for local as well as neighboring markets.

As the physical power of the motherland declines, her moral command over the Dominions will decline with it.

To such States as Australia and New Zealand, the failure of British sea power has become a matter of critical importance leading to the suspicion that their connection with Britain in the future may be more of a liability than an asset.

Within half a dozen years it will be no longer possible to protect the Dominions in the Antipodes through the medium of military aid extended from England. Under concentrated attack from Asia, help from these far distances in an era of matured air power would be both insufficient and too late.

What Britain calls the Far East is to Australians the Near North. If there is to be trouble in this corner of the world, the Australians will bear the brunt of it. Australia, in consequence, no longer can be ruled by Empire politics which do not reflect accurately the exigencies of her own position.

If not for the over-riding problem of race the natural consequence of Australia's geographical position would be to attach herself to Asia and find an enduring place in the future greater Asiatic economy.

Australia must survey with anxious eyes the power decay which will loosen the European grip on the arc of islands which surrounds all her approaches to the Northern Hemisphere like an iron collar. "Australia will be vitally concerned," said Foreign Minister H. V. Evatt, "as to who shall live in, develop and control these areas so vital to her security from aggression." [1]

The Dominion can find security only as a forward base to some huge air empire capable of rendering immediate aid in time of trouble, and of offering a natural reciprocity of markets and raw materials in time of peace. In this super-commonwealth, Australia would be a far-extended fist, connected with the parent body by the sinews and muscles of a solid framework of island bases.

Only one Power in the world answers this description. That Power is the United States of America, and it is toward its orbit that Australia and New Zealand visibly are drifting.

The security of the sister Dominions of Newfoundland and Canada depends no longer on British battleships but on the proximity of these territories to the United States. An invasion of Canadian ground by any foreign Power would produce an automatic declaration of war by the United States. An effort on the part of the Dominion to link itself with a Power hostile to the United States would invite almost immediate occupation.

The age of speed and mechanical weapons not only forces Canada's interests to run parallel with those of the United States, but makes it mandatory to American foreign policy to cause this to occur on all matters of essential importance to the politics, economy, or safety of this hemisphere. The Dominion is indispensable to the great air transport systems which ultimately will ply between Europe, Asia and America. It will become the aerial crossroads through which goods and men will feed over the short North Circle routes from the Old World into the Americas. Canada no longer is a free agent. It cannot disassociate itself from the United States and the predominant currents which will affect the destiny of the American Continent.

Where South Africa goes is uncertain. The tether which would

1 April 29, 1943.

hold her to a fading Empire is thin. A majority of the Dominion's white inhabitants are Afrikaans-speaking Boers, a great proportion of whom remain as violently anti-British as they were in the days of Paul Kruger and Louis Botha.

Under any circumstance the interests of South Africa are concerned with Africa alone. Here the Dominion possesses boundless ambitions and visualizes itself as the hub of African empire.

III

The heart of the British system has not been military exploitation, but banking and commerce. The welfare of Britain has depended on the ability of her traders to transport raw materials to her factory centers and re-export processed goods at a profit.

By her control of the sea routes Britain exacted a premium from a large part of the world's carrying trade. As an investing Power her lien on the basic resources, essential services and means of production of other States added materially to her wealth, prestige and authority. The Britain of empire was not alone the Britain of red-coated regiments, cannon, cruisers and dreadnaughts, but of merchantmen, mills, factories, bonds, securities and accrued interest.

This element of the British system, too, finds itself under desperate challenge and confronted with eventual disintegration and ruin.

British finance-capital must face the prospect of a world united in enormous economic blocs ruled by management corporations which neither can be coerced, cowed, bribed or turned from the path of their greatest ultimate advantage. For the first time in three centuries the superiority of transport as well as manufacturing position will be in non-British possession. Britain's manufacturers and traders will be forced into competition with great socialized national trusts having at their disposal unlimited resources, and expressing in their dealings not the search for money gain, but the political purposes of the total horde.

The already precarious competitive position of Britain industrially is complicated further by internal revolutionary causes, and labor's demand for wage increases and a cooperative economy. Britain's capacity to compete in the open markets of the world becomes less, not more.

When these developments reach their destined maturity the era of sea-borne profits by which city-States, or small faraway islands could dominate the commerce and trade of entire continents, finally will be ended. Britain which has worn the mantle of Phoenicia, Genoa and Venice, will share the fate of her predecessors and will be thrown back on her own resources for sustenance.

These trends clearly are visible now.

Their consequences will be grave.

Including Northern Ireland, Great Britain contains 47,676,000 people concentrated on 94,279 square miles of territory. England itself has a population of 39,050,000 of whom 32,507,000 are urban, and only 6,543,000 rural.

This serious imbalance is the outgrowth of the conditions of Britain's mercantile ascendancy. It will become measurably worse as her industrial lead continues to be whittled down by competing nations. Before the war England was compelled to import sixty per cent of her food, as well as the great bulk of the raw materials she used in industry. Though she possesses iron and coal, her physical position is on the whole not much better than that of Japan if she is forced to shrink herself to the frontiers of her native insular means and resources.

During the peak of British mercantile pre-eminence, the island kingdom had become the workshop of the world, far surpassing all others in the extent of her overseas trade, and in the amount of maritime tonnage which serviced her voluminous commerce as well as that of others.

In 1870, over twenty-five per cent of international commerce was conducted by Great Britain. By 1938 this percentage had fallen to fifteen per cent, and was continuing to drop under the competition of the United States, the Soviet Union, Germany and other countries.

This drop not only continued by percentage but also by volume. Even more important, the relationship between imports and exports changed for the worse, a growing mire of deficit in which the British ship of state continued to sink.

Up to the middle of the 1920's, Britain had possessed a favorable trade balance of around £150,000,000. By 1938 this had become an adverse balance of £50,000,000. The situation may be seen with some clarity in the trade figures for the latter year. An import figure of £919,508,000 contrasted painfully with exports of £470,-755,000. Re-exports of imported merchandise brought this amount to a total of £499,908. The differential in these figures, which otherwise would mean early bankruptcy, largely has been made up by so-called "invisible exports" or income from investments, shipping, insurance, banking and other essential services. For this period, banking and investment income was in the neighborhood of £200,-000,000, and shipping earnings around £110,000,000. Other receipts more or less related to British imperial position came to £60,000,000.

In these latter categories, too, an ominous blow has been struck for the British future. During the period previous to World War I, Britain had held just short of fifty per cent of the world total of foreign investments. In the year before World War II this had dropped to approximately thirty per cent.

Since that time the portfolio of British investments has been in increasing jeopardy. Assets located in the belligerent zones, such as the £190,000,000 invested in Shanghai or the £25,000,000 secured in Hong Kong, are almost certain to be among the casualties of war. They are not likely to be continued as income-producing assets in any event.

The nominal value of long term British investments overseas in 1938 was estimated by Lord Kindersley to have been £3,725,-000,000. Adding British investments in Eire and the value of gold and foreign exchange holdings, the actual market value of Britain's overseas assets and gold holdings are estimated to have been in the neighborhood of £5,000,000,000. *The Economist* (London, September 11, 1943) concludes that "the cumulative adverse balance of payments from the outbreak of war to the end of 1942 was of the order of £2,350,000,000." This, it will be noted, is somewhere near half the estimated market value of British foreign assets in 1938.

Part of this deficit was financed by the sale of £650,000,000 of gold and foreign exchange and the unloading of £875,000,000 of securities. Mr. N. Kaldor estimates that the loss of income through liquidation and war losses is in the neighborhood of £98,000,000 in investment earnings alone. The Foreign Policy Report, *"Britain's Postwar Trade and World Economy,"* concludes that Britain's investment receipts will not total more than £90,000,000 a year at the war's end.

The present tendency toward public control of national wealth is sure to end in the virtual expropriation of such properties as the British-owned Rio Tinto copper mines in Spain, or the Argentine railroad and electric light companies in which Britain has a stake of two billion dollars.

British capital has been able to preserve its Argentine holdings by the retaliatory threat to shut Argentine beef out of British markets if they are disturbed. As the Argentine begins to achieve a more symmetrical economic balance, foreign possession of her public utilities will become a major domestic issue, and she unquestionably will endeavor to curtail them.

In China a heavy percentage of British investment also is in transportation and public utilities, with other large amounts in banking, insurance, shipping, mines and heavy manufacturing. It is precisely these basic income producing properties which are sure to be taken over first in any nationalization program such as that to which China is committed.

In India British investments may come to £680,000,000, the greatest share of which is in heavy industry, banking, insurance, mines and transport facilities. These amounts, plus those invested in Ceylon and Malaya, are certain to be lost within the next decade or two under conditions which will approximate confiscation, the view being that continued payment of interest or profit to absentee owners is a form of tribute. The Dominions themselves, which now hold the bulk of British overseas investments, will tend more and more to resent the flow of money from their areas to a faraway banking center. This cannot fail to be considered in terms of un-earned increment, and consequently taxed out of existence.

British economists estimate that even though no payments ever will be demanded on the Lend-Lease account, "it is highly likely that Great Britain will emerge in the postwar world with only enough overseas assets to balance claims arising out of the overseas ownership of capital invested in Great Britain, or in other words, with a net income of nothing at all." [1]

The homespun American philosopher, Josh Billings, once said that when a man starts sliding all creation seems greased for the occasion. Britain's mercantile prospects, even in a reasonably peace-ful world, are bleak indeed compared to the privileged position she has occupied in the past. Even her important globe-girdling com-munications systems have been placed under challenge. The inter-national radio, telephone and cable systems as yet remain tightly held British preserves. This has ceased to be true, however, in that domain where once Britain had reigned supreme—the sphere of international shipping.

Britain's overshadowing rival for the globe's carrying trade will be the United States. America which entered the war with a marine tonnage of seven million, compared with Great Britain's twenty million, will end it with about fifty million tons against Britain's fifteen million. China has announced its determination to have a maritime service of its own adequate to the dignity of a great coun-try. The U.S.S.R. and others unquestionably will follow suit.

The situation in regard to air commerce is even more disquiet-ing. Due to the effective pioneering of the U.S. Army Air Trans-port Command, the United States holds complete mastery of the trans-oceanic routes covering the Pacific and the South Atlantic. In the North Atlantic it possesses a ratio of more than two and

[1] G. H. D. Cole, *The Economist,* London, December 12, 1942.

one-half to one over Great Britain. America's aviation as well as shipbuilding facilities are proportionately impressive.

If the British Government attempts to redress this unequal situation by subsidizing British airways, or excluding American aircraft from the strategically located chain of globe-circling British bases, unrestricted economic conflict could be the result.

Any all-out competition with either the United States or Soviet Russia for world trade would be calamitous to the United Kingdom. The overwhelming superiority of industrial strength possessed by either giant over the little island kingdom would guarantee the result. If to this competition were added the low-priced man-hour pool of China, the dispossession of the United Kingdom from major world markets would be a certainty.

The United States has made itself largely independent of British Asia in respect to raw materials. It now grows rubber, quinine and other tropical products in Haiti and the States of nearby Latin America. Under wartime pressure it has discovered substitutes or new sources of supply for most of the materials which formerly were imported from overseas. By closing its doors to the natural rubber of Asia and relying on synthetic production or rubber from nearby sources, as a measure of military security, the United States would ruin the British rubber industry of Malaya.

Soviet Russia too is installing machinery for the mass manufacture of synthetic rubber. The prospective surplus eventually will have to be disposed of on world markets.

England's future function in the world economy clearly will not conform to the exaggerated importance the little island has occupied in the past. Her almost grotesquely disproportionate economic power has sprung from a surpassing financial and naval power, and is following these into the haze of desuetude.

Britain's adverse balance will tend to become worse for yet other reasons. To satisfy its elemental needs the country will have to import immense amounts of essential goods. Certain industries such as printed cottons and textiles have all but disappeared. Manufacturing machinery suffers from depreciation and obsolescence.

Housing has deteriorated. Replacement needs will present a problem of incalculable dimensions.

It is conservatively calculated that Britain's annual postwar trade deficit will be more than £200,000,000. Even if she managed to retain the level of her pre-war commerce, the annual recurrence of these monster deficiencies would give Britain the simple choice between progressive impairment of her capital assets and bankruptcy, or of withdrawing from the free trade market and instituting a form of controlled economy.

Great Britain either will have to expand her export trade or accommodate herself to a far lower standard of living. She might attempt to achieve a better balance between agriculture and industry by a planned export of her excess population to the Dominions.

Under stress, land under the plow has been increased by fifty per cent; agriculture has been partially mechanized; but these measures are far from solving the problem. The explanation for Britain's difficulties is not found in some simple prodigy which requires mending, but in the fact that metamorphosis has overtaken all the forms of power. The economic foundations on which the present political order rests have been shaken to their roots. As one of the chief beneficiaries of the old power system, the United Kingdom finds itself correspondingly one of the primary sufferers in the revolution which is smashing it.

The single hopeful agency which remains to the United Kingdom is bilateral bargaining. This recourse, too, will prove ineffective, though it served the re-arming Nazi Reich well. As an instrument it is inoperable without major native resources and a plan of military aggrandizement which is its logical sequel.

With the exception of temporary gains which may follow the declaration of peace, Britain's exterior markets will continue to shrink due to an acceleration of the causes which operated before the war—the increasing competition of the United States and the continued industrialization of such lands as Soviet Russia, China, and probably India and Latin America. All of the formerly backward States, including the British Dominions themselves, are seeking not only to perpetuate their wartime industrialization but to equalize the prices of raw materials with those of manufactured goods. They are in short demanding a standard of living equal to that of the urbanized countries, a requirement fatal to the future of the small manufacturing State.

An influential section of British opinion now gropes for a means of effecting a reciprocal arrangement which would draw the United Kingdom closer to the U.S.S.R., with whom she would maintain a strong military and commercial alliance. The risks of eventual subordination to a Soviet-controlled Europe under this plan would seem to be inherent in the time equation and to follow it with mechanical faithfulness.

An alternative project involves the creation of a form of British regionalism on the Continent of Europe. Under this arrangement a federation of West European States would be set up as a counterweight to the economic power of America and the U.S.S.R. The Western European economy would be assimilated to the sterling bloc, forming a tightly knit unit largely insulated from outside influences. England's leadership would depend upon her ability to supply both finance and raw materials from her great colonies.

To counteract the advantages enjoyed by totalitarian operations, industry would be organized into a series of cartels with authority to regulate both output and sales. The existing German trusts would be taken over bodily under new management, and the fundamental basis of the greater European economy continued.

Certain powerful elements in Britain hope that America would agree to partnership in the control of these agencies—or would even consider a three-cornered partnership with the Germans. Markets would be allocated, and production restricted. The U.S.S.R. and China would be controlled by the threat of quarantine. By these means it is hoped that a critical and savage competition which Britain much fears, will be alleviated.

The hope of establishing close political ties with such footloose States as Holland, Denmark, Greece and Norway, or even France and Italy, is a mirage. After the liberation these countries will be in a state of revolutionary change, whether by legal or armed means, and will not have their destinies ruled by a declining, though still affluent island kingdom whose interests are intimately concerned with a continuation of the old order.

The practical men who are rising from the European undergrounds to take over the helm of government everywhere, would understand that any such engagement would represent a commitment to an antique era, and could not survive either its own contradictions or the hostility of the new universal Power taking shape on the Continent, Soviet Russia.

England, therefore, has little choice. If she is to continue as an independent Power she can do so only by an uneasy abandonment of Europe. She no longer will be able to dominate political events on the Continent. In the future she will be able only to buy or sell there, and may have to wall off her own economy to keep it from being swamped by unrestricted European competition.

IV

Though the British, like Job, are beset with troubles, they are a stubborn people who are not prone to accept defeat even under the most adverse circumstances. This trait served them admirably during the present war where a nation of lesser stomach might have yielded as did the French under Petain, and thus have changed the entire destiny of civilized man.

This indomitable people will attempt to retain their position until the last, seeking to hold their Empire and striving against all odds to recover their old footing in the world of trade, shipping and finance. This will-to-endure may be distinguished in the resolute tones of their magnificent Minister, Mr. Churchill. "I have not become the King's first Minister," he said, addressing the Commons on November 10, 1942, "in order to preside over the liquidation of the British Empire."

Notwithstanding this determination it is realized in high quarters in London that a far-flung empire may be impossible to defend in the air age, and that Britain may have to evacuate Asia and lose its markets.

The hope which now exists reverts back to Cecil Rhodes' dream of a solid red splash on the map of Africa from the Cape of Good Hope to the Mediterranean Sea.

If North Africa could be added to British holdings and if the peace could be kept in Europe for a period sufficient to allow a fair consolidation of this project, the African Empire might be held indefinitely.

The obsolescence of sea bases and the difficult supply problem which makes the present Empire so vulnerable to assault would not apply to a solidly-held Africa, which would fit nicely into the military aspects of the air age. Africa would yield almost every product which now comes from British Asia. The proximity of the territory to Europe would give it a real advantage in respect to the European trading area. The short route to South America would come under the British flag.

Africa as a permanent British holding has many attractions. It is not heavily populated. Its peoples consist of a wide diversity of races in various stages of culture, non-homogeneous, and speaking a bewildering variety of languages and dialects. The blacks are looked on as docile and willing to accommodate themselves to the imperial system. They are scattered, broken into many fragments, governed by innumerable tribal chiefs, beys and sultans, and are regarded as being incapable of organization in a modern competitive or revolutionary sense.

The material self-interest of the non-British whites, it is thought, will compel them to assimilate themselves to the British system as have the Canadian-French and South African Boers. Even the partial industrialization of the Continent under these conditions might be acceptable to the home country and would not be regarded as possessing excessively dangerous connotations.

This is an ambitious and brilliant vision, and has considerable possibilities of implementation. It would require the military support of the United States by which Russia and China could be held in check for a period of years to effect a gigantic, new balance of power design fabricated on a global scale.

What the British need desperately more than all else, is time.

At present the important Italian territories of Libya and Eritrea are in British hands. Ethiopia is occupied under an agreement similar to that with Iraq. British judges, officials and advisers "assist" the Ethiopian administration; the British Government may base its armies and air forces in Ethiopian territory.

The possessions of France, Belgium and Portugal, it is anticipated, would become tributary to the new empire though remaining ostensibly under non-British control. Portugal, itself, is expected to become completely dependent on Britain and perhaps even a member of the British community of nations. France is an unanswerable riddle, but is relied on to emerge as a second rate State unable to defend its holdings against encroachment.

As the different syllables of the charade are fitted into line it will be seen that this enterprise conforms to all the power requirements of the present century. It possesses the necessary space, and mineral wealth. It is near enough to home bases to be defensible.

The Continent presents many of the aspects of the two Americas under the Indians. It is three times the size of Europe and contains over one-quarter of the world's potential croplands.

No one knows exactly what Africa's population is, but probably 142,000,000 is a fair guess. Of these, 5,500,000 are Europeans, situated mostly in the extreme north and south portions. In addition, the fifteen million Arabs and Berbers of the North, and a portion of the Egyptians, may by a stretch of the imagination be considered Caucasian and included as a subcaste within the European category.

The existing demographic imbalance could be in part corrected by an influx of white settlers, so that quite a different situation would exist than has applied in the densely populated East where the Caucasian represents a ruling class of strictly alien sojourners rotated from the home country.

Africa possesses any quantity of land ideally situated for white settlement. Rhodesia and the great table-land of Angola are rich, virgin territories perfectly suited to mass European colonization. The Maghreb,[1] that long fertile strip of North Africa caught between the desert and the Mediterranean, is like the most desirable portions of Italy. Not one per cent of French Equatorial Africa has ever felt the heel of the plow. Even in the settled areas of Egypt no more than 3.7 per cent of the land is cultivated.

Africa's agriculture will grow anything that can be grown, ranging over the full roster of tropical, subtropical, temperate, rain area and desert products. Her timber, embracing an almost numberless variety of woods, is inexhaustible and extends in a solid block over a chunk of territory as large as all of the United States east of Denver.

In respect to those materials indispensable to industry and commerce, Africa is probably the most favored of all the continents. It possesses twenty-six of the twenty-seven principal minerals, most of them in abundance. French North Africa alone contains over thirty per cent of the world's natural phosphates. In the Katanga region of the Congo are the largest copper deposits in existence. The Dark Continent holds most of the world's bauxite, great amounts of asbestos, mercury, magnesium and sulphur. It has all of the ferro-alloys in abundance, showing a deficiency only in molybdenum. Gold, diamonds, tin and platinum, graphite, mica, chromium and iron are all present in more than sufficient quantities.

Africa has an inadequate amount of oil but this lack could be compensated for by the exhaustless British holdings in Arabia. Its so-far known coal deposits are also comparatively weak. This deficiency could be satisfied by shipments from England where coal is plentiful, or by utilization of Africa's potential water power sources, estimated to be more than that of all the other continents combined.

To anchor this project securely, it is necessary that Britain control the great peninsula of Arabia, and perhaps Iran. Hence, the

[1] Now held by the Spaniards and French.

other wing of British policy rests on a sponsored pan-Arabism which will enable the new empire to include the riches in oil, and the important trade routes which must some day traverse the Middle East.

British long range policy has concerned itself with Arab-Moslem politics since World War I in an effort to link up its Asiatic and African empire, to provide a cushion against Russia, and to hold a constant threat over the heads of non-Moslem peoples who might grow restive under British rule.

In addition to protecting the western flank of Africa this territory is destined to possess great commercial and military importance. It is the natural crossroads of three continents. Its oil deposits are the greatest in known existence.

London maintains its authority on the Peninsula in various ways. The Sultanate of Muscat and Oman, the Sheikhdom of Kuwait and the Kingdom of Iraq she occupies under treaty agreements which place these territories within the jurisdiction of British military units. Palestine and Transjordan are held under a mandate from the League of Nations. Aden and the Hadramaut are retained in fee simple; while the Hedjaz and deep interior of Arabia are in the hands of a friendly prince subsidized by Anglo-American capital, the gigantic Abd-ul-Aziz ibn Sa'ud.

Britain would prefer to see all of Arabia in some kind of confederation, feeling that the individual segments would be easier to control and less likely to fall under foreign influence. A unified Arabian empire also would have a plausible claim against all of North Africa, giving London a unique opportunity to put a pious face on its manipulations in that direction.

Internally, the situation is most favorable to imperial management. The Arabs, a motley mixture of races, presenting a pathetic picture of a people who were conquered by their own subjects via the institution of the harem, are indolent, scattered, and except for the Levantine elements on the coast, live in a primitive pastoral state. Their leaders are readily controllable by subsidies or by playing off against each other the various potentates, factions and princely families, whose rivalries and intrigues are eternal.

The Arabs have realistically accepted British beneficence though they cordially detest the officials and administrators who rule over them, a phenomenon not unusual to imperial enterprise. The only seriously untoward incidents which have occurred were those stimulated by Fascist propaganda and funds.

Pro-Nazi sentiment has been strong in Arabia. When Egypt was invaded not an Egyptian soldier lifted a gun to hold off the Axis armies. King Farouk and his cabinet did not endeavor to hide their sympathy for Britain's enemies.

For a time Iraq possessed a self-announced, pro-Nazi administration. On May 2nd, 1941, the Iraqis cut the vital pipeline which carries oil to the British Mediterranean fleet. The British airport at Habbania was attacked by Iraqi troops. This defection was put down by British troops in a short and vigorous campaign.

Britain has little genuine fear of the consequences of Arab recalcitrance. Arabs are easily influenced by emoluments of various kinds. The petty princelings, sheikhs, immans and effendis are amenable to manipulation and possess an incurable predilection for the winning side.

The Arab looks fierce and imposing astride his camel, but is of essentially non-military bent. Arab forays usually are bloodless and attended by shouted imprecations. As a race they detest discipline of any kind. In Egypt, they are willing to gather in shouting mobs denouncing British rule, but will go to the lengths of putting out their eyes to render themselves unfit for military service.

The British have, however, a real apprehension concerning European penetration of this vitally strategic area. They regard it as necessary to the success of their plan that no other Europeans be allowed to occupy territory in Arabia. The conquest of French Syria was a windfall which allowed British troops to spread to the Turkish border. In attempting to oust France permanently from the Middle East, the British bureaus who are the real rulers of Empire policy,[1]

1 It is these bureaus, composed of all-powerful, permanent officials, who run the expertly conducted business of the Empire. They are virtually independent of the electorate and are presided over by men who have been trained from boyhood for this

have followed a familiar pattern of instigation and abetment, making able use of the everpresent hatreds and rivalries. In the Lebanon region British functionaries encouraged a native "independence" movement, and in the resulting crisis solemnly intervened on behalf of the new "republic," forcing the chagrined French Committee of National Liberation to make the necessary concessions which split Lebanon off from Syria.

In the Mandate for Palestine which enjoined Britain to assist in the return of the Jews to the Holy Land, London was confronted by still another and even more disquieting threat to its plans. This trepidation was to prove fatal to the dream of a Jewish republic, for which purpose the Mandate originally had been written.

British alarm was governed by five self-sufficient considerations. (1) Palestine is the natural hinterland to the Suez Canal and guards its land approaches from the east. (2) It is the outlet to the Mediterranean for the petroleum pipeline reaching from the oil fields of Iraq. (3) It contains in Haifa a naval harbor second only to that at Alexandria. (4) It possesses in the minerals of the Dead Sea a chemical crucible of almost fabulous value. (5) It raises the nightmarish question of importing an aggressive European people to a portion of creation which is the very axis of the British imperial world.

British administrators had been impressed by the alleged conspiracy of the Elders of Zion, a forgery which a decade ago received enormous currency. More particularly, they were frightened by the factories which were promptly erected by the Jews in Tel Aviv and Haifa. They saw rising here a new Japan capable of intensive in-

---

function. To these administrators the slightest material advantage to Imperial business takes priority over any type of humanist philosophy or social code. They are masters of intrigue, of the charade of double talk, and have reduced finesse to an art. They possess an unconcealed contempt for elected politicians. Their method of parrying questions in Parliament is a marvel in efficiency. In the complex business of Empire and the closely held secrets of military and political maneuver, together with the long-range planning by which the future is safeguarded, these functionaries and the host of others behind them, shadows behind shadows, directly color, influence and even dictate the actions of their chiefs in the Cabinet. This impregnable web has rarely failed to enmesh every British Minister of modern times.

dustry and of exercising military control over the Near and Middle East and beyond. It was the famous Lawrence of Arabia who discerned early that the Jews "by the exercise of their skill and capital hoped to make Palestine as highly organized as a European State," and that "the success of their scheme will involve inevitably the raising of the present Arab population to their own material level, and might well . . . render them independent of industrial Europe, and in that case a new confederation might become a formidable element of world power."

As the result of a succession of carefully graduated steps taken for this purpose, the position of the Jews under the Mandate has been whittled down to the point where they exist in Palestine only under sufferance as a tolerated minority. Their development is hampered by all the familiar methods known to hostile central authority. Their immigration is limited to a mere dribble. Under the White Paper now in force, twenty-five thousand are to be allowed to enter over a period of time, after which the Jewish quota will be complete and Palestine will be hermetically closed against their further penetration.

Three quarters of the originally mandated country has been torn away and is ruled as the territory of Transjordan by the Emir Abdullah, an Arab prince imported with his tribe for this purpose. Transjordan is held by Britain directly under the Mandate, and its expenses are covered by taxes raised under the general Palestine administration. Jews, however, may not own land or settle there. Transjordan was the first of the countries of the world to become *judenrein,* or free of Jews.

On the left bank of the Jordan, in the Holy Land proper, the Jews are restricted to certain districts. The country is divided into three zones. Zone "A" where land may be purchased freely by Jews, comprises five per cent of the region west of Jordan. In Zone "C" consisting of 64 per cent of the Cis-Jordan area, all purchases of land by Jews are prohibited. In Zone "B" which covers the area remaining, Jewish land purchases may be effected if the consent of the High Commissioner can be secured.

The tension between Jews and the Palestine Government has long since hardened into one of active animosity, the two being united only in the exigencies of war against a common enemy.

It is crucial to the success of this brilliantly conceived project that no one Power emerge from the war capable of taking charge of the destinies of Europe. If this should occur the long-range scheme for a new Arabian-African empire becomes an impossible one and would have to be abandoned.

Britain then would have three possible choices. One would be to endeavor to maintain her independence in a heroic isolation, which in the end must result in her death by strangulation. Another would be to lose herself in a European federation of States.

The third possibility remaining to Britain would be to link her destinies with those of the United States of America, and become the European outpost of a new autarchic power-combine based on an altered alignment of peoples and strategically-located space, and on a revised conception of Britain's place in society.

England would cease to be an imperial ruler. Like Rome, the day of her glory would be done with the period which produced it. She would enter a new phase in which she would look forward only to being a busy and prosperous little green island on which men lived happily. Her wealth then would depend on the culture and capacity of her inhabitants, their ability to manufacture goods in competition, on great markets and unlimited sources of raw materials which automatically would be open to her businessmen, and on the fact that she would be the funnel through which the trade of Europe and America would pour back and forth.

Though Britain still would be open to attack from the European continent as before, her protection would lie in the point that war on her would involve immediate hostilities with some far more formidable adversary. The temptations which the prospect of a quick blitz success offers would lose the largest part of their allure.

XII

ASSIGNMENT TO CHAOS

THE termination of hostilities will bring to the United States of America domestic difficulties of the first magnitude, which are bound to reflect themselves in the external relations of our republic.

The United States will end the war with a machine tool industry increased by some three hundred per cent over the best pre-war year. It will possess a plant capacity dwarfing any known to history and designed for the latest production techniques.

Today our aviation plant is a twenty billion dollar business—five times as large as the spectacular automobile industry at its peacetime peak. The merchant shipping held by the United States will total more than fifty million tons, or almost the total gross tonnage of the world in 1939.

The Government will have on its hand twenty-five billion dollars' worth of war plants for which disposition somehow will have to be made. Our shipbuilding industry will possess the unbelievable production capacity of twenty million deadweight tons of merchant shipping a year. Electrical production capacity will have increased to about two hundred fifty billion kilowatt hours as compared to thirty-six billion during the peak of the last war. New tonnage highs will have been set for everything—synthetic rubber, aluminum, copper, zinc, and other industrial materials.

In almost every department this country is likely to possess a larger production machinery, more mills, plants, refineries, shops and power equipment than it possibly can absorb in peacetime.

The onerous question of a cost-price structure untried in free and competitive markets will further complicate our problems. This may be seen in the dollar growth of industry whose relation is not to normal competition but to wartime needs. For 1943 the monthly production all told, averaged 227 per cent above the level of 1935-39. Wage and salary income reached the figure of $101,-800,000,000 in 1943 as against $52,600,000,000 in 1929, the best pre-war year.

This immense growth has been based on the unnatural conditions of a forced draft economy. In greatest part it is like the totalitarian economies in that it represents a direct levy on the resources of the State with no accounting based on price levels, natural demand or conservation.

When the fighting ceases, over sixty per cent of the world's industrial production will be centered in the United States, creating a wholly abnormal relationship in our dealings with other nations. We will be in the position of the Cabots who talk only to the Lowells, who talk only to God. Everyone else will be poor and desperate and there will be no normal basis for the usual exchange of trade.

Europe and Asia will exist as doubtful outlets for our goods and services, if for no other reason, due to their inability to pay. South America will see the wartime price bubble burst and may find itself thrust into a savage competition with the raw material producers of Asia and Africa for existing markets.

The curtailment of debt expansion will bring with it disturbances to the entire economic equilibrium. There will be a public debt of around three hundred billion dollars. At two and one-half per cent the interest charges alone would be larger than the entire amount collected by the Federal Government in taxes in the best pre-war year.

On A-day the country will become suddenly aware of the extent to which war forces an industrial economy under the control of central authority. The Federal Government will be the sole buyer of seventy per cent of the national output. It will control the allocation of raw materials. It will have enormous investments in the capital structure of industry itself. It will be not only the sole customer for the great aviation industry but will have put up most of the money by which the plants were erected.

The Government will have maintained a rigid system of inspection and control over all manufacturing processes and hence will have passed close to the edge of State Socialism. In the various draft and rationing boards it will have developed an approach to government by soviets which is certain to affect the general view held toward free capital and enterprise.

The nation will have on its hands fantastic quantities of trucks, machinery and other war goods which either must be jettisoned or sold. If these were to be thrown on our internal market, they would carry it into an immediate tailspin of depression. If they were to be transferred to Europe or Asia, the arrangement would have to be on some long term basis which would take into consideration the probability that we never would be paid.

The transition to a peacetime economy may prove to be difficult and painful. The experience with total war is new and the adjustment back to peace represents the relinquishment of powerful bureaucratic controls which will be yielded reluctantly.

There will be serious engineering problems connected with the resumption of production for civilian use. There may be an economic crash of the shipyards; and unless government subsidy intervenes this will be true also in the aircraft industry. War plants will lack the requisite backlog of funds to tide them over the critical period when government orders fail. The problems of organization and re-tooling in transferring to peacetime operations will create bottlenecks in which the time lag alone will create perplexing problems of adjustment.

Commodities of every kind will tend more and more to be mass produced by precision machinery. The use of labor-saving devices, new materials and improved techniques will continue to result in an expanding output with a decreasing personnel. According to a Department of Commerce release, the entire output of 1940 now could be produced with nineteen million fewer workers. It is estimated that over the twelve-year period from 1929 to 1941 the nation's output per man-hour of employment increased thirty-four per cent. This was at the rate of two and one-half per cent per year compounded, a process which is likely to be accelerated rather than retarded by the years to come.[1]

As the employment index falls it will react upon the consuming market, bringing into view the possibility of spiraling unemployment following after a short period of feverish plenty.

The total of war workers who must be reabsorbed into a peacetime economy is around thirty million. This labor force will be augmented by at least another ten million men and women from the armed forces.

It is estimated that within six months after the arrival of A-day more than twelve million persons will be unemployed.

The problems of reconversion and unemployment obviously are as difficult and complex as any with which we have dealt in history. They undoubtedly will be met by one artifice or another. Great development projects and rehabilitation programs will cushion the shock of readjustment to peacetime function. Various means will be composed by which major mishaps can be avoided. The inherent good sense of the nation and its capacity for response, may be relied on to tide us over this troublesome period without bankruptcy or violent social change.

If these problems are to be soberly and intelligently answered, however, they will require a vision, prudence and sagacity which will test every resource of our republic. They cannot be handled independent of the world-wide revolution in ideas which is breaking the dikes of convention everywhere and from which the present crisis has derived.

In our own country this cynical disregard for the old legitimacies will result in material disarrangements in the old equilibrium. The divisions between capital and labor will be greatly sharpened,

1 Morris S. Livingston, *Markets After the War,* Department of Commerce booklet, pp. 2, 3.

with labor pressing forward for an actual voice in management. As capital steadily loses its wonted privileges it will seek recourse in diverse types of repression and violence. Labor in turn will tend increasingly to regard the end as sanctioning any means which might be required to achieve it. On both sides the problem of social morality will become acute.

Our young men will return from abroad matured and hardened, exposed to the germs of Communism and Fascism alike. They will have been inured to death and accustomed to grim risk and continuous excitement. To a considerable proportion of these men the technique of killing will have been reduced to a science in a way comparable to no other conflict known to our history. The aircraft men especially will have been taught to be quick and deadly, and to get in the first fatal burst of fire on a split-second schedule ahead of the enemy. They will return to a drab world, restless and unprepared to accept poverty and joblessness.

These men will find a world altogether different from the one they left. Many of them will resent the need for grappling with conventional living problems and will be seeking adventure. They will resent the presence of women in labor. They will discover the elderly, the weak and from their view, the non-patriotic, holding down positions which they themselves once had filled. The existing jobholders will be at pains to protect themselves against ouster by every device of unionization. In particular the labor market will be glutted with large numbers of skilled operators released from war plants and military service.

The total of the service blocs will be more than fifteen million. These men for the most part will be impatient with the stupidity and arrogance of the new bureaucratic rule. As their grievances mount, they will be the prey of agitators who will promise a radical and summary settlement of all problems.

Both with and without the stimulation of foreign governments, there will be a furious renewal of the effort to establish racial fascism in the United States.

During pre-war years, Hitler is known to have expended large sums annually in an effort to promote revolution in this country. According to the *Year Book of 1936* published by the German Foreign Institute in Stuttgart, there were over twenty thousand pro-German organizations in the United States. The German American Bund alone was said to have had a membership of over one hundred thousand, most of whom were drilled on a military basis. The Black Shirts of Salvatore Caridi, the Italian American Fascists, Inc. of Francesco Paolo Castorina, and others, had an equal number of organized pro-Fascist Italians.

In addition to the foreign groups, there were even more powerful transmission belts, such as the Christian Front led by the two priests, Charles Coughlin and Edward Lodge Curran. Coughlin's newspaper, *Social Justice,* at one time had a circulation of over one million. At a moment when he was confident of the quick victory of the Nazi world revolution, Coughlin did not lack the audacity to declare for his movement: "Rest assured we will fight you in Franco's way if necessary. Call this inflammatory if you will. It is inflammatory. But rest assured we will fight you and we will win."

Our society was permeated by these home-grown Nazis, American traitors, confederates and sympathizers with the world Nazi revolution. A Department of Justice survey demonstrated that there were no less than ninety-six pro-Axis publications in the country demanding the overthrow of the Government. In a single mass demonstration held at Madison Square Garden in New York, twenty thousand men, women and children were present together with a uniformed legion of twelve hundred men carrying swastika banners. In New York City and Boston it was shown that a large proportion of the police force was made up of followers of the revolutionary Christian Front.

The post-war attitude of these groups may be expected to continue as before. For a brief moment they have retreated into silence as a matter of provisional discretion. When the war crisis is over, they will emerge safely in the open.

They are led by men who have made a profound study of treason, who understand the art of revolution as a profession, and who will be financed and assisted both by elements within this country and abroad.

Under the ceaseless fomentation of these groups, race trouble of an increasingly inflammable nature will be studiedly agitated. Classic German anti-Semitism is certain to be promoted in its most sinister guise.

There is every indication that the Negro problem will take on a virulent form and that it will culminate in street warfare and riots, especially in our Northern cities.

This dread situation may assume the proportion of a militant pathology and be extremely difficult of control. It will be acted on by a complexity of causes additional to the historic animosity of the white man. In addition to the propaganda constantly at work on the Caucasian, will be that aimed at the Negro himself, astutely designed to erect a color solidarity with the Oriental peoples against the race assumptions of the white man.

The acute nature of the segregation problem is joined by still another source of friction and violence, the invasion of the skilled trades by Negro workers, an opportunity which was opened to them by reason of the wartime labor shortage.

There already have been strikes of workers to keep the Negro out. These will become more critical and determined as jobs become scarcer. "Watch out for the first symptom of a shrinking economy," warns the National Urban League. "Race tensions today are as nothing compared to what we may expect when the sirens blow . . . and peace comes again."

The drive of the Negro for equality and the stubborn determination of the white man to prevent it, are sure to meet in head-on collision. The Negro is actuated by a deep burning dynamism which his Caucasian fellows hardly understand. He no longer is patient, nor longer willing to accept his status as a suppressed minority. He is being victimized and agitated from all sides and has learned to consider the police as his enemy. He himself is given to violence, and it is no surprise that at least in the case of New

York City, the riots did not originate in any overt white move but by spontaneous action among the Negroes themselves.

To a degree a similar set of circumstances is visible in the ostracism of the three million Mexicans and other Latin Americans living in this country. The Jim Crow schools provided for their children, and the racial war in Southern California known euphemistically as the Zoot Suit Riots, furnish an unpleasant augury for the future character of our relationship with the Latin States.

All of these troublesome questions will be intensified by a result of mechanized war which is difficult to measure—the huge increase in psychiatric casualties.

The terrible agony of long eery nights in quivering mechanical monsters dodging the flak over enemy territory, or careening at enemy stations like so many dragons vomiting a staccato flow of fire and shell, will show itself in an impairment of the general mechanism of stability by which men are enabled to fit into conventional society. Dr. Thomas A. C. Rennie, attending psychiatrist at New York Hospital, estimated that mental crack-ups constituted twenty-eight to thirty-five per cent of all men discharged from the army, and that many of these would become lifelong responsibilities of the Government.

In Europe and Asia the psychoneurotic stage will be occupied by a myriad of Hamlets preaching to a people worn out by disease, violence and starvation. In the United States the psychic stresses and strains will not have been so severe since the calamities which induced them will not be so complete and all-pervasive. Nevertheless, they will be present in all classes of the population in the shape of war jitters, uneasiness and true psychic disease.

This web of emotional and material confusion will give rise to impulses which will be difficult to bring into harness. There could be an irresistible swing which would bring into power in the national government an isolationist program peculiarly suited to the new conditions. The constituents of politically-minded lawmakers will find a fascinating ring to the cry, "Cut down taxes," or, "Bring our boys home."

America may lean toward pacifism under the pressure of aroused taxpayers. Sheer distaste for the unhealthy growth of wartime bureaucracy may cause the Congress to ignore the plight the aviation plants will find themselves in when large-scale government orders are discontinued. It might even be urged with perfect plausibility that "We have plenty of airplanes now," ignoring the factor of military obsolescence which strikes the air arm above all others.

II

It is inevitable that the primary interests of Americans should center in the United States, and that their concern for the world around them should be circumscribed by a prudent regard for their own ultimate welfare. Any intelligible approach to the problems of peace must relate them to our own needs and social convictions, rather than to the profundities of international lawyers or the shortsighted guile of conventional politics.

We must examine the issues and endeavor to appraise them accurately without either haggling for mean advantage or attempting to achieve the millennium by a stroke of the pen.

It is useless to attempt to evade these issues by hiding ourselves behind the wall of our traditional engagements and policies. These commitments are being dissolved by the relentless hand of fate. They are succumbing to a new set of realities which must be faced if we are to control our own future.

The labyrinth through which our policy, both foreign and domestic, must pick its way is a highly complicated one. While the pattern is not altogether clear, it can be based on reasonable conjectures.

It may be accepted that this nation will face in the coming decades the most trying problems in its history, and that beyond rescuing us from the immediate disaster of a Nazi-Japanese world order the war will have settled nothing. Indeed, it will be discovered that it actually has stimulated the processes of social disintegration which are the major phenomena of this century, and will have exacerbated almost all of the major points of friction in our internal economy as well as in our relations with other States.

It is now pretty well accepted all around that we cannot extricate ourselves from the maze of postwar existence by receding into the classic isolationism which guided our policy after World War I. If it were a doubtful policy then, it is an impossible one now. The steadily broadening base of world intercourse of every kind renders such a course out of the question.

It is obvious that whatever affects the primary destinies of the Soviet Union and awakening China likewise will involve us; and that our foreign policy is so closely interwoven with that of the Anglo-Saxon motherland that we cannot evade the issues of war and peace which must arise from the mounting weaknesses of Imperial Britain in the political universe of tomorrow.

It seems equally plain that we cannot embark on the unmapped ocean of post-war existence in the assumption that this is to be an American Century, or that a Pax-Americana compounded of our present military and economic superiority, will be the regulating device by which the world will be kept in equilibrium. Such an expectation places an exaggerated importance on power factors which may be only temporary, and on achievements which might be surpassed by empires possessing greater resources in materials, manpower and space.

If the existing world relationship of nations could be permanently frozen, the United States would occupy an impregnable position. She possesses an area of almost three million square miles and an intelligent, able population, proficient in all the mechanical skills and unified in language and culture though differing in race. She is endowed with more than ample means in coal, iron, and water power, a wide category of minerals, and a rich agriculture. What she lacks, mainly in the products of tropical agriculture, can be supplied by the ingenuity of her scientists, or through the utilization of nearby territories in Latin America.

Within the past forty years the United States has achieved an industrial capacity of unexampled magnitude, placing her head and shoulders above all possible rivals.

The strength of the American postwar position will be measured by the relative powers of the competing large-space universes. As long as the present world distribution of power remains undisturbed the United States cannot be assaulted successfully except by the invisible weapons of psychological warfare.

In the past our security has been guaranteed by the pre-eminence of the British fleet, by the division of Europe into a host of States, by the isolation of Russia, and the ineptitude and powerlessness of the Orient.

To preserve its safety margin in the present world, the interests of the United States demand continued political fragmentation of Europe and Asia. The further consolidation of the two continents, so as to place them under the sway of any one dominant Power, would confront the United States with an antagonist overwhelmingly superior in every important respect, with whom it would be hopeless to compete.

The chances of such an outcome are far from negligible. They will increase as political failure sweeps in a train of hardships, terrors, perplexities, conflicts and trials too vexatious further to be endured. The existence of so much potential disorder and so many contradictory impulses, at a moment when the central drive of civilization is toward order and discipline, might provide the very setting needed for some new Caesar destined to subdue the nations to his will.

However visionary this possibility might be, the existence of an expanding U.S.S.R. and such coming power forms as the Chinese and Indian States, makes every spot on earth a determining weight in the gigantic balance of power system whose delicate equipoise will encompass the entire earth.

The United States as the richest country, and therefore the one with most to lose, must consider carefully its relationship to the future in terms of these new facts.

Any policy to be pursued by the United States must take into consideration the following absolute conditions:

1. The persistent and insoluble race problem which renders world union a practical impossibility;

2. The tremendous superiority in space, man-hours and raw materials existing in the Eurasian world;

3. The inherent weakness of Great Britain in the power firmament of tomorrow;

4. The presence of many small, weak and ruined nations caught in the midst of revolutionary tides and unable to resist either economic, ideological or military aggression;

5. The existence of a revolutionary Eurasian empire founded on principles seeking the establishment of a world union under the dictatorship of a militant proletariat;

6. The climbing population pressures and new world outlook of Asia.

Two additional facts seem reasonably clear: (1) If the Soviets decide to take over Europe either directly or indirectly, we would not be able to prevent it. (2) We will not be able to prevent an absorption by China of many of the policies which have guided Japan during the current century.

Our great nightmare would be the danger of encirclement on a global scale by some Power capable of achieving control over the whole Old World land mass. In this event the predicament of the United States, the richest prize ever dangled before the eyes of a military conqueror, would become precarious in the extreme. Except for the fact that the design would be drawn on expanded terms, our nation would be to its enemies as the Poland of 1939 was to the Nazi-Soviet alliance, outnumbered, outproduced, outgunned and outflanked in every direction.

On the Atlantic side we would possess a poor inner line of defense and no outer bulwarks whatsoever. The Canal Zone, though heavily fortified, could not be protected against a turning movement conducted from South America or the islands of the West

Indies. In the Pacific we would have little more than a patrol route running from the Aleutians to the Hawaiians and tenuously connected with the exposed outposts of Guam, Wake and Samoa.

Of the world's population of 2,200,000,000, we would command somewhere around 150,000,000. In a comparison of the mass resources by which wars are waged, we would come off poorly. Our physical position would be not much better. We should find ourselves almost completely encircled, locked in the center of a classic military envelopment movement blown up to global proportions.

On the Asiatic side in a situation profoundly altered by the bomber and transport plane, we would find ourselves connected with the Old World by an almost continuous land mass which would offer little obstacle to military penetration. The way to Europe would be over silent Arctic wasteland and short water gaps. The great circle routes which now add materially to the prospects of American commercial prosperity would become stepping-stones to attack, from either Europe or Asia.

It would be entirely feasible for a qualified commander to follow the polar pathways over Siberia, Norway, Iceland and Greenland to strike simultaneously at our East and West Coasts. Utilizing the same routes he could come down through the indefensible Canadian wilderness to smash with great sledge-hammer blows against our Middle West.

A carefully synchronized assault would be made by way of South America, hopping from Brazil to the islands of the Caribbean and thence to any point on the Southern American coast.

Two Powers potentially capable of performing such a function in history, already exist. They are the U.S.S.R. and China. While it is true that China and the Soviet Union are at present our allies and not our enemies, it also is true that in the normal evolution of power no one knows what ambitious conqueror is destined to succeed his more modest predecessors. The history of nations offers continuous illustration of the fact that great opportunities for power have invariably brought forward men capable of utilizing them. Bonaparte followed closely on the heels of the French Revolution. Hitler succeeded Stresemann and Ebert. Mussolini was once a candidate for the Nobel Peace prize.

III

The strategic frontiers of this hemisphere today are the Cape Verde Islands, the Azores, Iceland and Greenland in the east, and a line running from Seward Peninsula and Attu Island to the fortieth parallel and longitude 150 degrees East, thence diagonally to Luzon Island, and including all of the islands east of longitude 120 as far south as the Australian mainland, and thence east to the shores of the Americas.

Only by exclusive possession of the full aggregate of islands which dot the two big oceans could we achieve a counterbalance to the overwhelming superiority of numbers, materials and strategic situation a unification of the Old World would confer. Without them, profitable counterattack would be costly, painful and perhaps impossible. Their possession by an enemy would expose our production facilities and transportation centers to that methodical demolition which will be the primary task of all military commanders of the future.

These contingent shortcomings in our postwar power position must rightly be surveyed with some disquietude. Our greatest hazard, however, would lie on our southern periphery. In the event of an onslaught on the United States the true heel of Achilles of the American Continent would prove to be Latin America. The southern continent would be a military riddle almost impossible for our leaders to solve. As we have noted, our sister continent is for practical purposes, an island projected into the South Atlantic toward Africa. The travel distances to its most important points favor communication with the Old World rather than with the *Yanqui* North.

In the event our nation were under siege, South America conceivably could be found in the enemy camp. The Latin States have strong ideological ties with Europe, and an Old World mastered by a concert of dictators would move expeditiously to attach this area to itself as an economic vassal.

In an open competition with Europe and Asia for the good will of Latin America, the question would become one not of hemispheric solidarity, but of wheat, cotton, beef, leather, oil and tin; of profits, markets and realistic advantage. In such a competition, underwritten by dictators with the sole purpose of a peaceful conquest of Latin America, the weight of probability would be cast against us.

The persistently unfriendly nature of the Argentine and Bolivian Governments among others, renders possible an unpleasant surmise of what easily might have occurred had Fascist Europe been capable of substantial military action in this Hemisphere. It justifies the fear that new and more potent dictator Powers may be able to forge the Latin American coupling as the last link in a chain of military encirclement and isolation of the United States.

Although there is undoubtedly a great deal of ideological sympathy for the United States among influential strata of the American nations, the diplomatic alignment of these States with us in the present war largely may be credited to power politics aided by finance appeasement and overwhelming market advantages. The overmatching American military and economic power which for the time dominates the situation unconditionally, renders any other course unreal and out of the question.

As we shall observe, there are major prospective advantages which could operate to cement the interests of the two Americas and cause them to be perfectly complementary to each other. The paramount influences now at work, however, betray strong contrary tendencies. One is the militant provincialism of the Latin, his pride in his own civilization, and his deep-seated distrust of the Yankee Colossus. In many of their principal products, such as hides, wheat, meat and raw minerals, the Latin States are in competition with the United States and Canada for world markets. This fact plays directly into the hands of the *hidalgo* class [1] who possess a

1 Business men and landed gentry.

profound cultural attachment to Europe and to whom the North American is completely alien. The physical agency through which these influences are being coordinated and given a political complexion, is the Falange.

The Falange envisions the resurrection of a new and powerful political Spain based on the totalitarian unity of the Spanish-speaking peoples. It is a vital element in the web Hitler and his co-conspirators have woven to enmesh the Western World, and will not die with his defeat.

In his book, *Falange*, Allan Chase gives a vivid and frightening picture of the maneuvers which have brought this dangerous group into existence right at our back door. It was organized in 1934 by the German General, Wilhelm von Faupel, one of the most sinister of the present German crop of international adventurers. The Spanish *caudillo*, Francisco Franco, and his Fascist following, were used as the prime movers in this scheme which, like the original Nazi pattern after which it is drawn, makes a mystic appeal to primordial passions and hatreds, and holds out the stirring promises of revenge, glory and loot.

Falangismo demands unqualified adherence to three supreme principles: (1) The unity of all Spanish-speaking peoples of the world under the "revolutionary symbol of the yoke and arrow" (Falange), obeying the leadership of the Spanish *caudillo;* (2) the repudiation of the capitalist system in favor of State control by workers' syndicates, thus absorbing bodily the predilection of the Latins for revolutionary syndicalism; (3) the command that the National Syndicalist State merge with itself the totalitarian doctrine of the Medieval Church as being "the glorious and predominant tradition of Spain."

The Falange is violently anti-Yankee, anti-British, anti-Protestant and anti-Semitic. It is closely identified with the powerful Nazi groups representing a considerable section of Latin America's two million Germans. It has the support of the half million Japanese of Brazil, Peru and Ecuador and of the numerous Italian bloc.

Despite its hodgepodge of anarcho-syndicalist-religious doctrine, the Falange enjoys the ardent favor of Latin America's military caste and large landowners. It has the support, open or tacit, of Latin big business and a large part of the intellectual classes.

In the Argentine and Bolivia specifically, the far-reaching power of the Falange has been evident to all eyes. The Argentine rapidly is becoming a classic Fascist State. The press is gagged, and political parties have been repressed. The boundless ambitions and ego of the ruling clique is leading in the direction of a South American bloc under Argentine leadership, capable of competing in power with what it regards as the ultimate enemy, the United States.

The parallel use of finance appeasement and quiet intimidation by the United States, has placed a temporary damper on the more overt activities of the Fascist enthusiasts, but the Falange must be considered a potent factor even in such territories as Cuba and Porto Rico. In Mexico, where its activities must be regarded as particularly sinister, *Falangismo* operates through the powerful *Acción Nacional* and the dangerous *Sinarquistas* who seek to restore the old medieval order destroyed by "liberalism, Masonry and politicians." *Sinarquismo* is estimated to have over 600,000 members. Its announced foreign policy is flatly against Pan-American solidarity and cooperation with the United States. It is vehemently opposed to the Soviet Union but pursues a program of State Socialism of its own, and seeks the formation of an aggressive bloc of Latin American States cooperating in the international theater with Franco's Spain.

The highly disciplined, well-financed Falange should not be confused with some amorphous ideological viewpoint which will change with the times. The Falange is an expertly organized bund like the Nazi brotherhood, mystic, hypnotic, determined, devoted to the purposes of revolution and seeking military ends. It is capable of conducting espionage, psychological and economic warfare, and is fanatically devoted to the New Order.

As long as the Falange exists, our Caribbean life line is in serious jeopardy, and menaced by the dangers of international intrigue and mercurial political upsets. These countries will be subject to the manipulation of powerful authoritarian States, well organized for the conduct of political and economic warfare.

Most of the Latin States are single-crop countries whose whole economy depends on some one product such as bananas, coffee, oil, tin or meats. Great totalitarian empires accountable only to their own aspirations, could literally subsidize these States by the purchase of their entire outputs at premium prices, and by these means lift them out of our orbit and permanently secure them to the Old World.

An alienation of Latin American cordiality toward the United States likewise is certain to occur the instant this country terminates its wartime policy of appeasement by political loans, or the uneconomic purchase of quantities of cotton and other products destined to remain stored in the countries of origin.

Latin America is in default to the United States on its bonds alone to the amount of $1,720,000,000. We have nevertheless deposited funds to stabilize shaky currencies, placed credits at the disposal of the various States for the building of public works, roads, mills, power plants and other projects, underwritten key agricultural surpluses such as Haitian coffee and Peruvian cotton, purchased great amounts of strategic and miscellaneous materials under boom conditions, built airports, modern hospitals, model farm projects, opened up mines and factories and supplied the usual Lend-Lease airplanes, guns and other war materials.

The total expended in direct loans, leases, rentals, credits or outright gifts is said to come close to five billion dollars. In return the Latin States have sold us the products we needed, have taken a diplomatic stand against the Axis, and in some cases presumably, have made something of an effort to discourage enemy propaganda and espionage directed against us. Only Brazil has sent troops, token units appearing with the American 5th Army on the Italian front late in the war. None of the Latin States have furnished munitions, or have granted the United States permanent rights in air or naval stations. The bases we now hold are to be returned after the war, together with all improvements which have been installed. By any rational accounting system these outlays must be considered in the light of a subvention.

In a democracy such as the United States, subject to the will of the electorate, a policy of appeasement or of loan and purchase subsidies without profit or return revenue, in the end will be considered profligate. At some point the people of the United States will refuse pointblank to continue buying the support of the Hispanic half of this hemisphere. That day will introduce consequences of an incalculable nature in the internal economy of these countries and in their relationships with our Republic.

When hostilities cease, the sellers' market which has allowed Latin America an abnormal prosperity would come to a sudden and brutal end. The American demand for metals would drop rapidly the instant the United States went on the free market for what it required, placing South America in competition with the depressed areas of Malaysia and the East Indies. Our imports of hides, meats and grains would fall precipitously. The effect on Latin America could be both stormy and unpredictable, altering its structure swiftly in the direction of totalitarianism and throwing it directly into the lap of the Old World Powers.

IV

The gamut of shifting possibilities our nation must run in its post-war relations with other States is a wide and hazardous one. To meet its implications we should have to go about our business armed to the teeth, prepared to challenge instantly any Power which sought to upset the present critical balance either through military or economic means. Any type of domination which affected this teetering equilibrium would have the same fateful consequences to us and would have to be met with an immediate show of force.

Since all States are now near to us in point of time, and more or less locked up with our economy in terms of industrial sufficiency, everything which takes place anywhere on the globe must be marked by us.

It will be of primary importance to the United States as to who will own Manchukuo, or French West Africa. The control of international trade routes would have to be viewed with the same suspicious regard Britain historically has given the Suez Canal; and the grave events subsequent to the entry of India or China into the power competition of the future easily could become the central factors around which our entire policy would agglutinate.

An inflation or currency failure in any quarter of the globe must have the effect of disturbing the equilibrium of our own money. The attempt by any one country to implement the Socialist doctrine of full employment verges the State over in the direction of totalitarian function, creating a backwash which is felt on the economies of all others.

A planned autarchy on the part of a few countries favorably situated, will have serious effects on countries incapable of achieving a similar self-sufficiency. Autarchy in one State automatically creates the need for it among its neighbors, profoundly disordering the existing relationship of production to markets.

In a world thus interlocked, a radical revolution of any kind, anywhere, is certain to have its repercussive effects in our own social structure. A Pan-Hispanic movement in the Argentine possesses almost as much interest for us as it does for Spain. The wages paid a laborer in Rio de Janeiro or faraway Java will bear an increasingly important relation to the competitive powers of our own commercial structure.

The position to which this reasoning drives us is that of accepting responsibility for reshaping the political and economic destinies of both Europe and Asia, seeking to create those balances and compromises which will be tolerable to our continued existence as a people.

Since the United States cannot retire from the world, it has the choice of creating a reasoned international order or of continuing its military establishment on a full war footing. The total nature of present-day military preparedness makes it questionable whether the latter solution, by forcing us into a semi-totalitarian economy, would not mean finally our adoption of a totalitarian form of government.

In any event we must find ourselves mechanically sucked into the churning vortex of issues and problems which concern us only collaterally, and whose settlement will demand the active cooperation of States whose interests and ambitions run contrary to our own.

Our most pressing solicitude would have to be over the relations of China and the U.S.S.R., both to their neighbors and to each other. Despite a justified apprehension as to China's future military strength, in any quarrel between the two we should have to intervene on behalf of China in order to prevent the sovietizing of Asia. The latter possibility immediately would be seen as the greater of the two evils since it would mean the ultimate consolidation of the entire Old World land mass under a single totalitarian system, the nightmare of American politics.

Whatever the consequences of Sino-Russian rivalry, each will abet the other in a drive to force the Western Powers out of Asia.

The war has proved that it is only by the intervention of the United States that any part of Asia can be held in future by Europe. It may prove, too, that Europe itself will require the vigorous interposition of the United States if the present balance is to be preserved.

This contemplation forces us to re-examine in detail the commitments and policies to which we have been engaged.

V

For a nation engaged in the mightiest struggle in history, to proclaim its aims as being those contained in the Atlantic Charter, is to engage in the greatest of historic deceptions, or to be fighting simply for survival, without plan, without principle and without concept of tomorrow.

The Atlantic Charter is based primarily on the old ethnic principles of nationality and separatism which proved so valuable in collapsing the Central Powers during World War I. Today they would be directed by force of circumstances against the United Nations themselves. The principles of the Atlantic Charter applied to the English Empire would wreck it. The U.S.S.R. would have to abandon some of its most cherished territories. Even the Chinese Republic would be compelled to withdraw from Mongolia as well as Tibet, Sinkiang and Yunnan.

When Mr. Churchill was asked in the Commons whether Article III of the Charter which grants all countries the right to choose their form of government, applied to India, he condensed the total logic of the situation into the two words: "No, sir."

Even if one removed from the Russian prospect the three Baltic Republics, Western Poland, Finland and Bessarabia, a further question must arise in reference to the parts of Armenia and Mongolia held by the Soviets. Moscow holds Finnish Karelia, Mongolian Tanna Tuva and Mohammedan Central Asia. How would the ideology of the Charter apply to the portion of these nationalities held by the Soviets as against those parts which ostensibly are to be free? What would be its relevancy to a resurgent Slovakia or Croatia? Both these States have made their desire for independence clear, as they likewise have the form of government they preferred.

If we are to turn the clock back on the basis of the ethnic particularism which passed under the name of liberal thought a quarter century ago, we must recognize the claims of such regions as Spanish Catalonia, or French Brittany, as well as British-held Cyprus and Egypt. It would be necessary to recognize the independence of the Berbers in North Africa, or for that matter the freedom of the Kabyles and Senussi.

All of these areas speak differing languages and subscribe to separate social and political views. The Basque country has as much right to separate existence as Portugal. So has Macedonia which is a Poland in miniature, struggling bitterly for independence from the three possessor States of Yugoslavia, Greece and Bulgaria. Presumably such ancient European countries as Transylvania, Wallachia, Moldavia and Livonia, which have disappeared from the map but which still exist in the shape of peoples and provinces, might be riven from the parent countries and placed in charge of their own destinies, as might be the case too with the restless Walloons of Belgium.

A literal interpretation of the Charter would mean turning the Continent of Africa into slivers based on tribal hegemonies. It might conceivably end in the granting of independence to Wales where an insistent pro-Gaelic movement has existed for years.

Such a Balkanization of the map at the precise moment when larger rather than smaller spatial groupings are needed to meet the requirements of the machine revolution, would throw the world into permanent disorder and prepare it for conquest by some new mighty man of destiny.

If this concentration on the "rights" of native inhabitants is to be the criterion by which possession is to be judged, our nation forever will be debarred from holding military bases in the Arctic, Atlantic and Pacific, however necessary they might be to protect us from future aggression.

We have only to take the case of Greenland, poised like a huge ax directly over the heart of the Americas. In the hands of an enemy Power which controlled Europe, it would be a perfect stepping-stone from which to lash at every portion of our industrial East and Middle West. In an age where the power of the offensive grants overwhelming advantages to the aggressor, the question of who possessed Greenland might have a decisive bearing on our security.

The population of the big subcontinent is only eighteen thousand. Of these, some five hundred are of Danish blood; the rest, Eskimos. Greenland, theoretically, belongs to the Government of

Denmark. Denmark, as this is written, is an extension of Nazi Germany.

What is to decide the issue—the presence of five hundred Danes and 17,500 primitive natives and mixed bloods? Or might not a new principle apply based on the welfare and security of the 175,-000,000 people of Canada and the United States, or the millions more who live below the Rio Grande?

The old sacrosanct plebiscite system clearly is out of tune with today's realities. It poses the right of a stubborn and strategically-located minority to jeopardize the well-being of the majority; and its purposes easily can be controverted by a modern Power which possesses, like Germany, the will to do so.

Under the conditions the Reich has enforced in Poznan and other areas of Western Poland, a plebiscite would be a farce. The vanquished would find themselves in the nice position of being legal heirs to the patrimony of their victims. The Jews, whose properties have been confiscated, would be dead. The Poles and Czechs who have been expropriated would be elsewhere. Their places would have been taken by Germans.

If a plebiscite is to be held in the Pacific, the strategic Mariana, Caroline and Marshall Islands will have to be turned back to the sovereignty of Japan, since the population of these islands is now overwhelmingly Japanese.

The same condition applies in regions of old Greece where Greeks have been moved out and Bulgarians settled; and in portions of Yugoslavia, Rumania, France and Bohemia.

In addition to being committed to the absurd idyll which pledges them to no territorial changes "not in accord with the freely expressed desires of the peoples concerned," the Anglo-Americans also have charged themselves with responsibility "to further the enjoyment by all States, great or little, *victor or vanquished,* of access on equal terms to the trade and to the raw materials of the world which are needed for their economic prosperity." Theoretically, the Germans are to be given an opportunity to choose their own form of government after the period of military occupation is over.

As late as January, 1944, American planes were dropping leaflets over German cities, containing copies of the Charter printed in the German language. Either this is a gigantic swindle which will have as dangerous a consequence on German psychology as did the failure to implement Wilson's Fourteen Points after World War I, or it will give the Germans control of Europe.

On the basis of any possible peace along the lines elaborated in the Charter, the Reich would remain as a compact, highly organized body occupying a position in the center of the Continent making it the pivot of the entire European economy. It would retain the bulk of Europe's industry within its own frontiers. The balance of the European economy has been reorganized so that it funnels directly into Nazi hands. Most of the academic and intellectual leadership of the nearby small Slav States has been wiped out. The Jews who were considered potential business competitors, have been slaughtered *en masse*.

Hitler has attempted to create a new demographic balance in Central Europe favorable to the Germans, so that even if Germany should lose this war, its dominance in the *Lebensraum* it has set for itself will survive the defeat and become permanent. The Reich has followed a conscious policy of keeping the millions of French war prisoners in German camps in an attempt to destroy a whole generation of French youth. Millions of Polish men and women as well as those of other countries have been taken to Germany as indentured servants and thus prevented from breeding.

Within any European structure which can be envisaged, if the Germans are not placed under restraint they will possess the whiphand.

If the matter is to be one of implementing absolute justice, the question remains—justice to whom? Justice is not a disembodied entity. It cannot exist as an expression of mere abstract nobility and humaneness. It must retain within itself the fundamental elements of responsibility. Justice not only acts to forgive. It also acts to punish, and to restrain those anti-social elements whose continuing acts lead to the suspicion that the offenders are for practical purposes incurable.

The question then takes on the following aspects: Who is to pay for the spilled blood of our young boys who have been called out for the second time in a generation? Who pays for the heartbreak of American mothers, for the destruction of our wealth, for the wreckage in which human society finds itself the world over? If there is to be justice, as Professor Foerster [1] has pointed out, it must be justice toward all—not only to Germany but to the dead, the wounded, the orphans and all who today are wearing the garb of mourning. Those who stagger beneath the burden of the most colossal war debt the mind of man has ever conceived, also must receive justice, and so must those millions whose lands, homes, lives and goods have been ruined and pillaged. So must the millions of the unborn, who of right should be protected against another recurrence of this tragic period of death.

Under these conditions, the unworldly assurances of the Charter become self-evident rubbish.

VI

The big danger of declarations of this sort is not that they might be placed into effect; it is rather that they proclaim an unfortunate lack of direction. Under the sonorous beauty of these idyllic words there is no vision of tomorrow which spurs us on in an effort to realize the fulfilment of a great truth, or consciously to create the conditions under which the future peace can be realized.

We are not moved by the almost religious fervor of the Russians or by the Germans' fanatic hope of dominance. We do not struggle for freedom or racial equality as do the Chinese. Our policy, in consequence, having no great cause from which it can draw inspiration and faith, must become one which in the last analysis

[1] F. W. Foerster, *Europe and the German Question*, pp. 255, 256.

is guided by our mercantile interests, by pure pragmatism and by an attempted series of rationalizations.

Such a foreign policy is deadly. Its acts can have little cohesion. Its driving force will be vitiated by inevitable compromises and its attempted adjustments to many and diverse "realities" will leave it embroiled in a series of logical contraries which only can be reconciled by adopting a more and more reactionary view.

This in fact is the case as we find it everywhere.

In Arabia our policy is being determined by the rich concessions Standard Oil has been able to obtain there. In South America we endeavor to keep in existence undemocratic but "safe" regimes by a series of loans which never will be repaid, and by the uneconomic purchase of agricultural surpluses. In Asia, we have been moving circuitously in an effort to avoid setting off hidden land mines of antagonism.

In Europe our policy is one of frank expediency, which cannot fail to make us the eventual ally and protector of the most reactionary elements, and the final common enemy of all the European undergrounds.

A clear preview of the future was given in our dealings with the French Fascists in North Africa, as well as by our acceptance of the Italian General, Badoglio, as a "co-belligerent ally."

When our troops landed in French Africa it might have been expected that we at once would sweep away every vestige of the previous Nazi regime. We could be expected to liquidate Fascist laws, place active collaborationists behind bars, liberate our friends who were suffering in jails and concentration camps, and proclaim to the beat of triumphant drums the rebirth of the glorious French Republic.

Instead, we did just the opposite. We entered a prompt *mariage de convenance* with the resident regime of collaborationist functionaries. The vicious Nuremberg racial laws continued in full force. Some ten thousand refugee victims of Hitler remained in concentration camps in addition to droves of Spanish Republicans who were not released for fear of "offending General Franco."

These included French Republicans and followers of General de Gaulle, the one Frenchman of note who had stood his ground resolutely with us from the beginning.

The only people, in fact who were arrested were our friends, those who had helped us to make our landing. These were locked up as Elmer Davis later was to admit "because they were political opponents of the people in power."

Let us see who the people "in power" were by reference to their leaders. One was the notorious Darlan, pathologically anti-British and rated as number three man in Petain's cabinet. Another was General Auguste Nogues, who had resisted with military force our attack on Casablanca and who emerged as our "friend" only after we had won Algeria. Still another was a worthy who was not even on the spot and had to be imported from the Argentine, the notorious Marcel Peyrouton. This man had been Secretary-General of Police under Petain, and had been instrumental in rounding up the French patriots who were working against Hitler. When Minister of the Interior in the Petain cabinet, he had boasted: "I was the first Frenchman to introduce National Socialist methods in North Africa." This was the man to whom the Allies turned over the civil administration of Algeria.

The military chief whom the Anglo-Americans espoused was General Henri Giraud, an outstanding soldier, but an enemy of the French Republic. Giraud's political and social views may be understood from his explanation to journalists that he regarded the Jewish problem in North Africa as "his and France's affair."

In defending these actions against criticism, Robert Murphy, the State Department's adviser to General Einsenhower, asserted that "The Allies *never came to North Africa with a panacea to cure political ills, or to impose political doctrines on the inhabitants."*

This cynical appraisal ignored the fact that French North Africa was run under a full set of Nazi laws and by men who themselves were candidates for any future trials of Quisling collaborationists which might be held. Actually, Flandin, Boisson, Peyrouton and

Pucheu among others, were placed under arrest for treason by General de Gaulle's French Committee of National Liberation as soon as it attained the power to do so. Pucheu, who had been Vichy's Minister of the Interior and had been accused of helping Germans to slaughter his own French compatriots, was executed before a firing squad by a French court in Algiers. Others such as Peyrouton and the equally sinister Pierre Boisson were saved by the intervention of the American and British Governments on their behalf.

Sucked in by a policy which events had shaped for us, we thus had no other course than to interfere with the internal politics of France, completing the circle which this reactionary course had made inevitable. We insisted on foisting on the French a puppet regime of our own, comparable in a certain sense to those established by Germany and Japan. This authority was General Giraud and his entourage of Fascists.

In this manner we threw overboard the single French personage who had been our friend throughout, without doubt alienating his inner good will for all time to come. This was General Charles de Gaulle, idol of the French underground and sole rallying point of the French anti-Nazi resistance.

It was De Gaulle's men who with British help had campaigned against the troops of Vichy France in Syria and Central Africa, and who had continued the war in the name of France at a time when Petain had withdrawn the French Navy and had allowed the whole French Empire in Africa, Indo-China, Syria and the South Pacific to commit itself to collaboration with the Germans.

At a time when all seemed lost and the flabby Lavals, Petains and Weygands were to let France slip from their pulseless fingers into the hands of the enemy, De Gaulle had continued to urge resistance. Two days after France capitulated, this indomitable man was in England. Speaking from the BBC studios to a France broken and sickened by this incomprehensible surrender, his words rang in simple power to the world: "I, General de Gaulle, speaking from London, ask those French officers and soldiers now on British soil or capable of reaching it, I ask those French engineers and workmen now on British soil or capable of reaching it, to communicate with me immediately. France has lost a battle," he went on, "she has not lost the war."

For simple eloquence the words of this soldier may rank with those of Churchill, or of our own immortal Lincoln at Gettysburg. To the stupefied, crushed French, he cried: "Is all hope gone? Is the defeat final? No! Believe me, for I speak to you with full knowledge of what I say. The very same means that conquered us can one day give us victory. France is not alone! She is not alone!" In the face of the compromises in North Africa, he cabled in moving words to an American publication: "This war which has forced upon mankind such heavy and bloody sacrifices has no meaning and can have none unless a new world is to arise from its ruins and suffering, a free world in which liberty is no longer a word but a reality and the essence of daily life for every man and every woman . . . And how can one think of this revived world without that nation which has made of liberty and human dignity the time honored object of its thoughts and the vital object of its activities? How can one imagine it without France?" [1]

Our opposition to De Gaulle was based on many incongruities. One of these was that this stubborn man who had brought a price on his head by casting his lot with the United Nations in the dark days when Europe seemed irretrievably lost to the Nazis, was a Fascist. Another was that he was a Communist, and still another that he possessed a difficult character (to this, a British statesman commented drily that the "difficulty" might lie in the fact that De Gaulle was no Quisling).

Now it is this man who stands as the unchallenged leader of France, who has complete control of the French Committee of National Liberation, and who may see the future of France in collaboration with Stalin rather than in the unfathomable opportunism which has substituted for our political principles in North Africa.

Our record with the so-called neutral, Generalissimo Franco,

[1] *Free World,* June, 1943.

is not more reassuring. The Spanish *caudillo* is the frankly acknowledged enemy of the United Nations and of all the forces of liberalism to which we presumably are committed. When the Japanese-sponsored puppet government of Jose P. Laurel was established in the Philippines, Franco sent a prompt message of congratulations. In a broadcast made after our armies had landed in North Africa, he described the Axis New Order as "representing new faith and revolt against the hypocrisy of the old liberal world," demanding a resolute fight against "liberalism and all it stands for."

The Spanish legations are known to be centers of espionage and propaganda used against us. Madrid is the spiritual and financial headquarters of the anti-American Falange. A Blue Legion composed of a number of divisions of "Spanish volunteers," fought on the Eastern front against the Russians. These "volunteers" received by decree all privileges of service in the regular Spanish army including pensions and retirement pay. Franco's government has been the tube through which quantities of strategic materials have been siphoned off to Germany from the Western World.

Our relations with this Fascist State nevertheless have remained eminently correct throughout the war.

In Italy we followed a like course, accepting the Fascist General Badoglio together with the reigning House of Savoy, thus committing ourselves to the very political and social conditions which have brought on the present world disaster. If we have dealt with Badoglio simply because he offered to maintain order in Italy, there seems to be no reason why we should not deal with Goering, or a combination of the Junkers and a reformed Nazi hierarchy.

In defense of the American policy, it can be said that wherever an important Fascist leadership comes over to our side, we obtain easy victories as well as appear to save the lives of many men. Nevertheless, these political improvisations are more than overbalanced by a loss of moral tone, and by an utter confusion as to our ideals and ends.

It may be suspected that while from a purely material view we gain a certain respite in the sense of temporary stability in the conquered regions, this provisional gain will prove costly in the end. When we commit ourselves to these Fascist elements in Europe and North Africa, we are supporting the *status quo* against absolutely certain revolution. We are upholding regimes which not only have suppressed human liberties, but have been guilty of a far greater crime—that of failure.

To the emaciated people of Europe, wracked in body, sick of the world they live in, humiliated by the very conditions of existence, the declarations of our diplomatic leaders will seem empty and unattractive. Our program will have been prejudged by the acts which preceded it.

At the best, Europeans will be badly confused as to our purposes and our capacity to wield power. At the worst, we will become in their eyes the appointed champions of reaction and the enemy of freedom. In the guise of preventing Europe from becoming Communist, it is inevitable that we will join hands with the remnants of old reactionary regimes against the underground groups, assisting the Fascists in retaining control of the government, the press, the labor unions and the national economy, all in the name of the "Four Freedoms."

VII

In a society already writhing in the toils of political failure and threatened by the specter of total collapse, sides are chosen, and ideas harden, becoming cruel, rigid and uncompromising. Our occupation of Europe will not be that of a detached military authority fulfilling a commonplace function independent of local politics. This is no longer possible in today's world. If we are to associate ourselves with the present authorities in Europe, it is inevitable that we will be influenced by their views and will have the underground as our future enemy.

Our difficulties, minor at first, will increase rapidly. The German occupation taught the underground how to operate efficiently, but managed to keep it in check by shooting its members on sight or by exterminating entire villages in retaliation. This we are not likely to do, with the result that our rule will prove both oppressive and weak, a distressful combination.

The issues will be distinct and unmistakable. The Continent will be exhausted, in a dangerous revolutionary mood, and convinced that the old social order is on its last legs. The political and economic structure of traditional Europe will have been obliterated. Its old ruling classes will have been destroyed, its upper and middle classes on the verge of collapse. Whole areas will be depopulated, industry deprived of its markets, and civilized life demoralized. Boundaries of all kinds will have been broken, and cultural forms it has taken centuries to build, erased.

Almost forty million people will have been made homeless. Still other millions will be suffering from malnutrition, psychoneurosis and crippling disease. Eleven million foreign workers slaving in Germany will find themselves suddenly released, as will the broken inmates of concentration camps, ghettos, and jails, together with the embittered legions of war prisoners. These will be desperate, resentful men filled with venom and brute anger. Many of them will have been taught the vicious philosophy of the New Order, and will combine with their hatred for Hitler the dangerous conceptions of biological race supremacy.

In the German occupied countries a large section of the youth will have been corrupted by Nazi doctrines to which they have made an unconscious psychological adjustment. The cultural scheme which anchored them to the traditional past will largely have disintegrated.

Moral confusion and suspicion will permeate whole populations. Quisling groups of Frenchmen, Belgians, Dutch, Norwegians and Slovaks will have been trained into Gestapo methods of terror. Years of struggle will have taught the masses the strategies of unseen sabotage and guerilla attack. Many will have learned the old methods of Russian nihilism with its disrespect for all constituted authority.

Millions of small agricultural owners will be without farms. In-

tellectuals and white collar workers and skilled industrial operators will be unable to find jobs or make the psychological transition to new environments totally unprepared to receive them. The
sudden closing down of war industries may throw one hundred
million workers out of employment.

Europe will have been sunk in ghastly poverty, sixty per cent
of its livestock will have disappeared, irreplaceable farm imple-
ments will have been worn out, manufacturing machinery will
be depleted and the means of transport and distribution wrecked.

Economic Europe will be unrecognizable. Whole industrial areas
will have been devastated so that they resemble little more than a
cemetery. Great plants will have been dismantled and carted off,
while still others will have been bashed to bits. Entire cities will
have been dissolved as if in acid.

The once imposing manufactories of France, Belgium and Holland no longer will exist. Such machinery as will remain will be
in a serious state of disrepair and much of it will be fit for little
else than the junk heap.

Viaducts will have been destroyed and inland waterways rendered unnavigable. Harbors will be useless, land depleted of its
vital minerals and great forests burned to the ground. Reserves
of gasoline, rubber, metals and other critical materials will have
disappeared. Food stuffs will be at a premium. The greatest part
of Europe's rolling stock will have been confiscated or ruined. Currency disorders will be acute, and resulting inflationary movements difficult to control.

The term, "the former people," by which the old elite will be
known, will extend not only to political figures but to economic
classes and social institutions. These will have been despoiled of
their integrity as well as of their possessions. The major industries
of Europe will be "legally" owned by a few giant Nazi cartels. The
economy inherited from the New Order will depend for its efficiency on this set of monstrous controls from which it cannot be
disengaged without wrecking what is left of Europe's business and
well-being.

In this great tide of human misery there will be little idealism left. Europe is inexpressibly weary, the prey to terrible lusts and what may yet prove to be weird expressions of a universal paranoia. Our occupying armies will find a hotbed of friction and conflicting interests. In addition to the general psychosis of fear, resentment and apathy, there will be actual starvation everywhere.

Perhaps fifty million men have been under arms in Europe. They will return to civilian life and from their ranks will be drawn dynamic, restless and adventurous individuals capable of providing leadership for the most desperate and hopeless of movements. The lapse of years will find them returning as virtual strangers to discover other men in the few jobs which remain, and a world which has become alien to their interests.

The whole scheme of democratic approach as well as the mechanism of parliamentary rule will have fallen into discard. Europe will gravitate naturally toward military and party dictatorships.

The dying remnants of legally constituted Europe will make one last determined effort to assert themselves. The social democrats, clericals, Bourbon reactionaries and Communists who have been driven underground and have waited for this time with the grim patience of long, terrible nights of bitter brooding, will have whetted their knives for the Fascist bureaucrats who have so long oppressed them—and for each other. A vicious struggle may break out all over the Continent. National disintegration may have progressed so far that it might easily become a general conflagration, feeding itself on the universal forces of destruction which this war has aroused.

Throughout the Balkans and Central Europe millions of men and women will be at each other's throats. Revolutionary syndicalism will grip the Latin countries. Spain which still has more than a half million of its citizens in concentration camps, awaits only the signal of outside support for a dramatic battle to the death.

Poland and the Low Countries will be in ruins and blazing with the futile hope for revenge. The Baltic States, and perhaps Finland, will have disappeared from the map, and their exiled patriots will be conspiring in every capital of Europe. Hungary and Rumania will be quarrelling over the hopelessly mixed *irredenta* territories of Transylvania and the Banat. The internal conflicts of the Slovaks and Czechs will take on all the aspects of sanguinary struggle, as will those of the Croats, Slovenes and Serbs.

Everywhere in Europe once the ban is lifted, illicit armies representing the dissident factions quietly will take form, their emblem perhaps no more than the ubiquitous white socks of the pre-*Anschluss* Vienna Nazis.

The revolt against liberal democracy will become widespread, fanned by five years of intensive Nazi propaganda which has identified parliamentary rule as a synonym for plutocracy and capital-finance exploitation. The conservative forces will be tired, inert, and in many parts, almost pathologically indifferent to the future course of events. A few old-fashioned liberals will remain, hardened by the fire through which they have passed. More convinced than ever of the enduring worth of free institutions and basic human rights, they will if given a chance attempt to make over the governments in the mold of their own dreams. Against the true forces which are operating in the countries of Europe they can remain in power solely as puppets of an invading Anglo-American regime, the butt of ridicule and hatred, and the object of the assassin's bullet.

VIII

It is difficult to resist the belief that Europe is at the tide of history where Russia was when the Romanoffs fell, or where ancient Rome stood when the Goths, Huns and Vandals were gathering at her gates.

It is too late now to attempt a return to the familiar shape of the pre-war Europe. This is a role which has been played out and already belongs to history. The political structure of the old Europe is dead and cannot be restored.

If it is our policy to place Otto of the Hapsburgs on the throne of a reconstituted Austria, that policy will fail. We cannot hand back Europe to the clericals, the Polish landowners, the refugee royal houses, or the big banking and manufacturing families, without assuming an historical position which will appear in retrospect, grotesque. It is impossible to re-establish the French and English in Asia, or to restore the *status quo ante* in those territories or spheres of human activity which have been made the object of revolutionary change.

We cannot loose ourselves from the character of the times, which possesses powers equal to those of our arms, and more enduring. The effort to re-establish the old outworn legitimacies is hence a futile attempt to turn the clock back, which can last only as long as our bayonets are on hand.

Europe will not quiet down or Asia become a peaceful and respectable member of the world community until the peoples of these continents have been fitted into a permanent order which allows them to escape from the paralyzing chains of the antique world, and adjusts them to the physical needs of this century.

Two years ago we might have dominated the situation by proclaiming the existence of a free, united Europe, rid once and for all of its multitudinous boundary lines, tariffs, currency quarrels, disputes, and military establishments. By thus cutting the Gordian knot of European conflicts and ineptitudes we might have committed an act of supreme statesmanship and have prepared the way for a rationally planned world. Russia, reeling back from the Nazi invasion of her prairies, could not have objected. Our armies would have entered Europe to the wild enthusiasm of its people as liberators and as the saviors of the Continent, just as the legions of Garibaldi entered the crumbling city-States, republics and kingdoms of Italy three generations before.

This is a role which by default we may have given to Russia. It remains to be seen how she will acquit herself of it.

The Soviet Union will emerge as the strongest land Power on the globe and will credit her victories to her economic system. The influence of these facts on Europe will be magnetic. It will be the Soviet Union which will represent the source of authority, the stability and economic safety for which all Europe will yearn.

The Communist fold may yet prove to be the refuge of the ecclesiastics and the conservative elements of Europe against the growing violence of the Trotskyites, syndicalists and anarchists. We see this phenomenon in Yugoslavia where priests and a miscellany of bourgeoisie elements are gathered around the Communist, Josip Broz, as well as in the German underground.

Our nation becomes the chief actor in this drama by virtue of its comparative stability and its possession of most of the world's negotiable wealth. By a system of beneficence which did not too thoroughly conceal the iron hand hid beneath the soft glove, we might succeed in maintaining the existing political order over the world for a considerable period. Europe will look to us for quick rehabilitation. Russia will desire our financial and technical assistance. China will need the heavy machinery with which to construct her basic industries.

By shrewd handling, we could manage this role of international money-lender and earn for a short period that gratitude which, alas, in life is much too fleeting. We can distribute food at the cost of an irreparable loss of minerals from own soil, and we can ally ourselves with those presumably solid elements who with our assistance will be able to maintain the peace, though to do so they will be compelled to take greater and greater recourse to principles against which we have just fought a bloody war.

Europe and Asia both will need relief in huge quantities merely to keep body and soul alive. They will require clothing, consumers goods, and medicines, as well as machinery, fuel and housing.

If we are to feed the people of Asia as well as the untold millions of tragic Europe, and supply them with poultry and cattle as well as hospital buildings, medicines, machinery and other needs, we will find that we have let ourselves in for a large order.

Our propagandists in the war areas have promised much. We

expect to make our friends and to recreate the world on the basis of our inexhaustible wealth much as we have done in South America. As long as this largesse is forthcoming in sufficient quantities, the stricken peoples of Europe and Asia will welcome it eagerly and our moral position will be supreme.

At a certain point these handouts must cease since they represent a squandering of our own waning resources, which, whether justified or not, will never be tolerated by the Congress or the people of the United States. They will regard such a policy as unrealistic and will credit to it every evil which will affect our economy, and every strain on the American standard of living.

As the matter now rests, it is expected that we will assist England to retain its Empire, and the little countries of Europe in reconstituting themselves on the old pre-war basis. Russia and China are to remain impenetrable, but apparently friendly, enigmas. Everyone everywhere will have his hand out. From all points of the compass will arise a continuous cry from the small nations soliciting us to save them from the evils of their position. Since their facilities for manufacturing, as well as markets, will have largely disappeared, we will be asked to supply the machinery as well as the credit for rehabilitation.

It was suggested by British experts that America would be required to subsidize the balance of the world for an indefinite period of time at the rate of five billion dollars a year. In short, in order to bail out their bankrupt economies and keep these nations from the worse evil of political revolution, we will be expected like Atlas to hold up the world.

The question which would immediately arise is this: *What is Atlas standing on?* If this expectation is to begin in a set of logical incoherencies, it must end in a vacuum. Hence, Atlas will be found *to be standing on nothing.* While this proposition possesses the virtue of being unselfish, it may be suspected that it is also highly impractical.

It is simply impossible to attempt to underwrite the deficits of a bankrupt world based on the moral and financial hegemony of an American century. We cannot hand out money, machinery and materials indefinitely without depleting our own essential stockpiles and basic resources, which hardly can be regarded as inexhaustible.

Neither mercy nor compassion have had a sweeter flowering than in President Roosevelt's instructions to Governor Lehman to play the role of the *grand seigneur* in the devastated areas "through the provision of food, fuel, clothing and other basic necessities, housing facilities, medical and other essential services; and to facilitate in areas receiving relief the production and transportation of these articles and the furnishing of these services."

It is the general plan that, in addition to food, the needy nations of the world will get from us, without cost, machinery, fuel, breeding stock, raw materials, fertilizers and expert services of all kinds. We have already sent much heavy machinery to the Soviet Union and will be expected to send more to Europe and China. We thus not only will be exporting our products but our industry and know-how as well.

This is the most magnificent gesture of kindness and charity ever envisaged by a great nation, but unless it is correlated with a courageous effort to cast the conventional legitimacies aside, and reorder the failing political structures which already have brought so much suffering to the world, it is the economics and policy of Bedlam.

XIII

TREATIES, PACTS AND COALITIONS

IT is at this most climactic of all periods of modern history, when the old is being swept out and the new irresistibly ushered in, that the world has been pledged by its leaders to the so-called Four Power Pact between the United States, England, Russia and China.

To this Four Power directorate may be added hereafter either of the major defeated Axis Powers if by their good behavior they seem eligible for this honor. Associated with this all-powerful combination of States will be the smaller nations, either through a council with limited powers, or by corollary treaties and agreements.

Each of the great States presumably is to have its sphere of influence. Clustering around it like a series of moons will be its satellite nations.

This amounts to rule by condominium, by coalition, by conference—and by the force of superior arms.

Thus, under circumstances endowing it with new terrors, we return to an archaic pattern whose record is one of perpetual and dismal failure. Never has a concert of Powers started out with poorer prospects of success than this one.

This agreement by which equilibrium is to be achieved is entered into between the most imbalanced forces imaginable. These consist of a dying Empire, a great static commercial State interested in preserving its own mercantile supremacy, another great State just maturing from an acute revolutionary process, and a fourth State just entering it.

This concert of Powers enters existence at the very moment when

Europe and the world are in a spasm of violent change, when nothing is settled, and when whole continents are being rocked to their foundations by unsolved problems.

The different governments possess entirely different sets of ideas behind their foreign policies. What China seeks is not national independence but international freedom, equality and the right of her masses to move anywhere. The dying dynamics of British world finance will find itself confronted with the exultant powers of a new, triumphant and expanding Russia. The Russian drive is forced to conflict with every basic premise which lies behind the pre-eminent mass-production mercantilism of the United States.

The conflicts are fundamental both from an ideological and a material view. The grievances of the Orient, of which China will be the leading spokesman, can be satisfied only at the expense of one of the parties to the pact, Great Britain. China and Russia, as we have observed, have their own serious potential quarrels, but there are also strong attractions which draw the two nations together. The most powerful of these is the belief that in concert they would have the entire Old World land mass at their mercy.

If Britain and the United States refused to give Asia what it considers its due, we would be faced with the inevitable threat that the Orient would turn in a body to the Soviets, creating an irresistible wave which would flow over the earth. If we attempted to intervene against the political radicalism which is expected to throw large sections of Europe into turmoil, we conceivably could be presenting the Soviet Union with a *casus belli* under conditions which we cannot support by force of arms.

At the moment, these questions are obscured by the more pressing problems of war-making, and by the prospect of postwar gratuities. The Soviet Union will want our help in re-establishing her heavy industry in the devastated zones. We have been aiding China by friendly grants which reached the annual rate of five hundred million dollars in 1943. The Chinese will not wish this flow of funds to stop, and will be circumspect in reference to conditions which would affect it.

These circumstances obviously are transient. They refer to measures which can be of little durable value. Even though disguised under the cloak of deepest friendship, such palliations settle nothing, and may succeed in aggravating all problems by confining their distending pressures in a kettle without a vent.

This is not the first occasion in history where a concert of the major Powers has been inaugurated for the purpose of bringing peace and safety to the world. One can go down a tiresome and unending list of such coalitions based on what appeared to be the existing resources of power. There were so many triple and quadruple alliances, all entered into "for perpetuity" that no one knows quite which one is referred to when the phrase is used. They reach far back into the ancient world, even to the relations between the Egyptian, Assyrian and Hittite Empires.

The fate which has attended all such pacts may be seen in condensed form in the Quadruple Alliance between Greece, Serbia, Bulgaria and Rumania, by which the Christian Powers of the Balkans conducted a holy war against the hated Turks and swore peaceful allegiance to each other forever.

That war was brought to a quick and triumphant conclusion in 1913 by the utter defeat of Turkish arms. Within three weeks, the Quadruple Alliance which was to have lasted forever, fell apart under conditions of wild animosity, in which Turkey, the unspeakable enemy of a few weeks before, was allowed to join as one of the victorious Powers at the expense of Christian Bulgaria, the leading Power of the old Alliance.

The most impressive of the efforts to bring about a concert of Powers capable of keeping the peace was that which followed the fall of Napoleon. All Europe was actuated by a high idealism. Everywhere the liberal aristocratic view was in control. When the nations met finally at the Congress of Vienna in 1815, it was under the most salubrious of conditions.

Meeting around the mahogany tables were some of the most experienced and ablest negotiators Europe has produced. Wellington and Castlereagh sat for England, Talleyrand for France, Metternich for Austria, Nesselrode for Russia, and Hardenberg for Prussia. The leading Powers were determined to create a condition of permanent balance among themselves. Assurances were exchanged, and an article written into the compact binding the four great Powers to meet at fixed intervals to arrive at a pacific settlement of all problems affecting the peace of the Continent, and hence of the globe, which Europe dominated.

Thus the machinery was set up which was thereafter to be called the Concert of Europe. This arrangement looked forward to the final disarmament of the Continent, to the complete freedom of the seas everywhere, to the distribution of territory according to ethnic realities rather than by dynastic or imperial principles, and to the establishment of a Permanent International Court.

The Congress ended in the inevitable clash of interests. Instead of being reduced, militarism gained rapidly. All Europe became the prey of diplomatic finesse as each Power played its part to secure the utmost advantage out of its own peculiar position. Whatever good sense there was on the Continent disappeared utterly, culminating in the unhappy situation with which the world is now compelled to deal.

The spirit of calculated cynicism which has always characterized a Power-ruled world became evident at once in the deliberations which took place at the first Moscow Conference, in October, 1943.

These resulted in a vaguely worded declaration in favor of world disarmament, and the abolition of barriers interfering with the easy flow of goods in international trade. The Powers pledged that they would not use their armies in the territories of other nations without joint consultation. The Powers, henceforward, were to consult each other on major issues, and a Joint Committee was to be set up which would sit regularly in London and make joint recommendations. There was little else.

In view of the historical processes which we have reviewed here, this Agreement may be set down as an ephemeral arrangement to last only so long as the interests of the different participants are not adversely affected by it. The real condition may be seen in the tangible pronouncements which resulted from the Conference.

Here had been an historic occasion in which a shining opportunity existed to fire the imaginations of men everywhere, setting up a common goal for humanity and pointing the way to a reorganized world in which such catastrophes as we now endure would become impossible. At this moment when all men were groping for the light of reason in international arrangements, a bold pronouncement such as that which carried Napoleon's arms irresistibly over Europe would have marked one of the half dozen truly decisive moments in history.

The mountain labored and brought forth a mouse. There was no brave statement, and no proffered answers to those problems for whose solution humanity cries to heaven. Instead, the gentlemen pledged each other only one concrete proposition—the independence of Austria, a proposal which suffers from such obvious incongruities and disrelation to the times as to be fantastic. This pronouncement was offered at the very moment when the avenging archangel, Hitler, had among the few beneficent acts attributable to his career, swept Europe clear of boundaries and given it a single material economy and political status.

II

It is impossible to avoid the conclusion that while there is morality between individuals there is not and never has been morality between nations. There are no criteria which may be applied by which the actions of a single person, trained and adjusted to the pattern of social authority, may be compared to those of the great competing national States to whom the phrase "social authority" must by nature of the conditions dominating their existence be meaningless.

A swift backward glance at the circumstances applying in the relations between the victorious Allies after the capitulation of Germany in the last war, offers little in the way of assurance for the future of the present compact between the four great Allied Powers.

After Germany fell, the French were determined to annex the left bank of the Rhine as a matter of security. President Wilson, who regarded himself in the light of a great humanitarian, resisted this view as he did the insistence of our own General Pershing that Berlin itself be occupied and the basis of German military power permanently destroyed.

Despite our pledges to the other Allies, Wilson acted alone in offering terms to Germany. He was obsessed by the distinction he drew between the German Government and the German people, and felt that the establishment of democratic processes was sufficient to guarantee the peaceful inclusion of the German people in European society for the future.

The American President rode roughshod over the opinions of his various confreres at the peace settlement. He was insistent that it be based on an acceptance of his historic Fourteen Points [1] (later to become twenty-seven). These he had arrived at alone without consultation with the other Allies.

When the rest of the Allied statesmen informed Colonel House categorically that they could give him no assurance in advance of discussion that his proposals would be acceptable to them, House speaking as Wilson's representative immediately replied: "Very well, if the gentlemen refuse to accept the Twenty-seven Points as the basis for peace—the negotiations are thereby cancelled." He added meaningfully that the question would, however, arise "whether America would have to take these matters up directly with Germany."

Clemenceau inquired: "That would amount to a separate peace between the United States and the Central Powers?"

"It might," replied House, cryptically.

This bald threat, made the day before the American election, forced the Allies to agree at once to the American demands. "My

[1] Clemenceau remarked acidly, "Mr. Wilson bores me with his Fourteen Points—Why God Almighty has only ten!"

statement," House telegraphed the President, "had a very exciting effect on those present." [1]

This open use of the big stick by one of the parties to the conference, though in the name of high-flown idealism, was to have disastrous results for France.

To satisfy Paris which was determined to stabilize the French eastern borders at the Rhine, the United States and England agreed to demilitarize Germany permanently, to prevent the union of Germany and Austria, and to come immediately to the assistance of France if she were again invaded by her ambitious neighbor to the east. Under these circumstances, France was compelled reluctantly to yield.

Despite the fact that these unqualified commitments had been made by the President in the name of the United States, the American Senate rejected the entire premise on which they were based. It would not ratify the Versailles Treaty, refused to countenance our inclusion in the League, and concluded a separate peace with the Central Powers.

Whatever the intention had been, the physical result was to leave France betrayed out of her previous strong military position and faced by what inevitably must be a renascent and revengeful Germany.

France then rested her future policy on two instruments of international cooperation, the League of Nations and the five Locarno Treaties. Under the terms of the Covenant, the Versailles Treaty could not be altered except by unanimous decision of the League Council. This obviously never could be achieved as long as France was opposed. The Locarno Treaties themselves consisted of a mutual guarantee signed by Germany, France, Britain, Italy and Belgium, warranting forever the inviolability of the boundaries between these countries, as well as the permanent demilitarization of the Rhineland zone.

By these agreements the nations pledged their oaths never to make war against each other. Provision was made for a Permanent

1 Seymour, *The Intimate Papers of Colonel House*, p. 165.

Conciliation Commission in which all problems were to be solved with the help of neutrals. This was qualified further by the agreement that if no decision could be reached by the Commission, the dispute was to be referred to the World Court of the Council of the League of Nations. These compulsory clauses were reinforced by a series of bilateral agreements signed by France and Germany with Poland and Czechoslovakia.

A succession of *démarches* and unilateral actions which involved the sudden remilitarization of the Rhine, and the British denunciation of the clauses of the Versailles Treaty which prevented Germany from possessing naval and air units, completed the collapse of the safety provisions on which basis alone France had agreed to Wilson's Twenty-seven Points.

This ignominious collapse of a system based on guarantees, pledges and the most sacred of assurances gives a perfect picture of the certain fate which will betide all similar efforts to guarantee world peace and security. The handicaps simply are too much under any system which leaves the basic questions unsolved.

The whole of previous experience indicates that any arrangement short of universal empire amounts only to the setting up of new balances and equilibriums which promptly will be disturbed whenever the proper opportunity or provocation presents itself. The basic conflicts remain undisturbed, though obscured by a new haze of words and agreements.

A survey of treaties shows that invariably they have been honored more in the breach than in the observance, and that they represent a poor framework on which to build a lasting edifice.

It is not necessary to look far.

In the single case of Poland, there exists a series of treaties signed by that State with its neighbors. One of these is an arbitration pact with Germany which agreed to the settlement of all questions without the use of force. In 1929, Poland became party to the Litvinov Protocol, or Eastern Peace Pact. In 1932, she signed a non-aggression pact with Russia. In 1934, she signed a non-aggression treaty with Germany by which all differences between the countries were to be settled by pacific means.

At that time, Hitler told the Reichstag that he hoped "that this treaty would set an example of two nations settling their differences amicably between themselves and reconciling themselves to each other's right to exist." The Polish Foreign Minister Beck told the Sejm that "the Polish-German Pact is an example of that constructive work which we oppose to the pessimism which has invaded the international relations of the world." These pacts a few years later disappeared in the dust of the marching German and Russian armies.

It is rather freely believed that we live in a period of devious intrigue in which respect for the sanctity of treaties has disappeared. The premise is that a moral background once existed which gave treaties absolute validity and that this must somehow be re-established. It is assumed that if this dishonesty of approach were destroyed, the relationships between nations, by becoming honest, would become automatically sound.

This is worse than rubbish. There has never been a period in the world's history when treaties or arrangements of any kind, no matter how piously entered into, were regarded as binding when they conflicted with the vital interests of the States concerned. No treaty ever written could put into balance the shifting quality of trade advantage, the dynamisms of population growth, or the changes which affect political rule. Wherever treaties may conflict with the economic and political realities, they either will be evaded or ridden over roughshod.

The whole brittle succession of historic alliances, ententes, treaties, pacts and coalitions prove beyond the peradventure of doubt that any structure built on these arrangements is built on sand. They march like ghosts through the centuries, a long, shoddy list of contracts, all solemnly entered into by the most binding of ceremonies. No one of them settled anything beyond a new relationship of power. In each case they were made to be broken.

We see them in a row, rotating around central issues many of which have long since disappeared as the ebb and flow of struggle for advantage, possessions and priority took place between the contending States. Just as Lord Beaconsfield returning from the Congress of Berlin in 1878 was to announce confidently to the welcoming multitude: "I bring you peace with honor," another British Prime Minister was to wave a fluttering piece of paper before the applauding crowds on his return from Munich, and assure his compatriots of "peace in our time."

We examine all of these treaties in vain for a single sign that such instruments can survive beyond their period of usefulness to the stronger Power. A long list of alliances and inalienable promises were made and smashed in relation to the Balkan problem alone. As often as not the treaty which concluded one phase of conflict bred new and more destructive struggles.

Today the very names of these solemn conventions are practically unknown. The treaties of Tilsit, of Berlin, of Paris, of Bucharest, of Utrecht, of Aix-la-Chapelle, of Vienna, of Fontainebleau, of Westphalia and the Hague, of Sevres, Lausanne and Versailles, all have disappeared, together with the alliances, groupings and coalitions by which they were formed and guaranteed. In practically every case their stipulations proved to be, at the best, a pious fraud in which the power element entered as nakedly as if the treaty had never been concluded. The illustrations can be recited *ad nauseam,* though they have been buried and forgotten in the sea of subsequent events which has washed over them.

The pious vows which attended the alliance of the Central Powers did not prevent Italy from forsaking it in the last war and fighting on the side of the Allies, nor did it stop the German satellite, Rumania, from adopting a similar course.

We discover Pilsudski and his Polish Legions warring with the same zeal, first on one side and then on the other, for the independence of Poland. In the current conflict we find the French Government fighting against the Germans and later accepting a non-belligerent position in virtual alliance with them. We behold the

Government of Italy actively shifting sides, thus rupturing under stress one of the most intimate relationships which has ever existed between nations.

We see the Soviet Union and Germany abandoning what seemed to be an irreconcilable hostility under conditions which make one despair completely of any durable peace based on the moral ideals of nations. On August 24, 1939, Hitler presented the free world with a bombshell by which the safety of his rear was guaranteed, allowing him a free hand against the Western States. His former *Drang nach Osten* and holy war against Bolshevism was dissolved by a non-aggression pact between Germany and the Soviet Union.

Not more than a week later, the Nazi troops marched into Poland, there to be met at a predetermined demarcation line by the armies of the Soviets. Notwithstanding the solemn pacts which existed between Poland and these two States, they proceeded to divide up the prostrate republic and to absorb it into their political and economic systems.

Russia, which had a treaty with Finland of non-aggression, set up demands against that country and finally embarked on a naked war of aggression though the two States had previously been at peace. Power politics has never revealed as unrelieved and relentless a visage as that shown by the Soviet Union toward the three Baltic Republics as a result of the Russian deal with Germany. These, in consequence of a succession of increasingly harsh demands, found themselves absorbed as territories within the Soviet itself.

The attitude toward little Rumania was hardly better. As a result of an ultimatum without benefit of arbitration of any kind, that evil little kingdom was forced to hand over to the Soviet Union the province of Bessarabia. In addition, both Hungary and Bulgaria tore slices of Rumania away by the cold threat of brute force, though each had signed security agreements with her.

As part of this general mélange of double-dealing and faithlessness, a commercial betrothal had been vowed between Germany and Russia by which the Reich was to purchase raw materials valued at one hundred eighty million marks, and the Soviets were to purchase German machinery to the total of two hundred million marks. Mutual suspicion prevented the fulfilment of these provisions. Only token shipments were made on either side.

On the diplomatic front, however, Moscow supported Hitler's attempt to force a peace settlement on Britain and France on the basis of the division of Poland.

Finally, Hitler, himself, deeming the moment ripe from what appeared to be Moscow's abysmal failures in the war against Finland, moved for what he thought would be a triumphant march to the Caucasus and beyond. The result was to pitch the Soviet Union into a battle for life and death, and to throw it head foremost into the camp of the United Nations.

An analysis of the conditions preceding the Japanese grasp for world power offers little more in the way of assurance to global planners.

In 1898, the independence of Korea was guaranteed by four of the great Powers, including the United States of America. Three years previously, in the treaty of peace signed at Shimonoseki between China and Japan, both countries agreed to recognize "the complete neutrality of Korea." In a subsequent treaty of alliance between Japan and Korea, the object was stated to be that of "maintaining the independence of Korea on a firm footing."

Following the Russo-Japanese War in which Japan enjoyed the quiet but determined diplomatic support of the United States, it was agreed that China was to have exclusive administration of Manchuria and that both Russian and Japanese troops must evacuate that area.

Under the Anglo-Japanese agreement of 1902 between Great Britain and Japan, the high contracting parties mutually recognized the complete independence of China and Korea, and declared themselves "to be entirely uninfluenced by any aggressive tendencies in either country."

As a result of a series of progressive encroachments, Japan finally took over the postal, telegraph and telephone services of Korea and established herself permanently there. The modified Anglo-Japanese Alliance of 1905 now recognized that "Japan possesses paramount political, military and economic interests in Korea" and had the right to police it by force. In return the Japanese became a police partner to the Imperial West for the Orient, and unqualifiedly recognized the rights of the British in Eastern Asia and India. The contracting parties agreed to come to each other's assistance wherever these rights were challenged. At about the same time, the Government of the United States came to a secret agreement with Tokyo in which it, too, recognized Japanese "suzerainty over Korea."

By 1907 all pretense to Korean independence had disappeared, and the country was annexed to the Japanese Empire as the province of Chosen.

The Republic of France, in turn, had carved out for itself chunks of Southern China which it incorporated into its political system under the name of Indo-China. By the treaty of June 10, 1907, Japan recognized permanent French possession of Indo-China and parts of Siam. Paris, in turn, acquiesced to the Japanese aggression and recognized the rights of Nippon in Korea and her special interests in Manchuria.

This was followed in 1908 by the Root-Takahira Agreement between Japan and the United States by which tacit acceptance was given the Japanese conquests on the mainland. It was stipulated, however, that all countries were to possess equally the right of exploitation in China, though this passed under the euphemism of continuing "the independence and integrity of China and the principle of equal opportunity for the commerce and industry of all nations . . ."

As the situation unfolded, it was the United States which attempted finally to halt continued Japanese provocation in Asia. Britain, however, refused to go along and through its Foreign Minister, Sir John Simon, succeeded in halting any condemnation of the Japanese course by the then articulate League of Nations.

We find England as late as June, 1939, formally recognizing that extraordinary conditions exist in China, and noting that "as long as that state of affairs continues to exist, the Japanese forces in China have special requirements for the purpose of safeguarding their own security and maintaining public order," and that "His Majesty's Government have no intention of countenancing any acts or measures prejudicial to the attainment of the abovementioned objects by the Japanese forces."

In the meanwhile, Japan had gained support from the Western States by a series of unprovoked incursions against the Russians in Manchukuo and Siberia. The tension seemed to be greater even than that between Germany and Russia. Nevertheless, when Japanese provocations came to a head in the shape of the current war in the Pacific, Japan and the Soviet Union, with no treaties and no dubious pacts to blind them to the real course of events, remained at peace.

III

If the present Four Power structure is to constitute the foundation on which the postwar creation is to rest, the meaning to the United States is clear: We would be thrown right back to our own power resources.

Our policy then necessarily would be one of dealing with the most vulgar realities, and of weighing the most elemental suspicions and fears. We would have to be vitally concerned with the internal as well as the external developments in all countries. The growth of China to industrial competence would appear to be an unreserved calamity which would have to be prevented at all costs. Our relations with the U.S.S.R. would be no less difficult.

Our policy would be guided by the injunction "let not thy right hand know what thy left hand doeth." Our principal task in Europe and Asia would be that of giving tacit support to the lesser nations. Every small State would live in perpetual fear of this new rivalry between the giants, and would have to invoke all the classic evils of diplomatic venality to escape being crushed. Economic and ideological warfare would go forward quietly and without restraint.

Both Russia and China would have to be prevented from seizing adjoining areas, as well as kept out of South America. Our principal hope would be to keep both juggernauts at loggerheads over their conflicting ambitions, a matter which is likely to occur anyway.

An effort to seek allies among the moribund States of Western Europe would be a fatuous one unless we were to accommodate ourselves to the renewed aspirations of Germany. No other State in Europe has either the cunning, character or industrial capacity to withstand the disapproval of the Soviet bear.

The question of what to do about Britain would be a continual plague to any possible policy we would be able to improvise, because of the continuous embroilments in which the Empire will find itself.

We would be forced, whether we wished it or not, into an American Century, devoted to a gigantic balance of power scheme seeking to confine both giants by the use of various types of *cordon sanitaire*. It is doubtful whether either could be held in such a cage for long.

As a matter of sheer necessity, we should be compelled to seize all the islands of the Caribbean and to turn Canada into a satrapy so that her policy could be relied on to follow ours without argument or qualification in all essential economic and military respects.

We should be forced to erect the tightest wall we could against the Orient by taking over every Pacific island we were able to lay our hands on, forming them into a complex network of fortified points articulated by a matting of subsidized airlines and potential war plants.

The state of prolonged tension would be sure to show itself in shrewd propaganda aimed at the Mexicans, the Negroes, the proletariat, the industrialists, and whatever other groups could be stimulated into self-serving action. As the bullets of propaganda warfare turned our country into an arena in which the various Powers attempted to obtain possession of the American mind, a corollary economic warfare would be waged.

The day that one of the great Powers felt itself to be in a position to upset the military balance would find the other parties to the pact suddenly confronted with *faits accomplis*. Some mild warning of this is given in the unilateral attitude adopted by the Russians toward the question of Polish boundaries, the disposition of the Baltic States, and the demands to be made on Finland and Rumania.

In this kind of world we should have to get used to the fact that we could rely only on ourselves. This, in essence, would be a complete return to isolationism.

XIV

PANACEAS FOR PEACE

IT is pretty well agreed all around that if mankind is to avert the crisis toward which it is rushing, a new world outlook urgently is required.

The world shows an instinctive longing for unity and for a cessation to the general lawlessness which has prevailed in the relationship of peoples.

This longing for universal peace in which the enemies of man will be not other men but the contending forces of nature, is as old as civilization itself. The ancient Hebrews saw the ultimate role of man as being finally enacted under one roof in a millennium of goodness and peace. The Kingdom of Christ looked forward to an ultimate all-encompassing rule, not only in Heaven but on this planet. Peace was the final objective of even such violent doctrines as those which swept Mohammed and Omar out of the deserts of the Nejd to disembowel half the civilizations of the Old World.

Peace plans based on some sort of international unity have been advanced ever since the confusion and chaos of the Middle Ages. Until the last century they were mostly concerned with finding a substitute for the Pax-Romana by which the peace of the Mediterranean civilization had been kept.

As early as the Fourteenth Century, one of the advisers of the French king, Philippe le Bel, brought forward a plan for a Federation of Christian States in which he proposed a general council with a panel of judges to determine differences between the nations by arbitration. The poet, Dante, proposed a universal monarch (presumably Christian) who was to operate under the leadership of the Roman people whom he asserted best fitted for this role because they were the noblest of all peoples, and had been "ordained for empire by nature." [1] A succession of other designs centered mostly around an international parliament, or great council in which each nation would have representation.

In the Sixteenth Century, Emeric Cruce brought forward his *"New Cyneas, or Discourse of the Occasions and Means to Establish a General Peace and the Liberty of Commerce throughout the Whole World."* Cruce's plan differed from the others in the single essential that he made membership open to non-Christian as well as Christian Powers, thus creating for the first time a true concept of global federation. His proposal assessed in considerable detail the problems of the times and advocated methods by which these could be met on an international collaborative basis.

All of these projects existed either in the realm of noble conjecture or, as in the case of the Grand Design advanced by Henry IV of France, as schemes for freezing the existing balance of power. These plans hence bore the burden of being unworldly panaceas, or of reflecting still another phase of current political strategies.

The first concrete measures taken in the direction of international law and sanity were formulated by a political refugee from Germany, named Francis Lieber. These were issued by President Lincoln in the form of *"Instructions for the Government of the Armies of the United States in the Field."* Lieber's *Instructions* formed the basis for the body of laws regulating the conduct of war on land adopted by the International Conference at Brussels in 1874, and later revised by the Hague Conference of 1899 and 1907 in the form of the Hague Convention.

The next forward step in this direction was taken by an absolutist monarch, Czar Nicholas II of Russia. The proposal of Nicholas contemplated the limitation of armaments by mutual agreement, thus ending armed conflict by the use of mediation. It was carried

1 Sylvester John Hemleben, *Plans for World Peace through Six Centuries*, p. 9.

to the point where a number of committees actually were formed and met at the Hague.

This project failed, it is alleged, due to the position taken by Germany which refused to be bound by the stipulation preventing further increase in military expenditures. Nevertheless, out of this effort came the Permanent Court of Arbitration at the Hague which, for all its limited power, represented the first concrete stride in the direction of settling international problems by law rather than by force.

The weakness of the Hague Court was, of course, apparent, in that it represented little more than an ideal to which nations were bound only by principles of international morality and good will. The Court had no force or power of its own with which to make its decisions stick. It was in the position of a weak, central sovereign dealing with many nobles, the least of which was immeasurably stronger than he.

It was apparent that the decisions of the Hague could be adhered to only when they did not strike at the vital ambitions or prosperity of any one of the participating States, or where the balance of power between them remained so firmly established as to attend armed contention with grave and unprofitable risks.

The notion that aggressive war was an international crime became part of the belief of all nations, except the German. All, however, rationalized their aggressions wherever their own interests were concerned, into a matter of necessary defensive operations, a situation as true of the United States as it was of any of the traditionally warlike Powers. An example may be seen in the excuses sought by President Polk for war with Mexico, after negotiation for purchase had failed, to justify the seizure of territories coveted by the United States. It is perceived equally in the power politics utilized in our relations with weak but strategically located States; as, for example, our occupation of Liberia as a base for military operations, or our participation with Great Britain and Russia in the military seizure of Iran and the forcible deposition of its pro-German, though officially neutral, Shah.

The doctrine of an international moral responsibility on the part of nations seemed at first blush a plausible one. It proved to be rooted in ill-conceived legalisms which bore no sensible relation to the ethos in which the nations moved.

It was assumed that an identity of interests existed as between nations, that every country possessed the self-same stake in preserving the peace and that any State which attempted to break it was therefore both irrational and immoral.[1] This, of course, was in no sense true since to some degree or other the making of war continued to be looked on by all States as a necessary means for redressing problems which could not be settled in other ways.

Even the rules of war, while seeming to stem from purely humane considerations, arose from conditions immeasurably more practical. Belligerents found it to their mutual interests to distinguish between the armed forces and government of an enemy, and its merchants and workers, since the latter originally contributed little to the military effort.

This was the situation when at the conclusion of World War I President Wilson as the overshadowing figure among the representatives of the Allied Nations, determined to push through his plan for an idealistic association of States which would outlaw war for all time, insure commerce and guarantee the peaceful development of nations.

Mr. Wilson's views were crystallized in his famous Fourteen Points, founded on the principles of national self-determination and the association of all States, large and small, into a concert of nations. Here the nations would be bound by solemn convention to keep the peace and to take united action against any State which violated it.

The mortal weakness of this council of States which later became known as the League of Nations, was that in its founding principles it violated that first law of logic that "a thing cannot both be and not be in the same way at the same time." It attempted to curb the

[1] E. H. Carr, *The Twenty Years' Crisis*, p. 67.

States and in the same breath to guarantee their independence as sovereign universes.

Since its decisions were dependent on the voluntary acquiescence of the Powers, the League was unable to concern itself with those economic and social factors which were visibly rocking the conventional world, and engaged itself with political theory and legal definitions or with matters of relative unimportance.

The League essayed to set up a permanent world balance on that most unstable of foundations, the imperial control by small European nations of the great Asiatic masses, who were already stirring with a dream of their own destiny. Thus the larger portion of humanity either was not recognized at all or only nominally so. Above all the League was dedicated to that final incongruity of guaranteeing the perpetual inviolability of States whose relation to the machine age was such that they were already doomed.

In addition to being committed to these stagnating political frameworks which had been carried over from the feudal and late capitalist periods, the League was compelled to adjust itself to Mr. Wilson's principle of the freedom of nationality, by which the already serious disfunction of the world economy was made worse by splitting it up into still more fragments.

Irrespective of its economic and social consequences, this principle came to be regarded as the holiest of all regulations, endowing the right of secession with sanctity, however it might relate to the existing facts of commerce, markets, resources, or the general peace of the world. In Europe, the sickness of nationalism became endemic, so that a perfectly healthy manifestation was allowed to degenerate to the very edge of continental anarchy.

Every national fragment wished independence. In the four corners created by the juncture of Yugoslavia, Bulgaria, Albania and Greece, the bloodiest of revolutionary activities went forward in the shape of a demand for a new political sovereignty, Macedonia. In Spain there were grim rumblings where little Catalonia and even the mountain country of the Basques were touched by the compulsion for freedom. Even in France, railroads were wrecked and buildings dynamited by nationalist patriots who had become suffused with the urge for a free Brittany. Yugoslavia had three separate movements for sectional independence, and little Belgium, already too small for comfort in a modern world, was compelled to face the problem of a separatist Walloon movement.

Thus, not only were many small States created which had not existed before, but sympathetic attention was turned to many other fragments, such as Slovakia, which were raising the roof to achieve their complete "independence" of the national frameworks wherein they thought they were being victimized.

All of these States, new and old, observed in the internationally recognized principle of national self-determination a secondary principle of national superiority which was their title to independent existence. They also observed that despite high sounding phrases molded into the League framework, the actual condition existing was one of intensified competition which had outreached power politics alone and was stretching its grim fingers into economics, social habits and even cultural and ideological acceptances.

Despite the fact that each State felt the need for moving toward ultimate world organization, each became increasingly hardened against the consequence, which could be nothing else than the gradual limitation of its authority over its own spaces and its final dissolution as a sovereign entity. Unavoidably, within the apparatus by which the League functioned, isolationism flowered and matured, nursed by the self-same principles which it had been thought would lead directly to international cooperation.

The architects of the League failed utterly to probe the psychology which dominated the free voting masses of the member States. They assumed that these masses would be inspired by a general world outlook instead of by national hopes, follies and appetites as heretofore. In practice, it was found that no politician, no matter how altruistic, would dare yield the material interests of his people on the altar of international pledges and assurances. The character of the independent State and the very existence of its voting lists, demanded a seeking, not a relinquishing, of advantages.

Holland could not yield its tremendously disproportionate share of world trade, or Germany the power advantage of its overdeveloped industry. England would not forego the power value of either her fleet or her equally omnipotent finance system. With the exception of Japan, the Orient was a collective industrial zero, and was intended by the nations to remain so despite its struggles to escape into the broad daylight of social and industrial freedom.

The estates of all nations, in all their dimensions except that of high politics, were shut off from each other by the highest walls they were capable of erecting.

It will be seen that the failure of the League of Nations was not that of some blunder or fiasco in reference to the material details of organization. It was due more to the fact that the very organizing principles of the League, itself, condemned it to impotence and sterility. The League was a thin façade, not a vital expression of the living authority of the times grounded in the intimate decisions of day-to-day existence. Hence, it possessed no true force, and no powers of normal self-adjustment to shifting conditions. Had the League borne the same vital relation to the needs of men as the rude beginnings of American independence, or the humble origins of the Christian Church, it would have surmounted every crisis and have found an acceptable modification for every weakness and inequality in its structure.

As it was set up, the League betrayed the most astonishing belief in the restraining power of legal abstractions, and in the ability of a collaborationist society of nations to further these ends by invoking a higher law without the use of applying force or any lessening of sovereignty in the nations affected.

The complicated framework of the League reflected all of the evils arising from coalitions and consent agreements. The League in effect represented not a superior authority but a pool of multilateral treaties which though binding in theory could not be enforced when they conflicted with the national self interests of the States concerned. What actually was set up in this structure was a diplomatic forum where the balance of power theory received a clothing of plausible language which hid somewhat its uglier features.

The attempt to join in marriage two such thoroughly incompatible concepts as total sovereignty and international law could be reconciled only by reducing certain essential elements in the League's pattern to grotesquery.

Thus, in a situation which rested primarily on a division of the member nations into contending blocs, the principle was set up that all measures coming before the League Assembly, with the exception of questions of procedure and appointment to committees, *must be passed by unanimous vote*. When to this law is added the accompanying principle which called for the preservation unimpaired of the sceptered authority of the subscriber nations, we arrive at something bordering closely on a power vacuum.

The Covenant proposals for the regulation of economic policy between member States, obligatory arbitration of disputes, and abolition of compulsory military service, failed of acceptance. To include these principles would have been an infringement upon "national sovereignty." [1]

In addition to maintaining these self-nullifying canons, the League also committed its members to political archaism in a world where rapid change was rendering all boundaries obsolete. This commitment to resist the forces of growth and change was embodied in Article X which commanded all member States "to respect and *preserve* as against external aggression the territorial integrity" of all other members.

It was agreed further that before resorting to war international disputants would try every means offered by negotiation and mediation to settle their quarrels. Action was to be completed within six months of the time the dispute was laid before the League, and no war was to take place for three months after a decision had been reached. Thus absurdity was compounded with absurdity and the very aggressive and unmoral nature of war reduced to the ponder-

[1] Felix Morley, *The Society of Nations: Its Organization and Constitutional Development*, Brookings Institute, 1932, p. 218.

ous jousting conception of the medieval lists. Obviously, this ruling would remain a dead letter wherever one contender decided to apply the universal remedy of force, which in modern wars makes it necessary to utilize the strategy of surprise as well as to mobilize the entire economy of the State for attack.

By attempting the impossible task of standing on two sides of the same fence at one and the same time, the League could do little more than erect an elaborate structure based on the pomposity of words, its powers almost entirely circumscribed by the need for acquiring the consent of the nations to be affected by its rulings.

This situation was commented on drily by the meeting of Ministers of the Pan-American Union in 1942, where it was remarked that the scope of matters concluded under the League's jurisdiction in practical application "continues to be limited so that States resorted to arbitration only for the settlement of questions of secondary interest." [1] The Ministers also concluded that instead of the League influencing the policies of the great Powers, it was more often the great Powers which influenced the policies of the League, and "prevailed over the spirit of the Covenant."

When it suited the convenience of the Powers, they did not hesitate to conclude the most important agreements outside of the League's framework. Among these were the solemn pacts of Stresa and Locarno. These were presented to the League as *faits accomplis,* though with a sanctimonious mien which invited no conflict from that body.

A similar set of conditions applies to that coordinate of the League, the Permanent Court of International Justice. Although this body was brought into existence by the unanimous action of all member States, it at no time was able to take action in any affairs affecting the privileges of nations possessing actual power.

It did hand down a number of judgments and opinions on matters which were of secondary importance, and these were recognized by

[1] *Preliminary Recommendations on Post-war Problems,* Pan-American Union, November, 1942, p. 14.

the States affected. On the whole, however, its existence and its actions, together with the diplomatic privileges and immunities solemnly accorded its judges, were a matter of polite international humbug which affected the real decisions of no Power.

II

The miscarriage of the League's function, and its inability to fulfill the role for which it was designed, often has been attributed to the failure of the United States to participate. This explanation is a misapprehension. It is unlikely that the United States would have resorted to force against members who transgressed against the Covenant, or that any moral view of ours would have affected the basic power policies pursued by the other great States.

As it was, the United States though not a member of the League, participated actively in its deliberations. With the exception of the four permanent members of the League Council, the United States was represented on more committees than any other nation.

Neither can the fundamental impotence of the League properly be ascribed to the unwieldy character of its construction. In this respect the League presented no insuperable difficulties to efficient operation. The skeletal mechanism of the League articulated well, and the allocations of authority to its executive bureaus were comparable to those existing in any well-regulated State. The League would have possessed the entire apparatus pertinent to good function had it not been caught in a trough between the practical world inhabited by its members and the lip service these States were paying to the political idea of international collaboration.

The true status of the League could be seen in the circumstances connected with the payment of dues and contributions. When member States did not feel like paying, they did not pay. This did not prevent them from remaining, and even voting on questions of the budget in which they had an interest.

The original membership of the League consisted of those Allied Powers who had signed the Treaties of Versailles, St. Germain,

Neuilly, and Trianon with Germany, Austria, Bulgaria and Hungary respectively. Other members could enter and be accepted from time to time by vote, and any member could withdraw upon two years' notice provided that "all its international obligations and all its obligations under the Covenant were fulfilled." Or a member could be expelled by the unanimous vote of the League Council.

Although actually defunct, the League officially still is in existence. A short analysis of the mechanics of its operation will be of value.

The League is ruled by two bodies, each more or less competitive with the other. One is the League Assembly on which all member States are equally represented. The Assembly controls appropriations and all matters of financial administration. Together with the Council, it elects judges to the Permanent Court of International Justice. The Assembly also elects States to membership and elects the non-permanent members of the Council.

The Council in theory is the executive body of the League. Whereas the Assembly meets but once a year, the Council meets at intervals during the year. It supervises Mandates, appoints arbiters, commissioners and others under applying treaties, names practically all advisory and expert committees, acts as an arbitration body in inter-State disputes, and with the approval of the Assembly appoints the all-powerful Secretary General.

On this all-important body there are six seats permanently allocated to the great Powers, and eleven others elected by the Assembly and rotated among the smaller Powers. The permanent administrative works, similar to the Civil Service existing in the national governments, is undertaken by the Secretariat which in theory carries out the plans and determinations of the Council.

The Secretariat is an international governing bureaucracy in miniature, though without the requisite authority. Before World War II, it employed almost seven hundred people including the usual career civil servants and diplomats, who enjoyed the distinction of diplomatic privilege and immunity.

Executive functions theoretically exist in the Council but in most cases they originate with the Secretariat and are approved by the Council *ex-post facto*.

The Secretariat keeps all archives and does the publishing of all records, and is responsible for much of the technical work of the League. Most of the year it is left on its own resources without check or control. It handles the details of conferences and can exercise powers of decision merely through handling the order of the agenda, or by the selection of the chairman for a meeting.

Because of the infrequent meetings of the Council and Assembly, the Secretary General possesses great freedom of action and decision. Under Article II of the Covenant, he may summon the Council in case war threatens or on the request of any one of the fifty-five League members. His authority to act, though subject to review, is as wide as the powers exercised by the executive rulers in a modern semi-authoritarian State. The entire machinery of operation is in his hands. With the support of any single member he can create commissions of inquiry in reference to disputes. He has jurisdiction over the International Labor Organization, and is substantially unregulated. He may be ousted by unanimous vote of the Council, an action which also must be approved by the Assembly. For practical purposes this is an impossibility.

Noting that the Secretary General is subject to neither recall, impeachment or dismissal, Morley comments that "in the wrong hands in a League which had firmly established supernational powers, the unlimited authority of the Secretary General might become a most tremendous problem." [1]

All told, sixty-three nations have belonged to the League. The only countries abstaining from membership have been Saudi Arabia and the United States. The United States, however, consistently has cooperated through unofficial observers, or through such correlated bodies as the International Labor Organization, in which Americans have been especially prominent.

Though structurally incapable of fulfilling the mission for which

[1] Felix Morley, *The Society of Nations: Its Organization and Constitutional Development*, p. 314.

it was created, the League has performed a certain amount of useful work. Its greatest triumphs were in connection with the petitions
of small nations who did not dare move without the consent of the
great Powers.

It settled such disputes as that between Albania, Yugoslavia and
Greece, in 1921. It managed the Saar plebiscite and appointed the
high commissioners for Danzig and Memel. It has directed operations which the Powers regarded as intrinsically harmless, such as
disarmament conferences, committees on intellectual cooperation,
on general health, and on the refugee question.

The League was found additionally useful by the larger States as
a sounding board through which they could express policies for
which they did not wish to assume individual responsibility. This
was memorably the case in the British-inspired demand for sanctions
against Italy as punishment for her piratical aggression against
Ethiopia, where Britain had important interests—a subject to which
we shall shortly return.

In this case as in others, it all depended on whose ox was gored.
When Britain acted to contravene the terms of the Palestine Mandate and turn that little country into a puppet Arab preserve because it suited her interests to do so, the protest of the League's Mandates Commission denouncing this policy as one of "turning the
Mandate upside down" was coolly ignored.

Even the smaller nations flouted the League with impunity. This
was flagrantly noticeable in the handling of the "minority clauses"
by the countries concerned. These clauses had been inserted into
the treaties which gave birth to certain States, such as Poland,
Rumania, Czechoslovakia, Yugoslavia and Hungary. A representative instance is contained in the instrument signed June 28, 1919,
in which Poland guaranteed to all of its inhabitants complete equality before the law, and the right to use their own culture or mother
language in any district where a minority constituted a considerable part of the population. Poland recognized the obligation of
these clauses as "fundamental laws" which were not to be altered by

any subsequent legislation or administration, and which could be changed only by the consent of a majority of the League Council.

Nevertheless we find Poland adopting a rigid policy of repression toward its minorities. Jews were beaten and massacred and subjected to one of the most vindictive regimes Europe has ever witnessed prior to the Nazis. The Ukrainian, White Russian and Lithuanian blocs were made the objects of the crushing police power of the State in an effort to Polanize them by force. Poland thus placed more than two-fifths of its population under subjection, irrespective of the sacred promises to which she was sealed by the identical League of Nations which guaranteed her own independence.

In every case except that of Czechoslovakia these clauses were considered a dead letter and the minorities relentlessly suppressed. It was obvious that these clauses could be enforced only by direct armed intervention on the part of the other Powers, just as it was equally clear that any effort to supervise the treatment of minorities was an infringement on the sovereignty of the States concerned.

III

In considering the possibilities of an international society of free States operating without an authoritarian center capable of wielding police power, it is useful to review the relation of the League to the four international incidents which led in progression to the present conflict. These were the attack by the Japanese militarists on China beginning in 1931, the assault by Italy on Ethiopia in 1935, the Fascist invasion of Spain in 1936, and the initial flaunting of treaty restrictions by Germany's newly elected Hitler government in 1934.

The first of these major aggressions, which paved the way for the others, was the Japanese attack on Manchukuo. This vicious assault on a friendly government had been carefully planned and was put into effect with clockwork precision.

Contrary to treaty agreement, the Japanese Government had

maintained a full division of troops in the South Manchukuo Railway region in addition to numerous police and secret service operators. As a result of the presence of these functionaries, the adjoining Chinese areas were in a state of continuous disorder, punctuated by acts of violence against Chinese police and civilians. Japanese troops even practised mock warfare in the streets of Peiping, Tientsin and Shanghai, suspending business and communications for whole days.

When they were ready the Japanese used as a pretext an incident provoked by themselves, and marched in.

Secretary of State Stimson, acting for the Government of the United States, at once proposed to Great Britain that the Nine Power Treaty and the Kellogg-Briand Pact be invoked. This the British Government refused to do, but finally introduced into the Assembly of the League of Nations a resolution which called on the members of the League "not to recognize any situation, treaty or agreement which may be brought about by means contrary to the Covenant of the League of Nations, or to the Pact of Paris."

Instead of desisting from their operations, the Japanese spilled over the Manchukuoan frontier and occupied the border provinces of North China.

In the meanwhile, the League dutifully had been investigating the situation through the Lytton Commission which had been ordered to make an investigation. When the Lytton Commission reported the Japanese military operations in Manchukuo as a piece of inexcusable naked aggression in violation of all existing covenants, the Japanese delegation promptly walked out of the Assembly and announced its intention of withdrawing from the League.

When the Chinese proposed punitive sanctions, the British Foreign Secretary, Sir John Simon, bluntly opposed the demand as unjustified. This otherwise incomprehensible course arose from a violent inner hostility against the Russian Communists whom the British Civil Service, and Foreign Office in particular, regarded as the real enemy. They considered Japan as the policeman of the Far East who was entitled to an occasional free apple. They understood that the ultimate assault was to be on the U.S.S.R. and was to consist of an incursion over the Siberian border from the Manchukuoan plains, cutting the Trans-Siberian Railway and with it all contact between the Russian Soviets and the great body of Chinese Communists in the Northwest.

The opposition of Great Britain to any embroilment with Japan made action impossible and left the League declaration a mere piece of harmless palaver, allowing the Japs to continue their course of conquest on the Asiatic mainland uninterrupted.

The second unprovoked assault on a weaker nation was that of Italy against the defenseless Ethiopians. It again concerned Great Britain as the principal Power of the League.

Whoever held Ethiopia would be able to divert the headwaters of the Nile, which rose in Lake Tana in the upland region, and would be in a position to threaten the prosperity of Egypt. It was obvious that the question of Ethiopian sovereignty had become a matter of immediate and deep significance to the British Government.

Until the time of the Ethiopian incident, Italy had been looked on by British officials much in the same light as Portugal, as a friendly and perhaps satellite government. The Italian type of authoritarian government was viewed with approval by those real powers in British politics, the bureaus of Westminster and Whitehall. The early infiltrations into Abyssinia were made with the knowledge of the British Foreign Office and with the tacit approval of both London and Paris. On this point, it was charged by the Abyssinian delegate to the League, Tecle-Hawariate, that Sir John Simon and M. Joseph Avenol, the Secretary General of the League, had dumped Abyssinia's formal appeal into the wastebasket.

When the extent of the Fascist dictator's schemes and their dangerous implications to British power in the Mediterranean burst on the minds of the younger and shrewder officials in London, an appeal hurriedly was made to the League for the introduction of sanctions against Italy as an aggressor, and breaker of international law.

Speaking for Great Britain, Anthony Eden made a passionate plea before the League Assembly, demanding that the rule of force forever be abandoned, and that the League's principles be sustained. He was backed by Maxim Litvinov, the Soviet Foreign Commissar, to whom this was a decisive opportunity to test the future of European collaborationist principles. Nevertheless, Article XVI of the Covenant which demanded collective punitive action against aggressors, was ignored. Such sanctions as were applied by the various countries were entirely half-hearted and plainly in the way of a face-saving gesture. Even the United States, which was cooperating with the League, lumped Ethiopia and Italy together as common belligerents in refusing to sell certain products which could be useful as war materials.

Faced with this absolute test of principle, each nation decided to look out for itself, and though condemning the aggression in theory, continued to maintain proper relations with the aggressor.

It was clear that Italy had won a decisive diplomatic victory and would not be stopped from the lawless course it had set for itself. It additionally became apparent to the horrified British that Mussolini might be able to set Britain's historic sea control to naught and succeed in driving Britain out of the Mediterranean by the use of warplanes.

Totally ignoring her previous expressions on the subject of collective security, England suddenly revised her attitude. At the Stresa Conference, held outside the League's jurisdiction and attended by the principal Powers, the British Prime Minister, Ramsay Macdonald, treated the Abyssinian question as non-existent and neglected to mention it altogether.

A month later the Italian delegate to the League was offered the concession of special rights in Ethiopia by Anthony Eden, irrespective of the fact that the League in response to the British petition formally had declared Italy to be an open lawbreaker, and had recommended disciplinary action against her.

Thus this melancholy business went through its destined cycle of moves, all based on the application of unrestricted force to politics, and all under cover of the League's Covenant to keep the peace. On September 11, 1935, Sir Samuel Hoare had told the League for Britain that London stood ready for "collective resistance to all acts of unprovoked aggression." Acting on this demand, the Council of the League had found Italy guilty of violating the Covenant. A month later Hoare and the then French Premier, Pierre Laval, concluded a deal in Paris whereby Mussolini was to be given half of Ethiopia, an affair which caused such a wave of indignation throughout England as to force Hoare's resignation.

In the final act of this drama, sanctions were altogether abandoned. Eden went to Geneva where he endeavored unsuccessfully by parliamentary devices to prevent the Ethiopian Negus from making a plea in person to the listening nations. Despite these tragic circumstances, the Ethiopian ruler delivered his address, speaking with characteristic courage and dignity. His plea fell on deaf ears.

The League at last was rescued from its dilemma when it was able to declare the Government of Ethiopia non-existent and to assert that all resistance had ceased, and that there were no further armies in the field. The question, therefore, was settled by default, a matter considerably facilitated by the unaccountable loss of a telegram to the League from the Government of Ethiopia declaring itself still to be functioning and in armed opposition to the invaders. This message which had been routed through British Somaliland never reached its destination.

The whole affair came to an end with the Anglo-Italian Accord of April 16, 1938, where the Italian conquest of Ethiopia was formally recognized by the British Government.

When Hitler came to power in Germany as the result of an announced campaign to shatter European peace, the League and its members again followed the familiar channels of inaction. Hitler depended for his opportunities on a realistic appraisal of the European power balance. The real equilibrium, he surmised correctly, was not that contained in the noble phraseology of the Covenant, but rather that created by England's distrust of France as the major military Power of the Continent, and by her intractable fear of the U.S.S.R. and its social program.

Hitler concluded that despite the League, British policy not only would sanction but quietly welcome the introduction of a counter-weight to French power in Europe, and would regard with approval the creation of a new military establishment capable of challenging further Soviet extension to the West.

The German *Fuehrer* had risen to power with the indirect assistance of powerful reactionary British groups. Industrial giants such as Henri Deterding, head of the vast Shell Oil combine, and the immensely wealthy Guinness family, are said to have contributed heavily to the Nazi war chest. Lord Rothermere's influential *Daily Mail* did not hesitate to describe the German *Fuehrer* in terms of distinguished leadership. The *London Times* which was the unofficial mouthpiece of the Government, was strongly pro-German. Within the Government influential Bourbon politicians such as Simon, Hoare, Baldwin, and Chamberlain sought to halt the hand of time by espousing any reaction which promised to stop the flood of revolutionary change which threatened to swallow the world. They tended to regard the presence of Hitler and his gang as an act of Providence which should be assisted by the hand of man. It was their hope that a strong Germany would destroy the Russian bear, but emerge from the battle too weak to be of further menace.

Shortly after Hitler had been appointed Chancellor of the Reich, a plebiscite was held in the Saar Valley to determine whether that district was to go to France or Germany. Following the well-developed technique which later they were to apply in Danzig, the Sudetenland and elsewhere, Nazi hoodlums were organizing the vote by terror methods despite the presence of a British Commissioner appointed by the League. When the irked French consequently declared their determination to supervise the election with French troops, London let it be known that it would regard such a policy as counter to British interests. The election turned into an unopposed Nazi triumph.

On March 16, 1935, three months after the Reichswehr had paraded into the Saar as its new master, Hitler issued a bold proclamation repudiating the restraining clauses in the Versailles Treaty and reintroducing conscription. The French immediately made formal complaint to the League. Instead of acting in concurrence, Sir John Simon went to Berlin to confer with Hitler. Shortly thereafter Great Britain and Germany announced an agreement between them which amounted to a unilateral breach of the Versailles Treaty and had the effect of bringing that document down in a mass of ruins. The new compact allowed Germany to reconstruct her navy to within thirty-five per cent of that of Great Britain, and to build an air force. The angry French had not been consulted. Indeed, they were not even allowed to know the details on the plea that the agreement was a privileged one.

When Hitler invaded the Rhineland and remilitarized it in defiance of all treaty obligations, the anxious French urged that Allied troops be sent at once to force the Germans back. Again it was Britain which threw its weight against this action, compelling the reluctant French to remain inactive.

Faced with these humiliations, the League's Council passed a weak resolution deprecating German conduct, but proposed no concrete steps. An effort was made further to censure the Germans in the course of a Disarmament Conference, at which Hitler abruptly left the League, to which Germany had been admitted in 1926.

Hitler now was openly rearming on a total scale though continuing to assuage the British by his declarations of eternal friendship.

The arrogance of the Nazis and their complete indifference to pledges, began at this point to make it clear to a large section of British leadership that German military strength not only had become a counterweight to the French, but was rapidly outbalancing it. Many like Winston Churchill expressed the conviction that Britain had allowed the development of a Frankenstein in its backyard, and that Nazi Germany was becoming a greater menace than the Communist monster with whom it had been confidently expected to lock horns in a death struggle.

In all of this, the League sat supinely by. As the crisis began to become acute, the real masters of Europe emerged from behind the League's façade and no longer even bothered with the cumbersome pretense this cover had involved.

By October 1936, London was startled to discover that Italy and Germany had managed to patch up the differences arising over Hitler's ambitions toward Austria, and were now presenting a solid front. The same year brought to a head the existing pathologies which had distinguished the relationship between Right and Left in Europe. This was the so-called Civil War in Spain which the Fascist Powers now used as the battleground to test their theories of conquest.

The action started as an internal struggle by Spain to throw off the chains of the feudal order which had kept her mired so long in ignorance, backwardness and poverty. A general election in 1936 had brought crushing defeat to the combined monarchists, clericals, great landowners, and the clique of reactionary army officers. A republican government sat in the saddle firmly supported by the great bulk of the population.

On July 17, 1936, an army junta headed by General Francisco Franco invaded Spain from Morocco with troops consisting almost altogether of Moors and Foreign Legionnaires. These, together with their equipment, were ferried over to Spain by airplanes, which were soon shown to belong to the army of Italy.

At this point the League seems to have fallen apart completely, making no pretense to genuine powers which might be expected to influence the course of events. France was in the hands of a weak Socialist coalition headed by Leon Blum. Blum was at one and the same time attempting to assuage British suspicions in regard to his government, placate Herr Hitler, to whom he ignominiously referred in a message as "that distinguished front line fighter," and to prevent civil conflict from breaking out between the violent factions contending for power within his own country.

Without the support of Britain, Blum regarded himself as being in an impossible fix as far as any external adventure was concerned. This support Britain was resolved never to give, convinced more than ever that the true danger was a radical Leftist, Russo-French alliance joined by the nations of the Little Entente of Central and Eastern Europe.

When the Germans and Italians without effort at disguise, threw whole corps of men into the Spanish contest, the harassed French Government hurriedly announced its intention not to intervene in any manner in the "internal conflict in Spain."

London took a view from the beginning as if this were a struggle between equal belligerents who must be given an identical recognition, and not an invasion of a peaceful country by warlike Powers who must be quarantined forthwith, under the Covenant. English diplomacy was abetted in this conviction by the appearance of Russian planes and pilots on the Spanish battlefields as well as a pro-Government Brigade of International Volunteers.

London accepted the view that this was a struggle between the forces of Communism and those of a stable society. English diplomacy hence actively aided the cause of the rebels, as much by acts of omission as by any overt dealings. The English forbade fighting in Gibraltar harbor, thus blocking off the Spanish Government from attacking the rebels in their stronghold at Morocco. England's satellite, Fascist Portugal, was encouraged to adopt a rigid anti-Loyalist course.

Disregarding the League entirely, Britain in September 1936, called a Non-Intervention Conference of twenty-six States. At this conference, Portugal through which most rebel supplies were being imported, was noticeably absent.

The result of these activities was to prevent the legally constituted government of Spain from buying military supplies anywhere, isolating it from the world and placing it at the mercy of the Fascist Powers, who continued to pour into Spain a flood of mechanized troops and their equipment.

Thus the countries on whom the League depended altogether for its power, adjusted themselves to the strange moral principle by which one member, the recognized Government of Spain, was given a status equal in theory to that of a group of rebels. In practical application the position of the Government of Spain was the inferior one. Led by Great Britain, the mainstay of the League, the course adopted by the nations amounted to a grant of direct aid to the rebel cause by Germany, Italy and Portugal, and indirect assistance by the other Powers. In Lisbon, *Fortune* remarked caustically, "They were saying that the British were so neutral they didn't care whether Madrid was captured by the Carlists, by the Monarchists, by the Fascists or the Moors . . ." [1]

Even the United States participated in this tragic destruction of a new democracy which was bravely fighting for its life. When a delegation of American congressmen demanded of Secretary Hull that he apply the Neutrality Act to Germany and Italy because of their participation in the Spanish fighting, Mr. Hull is reported to have replied: "No, no, we can't do that. We must not do anything to offend Hitler at this moment." [2]

Frightened, but resolute as it watched this impenetrable wall of enemies close in on it, the Spanish Government desperately petitioned the League. It appealed to the democracies whose support gave the League whatever strength it possessed.

It was of no avail.

In March 1939, after almost three years of bitter fighting, the Republic came to an end. Germany is estimated to have contributed to the victorious rebels some fifteen thousand trained technicians, pilots and ground troops. According to *Forze Armate,* an official publication of the Italian armed forces, Italy had transported to Spain one hundred thousand troops together with an air force of more than six thousand men and extensive quantities of tanks, cannon, planes, munitions and other materials. Portugal, according to the Portuguese press, had provided ten thousand men. [3]

The stage was now set for still further adventures, shattering beyond any possible recognition the idea of collective security. Austria was taken by a sudden forced march. Czechoslovakia was dismembered and then swallowed. Little Albania was pounced upon.

In this final moment of disaster, the Society of Nations uttered no Jeremiad of protest. There was no indication of that unyielding

1 Issue of March, 1937, p. 154.
2 Robert Bendiner, *The Riddle of the State Department*, p. 58.
3 "Civil War in Spain," *Britannica Book of the Year, 1940,* p. 624.

probity and honor which had allowed the Spanish Government to struggle on to the end. The League simply looked the other way and pretended that it did not see. The Covenant was now as dead as the great auk, and the much feared general war became inevitable.

The experience of the League proved that the abstract concept of law removed from an apparatus capable of enforcing it, could not be made to apply in the mutual relations of States, and that wherever the authority of law applies, it does so only by the intercession of some recognized political machinery which in essence possesses the superior sovereignty.

XV

ORGANIZING UTOPIA

VARIOUS types of machinery have been proposed to remedy the glaring flaws exposed by the crumbling structure of the League of Nations, and to create in one manner or another an ideal international community.

These range from the mild scheme presented by Prinz Hubertus zu Loewenstein for a world-wide system of internationally subsidized universities for the purpose of training international leaders, to the outright demand for the dissolution of all political boundaries and the formation of a single world super-State.

The doctrinaire enthusiasts who think in terms of a world super-order are few, but they are also uncompromising. They look with justified horror at the terrifying problems which would accompany an attempted return to the *status quo ante*. Their proposals rest on the conviction that no plan for curing the deep-rooted ills of the world can be successful unless it is handled on an international scale and reduced to single points of control. They are in favor of liquidating all the difficulties and conflicts of the present order by one swing of the meat ax. Social and political evils which have existed since the dawn of Western culture are to be pounced upon, uprooted and cast out. Man who is inherently impure and imperfect, is to be made pure.

The means by which this is to be accomplished vary greatly. Some involve educational schemes for molding the mind of the growing youth. Others are auxiliary to plenary doctrines which would hammer the existing world economy into strange and unrecognizable shapes. A few call for the early creation of a total world State directed by a single world authority. Others recognizing the difficulties in bridging the wide gap which separates our present-day world from the millennium, outline variants of the old plan for a free association of independent nations.

Whether based on the principles of voluntary association or on actual coalescence into a single world unit, almost all of these plans suggest the use of force to intimidate would-be violators of the peace and to punish those who break faith with the mutually-held covenant. If any party to the scheme does not comport himself according to the rules, as they may from time to time be laid down, he is to be expeditiously ruined by sanctions, or is to be bashed out of existence by direct and concerted military measures.

That this would involve a complete liquidation of social forms and complex historical attitudes, and would at some point be stoutly resisted, is nowhere recognized by the authors. Nor is it recognized that the habit of confederation is to proceed by inexorable automatism to federation, while federation itself moves invariably forward toward a continually greater concentration of powers within the central authority.

The contention is that the primary defect of the League of Nations was its lack of physical power with which to enforce its decisions. Hence the argument is that if an international union is to keep the peace, it must be in possession of a police force of its own. This police body would be used against any aggressor who dared to challenge the orderly processes of international law.

The right of any nation to take the law into its own hands no longer would be an attribute of sovereignty. Only the community of nations acting through a centrally held militia would have the right to use force for any purpose whatsoever, including that of resisting aggression.

This international guard, while presumably possessing its own foot soldiers, artillery and navy, would rely largely on its air units, which would garrison internationally held bases at various strategic points. These stations, manifestly, would be located at such world crossroads as Pernambuco, Dakar, Hawaii, Singapore, Aden and Miami. The States concerned thus would find themselves with their key defense areas removed from their own jurisdiction through the establishment of what presumably would be international military zones.

The questions which rise to mind are these: Who is to control the manufacture of the heavy armament on which all modern police power is based? Who will control the police force itself? Who will give it its orders? Who will determine what constitutes an infraction of the law requiring the intervention of armed punitive power?

Such a force could be effective only if it were stronger than any combination of forces which possibly could be brought up against it, and would depend for its effectiveness on its ability to act swiftly and relentlessly against any State which broke the peace. A militia equipped with such powers would not be an instrument of law but of sovereignty.

The history of the world has been the history of the usurpation of power, and it may be relied on as a certainty that the moment the international militia was established, a conspiratorial struggle would go forward among the nations in an effort to control it.

The terminal result of such a project could be nothing else than the erection of a world super-State. With the surrender of their arms by the nations to the central super-authority there would come into existence a new Praetorian Guard, which like the Ottoman Janissaries and Saladin's Mamelukes, would contend for power, and perhaps establish itself as a ruling caste.

In a world inhabited by conflicting social systems and jealous, conflicting nations, whatever States gained control of the armed guard would be sure to find massed against them a coalition of the others. The war which would ensue would differ in no important sense from any other global struggle and would likely proceed from more or less the same causes.

If any reasonable amount of democratic procedure were observed in such a union, the force of events would continually conspire to place the real power not in the hands of theorists and philosophers, but in the proletarian masses. It is they who would have to be appeased and kept within bounds, and in the last analysis it is they who would wield the final and decisive influence.

The plain inference of these facts is that if we are to have an international society, it eventually will become a polyglot society, and that a new social order and new race of men would be the end consequence of this step.

When we discuss these matters of world federation, world police, and world government, we should be aware of the issues involved and the presumptions they contain. World unity means among other things, the right of men of all races to move about the earth just as this right now exists within the various provinces of the State itself. If one hundred million Chinese or Indians decided to move into the Amazon River Valley or to the West Coast of the United States, they could do so. The limitations now placed on them would be dissolved. They would demand and receive the same rights of global movement now pre-empted by the white man alone.

There are many barriers to world federation including those of vested interests, religion, social ideals, and political views. While these might be difficult to surmount they represent situations which time could be relied on to overcome. It is the question of race which is the true stumbling block on the path to world federation. All other barriers, whether of vested interests, social ideals or religious and political views, can be surmounted, requiring only the exertion of the proper force, and the healing hand of time.

It can be argued that the establishment of a world federation is merely doing on a large scale what already has been successfully accomplished on a small one. It can be pointed out that wars no longer are fought between Castille and Granada, or Languedoc and Brittany. Whatever the differences in local customs or even in language, Navarre today is Spain, Castille and the Asturias are Spain; the hot, dark blood of Andalusia is as much Spain as the mountain strongholds and foothills of the mysterious Basques.

There can be advanced also the example of the five Swiss cantons, and the pooling of interests which created the American nation out of the original thirteen members.

In each of these cases, however, the community of interests either existed before it was affirmed by law, or was forced at the point of the sword. In the case of the American and Swiss unions, the interdependence of the joined parts already existed, and the writing of articles of federation merely gave sanction to what was a *de facto* condition.

The internal quiet of States embodying dissimilar population elements is not attributable to the presence of a firm central authority alone, but rather to the interdependence of the various areas on the plateau of mutual acceptances and material well-being. The binding agent might be economics, geographical position, language, religion, or social beliefs. Whatever it might be, under its influence the fundamental interests of all strata of the State's inhabitants cease to be sectional and become national. That this process is not due alone to the holding of police power by some central hand is observable in the revolutionary ferment which has taken Ireland out of the orbit of the British Empire, and keeps Catalonia a sore spot in Spanish politics.

The concentration on the subject of "International Law" has become a sort of fetishism among many political thinkers, who fail to see that whatever part law may play in the relations of individuals to the State, it plays no such role in the relations of States to each other. The analogy usually drawn with the unchallenged authority enjoyed by the law courts, is not an altogether sound one. The morality of nations cannot be judged as if it represented an enlarged counterpart of the individual civic responsibility of law-abiding citizens subject to the overwhelming punitive power of the State.

Under normal circumstances individual citizens possess neither authority nor arms and have little choice but to submit to arrest and trial. This is not true of a nation, which has all the resources of power at its disposal.

Even the premise which would allow access by all countries to raw materials and markets, assumes a diminished sovereignty on the part of each State over its own space. Such a proposition is an impossibility as long as the State continues to exist, since, contrary to the individual, the State is an intrinsic power form which can exist only as it is free to exercise the unrestricted franchise of self-rule and is responsible to no higher authority. As long as the individual State retains jurisdiction over its own territories it will be able to determine, without reference to the welfare of the international community, policies connected with trade, tariffs, currency, immigration and labor, and its leaders will endeavor to exact the most from whatever bargaining position in which they may find themselves.

Professor Borchard points out that the major sources of international irritation involve no question of legal right or wrong, and that acting entirely within its legal rights, one State may inflict the greatest possible damage upon others.[1] As long as the causes of international conflict rest on an uneven division of the world's wealth, or marked differences in physical position, resources and population, the real provocations to war will remain untouched, and all that will be outlawed will be the resulting symptoms.

Wherever international law ran contrary to the stream of public opinion in each country it would be considered unreal and pedantic, and a means would be found to contravene it. Modern government cannot survive hostile public opinion and where favorable opinion cannot be created for governmental acts through propaganda or other ways, the government has no choice but to revise its policies.

As long as the system of independent States exists, the reigning interests of each nation would prove to be the decisive factor in international relations, since it is only the power, safety and prosperity of the State that its citizens possibly can be interested in, or that its politicians may seek if they are to maintain themselves in power. By the mere act of maintaining armies, navies and batteries of diplomats, or by the control of currency or the use of trade restrictions, each independent nation serves notice that it will seek to gain its

[1] Professor Edwin Borchard, *American Journal of International Law*, January 1943.

ends, in the last analysis, by the use or the continued threat of force.

Any system of true international collaboration would have to curb the powers of the existing States, who otherwise would enter the arrangement as so many unlicked cubs, whose views toward their essential prerogatives remained as unregenerate as ever.

Once these boundaries of power were destroyed in any sphere, social, political or economic, the sovereignty of the State would be impaired to that degree. Whether what followed would be a Pax-Romana under the thumb of the most powerful party to the arrangement, or an idyllic association of free peoples, would be determined by a course of events overwhelmingly weighed against the latter possibility.

It is necessary to go no further than the question of population movement for an irrefragable example. Thinly populated countries with vast surpluses of cropland would find themselves under mounting pressure from the Orient, which they would be sure to resist to the degree their possession of sovereignty over their own spaces allowed.

The claimant nations, in addition to their own pressing needs would have on their side the logic of international welfare, which could not fail to look on the exploitation of unused territories as a measure for the common good. In their corner, too, would be the moral equities, and what is even more important, a considerable proportion of the policing power. If the United States were one of the nations concerned, and if the World Organization were able to enforce its opinions contrary to the wishes of this country, the effect would be to reduce the President of the United States and the Congress to the status of a provincial governor and his assembly.

A contest would ensue as to the legitimacy of the orders of the Central World Authority wherever they ran contrary to established American views. If the loyalty of the people of the United States was to country rather than to World Organization, or was conditioned by prejudice and self-interest rather than the welfare of the least of the States, the World Union immediately would find itself bankrupt. The United States would be forced by its own public opinion to withdraw and if balked, to offer resistance.

A strong, enduring World Union quite evidently would require a shift of basic loyalties from the conventional State to the World Community. Neither racialism, politics, nor economics could fix separating boundaries, since the Union could be only as strong as the allegiance of its individual members permitted.

Though there exists a genuine craving for some kind of world order by which the nations can be regulated against their own lawless propensities, humanity is far from ready to pay the price demanded by such an order.

Even were a universal political system possible, it must be accounted to possess highly undesirable features. Competitive spirit which ran counter to the interests of constituted authority would be instantly repressed as is the case in Russia or Germany. Political experiment by which the world is kept resilient and prevented from freezing into a spiritless and all-powerful matrix, would be practically ended. That historic haven for the noble and dissident mind, the place of sanctuary where the long hand of retaliation for political crime may be stayed, would disappear.

The trend toward everincreasing centralization must be recognized as a tendency toward repression and toward the decay of the human spirit, where the free individual finally will be confined by the robot mass and imprisoned by the limitations of a purely mechanistic society.

II

Many of the proposals which have received serious consideration involve the establishment of either a single house of parliament, or of a congress patterned after that of the United States. Winston Churchill has advocated a postwar "world organization" armed with "overwhelming military power" to keep the peace, but has been silent as to the details. The United States Government favors an international security organization built around "a council" annually elected by the nations, which would operate in conjunction with an International Court of Justice, but be "without a militia and other paraphernalia of coercive power." This is the plan which is receiving the most serious consideration currently. It amounts to an uneasy alliance of the victors, each of whom is to police his own quarter of the globe. No itemized account has yet been given of this proposal, which would appear to be the old balance of power scheme in a new dress, and blown to global proportions.

Among the projects which have had public discussion, the best known is the plan advanced by the former Governor of Minnesota, Harold E. Stassen. It proposes a single parliament on a membership basis computed from the number of literate citizens of the member States, their resources and the amounts contributed by them to the expenses of the joint government.

This body would elect a chairman who would appoint a council of seven members which would be the executive branch of the United Nations Government.

The function of this authority though supposedly limited, would be potentially of unlimited power since it would administer the international airports, regulate the airways and direct interstate commerce, shipping and other business of global dimensions. Its ultimate influence is guaranteed by the fact that it would have at its disposal a United Nations army to enforce its decisions.

Another project which has attracted wide attention is that proposed by Clarence Streit. This would restrict membership in the World Union to democracies only, that is to those States which guaranteed to their citizens the Union's Bill of Rights.

Under Mr. Streit's plan there would be a House of Deputies in which would sit one representative for every half million or million population; and a Senate with two representatives for every country of twenty-five million or less, two additional Senators for every added twenty-five or fifty million. There would be an Executive Board of five persons, one selected by the House, one by the Senate and three by popular vote. This Board would appoint the Premier, name judges, run the International Army and be able to dissolve the legislative branch.

While it is planned that the Union is to operate within narrow limits so as not to encroach on the suzerain rights which the constituent States will reserve for themselves, it will be able to raise its troops directly, without reference to the States, and may tax their citizens.[1]

It cannot fail to be noticed that on democratic grounds the Western nations would be outvoted by the great masses of Eastern Asia, who would not fail to combine against the presumptions of the white man.

If it is contemplated that the repugnancies existing between revolutionary States, conventional States and archaic States are to be reconciled in a common world order on the basis of an International Bill of Rights, the franchise would have to be limited on a racial basis so that it would not apply in India and other territories under British jurisdiction. To do otherwise would be to blow up the British Empire and place the majority voting power of the Union overwhelmingly in the possession of the dark peoples. The same principle would exist with reference to other nations such as France, Portugal and Belgium, which hold colonies whose populations far outnumber those of the mother country.

Modifications of these proposals have been suggested in the direction of regional federations, or of an international society composed of loosely organized blocs of nations. It is argued that in this way an authentic community of interests would be assured, and the much desired larger groupings brought about.

This compromise would appear to suffer from almost every evil of the two shores it seeks to span, without possessing the advantages of either.

[1] Mr. Streit subsequently modified his plan to one favoring the amalgamation of the United States and the British Empire as the first step in the historic process he proposes. This measure would appear to involve the creation of opposing and hostile coalitions among other Powers who would feel themselves menaced.

One of these schemes was to take the form of a *Katholische Federation der Donaustaaten,* or Catholic Federation of Danube States. Another was a projected Confederation of East European States. Still another, a Federation of Balkan Nations.

For a while these plans seemed far advanced. President Eduard Beneš of Czechoslovakia announced in January 1942, an agreement with Poland looking to this end. At about the same time the Greeks and Yugoslavs came to an arrangement as the first move in establishing a similar federation in Southeastern Europe.

After the Soviet Union discovered the strength of its own armies, Moscow began to speak up in frank resistance to these plans, regarding them in the nature of springboards for launching new reactionary attacks against the Soviets. This fact in itself was sufficient to capsize the regional blocs since no possible world order can be envisaged without the cooperation of the U.S.S.R.

The proposed blocs contain all the old weaknesses which characterized the functioning of the League of Nations, with a few new ones added for good measure. Within each of these associations the old national sovereignties are to persist with only slight modification in the way of common agreements on economics, finance and defense policies. No political or military union in the sense of a complete pooling of interests is contemplated. As far as military and foreign policies are concerned, the arrangement would be one of consultation rather than compulsory common action. It is hoped that unity could be secured on the questions of tariff and currency, and in those economic matters which affected the region generally.

Within the apparatus provided by the blocs, a desperate battle would go forward for control, in which the larger and more powerful States would find the smaller lined up in coalitions against them. The explosive dynamisms thus engendered unfailingly would be communicated to the external relations of the blocs themselves, representing a wide field for disruptive propaganda and undercover conspiracies on the part of aggressive outside Powers. Forewarning of this may be seen in the crumbling internal relations of the Yugoslav State, terminating in the Nazi-inspired secession of Croatia, or of the similar experience of the Czechoslovak State with its component part, Slovakia.

It should be noted that the countries which would compose the blocs, though neighbors, do not necessarily possess common interests, nor do they necessarily complement each other in the raw materials and markets fundamental to their prosperity. A bloc composed of the Balkan nations would be without a metallurgical industry for lack of coal, and would possess no compensating prospects of hydroelectric power. The member States moreover would compete with each other on almost exactly the same type of exports, the great bulk of them derived from agriculture.

The whole concept would appear to represent the worst of improvisations, creating blocs of unequal power, not self-contained in relation to their own resources, and in which the constituent parts remained more or less autonomous. Whether within or without the apparatus of international organization, the weaker blocs could not fail to succumb to the economic and political pressures exerted on them by strong outside forces who would quarrel among themselves over the prey.

The varying degrees of strength and weakness presented by the blocs in relation to each other would make it mandatory that they pyramid themselves into a collective system for world security if any part of this proposition were to have the slightest value. This would appear to bring back to life the same old paraphernalia which time has discredited, the World Court and the machinery for arbitration, as well as the projected international military elements which are to enforce the will of the Central Authority.

The most elaborate of these plans and the one which epitomizes much of the current thinking on this subject, is that offered by Ely Culbertson. This proposal would create eleven regional federations out of the present seven score independent members of the society of nations.

The nations composing these regional groups would be "held loosely together by a regional government modeled after that of the world federation." Any State would be free to join or not, or it might join any neighboring federation.

The Dutch East Indies would remain under Netherlands sovereignty and Indo-China under French sovereignty. The Japanese islands are paid the compliment of being a complete federation in themselves, and Japan is left stranded with its large industry, without access to raw materials or markets. The United Kingdom and the British Dominions, an anachronism in terms of either sound economics or military logic in the world of tomorrow, are to be another federation.

There are to be three governmental branches, the executive, legislative and judiciary. A World President is chosen from each Regional Federation in turn, while each of the eleven Regional Federations provides a single World Trustee. There is also to be a World Supreme Court to interpret the Federation's constitution, and a World Court of Equity to deal with economic or territorial disputes between the nations.

Except for the trimmings, this plan does not differ materially from the world-wide multilateral, anti-war pact proposed by the French Foreign Minister, Aristide Briand, in 1927. This was solemnly ratified by forty-five nations, including all of those now at war. Article I of the treaty starts with the forthright pledge that "The High Contracting Parties solemnly declare, in the names of their respective peoples, that they condemn recourse to war for the solution of international controversies and renounce it as an instrument of national policy in their relations with one another."

It is assumed that the conspicuous fault of the Briand Agreement was not that it represented a shabby piece of rhetoric belonging to a dead era, but that it wanted the machinery to make its obligations felt. This machinery the Culbertson Plan attempts to provide.

It is not intended that the project is to be a super-government. The nations are to remain independent. "Those of its powers which are enforceable by military means are sharply limited to one and only one object: the prohibition and prevention of war. No nation gives up any of its essential sovereign rights save one: the right to wage war." [1]

To make this system effective the author accords the Central Authority overwhelming force, "armed, composed and distributed according to a new technique." This policing machinery would consist of National Contingents "held in reserve in the country of their origin" and a Mobile Corps of shock troops who are to consist of "highly paid, highly educated volunteers." The possession and manufacture of heavy weapons would be apportioned on the same quota basis.

The countries themselves though "independent" would be allowed to possess no troops except local police forces, armed with nothing heavier than machine guns. Each National Contingent, on the other hand, though maintained and paid for by the World Federation Government, is subject to the World Federation's orders only in case of war. In peacetime it remains the national armed force of its own country, where it remains stationed and is trained by its own national officers in its own particular military practices and tradition. The Mobile Corps, on the other hand, will be directly under the orders of the Central World Authority at all times. It will be recruited from the smaller nations only.

It is noticeable that the United States will possess twenty per cent of the quota for the World Police as against four per cent each for China and India. The Chinese quota would be exactly equal to the Turkish, a situation which could last just long enough for the outraged Chinese to acquire sufficient strength to cry, "discrimination!"

The fundamental logic of this plan is that national sovereignty will not essentially be interfered with except in the case of "aggression." It is assumed that the Central Authority though without governmental powers, will enjoy the absolute loyalty of the heterogeneous national forces, which will remain under the various national commands up until the moment the Central Authority deems it wise to invoke its own prerogatives.

All this obviously is a fantasy. Unless one were to grant the World

[1] Ely Culbertson, "A System to Win This War," *Readers Digest*, February 1943.

Authority sufficient strength to form the entire globe into a single empire under its suzerainty, the same fundamental difficulties remain. The States will have their individual problems; they will be unequal in strength, in resources, in energy, and in the social standards by which their external policies are fashioned. The Western nations which are a minority in the world's population will continue to hold the bulk of the world's commerce. They will remain in control of almost eighty-five per cent of the world's surface, thus precipitating the inevitable struggle with the crowded East.

These are the real questions and they cannot be avoided by constitutional provisions which, like King Canute addressing the waters, would call on these problems to yield their kinetic force and become forever still.

III

The ideas of many thoughtful men penetrate beyond the horizons of purely political thinking and demand a managed world economy capable of exercising some measure of control over international finance, production and trade, and of preventing the more flagrant types of exchange discriminations and trade abuses from running amok.

The modern problems of war and peace are seen to be less rooted in some malignancy requiring world pledges than in mechanical maladjustments resulting from the machine age itself. The logic of these assumptions follows a school of thought which sees the attainment of economic world unity as the basic presupposition of modern industrialism. If this indispensable prerequisite to the future of industrialism cannot be achieved, asserts Toynbee in his classic *A Study of History*, "it seems doomed to die of asphyxiation." [1] The identical contention is offered by Lewis Mumford in his *Technics and Civilization*, declaring that mankind "has no other alternative than to organize industry and its polity on a world-wide scale." [2]

[1] Arnold J. Toynbee, *A Study of History*, Vol. IV, p. 180.
[2] Eugene Staley, *World Economy in Transition*, p. 35.

Thus, according to the best of modern thinkers, a functioning world order is required, if only to provide the institutional framework for what will be tomorrow's universal trade. It is perceived that the parochial, segmentized sovereignties into which the world is walled off, must somehow be delimited before they wreck the very basis of the technology on which their own welfare depends.

The efforts to secure this result within the present political dispensation, propose a hopelessly discrepant task, that of displacing the State from jurisdiction over its own vital affairs, while at the same time conceding its final authority as a free vested entity. This, of course, is fantastic.

It is impossible to expect of a State that it will act contrary to its own welfare in the interests of a set of standards only remotely beneficial to it. The Soviet Union, for instance, is not likely to acquiesce to any international agreement which limits her industrial expansion. In this she would be joined by China and the Latin American countries.

Neither is it probable that the United States or Britain would yield their industrial pre-eminence in the interests of a fairer distribution of world trade. For such States as Holland and Belgium to do so would be to sign their death warrants.

An effort to regulate competition by the use of price agreements among the producing countries would hit heavy snags based on differences in local conditions, and in cost of production. Cotton is a fair example. China, the Near and Middle East and South America will want to grow more of it. So will the Soviet Union. They will not welcome an arrangement which freezes an important element of their economy. The price of Brazilian cotton at Sao Paulo in 1941 was 8.42 cents a pound. American cotton on that date marketed at 18.30 cents a pound. When peace comes there will exist an accumulation of fifteen million bales of foreign cotton ready for export, whose owners could not agree to price restrictions which would cause it to be a dead commodity on their hands.

It may be said of these projections in general, that they are impractical and can only exist as they are forced on the weaker nations by the stronger, or as they may be supported by the unlimited bank account of the United States of America.

International direction of the world economy now is planned both on the production and consumption ends, with various central authorities operating by common consent to create world order out of the current economic anarchy.

The overall world economic executive would attempt to prevent world-wide unemployment and the political instability which goes with it. It would offer to rehabilitate the war-battered countries and to assist in the creation of a sane, economic society with guaranteed access by all to raw materials and markets. Obstructive and unfair practices would be regulated and, presumably, fair quotas arrived at in a general all-around balancing of international accounts.

The International Economic Authority would supervise a multiplicity of lesser bureaus connected with making the best possible use of the world's resources. There would be a World RFC which would direct investments and undertake the handling of huge international projects, principally in the domains of the undeveloped nations.

Railroads, airports, great irrigation works, huge water power developments, would spring into existence. An International Agricultural Authority would determine the broad outlines of what was to be raised, and where. There would be an International Labor Office, an International Health Authority, and a World Commodity Credit Corporation by which the prices of raw materials would be kept in equilibrium and necessary subsidies granted.

Among the variants suggested has been an United Nations Investment Corporation which would operate an international network of airways and provide capital for world-wide reconstruction. Vice President Wallace suggests that the function of this contemplated power house be both military and commercial. It would have two jobs, one to carry passengers and cargo, and the other to bomb any nation which violated the International Code.

Theoretically, these monumental undertakings would be the responsibility of the concert of nations. In practice, the United States would be asked to subscribe the great bulk of the funds required and to support these ventures on an indefinite time basis, though not possessing a proportionate influence in the making of their policies.

Serious consideration has been given proposals for a great postwar World Bank and International Clearing Union which would stabilize national currencies and provide the credits for foreign reconstruction. These propose to control trade cycles and reduce practices which hamper world commerce, by introducing a mechanism to regulate credit expansion and restrictions.

Two major proposals exist, one brought forward by Lord Keynes; the other known as the White Plan and credited to Harry D. White, Director of Monetary Research for the U. S. Treasury.

Under the Keynes proposal there would be a world bank in association with an international police body to force payment by defaulting nations. Such nations additionally would be subject to financial quarantine and thus starved into submission.

The bank would have veto power over the trade policies of any State which in its judgment was not operating in harmony with what it construed to be world interests.

The White Plan involves the establishment of a bank with an initial capital of approximately ten billion dollars subscribed to by the associated countries according to quota. This bank would have great latitude. It not only could make loans but could guarantee loans made by private capital to any member nation. It could finance industrial and business enterprises anywhere. Payment would be guaranteed by the government of the constituent country in which the loan was made, whether to a private enterprise or to the State itself. The voting power of member countries would be related to their shareholdings.

Each of the plans provides for a unit of international currency. That of the Keynes Plan is known as the *bancor*. In the White Plan, it is called the *unitas*.

These plans would undertake to prevent dangerous shifts in the value of currencies and would determine the par value of the money of all States, to enable an equitable settlement of exchange balances through the International Clearing Union. Nations with adverse trade balances would come in just as individuals do now to private banks, and secure credit to tide them over, or for development purposes.

The capital of the White Plan bank largely would be tied to gold. Countries entering into the arrangement would have to agree to maintain exchange rates set by the bank, and to submit to the general practices and restrictions approved by the bank.

The White Plan is favored by the United States. The Keynes Plan which also tacks off toward the gold standard, is favored by the British who are particularly anxious to clarify the postwar financial situation in an effort to ward off the unprincipled competitions they fear will come if no restrictions are in existence. This sort of plan cannot function by consent or on a scheme of collaboration by free and equal nations. It would last only so long as the member Powers did not feel that it was operating to their disadvantage, or were compelled to acquiesce by the stark threat of armed force. Both plans, by reason of the executive mandate their operations would require, would impinge directly on the sovereignty of the component countries. The punitive content of each is obvious since they rest on their capacity to discipline a defaulting or recalcitrant nation.

The international governing body controlling the bank soon would acquire powers of life and death over the commerce of at least the smaller States, giving the bank a peculiarly decisive political position.

The introduction of any of the control forms referred to would create a new series of mammoth superbureaucracies with all the vices inherent in such structures. These bureaucracies, or the bodies which controlled them, would be the real wielders of power and would themselves become the object of competition and seizure.

The totalitarians with their planned production and socialized controls would make better adjustment to international economic regulation than would the free trade countries. They also would show infinitely more skill in evading those portions of the law which proved onerous or profitless. The introduction of an international regulatory apparatus accordingly would enable any powerful authoritarian country of dishonest bent, to wreck the business of the free trade States by subtle methods not easily recognized early enough to be of value. The alternative would mean continually tightening controls, with price levels and conditions of operation fixed everywhere on everything, as in the present wartime crisis.

Such a state of affairs would force the Western countries to adjust themselves to a permanent, planned economy of more or less total type.

What has been planned as a simple and moderate remedial measure thus would become a managed economy with a vengeance, and result in a true authoritarian world.

XVI

THE TRAGIC STRUGGLE OF RACE

AS if the troubles which accrued to him naturally were not complex and impenetrable enough, Caucasian man must needs complicate them by bedevilling himself with yet another and worse one: the tormenting obsession with race. Even were civilization able to answer all the major conundrums on which its fate depends, it still would have to deal with the furies engendered by this overriding presence.

The worship of race and the tenacious belief in the destined triumph of biological Aryanism may prove to be the most dangerous body of doctrine ever to take shape on this planet. It is a persuasion which may bear the same relation to the Twentieth Century that Islam did to the Seventh, and be answerable only in a bath of blood.

There have been many pictures of racial fantasy in the past. The Incas considered themselves descendent from the Sun God, and hence unique. During the first rich flush of Anglo-Protestant zeal, it was believed by large sections of the British people that they were descended from the Lost Ten Tribes of Israel. This conviction was passionately held by such notable figures as Queen Victoria and the Irish General, Vallancey.

These claims existed purely in the realm of assertion. They were backed by no proof and did not purport to constitute a way of life or explanation of the universe itself. They derived simply from the myths surrounding the antiquity of the race.

They did not contravene the doctrinal belief in the rights of man, or the inalienable oneness of science, truth and justice. It was pos-

363

sible for Napoleon to award prizes to English scientists even during the midst of his wars against Great Britain, or for the English scientist, Michael Faraday, to go to Paris in the midst of the Franco-British wars in order to compare notes with his French colleagues.

The so-called racial movements of the past received most of their formulation from linguistic affinities, or from national patriotism in the geographic sense. National divisions were determined by religion, language or general commonalty of interests. The Crusaders intermarried with the peoples they found in the Levant. The Romans merged their blood with almost every conquered type. The Mongoloid Magyars intermixed to such a degree as to cause themselves to become indistinguishable from other Europeans. Even the Pan-German zealots, fanatically devoted to the theory of German mission as they were, went to great pains to Germanize the Poles, and strenuously proselytized the Jews.

Up until the present century, a Frenchman remained a Frenchman whether descended from Italian-speaking Savoy, Celtic Brittany, Scandinavian Normandy or the country of the Basques in the Pyrenees. The Jewish Disraeli, or the Welsh Lloyd George, remained as positive expressions of British imperialist culture as if they had stemmed from the fierce Angle and Saxon swordsmen of Hegira, or the wild invading knights of William the Norman.

Anyone who accepted the community of Christ was a Christian. All Greek Catholics who spoke Russian and accepted allegiance to the Czar were Russians, whether they betrayed the Mongol eyes and high cheek bones of the old Altaic blood of Central Asia, whether they were short or dark, squat or tall, and whatever their head shape or other physical configuration.

Modern racism represents the successful completion of what would at first flush appear to be an impossible merger—that of modern material science with the most primitive pagan mysticism. It is far removed from those "recognizable lines of nationality" with their historic rights of autonomous development covered in Wilson's Fourteen Points. Though it is completely intolerant, it is not bigotry in the traditional religious sense but something far transcending this. It is a true part of the world revolution, of an attempted adjustment of the psychologically sick body of mass-man to the machine age. Just as the ape and man developed in different directions from intermediate ancestors, so we have this separate evolvement, tracing from the same common problems which have led to the concept of proletarian universalism.

Racism is not only an expression of group consciousness—it is a doctrine, a science, a political movement, a religious cult, and a complete philosophy of life. Its dogma is based on an interpretation of the Darwinian solution to the natural order, and assumes the world to be a primordial wilderness in which the races struggle with each other for survival. It postulates the arrival of a new heroic age in which the Aryan man will be supreme.

The advent of racism represents a beginning in time, a doctrine as radical in its impact on the human mind as the revolutionary teachings of Jesus, Mohammed and Lenin. It comes at the very moment when the nations of the world have been thrown more closely together than at any time in history, and when mankind either must find some rational form of international organization or perish in a series of ungovernable global conflagrations.

The racial creed has reached a pathological pitch of intensity in the German Reich which it has developed nowhere else; but it is evident as an influential element in every sphere in which the white man moves. It constitutes a growing and already impassable barrier to any sane working agreement between the nations for the postwar period. It accounts for persistent external policies on the part of various Western States which otherwise would be inexplicable. It is observable in the ceaseless jangling which threatens their internal peace. It is seen in the morbid increase of anti-Semitism, and in the universal social stigma attached to the yellow and colored races.

Racism is almost altogether a Caucasian phenomenon. The brown and yellow peoples possess no overmastering consciousness of race in the sense that it exists in the Occident. Various powerful frictions do indeed exist, as the considerable dislike shown for East Indians in the Malay States and Burma, or the incipient feeling against the wealthy Parsees in India. Nowhere, however, does it reach the proportions of the Nordic creed preached in Germany, and which is spreading from there to all parts of the Caucasian macrocosm.

The difference between modern racism and racial prejudice is the difference between a bias in which the most decent men of the race find nothing but shame, and a doctrine which is represented as authoritative anthropological science. The lines of old-fashioned racial prejudice tended to be elastic if not altogether confused, resting on habit and classic predispositions rather than on some scientifically clear differentiation. It was possible for La Marr, apostate son of a Jewish actor, to be one of the foremost exponents of pan-German anti-Semitism, just as it was possible for the Czar's government to show every favor to converted Jews in order to make the transition attractive, or for Bismarck to advise Junker officers to marry into Jewish families in order to improve the intellect of their progeny.

Manifestations of racial exclusiveness in one form or another have always existed. They may be traced in the anathema pronounced by the Prophets on Jews who had married women of Ashdod, or of Ammon and Moab. These expressions of prophetic anger may be laid largely to the fear of the corrupting influence of foreign women in the struggle then going forward between the priesthoods of Jehovah, Baal, Chemosh and Asteroth. We note, for example, that Ruth, one of the most luminous of all the Biblical personalities, was a Moabitess.

It is doubtful if any of the ancient races had any understanding of differences between peoples except as these might be visible to the eye, and even then, only as they were reflected by current cultures. Just as the Spanish people mingled their blood with the Negro and Indian races on the American Continent, Europeans did with the equally diverse Mongolians. Whole sections of Russia are perceptibly of Mongolian mixture. Mongoloid blood is apparent in much of Eastern and Central Europe. Such a State as Portugal is an olio of everything, with a strong Negroid caste.

Differences of race everywhere have tended to be confused with differences of religion and culture and nationality. The Beirut Arab of Latin physiognomy could hardly see anything in a neighboring Bedouin of black skin and kinky hair, but a fellow Arab.

In a country like Honduras, where members of every section of the human family have been stirred into the common melting pot, differences of physical type are not identified by those distinctive characteristics of separation we refer to in the social sense as racial. Here a Negro is but a dark man with certain accompanying personality traits, just as a red-haired man is distinguishable among Caucasians for his translucent skin and volatile temperament.

From any rational view the racial concept often degenerates into grotesquery. We have the record of a Rumanian mob chasing a blond German diplomat who had been mistaken for a Jew since Jews were the only blonds with whom the Rumanians were familiar. In the United States it is common to see some dark and aquiline featured female wearing a cross upon her bosom to make certain that she will not be mistaken as a non-Aryan. On the basis of race she will be socially accepted in the very places from which some blond and blue-eyed Jew who conforms rigidly in type to the theoretical "Nordic" standard, is excluded.

A chocolate colored man from Madras may go anywhere provided he keeps a great mass of swathing around his head in the form of a turban. A man of manifest Negro blood who enters this country as a Brazilian social figure may also be accepted; but an American colored man of the most remote Negro ancestry may not enter a restaurant or be employed in certain industries, even if he be the living counterpart of the classic Aryan of the picture books.

The scientific background for modern racist doctrine began to take form following the investigations of the philologist, Sir William Jones, in the late Eighteenth Century. It was crystallized by the work of Friedrich Max Mueller who held that the likeness of the various European languages indicated a common descent from a people who once had been housed somewhere in the world under a single roof. This people whom he asserted to be the great catalyst of civilization, he gave the name of Aryan. Later, Mueller, the prophet and pioneer of these discoveries, was to reject the entire system of racism which was erected on them. "I have declared again and again," he stated bitterly, "that if I say Aryans, I mean neither blood nor bones nor brain nor skull; I mean simply those who speak an Aryan language."

As we have noted in our discussion of the Germans, the new religion of race acquired a high priest in the French count, Arthur de Gobineau, who maintained that the question of race was the key to all other questions and loomed gigantically over every problem of history. These theories, though still liquid and shapeless, began to find followers and exponents among all the North Caucasian peoples, though nowhere with the same eagerness and passion as in Germany.

In the United States the movement, scarcely recognizable for its true content, followed in the wake of the forces which were agitating Europe. It drew its inspiration from such books as Madison Grant's *The Passing of the Great Race,* and Lothrop Stoddard's *The Rising Tide of Color.* In a mild form it has tinctured the official policy of America for a number of generations. Its influence may be seen in the very existence of the present Immigration Act which represents a transparent effort to fix percentages of those who may enter the country, based primarily on the possession of "Nordic" blood. To accomplish this purpose, the Act, which was passed in 1924, used 1890, the year of greatest migration from Northern and Western Europe, as the census year from which the percentage of each nationality to enter this country was to be computed.

The racist doctrine has continued to spread despite the war, seeping into all corners of the West in a steadily rising flood. It gains power as disrespect for the old free-capital, parliamentary society increases.

In England and the United States the movement is vague, uncertain, and except for its nucleus of zealots, not well-formed, but its influence is profound and gaining with dangerous rapidity. Even while the military struggle is being waged, English Fascists have been campaigning with the slogan, "Put Moseley in power." In the United States, thousands of similar groups and organizations exist. Their publications, the so-called vermin press, are vociferous in their barely-concealed pro-Germanism and hatred for conventional society.

Racism will not die with the defeat of the German arms, or even with the death of the German economy. It has become a universal disease affecting the white race, and perhaps the symbol of its decay and approaching dissolution. It will feed on the great global neuroses resulting from privation, shock, fear, and long-continued anger, and which will spread like a virus from people to people.

The movement has its followers among all races claiming to derive from Caucasian stock, except the Hebrew. It is led by men who believe themselves to be the broom of destiny, which will sweep away the outmoded, the antique and the archaic and bring a new heroic future to birth. It shows every evidence of irrepressible growth. Even though its military centers in Berlin and Munich be destroyed, its spiritual centers will remain there with the same enduring power which draws the faithful to Mecca and Medina to this day.

The Nazis themselves regard their view as irresistible. Hitler asserted in his speech of January 31, 1944, that regardless of the military outcome, Nazism would conquer the world. He predicted that "millions of soldiers and war prisoners will become millions of propagandists" and that the ideals of Nazi Germany "will appear not only worth imitating but natural" all over the globe.

In this hypnotic vision is observable a fanatic ferment of reckless challenging force, which like the heedless march of the lemmings is moving toward renewed social and political disturbances on a gigantic scale. It drives the world irresistibly forward through fear, distrust, arrogance and hatred to the third phase of the great global struggle which has been known as World Wars I and II.

The task of the new Germany will be to stimulate and form this sentiment in all its mad megalomaniac glory, utilizing it as the prime weapon to win friends to its side again among the victorious nations, and finally to find among them allies for a last fratricidal struggle for control of the white world as the prelude to global conquest.

II

Scientists and logicians may inveigh against the racist proposition as a dangerous piece of lunacy; they may assert that though there are marked differences of character and characteristics between races, these do not obliterate the likenesses any more than they do in the differences between families; they may prove that to a Chinese not inured to the delicate details of Caucasian prejudice, there is no discernible difference between one type of blond white man and another, or between a brunet Castilian and his counterpart from Munich. Such rationalizations will not be resisted. They simply will be ignored wherever the racial belief has taken hold. Racism no longer is the result of emotional reaction, but is a political and cultural concept imbedded deep in the consciousness of Caucasian man. In many aspects it constitutes a new area of religious conviction. As such, it is the center of world unrest for the future and will be the rock on which the ship of white civilization may be destined to crash.

It cannot fail to become more and more schismatic in its relations to orthodox religion since it possesses within itself all of the seeds of exclusiveness. Racism categorically rejects the premise on which the great religions were founded, the ultimate brotherhood of man and triumph of universal morality, the sacred character of the human soul, and the supreme worth of abstract virtue.

No less than Communist doctrine, racist philosophy regards

orthodox religion as a detestable superstition and outmoded relic of antique society. Such organizations as the Roman Church are considered to be insufferable competitors for political allegiance and power, who in the end must be destroyed. Though authoritarian logic has received much of its stimulus from the clerical mind, and has become heir to the traditional struggle of the Church against liberalism, the inevitable result must be that the totalitarian racial State and the Church cannot exist together on the same planet.

If history is to be rewritten by the Nazis, Jesus of Nazareth will be represented as a weakling of inferior breed whose system of pity-ethics was doomed to be overtaken by the heroic sword of the Nordic Wodin. Wherever racism has obtained full sway, Jesus either is rejected or represented as a pure Aryan. Nazi youth marches the streets chanting

> "Pope and rabbi shall be gone;
> We want to be pagans once again,
> And no more creep to churches."

Hitler is the new hero who has been impressed on the Nazi youth as a god. He is variously described as "the true Holy Ghost," [1] or as a savior "far too great to be compared to one so snivelling and petty as Jesus." [2]

It is the unlimited assimilative property of this doctrine with its capacity to absorb local dogmas without impeding its course of progress, and its baffling independence of every other type of logic, which makes it so powerful a potential factor in the determination of the world's future.

The strange mentality which is fascinated by the racist view seems capable of accepting any inconsistency. Racism can base itself on the pure Nordic characteristics of long-headed blondness and yet be led by the dark Hitler, Goebbels, Goering, and Hess, whose

[1] By Reichsminister for Church Affairs, Hans Kerrl.
[2] Julius Streicher before the German Academy of Education, Munich, July 20th, 1935.

combined coloring, head and body shapes refute its doctrine to the point of buffoonery. Although his movement advocates the destruction of private capital, Herr Hitler could get a great portion of his support from the big Rhineland industrialists. Though the intellectual goals of Nazism are violently pagan, he could receive a considerable portion of his early help from the Church. Though he affects to despise the colored races, Hitler could be allied with the Mongoloid Japanese against the Aryan English.

The racial doctrine is quite capable of including the Slavs, Latins and Celts as part of the Germanic world super-order while at the same time marching vigorously toward their exclusion. It can accept the Mongoloid Finns and Hungarians, and the largely Semitic Spaniards, and yet reject the blond Russians. It can proclaim the Persians as Aryan ancestors though the bas reliefs these ancients have left show a hooked-nosed people whose features are almost a burlesque of traditional Semitism.

It may claim all culture to be solely the product of the Germanic peoples despite the fact that these races entered civilization as barbarian destroyers, and that in Germany, itself, "the Nordic type is purest in those parts which lag far behind the rest of the country in cultural achievement." [1] It can distort history out of all sense but the persuasive quality of its doctrine remains unaffected.

If all this seems like the politics of Bedlam it is none the less real. Like Nietzsche's "beyond good and evil" it is beyond and above any other competitive logic.

III

To this body of beliefs has been added an opposing principle, that of the eternal Jew who is represented as the antithesis of all that Aryanism has come to mean.

In the vernacular of racism the term non-Aryan hence has taken on the meaning "Jewish." Neither the Italians, the Mongoloid Hungarians or the Ibero-Semitic Spaniards are non-Aryan in the

[1] Dr. I. Zollschan, *Racialism against Civilization*, pp. 40, 41.

particular sense the word has come to possess. In racist argot it has become a symbol of natural inarticulate evil, of eternal lustfulness and depravity, of ratlike fears and hates.

The Jews were made the personification of all that was wicked and ignoble in life. They were accused of every vile and misbegotten crime on the calendar and held responsible for every misfortune affecting the human race. It was they who brought about wars, who manipulated currencies, and struck at the roots of society in an effort to destroy it for their own ends. They were responsible for plutocracy and Communism alike. Though few, and without a political State to back them, this minor and almost helpless people was pictured as the resistless ruler of the universe, a terrible and omnipresent force which made all nations their puppets, and against which the embattled Aryan must expend his last brave breath in struggle.

Universally they were made the victims of the most unscrupulous and poisonously successful propaganda the world has ever seen. The extent of the successes of the racist revolution could be measured in each country by the extent and quality of the campaign of vilification against the Jews. "Forget all other issues," Hitler advised his English follower, Moseley, "concentrate on the Jews."

The presence of this ancient race in Europe was a windfall to the masters of Nazi strategy. In their hands anti-Semitism became a weapon of such formidable proportions as to be capable of giving Germany ultimate and perhaps bloodless victory despite the impending defeat of German arms. "The Jewish problem," Werner Best, legal adviser to the Gestapo, told a group of SS leaders, "is the dynamite with which we shatter the bastions where the last snipers of liberalism have holed up. When nations smash their Jews," he said, "they give up their former Judaized manner of life, which rests upon false ideals of freedom. Only in this way can they take up their places in our war for a new order."

The result of these tactics has been the destruction, not only of liberty but of sanity over large portions of the globe. Millions of unoffending people have been butchered in a continuous pogrom which the Archbishop of York has stigmatized as "the greatest crime in history." They have been tortured, degraded, burned, robbed, gassed and machine-gunned in whole community batches. Many were buried in mass graves before they died. Eyewitnesses state that the earth trembled in the convulsions of their last agonized breathing.

Another two million have become broken wanderers, their property seized, their bodies racked by disease and privation, their entire adjustment to existence destroyed. They have become the true outcasts of the Twentieth Century. None speak for them and no one defends them except a few idealists and brave, generous men who for the most part lack both practicality and power.

One is compelled to stand aghast not only at the brutishness which created these acts, but at the indifference toward them displayed by the Western World. Despite the mass tragedies which took place every day and every hour, there was no audible protest, no outraged demands that these mass slaughters cease. Not even when the last thirty-five thousand Jews of the Warsaw ghetto heroically fought off the Nazi troops with their bare hands in what was the first open mass revolt against German rule, was a note made of the tragic heroism of this beleaguered people. In this three week battle greater destruction occurred than during the entire Nazi siege of Warsaw in 1939. Every house was defended to the end.

When at the first Moscow Conference a Joint Statement of warning was issued by the leaders of the United Nations, pledging punishment for the atrocities committed by the Nazis against the civil populations of the conquered countries, the Jews were not mentioned at all, though account was taken of the sufferings of even such minor groups as Cretan peasants. Rather than run the risk of laying themselves open to the familiar charge that the war was being fought in the interests of the Jews, the three Allied leaders circumspectly by-passed the subject and pretended that this people did not exist.

In this ugly silence, so different from the once proud character of the West, is indicated an inner and unseen demoralization, a terrifying alteration of standards which should well give the West fear for the future. It comes at one of the most critical moments in history, when all the resources of compassion, moral courage and social wisdom Western man possesses will be required to keep his institutions alive, and himself from destruction.

By becoming the special target of the Hitlerian racists, the Jews have become the test of Western professions and principles, and as Lord Davies has put it, "the very personification of the issues involved in this world struggle."

In the carefully weighed expediencies which have characterized the attitude of our statesmen toward these people, there is little which speaks for the brave new world allegedly in the making, and little to assure the outcasts, sufferers and pariahs who today are the majority of humanity.

Among the multitudes of the East, too, to whom the Jews look exactly like all other Westerners, is deeply engraved this thought: "If the white man can do this to his own, what will be finally reserved for us when the great test of strength comes?" The eyes of the East gaze on us with curious distrust, with unquenchable suspicion, and growing contempt and hatred. Not because the East is humane, but because its own fate now lies in the balance, and all which reflects the soul of the Western World will reflect as if in a mirror the destiny of the Orient.

Because it is a catalyst favoring the forces of social unhingement and national disintegration, the question of anti-Semitism has become one of the prime problems with which the West must deal.

A great deal of learned analysis has been made of this phenomenon. The erudite discussion has arisen as to whether the Jews were a race, a religion, a culture or as the Marxists allege, a social class which requires liquidation.

Such authorities as the anthropologist, Franz Boas, assert that the Jews are an ethnic mixture of many peoples and have been so from the earliest times, and moreover, that the Jewish type varies in each country according to the general racial picture which is presented.

A considerable part of the Jewish community itself considers its Jewishness to be solely a religious manifestation. Jews are also vaguely defined as "a people with a peculiar cultural genius," and as a nationality who in the fulness of time will be reconstituted in their ancient home in the Levant.

Whatever the scientific validity of these niceties of distinction, the fact is that Jews do exist, that they have been murdered and tortured in whole masses in Hitler's Europe, and in many other places in the world, harried, ostracized and abused; and that the technique by which the Fascists have risen to power in every State has centered around a mobilization of anti-Jewish prejudices.

The comparative unanimity of bias against Jews, results from a complexity of historical causes. The most important for its immediate effect has been the calculated propaganda of the racists. The predisposing emotional factors stem from the early theologic teaching that the Jews killed Christ. It is expressed in the accusation of the Fourth Century saint, Chrysostom, that "the Jews have crucified the Son and rejected the Holy Ghost and their souls are the abode of the devil." The ensuing aversion showed itself in periodic massacres during the Middle Ages when wandering mobs led by worthies who proclaimed themselves appointed by Heaven for this purpose, placed hundreds of Jewish communities to the sword, burned them alive in their temples and despoliated them of their possessions.

Anti-Semitism has become a sort of social habit among the Western peoples. Other and more practical factors have contrived, however, to add fuel to this enmity. One is the competitive struggle in the professions and business. The Jew as a symbol of Communism has made a deep impress on minds already indoctrinated with the anti-Semitic virus.

Other antipathies resulted from the identification of the Jews with the existing world order, in which the active participation of Jewish minds is everywhere to be seen. To all the revolutionary classes, the Jews became the very symbol of a parliamentary, commercial, finance and individualistic age they hated. The Fascists taxed them with alienism and with responsibility for the evils of the present order. To the Communists they were not even a race, but a social class, emblem of all that was wrong with society, the very epitome of exploiting plutocracy. "The bowels of civilization," wrote Marx acidly, "are continually producing Jews."

In any but a Utopian consideration of the question, anti-Semitism must be weighed as a serious factor in the life of postwar Europe. It is doubtful whether the Jews could remain there under present political circumstances even if they wished to do so. Their existence would be complicated by the psychology of fear and mistrust, and by the memory of unforgettable days of horror.

They would be the target of the running fire of the political racists. In countries like Poland they could not forget that long before the Nazi invasion they were anxious to escape from the grim circumstances which suffused every step of their lives there. They would find on their return a new elite. Their former businesses, trades and professions would be occupied by Christian Poles who would stoutly resist any effort of the newcomers to displace them. They would remain footloose and rootless, the objects of an implacable hatred and without the vaguest possibility of integrating themselves with the national life.

European anti-Semitism may be condemned as cowardly and brutal but this will have no effect in ameliorating the situation. The concern manifested by a small stratum of liberal European leaders over the rights of these people will have no more consequence than the drumming of a woodpecker on a great oak. It will lead to no effective steps and will provide no practical remedy.

The Jews of Europe understood long ago that the only possible course for them was removal, and that the idea of an autonomous Jewish State was perfectly rational and represented a reasonable settlement of a problem which has followed them through all of their generations.

It is true that Europe, as all the world, must be free, but it will not be so long as any fundamental issue remains unsettled. It will be useless to point out that by invoking race and religious hatreds during these complexly troubled times, Europeans will be wrecking not only their own economy but that which will be inhabited in the future by their children. In these situations, academic logic falls on deaf ears and even good sense is abandoned for the unwritten law of the horde.

If ever an argument existed in favor of a prompt and decisive settlement of basic problems, it exists in the frightful fate of these people, who could not even die until the conditions of their existence were already beyond sanity and human endurance.

Of those who managed to escape the Nazi nemesis, more than half were absorbed in the tiny community of Palestine, to which the eyes of these forgotten children of the Twentieth Century had been glued pathetically for a generation. No other place would have them. Were it not for the opposition of the Mandatory Power which blocked the way, the entire problem might have been settled there.

IV

The terminal crisis toward which the racial question is moving pivots on still another and more universally menacing problem: that of color. It not only applies to the Negro, but is one of the primary concerns of the Indians, Japanese and other Asiatics. It has developed into a sort of *Weltanschauung* or obsession with the fact of skin pigmentation. It has created, to one degree or another, a remarkable solidarity over the globe between the principal non-Caucasian races.

There has grown in the subjugated and socially excluded Oriental peoples a fixed dislike for Caucasians which will bode ill for the future of humankind as it gains momentum. Coincidentally there is observable a new and defiant attitude on the part of the Negro, who is in a revolutionary mood and no longer impressed by the white man's estimate of his own worth. It is only the political and economic weakness of the black man, and the unreadiness of the

Orient, which keeps these resentments in check and prevents them from flaring out in openly expressed challenge.

The dark peoples are convinced that the true meaning of the war is not one of struggle between the ideals of two contrasting social philosophies, but between the rival imperialisms of the played-out white races, whose brief tenure of world rule is drawing to a close. They see their own appointed task as that of hastening its end.

As they move forward to a fuller consolidation of economic and political power the yellow and brown races will set themselves adamantly against the social conceptions imposed on them by the white man. It will no longer be possible to maintain a social club in Bombay from which Indians are excluded by rule, or to compel Chinese to ride second-class on boats plying Chinese waters.

The colored peoples will move to end every type of exclusion, social or economic, and will see such discriminations even where none exists.

If the yellow and brown races are scheduled eventually to emerge as power factors, the demographic balance between the races becomes a matter of critical importance. If in addition to their already predominant numbers, the colored peoples are favored by the population projections for the future, it constitutes a portent which may not safely be disregarded.

The figures are far from reassuring. Assuming a total world population of something like 2,200,000,000, it may be accepted that under the most liberal estimate the white race represents no more than 725,000,000. Moreover, outside of the Continent of Europe and the areas above the Rio Grande in North America, the whites are badly scattered in a series of Indo-European and Semitic population islands which are washed by a great sea of colored races.

Even the estimate of 725,000,000 errs on the side of generosity. It includes in the Caucasian category such peoples as the Arabs, Berbers, Copts and Persians who, whatever their original stocks, are now plainly polyglot-mulatto in type and have as much reason as any to resent the social arrogance and material rule of the pure Caucasian.

In Asia, situated in one solid impervious bloc, are some eight hundred million people of the Mongolian-Ural-Altaic strain, the so-called yellow races. These are flanked by another solid bloc of almost four hundred million of Indo-European language, but brown skinned, who inhabit the great peninsula of India; and another eighty million similar in physical appearance but of Malayan and Polynesian blood.

In addition there must be close to 210,000,000 in whom Negro blood predominates, and perhaps fifty million so-called red men, who are undoubtedly of Mongolian derivation.

Latin America, generally considered in terms of the dark Caucasian, contains only twenty million of white race, and not all of these are without some slight admixture of colored blood. According to the best available estimates of Latin America's 128,000,000 people, seventeen million are pure Negro, nineteen million wholly Indian, and sixty-six million of varying degrees of Negro, Indian and white mixture. The State of Paraguay is so completely Indian that the Guarani language is the common tongue. Only the Argentine, Uruguay, and possibly Costa Rica, are preponderantly over on the white side.

It is calculated that the black, brown and yellow races are expanding at about twice the rate of the Caucasian peoples. Among the whites themselves, the proportion of increase is weighted heavily on the side of the Latin and Slavic peoples, with the so-called Western races tending to become stationary.

Europe already has completed its cycle of fabulous population growth, increasing from 187,000,000 in the year 1800, to 533,000,000 in 1936. By 1975 it is calculated that Northern and Western Europe will have lost population over the 1940 figure, while Southern and Eastern Europe will have made a somewhat substantial gain. The United States as we have noted, will show a slight increase, while the Orient will grow out of all bounds. As sanitation and the improved nutrition of the industrial age lengthen the average life span of the Oriental peoples, the population of the already over-flowing East may come close to trebling itself in a century.

These events will present quite a different picture of the world than that which now exists, and would appear to attend a policy of racial incendiarism with the gravest possible risks.

V

The rate of increase of the brown and yellow peoples will be fully matched by those of the blacks.

The problem of the Negro is an integral part of the turbulent stream of world-wide social unrest. It is a chronic blight which has grown with the absorption of the African races into a world community dominated by the white man's weapons and culture.

It cannot be cured by pretending that it is not there, or that it has disappeared like some bad dream in the warm sunlight of the Four Freedoms.

The glaring inconsistency between declarations of universal brotherhood and the actual facts of social ostracism which have left this race completely without hope, cannot be reconciled. The pretense that the Atlantic Charter or the Four Freedoms applies also to Negroes is a gigantic swindle, not only against the Negro himself but against the balance of mankind since it nurses what is already a focal point of trouble.

Though the black people of the world are estimated to number around 210,000,000, no complete census has ever been made to guarantee the accuracy of these estimates. About 160,000,000 live on the Continent of Africa. About thirty-seven million inhabit the two Americas, of whom thirteen million live in the United States.

The single outstanding fact which unites all these dissimilar peoples, cultures and inheritances is the universal prejudice against their black skin. The Negro occupies different levels of acceptance throughout the world but nowhere is he received without comment as a complete social equal. In most localities he is made the object of intense economic, as well as social discrimination and is brusquely relegated to a position of unchangeable inferiority. Practically everywhere he is subjected to humiliation and a hopeless unbending discrimination which holds every man, woman and child of the dark people with all the terrible certainty of a steel trap.

In the United States the Negro is assured that he is constitutionally equal to all others, while at the same time he is prevented from exercising the largest share of these rights. The social contrarieties this involves can be understood from the educational figures for 1941. In addition to the millions who received public schooling, 4,800 Negroes were given college degrees in engineering, chemistry, science and the liberal arts; and 56,000 completed trade, industrial, professional and clerical courses. The opportunity for young Negroes to utilize any of these skills is slim.

The economic discrimination suffered by this people is, on the whole, worse in the American North than it is in the South. In cities like New York, prideful of their democratic views, no white person would dream of utilizing a colored barber, or employing a colored plumber, actions which are commonplace in the Southern States.

The result of thus turning a whole people into a race of pariahs has been to poison the normal life of the nation. It furnishes the United States with an acute and growing problem which in the presence of American racism will become immeasurably worse.

The popular justification for anti-Negro sentiment ascribes to the black man an inborn and constitutional inferiority which makes him a menace to the white race in whose midst he dwells. He is credited with high criminal tendencies, and is said to be childlike, shiftless, immoral and no lover of hard work. In the southern part of the United States his existence is the pivot around which all other problems revolve.

Many of the limitations of which he is accused are unfounded. Others undoubtedly are due to the depressed social status he occupies and the psychological abrasions this has created in his consciousness. Comparative intelligence tests show the Negro to possess a considerably lower I.Q. rating than that of whites generally; but so do similar anthropological studies of Portuguese and others who succeed in maintaining themselves in civilization. Whatever the reliability of these collective estimates, a wide latitude of individual difference certainly exists, gifted Negroes often far surpassing ordinary whites. There are few poets more significant than Pushkin, or scientists of finer creative genius than George Washington Carver. Brazil's greatest novelist, Machado de Assiz, is a mulatto.

It is in Africa, the country of his origin, that the condition of the Negro is the most wretched. Nevertheless, since he is here overwhelmingly dominant in numbers, his subjection by relatively minor groups of whites is likely to prove bootless and impermanent. As fast as the Negro steps out of tribalism, and is acted on by the currents of revolutionary philosophy which are spreading over the earth, he will be galvanized into resistance and anger. He will not lack friends in the peoples of the East, who will see in his problem a common purpose, and in the territories he inhabits a rich inheritance crying out for exploitation and development.

The detribalization process in Africa has gone forward with an almost complete disregard for the welfare of the natives or of future consequences. The Negro has no political rights whether he be a half-caste or pure breed. He is viewed with a mixed attitude, as being something not altogether human in the white sense, picturesque, but a bit of a nuisance and under some circumstances as dangerous as is a buffalo when it runs amok.

With the exception of Liberia, Abyssinia and to a limited degree, French Senegal, Africa is governed by a strictly racial caste system. A typical example is mandated Tanganyika where nine thousand Caucasians and twenty-five thousand East Indians find themselves submerged among a great black mass of five million five hundred thousand. Under the constitution of 1926, the Legislative Council consists of twenty British Europeans and three British Indians.

In the Union of South Africa, blacks are eighty per cent of the approximately ten million population. With the exception of the few hundred thousand East Indians, the rest are Europeans. It is mandatory that members of both the Senate and House of Assembly be British subjects of European descent. When Gandhi came to the Dominion to practise law on behalf of his Indian compatriots, he was not allowed to enter one of the great public office buildings because of his color, a fact he never forgot.

The presence of this overwhelming mass of blacks is creating an industrial problem of the first magnitude. The decline in white prestige throughout Asia, accompanied by persistent Japanese and Communist propaganda, is bringing about a vague but growing restlessness on the part of the Negro. The black man has begun to sense the power which comes with numbers. There are already strikes and increasing rumblings of violence. This is a sinister situation which as we shall see, could have far-reaching results.

The situation of the Portuguese and Spanish colonies is about the same as that of the British. That of the French areas is a little better. Senegal is represented in the French Parliament by a single black deputy. Senegalese troops wear French uniforms and recently the French Committee for National Liberation has taken the radical step of appointing a black governor for French Equatorial Africa. In most of French Africa the local chiefs are given a sort of limited autonomy which grants them jurisdiction over the collection of taxes, and by delegation, the preservation of order.

Africa is the scene of the worst set of working and social conditions to be found anywhere on the globe. Forced labor is common and is accomplished either by direct recruiting or seizure, or by the indirect method of taxation, which in the absence of money must be paid off in labor.[1]

The tax levied on the native is not related to capacity to pay and is imposed regardless of social consequence. Its sole purpose is to force him into activities in which he otherwise would not engage.

By Act of 1925, in the Union of South Africa any European policeman may demand production of a tax receipt. The native who cannot show one is liable to imminent arrest. The cattle of

[1] See Lord William Malcolm Hailey, *An African Survey;* G. St. John Orde-Brown, *The African Labourer;* and J. M. Tinley, *The Native Labor Problem of South Africa.*

defaulters may be rounded up and requisitioned, or the culprits placed in detention camps to work their debts out.

Native life is altogether demoralized by this system, which involves the migration of great numbers of men from their homes to distant places, subjecting them to social and health problems of a serious nature. The death rate of these impressed laborers is often exceedingly high due to disease, depressed psychology and separation from the tribal organization to which the native is used. Usually, happy-go-lucky, generous and carefree in his own environment, the native becomes fretful, sullen and depressed. The relative sanity of his previous life turns to a chronic morbid neuroticism.

Another of the devices by which natives are segregated and held in the labor pool is the so-called Pass Law. These were originally police regulations but now are used to guarantee what is a form of indenture. When travelling into the European area, or when moving from one region to another, natives are required to carry travelling passes. In the mining territory of the Union, a laborer must receive permission from his employer if he wishes to leave the property on which he is employed. In the Transvaal and the Orange Free State, a black man employed on a private farm must have a document of identification before he can go any place other than to his home. No one may hire him unless he carries an endorsement from his former employer authorizing him to seek a new job. In South Rhodesia, all natives must observe a curfew law and be indoors between the hours of nine p.m and five a.m. except by special sanction. Similar restrictions operate in the French, Belgian and Portuguese colonies.

Throughout most of Africa, and in all of the British portions, natives are restricted to heavy labor. All skilled occupations are reserved for Caucasians. The general ratio of wages between Europeans and natives in the mines is eight to one in favor of the whites, and in the secondary industries five to one. Europeans also get pensions, holidays and other social benefits to which the blacks are not entitled. The average wage paid natives in the mines is around fourteen dollars a month. The wage scale in Rhodesia hovers around five dollars a month with food. Farm wages may be as low as one dollar and fifty cents a month with food.

Natives may not join the white trade unions. Activities under their own permitted unions are severely restricted. If a black man strikes, it is a penal offense under the Master and Servants Act.

A somewhat better condition exists in the French and Belgian colonies where economic segregation is limited and natives may take most types of employment if they are fitted for them. Recently, in Kenya, due to war needs, army schools have trained African artisans for military purposes. These have turned out many thousands of masons, carpenters, electricians and mechanics, who presumably will not be allowed to compete with white labor in these occupations during peacetime.

As might be expected, criminal law is different for the black man than it is for the European. In addition to offenses against the Pass Laws, a Liquor Regulation Act applies to the native. The breaking of a contract for service, or the non-payment of taxes, is a criminal offense on the part of a native, and he may be subject to prosecution for carrying sticks larger than specified in urban areas, for non-payment of rent, or for being idle in a native location.

The native also finds himself dispossessed of his lands by legal processes which he does not understand and which completely ignore him. In the Union of South Africa, more than two-thirds of the country is under European farms. In Kenya, all of the good agricultural land has been restricted for the plantations of the eighteen thousand resident Europeans. In Southern Rhodesia, white farmers who constitute less than four per cent of the population have taken over almost all of the fertile areas, isolating the Negro to the remaining marginal lands.

Such a system as that which now exists in Africa cannot possibly survive the industrial revolution. In the entire area south of the Sahara Desert there could be no more than two and a quarter million whites who are literally lost and swallowed up in an ocean of anonymous blacks.

As fast as the Negro is sucked into the working apparatus of the machine age, he will begin to become competitive to the white man and will seek to break down the prison walls which hedge him in. He will carry his resentment to the point of extreme violence wherever he is able to do so.

Africa will become the scene of savage political disorders, of sanguinary struggles comparable on a larger scale to those harrowing conflicts which took place in Haiti when the blacks rose in a grim tide of revolt against their numerically inferior white masters. When on January 1, 1804, Haiti declared itself independent from France it was determined by the Assembly to put the entire French white population to death and to take over their property. There were no exceptions. Planters, merchants and professional men, all were decapitated, bayoneted or shot. "Their bodies were thrown one above the other so as to form a mound . . . for the country Negroes, as Governor Dessalines said, to look at their masters." [1] When this slaughter was over, of an original French population of about seventy thousand, not a single French white inhabitant remained alive on the island.

This terrible memory may well exist as a sinister warning to the numerically feeble whites of Africa. There may be expected, in the future, periodic clashes quite different from the Kaffir, Hottentot and Bantu wars which characterized black resistance to European alienation of their lands. A large scale disturbance such as might sweep the Continent within another generation, would take flame as an acknowledged racial war which in the present state of the world would prove too inflammatory to be confined to the borders of Africa.

In various parts of the world a considerable pan-African movement has taken shape. Particularly in British West and South Africa, centers of Pan-African propaganda are flourishing. There are signs of this also in the British islands of the Caribbean and to some degree in the United States, where an intense interest has

1 Pierre Etienne Chazotte, *The Black Rebellion in Haiti,* edited by Charles Platt, privately printed, Philadelphia, 1927.

developed among American Negroes in the fate of the Dark Continent. When Mussolini invaded Ethiopia the Negro press expressed almost the same tempestuous indignation as if the victim had been Harlem.

The aims of Pan-Africanism are not altogether clear. The movement suffers from a lack of political coherence, due to the many factions into which the Negro people are broken, and to the extreme differences in their mode of life. The movement for the present remains essentially one of resistance to the tyranny of white social convention. It smolders deep in Negro consciousness, far more than the white man realizes.

A generation ago, a back-to-Africa movement led by a Negro from Jamaica named Marcus Garvey, managed to attract an extensive following in the United States, centered around the demand for a free republican Africa. Garvey eventually was deported to his native Jamaica and his movement subsided, though it may be suspected that the effect of his activities remains, ready to be called forth by still another Messiah.

This remarkable man did not hesitate to declare with blunt directness that "there is no white supremacy beyond the power and strength of the white man to hold himself against the others. The supremacy of any race is not permanent. It is only a thing of the time in which the race finds itself powerful."

"Every impartial student of history knows," he wrote, referring to ancient Egypt which he assumed to have been a black civilization, "that the Negro once ruled the world when white men were savages and barbarians living in caves."

It is evident to those with eyes to see, that the Negro is developing an ego of his own, quite as sullen, intractable and murderous as that of the white man. It will grow in the proportion that it is acted on by white chauvinists, to whom he is little more than a draft animal, and by the contrary propaganda of the enraged Oriental peoples and Marxian revolutionaries conspiring in turn to bring an end to the tottering white imperial world.

VI

None of these chronic, festering problems can be corrected short of a world-wide settlement of basic issues which would seek to place them into self-regulating balance, removing them altogether from the conventional realm of prejudice and disputation. In the meanwhile the unchecked beating of the drums of hate by organized political forces must be considered a manifestation of social disease, which will lead unfailingly to external wars as well as internal violence, with attendant changes in our form of government.

Apart from the inherited social prejudices which may be expected to act normally on the situation, the main body of this poison is flooding in on the West from the outside. It is the product of a carefully stimulated stream of political nihilism designed to promote the final victory of the Aryan world revolution. The political headquarters of this flow of incessant conspiratorial activity is Germany. If the Reich is manacled by a resolute occupying authority, the central direction temporarily will shift under Nazi leadership to Spain, the Argentine, or even the United States.

The objective of these attacks is the quite practical one of dissolving the character of Western resistance to a renewed Nazi effort at global control. For this purpose whole sections of the population are being turned against each other, race against race, religion against religion and social class against social class. The skills and mediums involved make use of all the classic forms of war. There is a mobilization of powers, a plan of attack, a strategy and an organized leadership. There is the external enemy and there are the internal traitors, exactly as if the struggle represented a resort to arms rather than the more nebulous combat theater of idea.

The question as to what can be done in this difficult situation appears to be anybody's guess. The enemies of the parliamentary States possess wide latitude for their intrigues, and are sheltered by the identical free institutions which by their activities they seek to destroy. The racists, hence, are able to proceed more or less openly with their program without risking the dangers of repression, since repression would mean the end to the freedom of the State itself.

Thus, the West is in the preposterous situation of being forced to allow itself to provide the very tools to its enemies by which the State ultimately is to be destroyed. This was conceded with contemptuous candor by the Spanish Fascist, Gil Robles. "For us," he declared, "democracy is a transitory means of influencing the politics of the country . . . What I do is find a supporting base on whatever offers itself to me, in order to transform it and if necessary to destroy it."

One method of dealing with this situation would be to ignore it in the assumption that it will lie buried under the enthusiasm and hope of an expanding industrial economy. Another would be to outlaw racial assault and the violent slander on which it feeds, as was done in the Soviet Union.

To outlaw prejudices by legal enactment would mean that whatever was forbidden would only await a favorable moment to reappear more virulent and relentless than ever. Whatever must be interdicted by law can be relied on to continue its existence extramurally, and in the natural cycle of events may be expected to reacquire respectability and exist legally.

It must be accepted as one of the central realities of existence that outlawing a prejudice without making provision to liquidate the pressures which keep it alive, will only increase it in the long run. It seems necessary to take a broad view of the problem as a piece of social engineering, and to measure it in relation to the universal questions which simultaneously are to be solved.

These are in part psychological. They are in part posed by the maladjustments of the scientific century. They represent a great complication of emotional as well as material problems. It is doubtful whether any ideology can remove them entirely.

It seems fair to assume that at least there is need for an airing of this question. It should not be allowed to lie hidden under a

THE TRAGIC STRUGGLE OF RACE

blanket of diplomatic niceties, to become purulent and poison the entire bloodstream of humanity.

If it can be dragged out into the open, a determined effort can be made to liquidate its basic causes. This would involve a redistribution of the world's resources and frontiers. It would include the moving of repressed or endangered minority peoples into areas of self-jurisdiction, requiring the use of social engineering on a grand scale never before visualized.

If the question is to be acknowledged in its proper light, it must be seen that the globe is possessed by a number of varying peoples. While the minor ones summarily may be disposed of, the major races are too numerous to be easily destroyed. They are here to stay and will continue to occupy the same earth with the rest of us.

It may be assumed that the goal of racial dominance cannot be secured without the forfeiture of all internal liberties, and the formation of an authoritarian military State. The result, moreover, would be to rob the world of the glory and beauty of those individual and family differences which, were they demolished, would leave existence infinitely poorer, and drab beyond description.

There are no pure races. Within certain broad brackets all nations are of mixed inheritance. Within every national family may be found wide variations of type, of head shape, body build, coloring and temperament, which must have derived originally from unlike racial progenitors. A study of seven million German school children, made under the direction of the Berlin Anthropological Society in the 1870's, reported a variation in the blond type ranging from nine per cent in South Germany to fifty-six per cent in Oldenburg. On the other hand, blond Israelites may be found prominently represented on the sarcophagi of the ancient Egyptians.

It is at this point that the theory of political racialism begins to lose all connection with common sense. Nevertheless, though the range of physical, mental and emotional traits is great within each race, so that no racial criterion can be accepted as conclusive, it is equally preposterous to assume that there is no difference in the characteristics of the races, or in their ability to adjust themselves to the various phases of modern existence. This is a physiological untruth which leads us nowhere. The assumption that men do not differ from each other in capacity, stability, intelligence and instinct obviously leads to the most nonsensical and contradictory conclusions. Races may be seen to be dissimilar in temperament, mentality and appearance, much as their own individual members vary from each other.

The contention that every individual born is exactly equal to every other individual except for the accident of environment and opportunity, is a religious, not a scientific conclusion. Instead of leading to a cheerful and intelligent acceptance of the fact of difference, common reason must rebound from these claims and be attracted to the sinister orbit of Nazi racial doctrine.

It must be accepted that among every people, no matter how primitive, there is a peculiar genius and capacity to contribute to the general welfare. These gifts not only include artistry and intellect, but foresight, tenacity, will, strength and courage. They may be stretched to include gaiety and generosity and a sense of the general graces, as well as the capacity to do a hard day's work. Indians on the whole make quite low scores in comparative intelligence tests; but no one who has visited the State of Yucatan, inhabited by an almost pure Maya race, can fail to be struck by the fine type of agricultural civilization these people have created. An Indian, Diego Rivera, is the greatest artist in Mexico.

In the Latin countries, all of the races, Negro, Indian and white, have added to the common cultural unity. There is no race problem based on the ironclad ostracisms which we invoke. An Indian artist in Brazil is not an Indian but an artist, and a Negro scientist is not a Negro but a scientist.

The relaxation of economic and cultural barriers need not result in the degeneration or death of the white race, but in a deeper and richer civilization unaffected by problems which now bid fair to destroy it. In Brazil the superior adaptability of the Caucasians in relation to the general urbanizing process shows itself in every strata of society. The blacks and darker mixed bloods ordinarily occupy the lower economic levels, the mestizo and mulatto mixtures the middle position, and the whites the upper stratum. The problem loses its intensity as one of racial conflict and, in its economic acceptances at least, begins to approach a rational solution.

New Zealand has proved conclusively that segregation is not a necessary concomitant to a successful civilization, or even to the maintenance of racial integrity. The dark-skinned Maoris who comprise some five per cent of the population, play an equal part with all others in every realm of life. There is no color ban and no discrimination. There is at present a Maori minister in the Cabinet and four Maori Members of Parliament.

The Mexican Secretary of Foreign Affairs, Dr. Padilla, believes that it is the mestizo, or mixed blood, who will inherit the future and become the genuine American type. He feels that this type will be invigorated with the good qualities of each race and that the task of the future is that of consciously improving the biological quality of the American by means of eugenic racial crossbreeding to furnish civilization with a new and superior being.[1]

This question is one of the great conundrums of the future. It is a process which the hand of the Caucasian cannot stay, whether he wills it or no. It proceeds steadily on both continents, though at a more measured pace in the English-speaking North. French Canada has a strong Indian infiltration as do parts of the United States. The Negro, particularly, has received much Indian blood, though the memory remains only as a local tradition in a few isolated Negroid communities in Maryland and the Carolinas. He has also absorbed great quantities of white blood of every description. There is probably a higher percentage of Anglo-Saxon blood running in the veins of Negro Harlem than there is for the average of New York City generally.

There is an opposite phenomenon which is common throughout Latin America and in some other parts of the world, but which to

[1] Ezequiel Padilla, *Free Men of America*, p. 109.

a limited degree takes place in the United States—the absorption of colored families into the white race. This is a process which is known to the Negro as "passing." It is estimated that from ten to twenty thousand escape from the colored into the white group each year.

The union of peoples more or less alike physiologically, has produced brilliant results. The British are one of the greatest amalgams of races on record. It is said that all great historical civilizations have been the result of a meeting of nations of divergent origin. This was true of the Egyptians, the Greeks and the Romans. The latter received much of their stimulus from a merger with the Semitic Etruscans, as did the Greeks from the Phoenician seafarers and colonists.

The mixture of races possessing strongly diverse characteristics does not appear to produce as happy a result. In Iran, Egypt and the Middle East where peoples of every kind, black, yellow and white, have been intimately intermingled for centuries through the agency of the harem, the consequence has been far from impressive.

Judging from the registry of the past, these peoples might have contributed more to civilization and to their own happiness had they continued to live side by side, developing their own peculiar cultural legacies, rather than by losing themselves in the general patchwork of polyglot confusion. Here would seem to be one of those questions which history will answer in her own way, irrespective of the puny restraining hand of man.

Whatever the virtue of these speculations, it is apparent that no political adjustment in the way of a coalition, sectional grouping or international league of nations has the slightest chance of success if the race problem is left dangling or is bypassed. This overriding question which merges with that of the economic and social organization of the world, no longer can be restricted to the shadows of hushed private discussion.

XVII

THE DOCTRINE OF FREE MAN

THE knotty snarl of problems which will survive any purely political determination of the peace cannot be met by the habitual method of leaving them to take care of themselves. Some, it is true, will do so. Others will become more menacing and intractable with the years.

The belief that one may secure peace and prosperity by not earning it, or through the intercession of magical methods, has no place in modern civilization. When challenged by evil circumstance, man has always taken recourse in rituals and rubrics, rather than employ the sweat, labor and common sense necessary to acquit himself of his troubles.

The Nazis believe that the conventional States will not take the steps necessary to place themselves in sound relation to the changed conditions of the technical epoch. The postwar world, they consider, will not be created by plan but by the usual hodgepodge of expediency and power politics.

Revolutionary racism assumes this inability to command our situation to be a sign of progressive deterioration. The Nazi belief is that we are not only losing control of our environment but of our political faith as well; and that our civilization lacks the pliancy to make the adjustments to the new realities which have grown out of the collapse of the antique world.

The underlying system of moral values which enabled Nineteenth Century liberalism to dominate the age is considered to be bankrupt and in hopeless disorder. The Nazi, who does not hesitate to employ the principle of unlimited falsehood and duplicity, regards all moral codes as an archaic fetish which has no place in the struggle for existence. He looks on them as ridiculous relics of a dead age, which have long since been discarded in the grim business of real fighting.

This is the challenge we must face: even after the defeat of Nazi arms we must reckon with a revolutionary racism which is at one and the same time shrewd, magnetic and as unrelenting in its appetites as a starving tiger which stalks its prey at night. We must deal with the fact of a Fascist doctrine which though unfree is practical and equalitarian; while democratic society, though granting the free rights of man, has also abandoned him like a little child lost in a dark and fearful woods, to the chaotic complexities of an unregulated industrial society.

To the troubles which plague international society the racists have an answer—that of a single world order in which the managers will be the new racial elite. In this society, man will take the position of a well-fed, well-tended cow whose only rights will be those of production and consumption.

Unless we reorganize our own appraisal of values and readjust their relationship to the processes of organic existence, military victory alone will not serve us. We will find ourselves conquered by the very ideas against which we have attempted to fight. By reason of their racial content alone, this means final war on gigantic, global terms.

The power of the German world revolution lies in its rejection of the old world order with its shabby failures and petty egoisms. Our view will have to be as strategically sound, with the addition of that single ingredient on which all freedom has its foundation— the basic rights of man.

If we are to bring order, logic and faith once again to the Western peoples we cannot extenuate the morbidities which have sapped the vitality of this generation, nor gloss over the cumulative failures which have gradually embittered men everywhere and made them sour and cynical.

We must recognize the utter failure of diplomacy as we have known it, the archaism of present political boundaries, and the low state to which our moral courage has sunk. We must understand above all that though totalitarian efficiency is new to our age, it is an old story in history, where the reaction of human society to disturbances and problems it could not master has been always the same—repression, regimentation and slavery. Since the totalitarian edifice is conditioned entirely by power and efficiency, it can deal only in those terms. The result must be continuous rearmament, suspicion, fear and finally, when the moment comes, conflict on a total and grand scale.

It must be acknowledged that some modification is required in the present political systems of the Western countries to adjust them to the new techniques which actually rule existence. However, in reference to many of the deficiencies ascribed to the democratic system, it is easy to agree with Padilla that they "are in reality faults of man himself and are also found in the dictatorships," the only difference being that in the democratic system these errors receive wide publicity, while under the dictatorships they are covered with a veil of falsehood and terror.[1]

The mere fact that free government has difficulty in dealing with authoritarian competition does not remove the desirable features of democratic rule. Quite the contrary, it merely proves that in the jungle provided by modern military and social techniques some type of organization on a global scale is required, and that republican and free trade countries cannot exist easily in a world of ruthless and conspiratorial dictatorships, which have them at a disadvantage equal to the measure of their freedom.

It is obvious that we will require something more than reason and expediency, and the logic of the machine age. We will need to recover not only sanity, but a measure of belief in the divine pattern of goodness. If we are to contend with a Hitler and the ideas which make his revolutionary New Order a compelling influence on the minds of men, we must know what we are fighting

[1] Ezequiel Padilla, *Free Men of America.*

for, and state it in clear and unmistakable terms. We must seek to erect at some future determinate period, a new society in which such catastrophes as that we now endure, will not recur.

Otherwise when the historians of the future reduce the facts to the limited pages at their disposal, they will note that when the crumbling world looked to us for spiritual strength and moral comradeship, we were found dealing with Darlan, Badoglio, Franco and the petty Fascist functionaries of North Africa and Europe. It will be said that we fought a war in defense of a better imperialism as against a worse one, and that we had nothing to offer history in support of the rights of man but a so-called Atlantic Charter in which no one believed, and which itself belied the actions of the participant nations.

It will be noted that we proved ourselves the champions of the *status quo,* whether this referred to those wicked men who are themselves responsible for the travail of Europe, or to some Royalist defender of the faith who was long before rejected and ridiculed by his own people.

Such a situation is wholly preposterous. If we are to recover our historic character, we must first rid ourselves of the hoax of superior functional worth which years of unchecked authoritarian propaganda has fixed in our minds.

We can start with the view that a sound, organic society exalts rather than crushes the basic rights of man. We may assume that in the long run there is more practicality to this view than there is to that of the slave society. Slavery is a failing institution, outmoded by the development of the machine. Modern industry demands initiative, skill and know-how, qualities which are not the product of slavery.

We must recognize that a purely economic interpretation of history is an error, and that one cannot brush aside the psychology, traditions and inheritances of man in favor of a rigidly mechanistic explanation of the universe.

It should be accepted as axiomatic that no matter what rational schemes for social control may be evolved, lurking in their background must always be the conception of moral sanity. If man is to progress he must at least be willing to do so, and if he is to keep the peace he cannot be compelled to this view by being bludgeoned into compliance.

The idea that the application of unlimited force can create a permanent peace is, as we have seen, pure fantasy. In the last analysis, repression never creates anything but the need for permanently dissolving it. The future of the world lies not in further authoritarian and more powerful bureaucracies, but rather in such decentralizations as can within reason be accomplished, plus, as we have noted, free movement in wide spaces equipped with extensive resources.

As far as the needs of our social system will allow we should be ruled by the axiom that that government governs best which governs least. We should endeavor to construct a society which will allow room for full human dignity through the complete exercise of liberties of every kind, academic, civil, industrial, religious and political. As far as possible we should endeavor to keep ourselves free from those bureaucracies which historically have strangled every system, beneficent or otherwise, which has ever come into existence on earth.

The Western nations studiously avoid the use of the word totalitarian, and refer rather to a managerial economy. The obvious belief is that in the efficiencies of managerial operation, the problems of manufacture and distribution will be solved, and yet the democratic content of the political structure be left unimpaired.

No matter with what high hopes it is entered into, collectivism has historically implied government by decree rather than law. It involves the use of devices which in themselves centralize power and create areas which cannot be reached by the voter lists. By this concentration of the most powerful instruments of the State into a few hands, it creates as in Germany not only ample opportunities for war, but the actual war psychology itself. For indecision and compromise it substitutes powerful, ambitious leaders

who can by the simple act of pushing buttons influence the electorate in almost any direction.

There are no greater power concentrations than those of government. When government goes paternal it verges into dictatorship. This is the inevitable end in the chain of cause and effect.
The tendency in a planned economy is to hand over the government of the country to trained civil servants who in due course
become a law unto themselves—the classic bureaucracy.

Thus out of the welfare State which devotes itself to caring for
all the needs of the citizen, comes a coddling process which sooner
or later reduces him to an industrial robot.

Whatever the theory might be, the State in practice obtains absolute power over the individual, so that even an attempt to remedy
the more flagrant abuses of power results in pitting single individuals or groups of individuals against the massed resources of
the State. Such an unequal contest only can end as it invariably
does end, in the crushing defeat of those who contest the will of
the bureaucracy, whether that will be for war or for whatever purpose.

Worship of the State suffers from the palpable weaknesses of
worship of Baal. The god can be demonstrated to have clay feet. It
possesses bureaucracies and evils which can be named. It is selfish,
greedy and cruel, as well as beneficent. It is essentially inhuman—
therefore, it has neither compassion nor ultimate power to dominate the human soul.

Whether in the form of Communism or Fascism the idolatrous
worship of the State can end only in a new relationship between
the State and the mass workers who compose it. In a thoroughly
socialized community there is no sanctuary any place for the man
who by reason of religion, race or opinion finds himself excommunicated from the group. Prejudices become rationalized and
discriminations which once were applied by subterfuge, become
written into the law. Whatever constitutions may proclaim, as in
Germany, Russia and China, the one party system comes firmly
into power and cannot be removed except by armed revolution.

A typical result of the long process of deterioration of the constitutional State which has lent itself to collectivist principles, was evident when Adolf Hitler was appointed chancellor of the Reich on January 30, 1933. Step by step under socialist rulers, the constitutional guarantees of civil liberties had been eliminated in the name of efficiency or emergency. The transition phase from socialism to fascism, the second always an inevitable consequence of the first, had been completed.

Stolper describes the situation when Hitler strode for the first time to the Chancellor's chair to seize the helm of a State whose constitutional safeguards already had been destroyed. "There was in all Germany not a handful of men independent and willing to resist. The machinery of the State was finished to the last touch, holding in its grip every individual citizen in every walk of life. Hitler had only to press the button and the machine was ready to work. His predecessors had done for him everything he needed . . . the State owned the banks, the banks owned and controlled business, business controlled the jobs, and the masses who wanted the jobs had been trained by Marxist and anti-Marxist leaders alike to look to the government for whatever they asked of life." [1] All of Germany had fallen into a single bureaucratic design. Labor, industry and the whole economic structure had been swallowed and digested.

This tendency to organize life down to minutiae is not favorably regarded by all. Many point to the breakdown of the Italian totalitarian system with its vaunted efficiencies, under bombing attacks of a type which in the Battle of London only stiffened British resistance. It is shown that there is little difference between government monopoly and private monopoly and that anything but free enterprise will in the end stultify the entire economic system, entrenching in power both inefficiency and corruption, and necessitating a complicated type of direction which all the wisdom of Solomon could not handle without final disaster.

The Parliamentarians point out that the curse of this age is the growing might of the bureaucracies, which have reduced all human

[1] Gustav Stolper, *German Economy 1870-1940*, pp. 19-20.

feeling to power calculations, and all morals to the specter of utility. They assert that most of the difficulty between nations is due to other causes than lack of government control, but that one of these is government interference in the normal laws of economics and trade. They aver that it is the very lack of flexibility of the managerial State which pushes it headlong into war in an atmosphere of general predatory aggression which even the largest private corporations could never manage.

One is forced to believe at least this, that whatever the worth of the collectivization scheme into which we precipitously are plunging, none of its evils may be mitigated or avoided. The very existence of the controls provided by governmental monopoly creates centripetal forces which put an end to independent competition whether in identical or related economic fields. Since the actual source of power in the industrial State is industry, control of these sources by the government will nullify all other political balances and reduce them to zero.

The electorate and the jobholders by becoming identical dispose of the fiction of independent political parties. The totalitarian State becomes a fact, and with it new rivalries of a more heartless and inflexible nature.

It is through the nature of a balanced economy, rather than through force and compulsion, that we should find expression to those social ideals to which the race aspires. It is patent that the solution to the poor living standards of the Chinese peasant is not to be found by allocating absolute powers to central bureaucracies. It required no such intervention to create the high standards enjoyed by the Midwestern farmer or the high wage of the skilled worker of our Northern States. This was rather the result of intelligently guided self-interest, involving a minimum of legislation and governmental interference.

The purely mechanistic view of existence will always prove a frail reed on which to lean. The unadulterated pragmatic ideal is seldom any sounder than the hedonism to which it leads. We must recognize that there is a separate set of purely spiritual values which bears on all the issues of life with a strength and power which cannot be safely ignored. It is these which keep a functioning society in equilibrium. They are the prophylactic against the social pellagras and moral leprosies which otherwise corrupt mind and soul and reduce men to the status of grubbing animals. In this important sense moral responsibility has a material worth. It is the required counterbalance for social achievement, and is one part of a well-ordered universe which may not be dispensed with.

The great truth we must arrive at and proclaim is this, that the greater the power and the more significant the gains of material science, the more necessary a system of viable ethics becomes if the structure is not to collapse through its own dead weight. In short, morality pays off.

This is not an easy concept to sell. It appears to possess obvious weaknesses which cancel out its great truths.

Nevertheless, in no other way can we avoid the universal neurosis which grows with the achievements of the industrial age and which is its heel of Achilles. We must reach the view that this will either be a moral world or civilization cannot survive the machine.

If the gentlemen believe they can achieve a permanent peace on this earth without reference to these propositions they are quite mad.

Without this common faith in man's destiny and in the purposes and objectives of life, even material science can have no goal. This may be seen in the warped and distorted views held toward scientific achievement in Nazi Germany where the mechanistic interpretation of society vies with the mystic faith in "blood" for dominance over the German mind. Here there is no common pursuit of truth, and even scientific discovery and intellectual achievement is subjected to the scrutiny of racial interests.

Thus we have the twin error that material science and technical proficiency will solve all problems, and that the ability to master these issues rises from race alone.

Even in its mysticism, this view represents the distilled thoughts of the managerial revolution perverted to the purposes of a single nation. Its inevitable consequence is the view the Nazis hold toward man himself, that he is made to serve the State and that he is actuated not by principles, but by envy, hatred, greed and bestiality.

It is this cynicism toward the essential goodness of human nature which renders Nazi principles not only malign, but unsound. It is not the abhorrent nature of these dogmas alone which makes them undesirable but their essential impracticability. Hence it is not their depravity and wickedness which must be stressed if they are to be cleansed from the Caucasian mind, but their unsoundness.

If freedom, democracy, mercy and compassion appear to have lost their meaning and to be mere empty rubbish, and if they seem to bear no real relation to the problems posed by today, it is because humanity for the moment has lost its sense of eternal truth. We are unable to see that society is built on faith as much as power. It is cemented by acceptances, by the willingness of the son to take care of his aging father and the mother to suckle her newborn babe. It is only when it is anchored in the pursuit of true happiness that it can be successful or can be reasoned into well-ordered sequences.

It is this contempt for humankind and for personal happiness, which makes Germany the supreme danger point by which the world may be contaminated and Western civilization brought down in ruins. In defeat, the Germans may prove more menacing and more invincible than in victory through imparting this spiritual sickness whose growth has not been halted even during the war. Prussia having conquered Germany may finally be found to have conquered the world, though having twice lost a contest of arms.

Before any physical schemes of salvation can be advanced, the moral foundations on which they rest must be firm. If these are corrupted, the entire structure crumbles. These facts will not emerge from the vulgar realities of the diplomats, or from the half-truths by which the politicians pander to the mass in their quest for power. They can come only from the will of men who are determined to remain free, and to whom no sacrifice is too great if it serves the attainment of this goal.

Unless a projection can be made on a broad canvas, which in practice liquidates the difficulties associated with national self-interests and the prejudices of many lifetimes, our alliance with the principal members of the United Nations will have to be viewed with one eye cocked warily to the time when it will find itself in practice, dissolved. This will occur whenever the fundamental interests of the other big States become clearly alien to our own.

This dénouement, and the internal collapse of the West, is what the Germans have been counting on. It would again presage *der Tag*, the advent of the third modern Punic War. The Germans would hope for bloodless victory. Their undiminished megalomania would see in all this turmoil and disaster the future of renascent Germania, and the triumph of a war fought with economic and psychological weapons.

Thus would be remedied the great mistake which from the German computation Hitler made by resorting to arms before the field had been made ready.

Against this sinister project we have to establish a reasoned and logical world backed by a total faith in the destiny of those things we hold to be true.

XVIII

THE QUESTION OF OUR DEFEATED ENEMIES

AFTER our enemies have been brought to heel, the problem represented by each of them will vary greatly. Italy will be abject and drained of the short spurt of energy which her last abortive Caesar had stimulated in her. Her people will be embittered against nationalism and perhaps against all constituted authority. The problem will be one of ideological wrangling, proletarian movements, and impassioned violence founded on a fully aroused and quixotic Latin idealism.

The questions of Finland, Rumania, and Bulgaria will be matters of negotiation with the Soviet Union, as those of French Indo-China and Thailand will be with China.

What the view of the Western States toward a defeated Japan will be is hard to foresee. That it will be complicated by fear of both China and the U.S.S.R. may be deemed certain.

Deprived of its normal expanding economy, Japan will be helpless. Without the markets and sources of raw materials provided by her captive territories, she will be in an impossible economic situation. Her heavy industry in Manchukuo will be lost to China. The Chinese Republic will demand and probably receive the Japanese mercantile fleet and that portion of Japanese industry which can be dismantled and moved to the mainland.

The great Japanese problem will become one of evacuation. There will have to be an orderly migration from the Nipponese islands, which no longer will support the human masses which now crawl over their rocky surface.[1]

The factors bearing on Japan's postwar behavior may be disposed of by simple reference to one of them, the glaring weakness of her situation in space. Once Japan is robbed of the armored chain of islands which safeguard her main living areas from direct frontal attack, she lies in a wholly unprotected situation. Her position directly off the east coast of Asia, once a source of strength when she was able to control the Yellow Sea with her warships, will expose her crowded cities to quick assault, making them as vulnerable as so many partridges on a limb. This factor, the product of the airplane and the new technology, dooms her to oblivion as a military Power.

Japan can emerge as a potential military competitor again only if China is convulsed into fragments by recurring internal disorders, and if Japanese industry is allowed to remain intact and given guaranteed access to desperately needed raw materials. Nippon otherwise has none of the geopolitical advantages which would enable her to become a factor in the power politics of tomorrow.

Her sources of industrial strength will be under alien control, which must have the effect of permanently disabling her as a first-class nation. Like Carthage after the Second Punic War, she will be compelled to devote her energies to small commerce and to become a military vassal of some stronger Power. This Power may be Russia, China or even the United States. It is quite possible that as a regenerate China progresses down the path of its destiny, the final role of Japan will be that of an island outpost of a great Oriental empire. Due to the energies of her people she may become politically influential within the estate of the Chinese giant. She may be to China what Wales and Scotland have been to Britain, but this is the best she can hope for.

It will not be necessary to raze the great shipbuilding works at Yokohama, or the heavy industries on Honshu and Kyushu as a

[1] Japan's present density of population is one of the greatest in the world—over 400 per square mile.

protection against Japanese-inspired war of the future. These imposing adjuncts to military power will be quite impotent.

It may be taken for granted that her armies as well as her military equipment will be summarily demolished, and that she will lose the islands of the South Seas in addition to all her possessions on the mainland of Asia.

Since Japan can live only by importing raw materials and exporting them in the shape of finished goods, she will be abjectly dependent on the good will of those who control her sources of supply, as well as her potential markets.

Though Nippon is the third largest rubber manufacturer, she will have to import her entire supply of crude rubber. She must import more than a third in value of all the raw materials she uses in her industries, and must bring in from abroad the great bulk of her iron ore as well as scrap iron.

Her present insufficient resources of petroleum are all on the island of Sakhalin, which presumably will be re-annexed to the Soviet Union. Japan has some reserves of coal but these are of mediocre quality. Her total iron reserves do not come to half the amount used in a single year by the United States. While Nippon is self-sufficient in sulphur and almost so in chromium and copper, she possesses almost none of the ferro-alloys. She must import all her nickel, vanadium, bauxite, tin and mercury.

With the exception of copper there is no major raw material with which Japan is endowed in sufficient amount. She has neither wool, cotton nor nitrates. Even the pulp for her great rayon industry must be imported. This is true also of a great part of her food, only her fishing industry being sufficient to give her an independent position in world markets.

The Japanese market in raw silk is likely to suffer badly under Chinese competition, as well as from that of the new synthetic materials which soon will be produced in quantity by all of the industrialized nations. Her single major asset, which may be useless for want of raw materials, is her fine resource in hydroelectric power.

Thus everything from Japan's number one export item, cotton goods, down to the very products of her synthetic dye industry, would depend on outside sources of supply as well as outside markets. Such a position as this in a conscienceless and highly competitive world is a precarious one, to say the least.

It would appear as if the Japanese problem will be self-liquidating and that Japan will never again rank among the Great Powers. What should be done with the Emperor, the ruling class and Japanese industry will be an incidental rather than a crucial question.

It will be evident that no plans can be made in relation to the future of Japan without China and the Soviet Union. The last word will be spoken by them.

II

The problem of the German Reich will involve far greater difficulties.

Germany will continue to occupy a geographic position in the very center of Europe. She will hold within her borders the greatest percentage of Europe's heavy industry. She will possess some two million industrial establishments, in which more than forty-five per cent of her working population will be employed.

In the course of their adventure across Europe, the Germans have relentlessly subverted the institutions and cultural forces which might have placed a brake on postwar German leadership. The Reich has dismantled industry, destroyed schools and universities, and in the Balkans and Slavic East has all but liquidated the intellectual and ruling classes.

Europe will enter the postwar period with her energies depleted and functioning in a void. Nazi policies have effaced all areas of stability, leaving behind only the prospect of administrative disorder and political chaos. All of the forces of economic balance will appear to be centered in the Reich, which consciously is creating this situation of automatic leadership in an effort to pluck victory out of defeat.

The huge German trusts will be represented as the sole guarantors of equilibrium in Europe. The Continent will be served by a tremendous economic empire run on totalitarian lines. This empire will be legally in the hands of German owners and technicians. It will provide an urgently needed instrument for the postwar reconstruction of Europe. The tendency on the part of the conquerors will be to leave it undisturbed. They will be more concerned with the fact that Europe will be starving and ready for radical mischief.

The Germans will attempt to prove that their system of orderly administration is the last barrier to chaos. They will retire to within their own borders, but their control of economic Europe will remain.

German reasoning on the situation is simple and logical. The military element of war today is only a single phase. The other theaters in which a struggle for mastery may be concluded successfully, are the trading and industrial economies, psychological warfare and the proselytizing use of idea. All of these methods played an important part in the Reich's amazing bloodless victories prior to the opening military assault on Poland. They were factors in the fall of France and the Low Countries, and were influential in the pacifist position taken by Great Britain and the United States.

With the lesson of the last postwar period in mind, the Germans will by no means view the situation resulting from their defeat as hopeless. They are convinced that an outward alteration in Germany's political structure in the direction of free government, will allow them quite decent peace terms with the possibility of early rehabilitation.

Individual leaders whom the United Nations can regard as trustworthy are being groomed by the Germans now to play this role. The German Badoglios and Darlans will have even more reason for existence than the Fascist functionaries already found acceptable by the Anglo-American leadership.

Immediately upon the resumption of international trade, American and English business men unavoidably will find themselves dealing with Germans. The shipping and mining interests, together with almost all heavy manufacturing, will be owned by immense German trusts. Such organizations as the Reichswerke Hermann Goering, I. G. Farbenindustrie and Kontinentale Oel A.G., hold the factories and raw material sources of Europe in an immovable grip. The aggregate financial structure of the Continent funnels into half a dozen banks in Germany. The unpleasant fact is that all of the physical resources of Europe are legally subsidiary to the German system, and can be disentangled from it only by force.

The Germans will seek and find allies in many directions. They believe they will win friends in powerful financial and industrial circles of London, New York and Washington as they did in the early days when Hitler was rising to power as the foremost opponent of social reform. They see in their camp powerful elements in the United States, pathologically anti-democratic and fanatically dedicated to the cause of the right wing revolution.

German leaders see the Anglo-American coalition entering Europe as the champion of the old order, of stable business conditions and of the conservative approach to life. They believe that all revolutions of a popular nature will be ruthlessly suppressed by the conquerors, who will be compelled in any case to deal with the great body of Nazi functionaries in order to preserve order. They take it for granted that while a few top heads will roll, the basic German structure will remain unaffected, waiting on the inevitable time when the French and English leave and the Germans once more take over undisputed control of their own country.

They believe that by the very nature of our own problems we cannot undertake permanently to police Central Europe or to maintain long term control over the policies of German educational institutions. They feel that since policing will prove unprofitable our soldiers eventually will be withdrawn by public opinion at home, and that the German propaganda machine, so successful in the past, can undertake responsibility for this task.

When the Nazi Party closes up shop and is driven underground, these agencies will be ready to renew the struggle. The loss of the battle of Germany will be conceived of as a single phase in a deadly contest between primary and universal forces, in which the Germans do not doubt their final success. The loss of this war will not convince them of their weakness but rather of the inevitable destruction of the old order.

In the bitter realization that victory has been torn out of her very grasp, in this brilliant gamble to possess the earth, the Third Reich will move with quiet calculation to prepare for that next phase which is to bring final victory. In her vision is that which sober conventional States will never understand—the frenetic search for triumph, the haggard demand for self-justification, and the longing for a new order which will portend the heroic age. Here the German Siegfried, so long thwarted and so many times reappearing to contend with renewed strength against the enemies of Germanism, is at last to sweep all before him and gain the ring. This dream conception would not be altered by a shift in the political fortunes of the country in the direction of Communism. It endured and flourished through the monarchy, the republic, and the authoritarian regime of Hitler. It will adjust itself to the next epoch with equal facility.

The war party easily could figure the present enterprise as having been a profitable one despite German reverses. The Germans have proved that there is no power in Western Europe capable of resisting their arms for more than a few months in any military operation which can possibly be visualized for the future.

Germany could hope to neutralize Russia, and by the tactics with which we are familiar, to corrupt America and eliminate her as a force for the next war. Economic and psychological weapons have placed in the hands of the Reich unlimited opportunities to recover. They have made her an omnipresent menace, not by reason of her possessions and position in space alone, but by virtue of that enduring will which is the final master of all things.

Surveying the conditions which resulted from the last war, Germany cannot fail to note the truth of Tardieu's bitter remark that if the Reich lost the war "she won the peace after the lapse of fifteen years." [1] During this period Germany maneuvered her conquerors into shelving the reparations to which she had agreed. She succeeded in getting them to revise the treaty by which the Western States had secured some measure of safety against renewed acts of violence. By what were for the most part perfectly legal means, she was able to secure the restoration of her armed forces.

In their preparations for the next war, the Germans see the following conditions: 1. A weakened Europe. 2. An entirely different military situation than applied in the past, suggesting that the weapons of the victors might again be rendered obsolete. 3. The elimination of England as the pivot in the balance of power system. Germany foresees certain conflict between the Soviets and the Western World. In this tug of war she visualizes herself in the position of the actual balancer, capable by reason of her heavy industry and central position, of commanding the attentions of the Western Powers, who would be forced by fear of the Russian colossus to forego any threats of punishment.

As long as the Germans are able to maintain commercial mastery over Central and Southeastern Europe, the Reich will be capable of fighting a successful war. The potentials of Germany's military position will be dictated by her strength as a manufacturing nation, plus the power of her communications, which are incomparably the best in Europe.

Germany continues to see the position as that of a semi-agricultural continent dominated by a great industrial power center. She relies on the supposition that nothing can be done to alter this situation except by methods which in themselves would impair the residual economy of Europe and render rehabilitation more difficult.

The Nazis assume that the United Nations will follow the path of expediency throughout, and will not for the sake of long range safeguards risk complicating the immediate task. The Teutons

[1] André Tardieu, *France in Danger.*

hence believe that the conquerors can be subtly blackmailed into leaving German industry alone.

Germany must be regarded as the sore point in the Western universe, a nation utterly irreconcilable in any terms which the West could find acceptable. One thing is certain: no sound functioning basis by which Western society can endure may be found as long as this paranoiac and conspiratorial State exists.

The grave danger is not that the Reich will be able to conquer the world again. She will not be able. The time for that is past. The entry of the East into participation in world affairs will reduce the Nazi schemes to pallid provincial incoherencies.

The power of these conspiracies lies in another direction—in their effect on the mentality of the white world generally, and their crippling result on its psychology. The entire well of civilization has been poisoned by the tactics of German psychological methods, almost beyond redemption in our time. Postwar Germany easily could become the infection point by which a creation already corroded with the virus of moral decay, might acquire its last mortal sickness.

The techniques employed in the succession of Teutonic thrusts for world domination has left on the body of civilization lesions of the gravest consequence. Tensions between colored and white, Gentile and Jew, Celt, Slav and Teuton, capital and labor, Catholic and Protestant, have been stimulated to risky proportions. There has been a breakdown in moral tone, and in the general sense of security within the nations, as well as in their external relationships.

If the Reich again should seek to tread the path of military glory, the first fury of this sinister State must as always be directed against her associates among the Western nations who, like the Jews, she regards as standing in the path of her destiny. If there is to be another fratricidal contest among the white races precipitated by the historic German determination on power, it can end only in the failure of Western civilization, which will be an easy prey to the forces gathering in the East. For these reasons it is imperative that the traditional ambitions of Germany be neutralized and that the Reich's attempt to seize leadership in the Western World be halted once and for all. Otherwise we will find ourselves, win, lose or draw, in an inevitable conflict with the East in which the prize will be the future of man on this planet.

What happens to ambitious Nippon, vicious little Slovakia, treacherous Croatia, Rumania and Italy, or foolish Bulgaria, Finland, Hungary, Thailand and Burma, is not apt to prove of decisive consequence. But the question of what disposal is to be made of Germany is unmistakably the central issue of the war and the criterion of the peace which is to follow.

In the coming occupation of Germany, Russia and the Anglo-American partners will sit in the territory of the Reich like two strange cats guarding the same bowl of milk. If on the surface everything appears calm and serene, the tension beneath will be the more painful.

The Russians and the Anglo-Americans will be absorbed with two different conceptions of the future into which postwar Germany must fit. Despite the lip-service paid to unity and collaboration, when put to the test of practical politics, these divergencies of view may vary so greatly as to be unbridgeable.

This is Germany's hope. Instead of being prostrate before the triumphant Allies she would find herself once again in a bargaining position, ready to take up the threads which would weave the next phase in the still undecided struggle for mastery of the globe.

The Kremlin will want a Germany either under a strong government sympathetic to Russian ideals, or dependent on the Soviets for support. If Russia retains the deeply ingrained fear of Western imperialism which has haunted her for a generation, she will require German industry integral and unbroken. Possession of Central Europe would render completely ineffective any *cordon sanitaire* which could be erected on the Continent against her, and would add immeasurably to the power of her weapons.

The possibility of fresh quarrels with England and America is not overlooked by Stalin. The question of Poland and the Baltic countries has not been settled. Neither has the question of access to warm water on the Atlantic or on the Southern oceans fronting Asia. Stalin will want a free hand in the Balkans, the classic objective of Russian policy.

The United States whose political course is for the first time in its history veering sharply to the right, is adopting a view dangerously close to reliance on an American Century. England which will feel itself directly imperilled by a further extension of conflict, will seek to mediate the difference between the two attitudes and to balance them to her own advantage. The struggle for power conceivably might become a naked one.

The Germans will observe their opportunities in this situation with eager and alert eyes.

The question of Germany, therefore, is more than a question affecting a single defeated country. It is a question of a world settlement which looks forward to the rationalization of all problems which might disturb the future peace. Anything less than this leaves Germany as an arena of conflict for the various powers, and will create a truly diabolical situation in which possession of the friendship of the Reich may become the eagerly sought-for prize.

When the United Nations face each other on the two sides of the Wilhelmstrasse in Berlin, they could very well be standing at Armageddon. The crisis which has derived from the assault made by Germany on the world, will be transferred to their own relations.

If we are to deal with this problem and insulate ourselves against further trouble from this quarter, we must weigh with great care the nature of the question as it relates to German character and history itself.

To arrive at any collective estimate of the Germans must be acknowledged to be difficult and subject to all the errors inherent in such generalizations. Yet not to do so would be foolhardy. A serious miscalculation in conclusion could well cost Western civilization its future.

III

It is cardinal to any realistic settlement that human society must be reckoned as an organic structure which derives its primary character from its antecedents. It has a genesis, and it is admittedly subject to pressures as well as impressions and accidents. It is made up of men, and men relinquish tradition reluctantly. The distinctive features of a culture, as the common traits of human personality, are never altogether abandoned. They simply are given new names and diverted into new channels.

The real question is whether what we have witnessed in Germany is a passing occurrence or the result of characteristics so deeply engraved in the nature and lives of the German people as to offer little hope of early eradication. The German problem should not be seen as a question of crime and punishment alone, but in its relation to the future of the world and for its effect upon the common purposes of humanity.

The history of German rearmament has proved clearly that there is no system of control whether imposed by military occupation, reparations or treaty, which cannot be evaded by a resolute people. All military history proves that peace is not the product of law, or of sanctions, and cannot be imposed unilaterally in a scheme which runs counter to the dynamics of the nations who are affected.

All treaties of peace and their aftermath have shown, if they show anything, that enduring peace can only derive from one of the three following: 1. The loser, as in the case of the Carthaginians, is dead and his cities plowed under. 2. The loser has lost his capacity to make war in terms of the weapons available to the victor. 3. The loser merges his interests with those of the victor so that the dynamisms of each present no basic contradictions.

It should be regarded as axiomatic by the peacemakers that wherever any fundamental conflict of interests remains as a residue of war, a vigorous people sooner or later will render the fact of their defeat meaningless. A new trial of strength is certain to ensue at the first acceptable opportunity.

These are the realities with which an intelligible peace must be concerned. Any proposal which fails to take them into consideration, particularly in regard to Germany, is the product of wishful thinking and can lead only to disaster.

It may be assumed that the coming peace, no matter how lightly imposed, will prove burdensome to the Germans, and that they will endeavor to circumvent it. The nature of that attempt will have a determinative bearing on the impending course of world events.

Among the statesmen of the United Nations various explanations are offered for Germany's warlike behavior. These range from official expressions of Marxist dogma which assume it to be an expression of class psychology, through the middle ground of those who credit it to pure reaction against the iniquities of the Versailles Treaty, to those who share with Lord Vansittart and Clemenceau the belief that the Germans are fundamentally atavistic, of violent mentality and permanently arrested moral development.

Whatever may be the truth of any of these assertions, it cannot be ignored that for the second time in a generation these people have flung themselves against organized Western society in a fanatic determination to enslave it. Now that they again are about to fail, the question is whether they are to be cured, punished, or perhaps even expunged as a nation.

It must be acknowledged that a society based on the idea of revenge possesses within itself the seeds of its own destruction; but a society based on an incapacity to control periodic lawlessness cannot exist at all. License in international relationships must bring with it the ultimate necessity for dictatorship. Its result will be precisely the type of world military government proposed by the Nazis and the Japanese.

The fear of punishing any nation for the crimes it has committed against collective society is not an expression of humanity but rather of that type of weakness which formerly went under the name of appeasement.

The question is not one of what we should do, but rather this: *what will we be able to do?* There can be no question of being harsh with Germany. The problem is only whether a peaceful and progressive Germany can be created.

It may well be that German history was a lie, and that the Germans were about to escape it when they themselves were enslaved by Hitler and the adventurers who followed him. It would seem to make little difference whether this vicious circle followed on the corruption of the millions of Germans by the Nazi *Fuehrer,* or existed as an inalienable element of the German character. The probabilities are that there are no inalienable characteristics in nations, that the traits and actions of nations are the outgrowth of tradition and habit, situation in space, psychology, opportunity, and a myriad of other factors additional to those of heredity. Whatever they may spring from, however, national characteristics are visible and recognizable. The plain fact is that they exist.

Even though a pathology may be most innocently acquired, it does not follow that it may be as easily eradicated, or that it may be eradicated at all. To cure Germanism, it may be necessary to destroy the political, economic and sociological structure which brought it into existence and on whose teats it has been nursed through the centuries.

The record as we have surveyed it is not good. It does not validate the theory that Germany may be bribed into subjection, that on the premise of a prosperous Germany being a peaceful Germany, the Reich should be assisted in reviving her commerce and industry rather than subjected to penalty.

The record everywhere disputes any effort to explain Germany's behavior in terms of poverty or economic repression. In 1914 when the Kaiser threw his legions against France, the Reich was the most prosperous of all the European States. When she behaved herself the best, Germany was at the lowest ebb of her fortunes.

Wherever we look at the German situation, we see unmistakable warning that it would be a tragic error for the democracies to settle this problem as if it related primarily to a man named Hitler and his restricted group of accomplices.

Long ago it was observed by that strange hunchback genius, Homer Lea, that governments are only an expression of the collective ideals of the individuals who are governed; [1] a fact noted also by Le Bon, who pointed out that "peoples are not governed in accordance with their caprices of the moment, but as their character determines that they shall be." [2] Whatever the passions, circumstances and standards of the mass, they will be reflected in the long range conduct of the ruling authority. This is exemplified by reference to England which remains a democracy though under a monarchial regime, and to certain Spanish American republics, where the most oppressive despotisms exist despite their republican constitutions.

To argue against this thesis would seem to argue that men are clods without free will, and that their relationship to their own government is a nullity. It would have to be assumed that their loyalties, enthusiasms, emotions and attitudes generally, were like putty, capable of being transformed to his own purposes by every adventurer who imposes himself upon them. This, of course, is nonsensical.

In our analysis of German history we have noted that the scheme of ruthlessness, the desire for rule, the implicit belief in brutality and force, and the concept of mission by which the *herrenvolk* are to take charge of the destinies of the globe, are constant elements in conventional German thinking. The pattern is at least as old as the Pan-Germanism which began its course in the middle of the Eighteenth Century, and probably reaches back to impulses derived from that predatory blood brotherhood, the Order of the Teutonic Knights.

Rejection of customary morality may be seen as easily in the

1 Homer Lea, *The Valor of Ignorance*, p. 101.
2 Gustav Le Bon, *The Crowd*, pp. 97, 98.

Socialist Stresemann's remarks that "it is the policy of force which always finally will triumph," as in the comment of Frederick William IV that "all charters are only scraps of paper."

The schemes for expropriation of Germany's European neighbors extend to before the time Hitler emerged from his mother's womb. As early as 1895 the Pan-German League was publishing pamphlets urging that other Europeans be relegated to the more menial forms of labor with only racial Germans enjoying political rights, operating businesses or owning land. Only in Germany could a public figure like General von Bernhardi have proclaimed war to be "an indispensable factor of culture in which a truly civilized nation finds the highest expression of strength and vitality."

It can be argued that the huge majorities given the Nazi Party at the polls were synthetic and the product of coercion. Some of them undoubtedly were. But it is useful to observe that in Germanic areas under foreign jurisdiction, the populations turned to National Socialism with the same unswerving faith and enthusiasm as in the Reich itself. The Sudeten areas of Czechoslovakia went solidly over to the Nazi side, as did German Memel and Danzig. In Austria, National Socialism grew irrepressibly. The popular support upon which the Austrian Government rested was destroyed long before Hitler's legions triumphantly crossed the border to the wild acclaim of the population.

There are, of course, individuals in the Reich whose minds have not been corrupted by these clouded fancies. Many of them were forced to flee during the time of Bismarck. The others were done away with by Herr Hitler with that German thoroughness which leaves no stone unturned.

Practically speaking, no democratic German underground exists. The forces which are functioning relate to the Communist dream, to the theocratic philosophy of the Centrists, or to the manipulations of the dispossessed financial oligarchs. There may be disorders after the fall of Hitler but the net effect of these would not be in the direction of the establishment of a free society as we know it.

How little the world understood the malignancies eating at the heart of the Reich is no better illustrated than in Sir Neville Henderson's statement that "Herr Hitler and Nationalism are the products of the defeat of a great nation in war and its reaction against the confusion and distress which followed that defeat." [1]

Despite the claims subsequently made against it, the Treaty of Versailles was as equitable a document as could have been drawn under the circumstances. While it created an economically unstable and politically unsound Europe, it did follow with some accuracy President Wilson's ethnographic convictions. It was the closest approximation of cultural and natural geographic frontiers ever to be achieved in Europe.

The failure of the Weimar Republic is no more attributable to the Treaty of Versailles than the success of the Bolshevik Revolution is traceable to the harsh Treaty of Brest-Litovsk imposed by the Germans themselves on collapsing Russia. [2]

After the Peace of Tilsit, the rigid disarmament clauses inserted by France were evaded with the same skill which characterized the evasions after the Peace of Versailles. Then the Prussian minister, Scharnhorst, introduced the modern system of compulsory

---

1 Sir Neville Henderson, *Final Report of the Rt. Hon. Sir Neville Henderson on The Circumstances leading to the Termination of his Mission in Berlin, September 20, 1939*, p. 2.

2 By this Treaty, forced on Russia on March 4, 1918, the Ukraine, Poland, and the three Baltic provinces were severed from the Empire and placed under the protection of Germany. Russia lost thirty-four per cent of her population, fifty-four per cent of her industrial undertakings and almost ninety per cent of her known coal. She was compelled to agree to become an economic lackey to the Reich, giving most favored treatment but receiving none in exchange.

Together with the severed Ukraine and the Baltic States, Russia was to become an agrarian hinterland and raw material supplier for Germany. This plan itself, as drastic as it was, was regarded by the Germans as a temporary expedient. The ultimate scheme of partition was revealed in a letter by Kaiser Wilhelm II to the Hetman of the Don Cossacks. It was proposed that the balance of Russia be divided into three parts, all under German control—the Union of the Southeast (which was to include the Caucasian oilfields), Central Russia, and Siberia.

short service for the purpose of creating large reserves, just as the modern Nazis circumvented the strictures of Versailles by creating the mechanized professional army.

Since the time Prussia became a State and galvanized the German-speaking duchies and kingdoms into the conception of nationhood, there has been little in the German record which promises that any Germany, no matter how conceived, could be a safe neighbor. The end of each frustrated attempt at conquest has seen renewed preparations for a new one, the scheme merely being revised to cover the mistakes its authors conceived to have been instrumental in the earlier failures.

The spiritual inheritance which Hitler received from Ludendorff, Bismarck, and Frederick the Great, will be handed down to the next generation intact. The Nazis have done a thorough job of indoctrination. Hitler knows the power of ideas and understands their indestructibility. "An idea which has been avidly absorbed by millions," he wrote, "cannot be destroyed by violence, unless the sword itself has the power of an electrifying idea." [1]

The whole younger generation of Germany has been poisoned beyond redemption by the total tactics pursued by the Nazis. For all practical purposes they are incurable. These boys have been brought up to worship adventure, to despise and hate aliens and to gaze on the operations of a peaceful, moral society as decadent and contemptible. The acid has bitten to the core of the nation and has created a regimented, fanatic, and conscienceless youth whose entire dream is the glory of the warrior.

Added thus to the existing megalomania, which has been Germany's curse, will be the ardent conviction ingrained in the German youth by years of intensive propaganda, that they have been cheated by a quirk of fate of their appointed place in world society. The effort on the part of the Poles, Yugoslavs, Czechs and others whom the Germans regard as subraces, to erect their own industries and assume an equal voice in the affairs of the Conti-

[1] Fried, *The Guilt of the German Army*, pp. 88, 89.

nent, will be looked on as a dastardly presumption which one day must be liquidated by airplanes, tanks and demolition bombs.

Hundreds of thousands of Germans, the most active and enterprising of their race, have found lucrative positions under the New Order. Farmers who had possessed but a pittance, now own large estates in the conquered areas. "Clerks in German banks became managers in Polish or Czech banks. Department heads in German stores became managers or even owners in conquered stores. Petty government officials of every variety moved from insignificant and unpromising posts in Berlin to what corresponds to cabinet rank in Copenhagen, Brussels and Paris." [1]

Had the conquest been permanent, the future of these Germans would have been lush indeed. These fantastic achievements occurred virtually overnight, and the adventuring German executives, farmers and business men who will be thrown back on their heels into the old Reich, are not likely to forget. There is no humor or moral side to the Germanic influx which seeped over Europe. The German regards possession of these things as his patrimony and his destiny, and is inclined to look on any resistance to these acts as sacrilege.

It would be a mistake to believe that any people have ever forgotten their past glories or ceased living in anticipation of reclaiming them. Even today, after more than a generation of exile, the scattered and poverty-stricken White Russian émigrés still live in the dream of reforming Russia on the old feudal pattern and recovering their ancestral position.

Nazi teachings and years of looting, rape and murder, have taken a fearful toll of German character, which will show in uncompromising viciousness when the Nazi Party has been driven underground and becomes a league of secret and fanatic executioners, similar to those who took the life of Rathenau and other moderates among the German statesmen. These men will form the worst group of disciplined hoodlums ever to be let loose on a

1 Joseph C. Harsch, *Pattern of Conquest*, pp. 46, 47.

nation during peacetime. They have been taught to unleash the lowest instincts of human nature and to regard the balance of humankind as their natural prey, against whom almost any excess is permitted.

In Hitler's elite Black Shirt bodyguard, the Schutzstaffel, were more than five hundred thousand of these youths by the beginning of 1942, organized on a pyramidal cell system and capable of functioning as a disciplined underground body. The Brown Shirt storm troopers were still more numerous. These shock troops in themselves are sufficient to constitute a catalytic force which will act irresistibly on any post-war Germany which can be set up. They are the Janissaries who have been trained to unconditional obedience to the racial and geopolitical concept of the world, and to Germany's place as the central court from which the uncompromising *Uebermensch* will rule for the future.

Those who have dealt with Nazi prisoners see no evidence of contrition, or lessening of the perverse complexes which have distinguished their conduct throughout the war. Their arrogance remains undiminished. Quentin Reynolds says that he talked to at least two hundred German prisoners and "never met one who was anything but an unregenerate, hundred per cent supporter of every theory which Hitler holds." What to do with this brutalized Nazi youth is one of the most perplexing parts of the question of Germany.

There is also the problem of what to do with the numerous Nazi Party officials, hardly less saturated with Pan-German doctrines. These occupy every job in the government, judiciary and schools, as well as in government-controlled labor and industry. Under the socialized scheme of German existence they are everywhere.

It is fanciful to believe that it is possible to impose on a people such as this a different view through control of their educational system. Neither legitimate nor paranoid responses can be revised by this means. The full power of the Russian Government was unable to Russify Poland under the Czars. The Jews survived all efforts to Christianize them during the inquisitions of the Middle

Ages. The attitude of the South toward the Negro lived through the carpet-bagging period, if anything, intensified.

Nations cannot have education thrust upon them. The process starts from within and grows from natural foundations. This is nowhere better illustrated than in the unavailing efforts of Chancellor Dollfuss to outlaw the growing Nazi Party in Austria, his repression going the length of abolishing their right to free speech, press and assemblage.

Neither can standards be overturned and facilely re-erected later, as anyone who has had experience with deterioration in moral principle can testify. The miscarriage of a criminal enterprise usually does not lead to reformation but rather the reverse, the criminal always being able to see by hindsight why he failed, and of ready conviction that next time he would succeed. This, indeed, appears to have been the case with Germany.

The blueprint for reeducation also presumes that the leaders of the United Nations are themselves democratically inclined and will not be swallowed up by their own bureaucracies. All the automatisms are against this. The Western States themselves will have a difficult enough time maintaining their own democratic character at home.

The temptation to deal with a reformed government, or with industrialists, clericals, military leaders and others who have on their side the guarantee of "stability," will be an overwhelming one. Yet here is the path to danger which will lead Germany again to recovery and involve the world once more in an unlimited disaster similar to that from which we are emerging. It leaves in power all of the agencies and institutions which will make such a renewed attempt inevitable.

Presumably, the German army will be disarmed and disbanded with the exception of a small nucleus which will remain under the supervision of the Allied High Command to assist in policing the country against political disorder. The German Officers Corps which is the center of any future German military economy, will remain, if only as an illegal or quasi-social organization. Its traditions and iron discipline will endure. The vast collection of military literature on which its philosophy and logic depends will survive as a source of inspiration and instruction to a future revived Reich.

Though disarmed in other respects, the Germans would retain that formidable weapon whose employment they have reduced to one of the great military arts—the propaganda arm. The propaganda machine, whose activities extend in an unseen web into almost every phase of organized German existence, has become an integral part of the German social apparatus. Dissolving it will not destroy it, but cause it to be cunningly hidden in the activities of German police officials and civil functionaries, where it will continue to operate under the very noses of the occupying authorities.

In ways which cannot be controlled, the Germans carefully will direct their propaganda to alienate our own occupying forces from the philosophies for which they have fought. The contamination of Nazism should not be underestimated. It is forceful and potent, and quite capable of reaching deep into the minds of the Americans and Britishers stationed in the Reich. It will be unconsciously absorbed during friendly contact with the German population. Its propagation will be regarded by the German underground as its chief task.

No amount of police power will alter this situation in the slightest. Even the limited policing done west of the Rhine after World War I, ended in the total discomfiture of the policing nations.

The job of policing this powerful State would soon be found to be an unprofitable one. Advantageous policing can be done only under the German *Gauleiter* system, with the local population reduced to actual slavery. Any system less brutal than this cannot be enforced. It invites resentments, angers and boycotts. The workers will not work, business men will not cooperate and government functionaries will find ways to sabotage the administrative machine. Those who work with the invaders will be regarded as

Quislings, men who in the future must be violently punished for their acts of betrayal.

As we continue to police, jaded weariness and surfeit will succeed the first enthusiasm of occupation. The people at home will demand the return of their boys. The Germans by degrees will begin to take back their country. .

No large and vigorous nation can be policed forever. If they have the power to last, it is the resident or conquered population which will emerge from such a contest triumphant.

IV

It may be taken for granted that the Reich will be disarmed and forced to evacuate all non-German territory. Some sort of civil government will be set up with military advisers from the armed forces of the United Nations, who undoubtedly will retain the real power.

Quite independent of any convictions we may possess with reference to Germany's guilt in precipitating the war, she will be granted relief in the way of food, medicine and other commodities. A German interim government undoubtedly will agree to a revamping of the school curriculum under the supervision of advisers from the United Nations. The greater body of the Nazi laws will be rescinded and the Nazi Party itself liquidated, after which it will continue its existence underground.

We then will be faced with the real question: *what to do?*

There will be an atmosphere of strain and uncertainty attended perhaps by some internal violence as the underground groups settle scores with their enemies. Some elements will place themselves at once at the disposal of the occupying forces. The larger number of Germans will remain sullen. For the moment stunned and apathetic they will present to the invaders an aspect of being decent, stolid people who somehow managed to get themselves roped into this business and are now a bit aghast over it.

If we do not enter Germany with a predetermined plan which

we are committed to carry out, our moral resolution will crumble. We will see not an enemy but stout, bewildered burghers apparently willing to cooperate to set their house in order.

What can be done?

The usual plan advanced is the partition of Germany. This assumes that the evil of the contemporary Reich arose from its unification by Bismarck in 1870, and can be cured by turning the clock back and resurrecting the antique period.

This is a futile hope. The partition of Germany either along religious or sectional lines would only add fuel to the fire. The severed parts would be galvanized into action from the beginning, writhing and struggling to obey the central magnetism which was drawing them together again. This would be as true of Austria as of Bavaria, Prussia or Württemberg.

Such a solution moreover would be directly contrary to the material conditions of the age. Air power and modern communications have eliminated the principal significance of boundaries and have rendered buffer States useless. Strategic frontiers have ceased to have a meaning. Partition would add new and uneconomic sovereignties at the precise moment when the failure of small political entities had become apparent to all. It would represent an ugly current contrary to the needs of the times and would result in economic chaos and recurring political anarchy for all Europe. If Europe is to survive its troubles, it requires economic and political unity, not separation.

Breaking up Germany into bits will not liquidate the German drive for domination, or free the neighbors of the Reich from the perpetual menace of its military will. The Treaty of Versailles stripped Germany of her armies, and deprived her of much of her European territory. Germany lost valuable industrial regions, containing a great share of her iron ore, blast furnaces, foundries and rolling mills. Nevertheless, the Reich eventually was able to frustrate the restrictions placed on her, and to render these as ineffectual as if they had never existed.

The effort at beggaring the Reich by forcing her to pay reparations will prove equally unworkable. The amounts to be retrieved in themselves will not be important compared to the tremendous wreckage left behind by the German bull in its wild careening course through the world's china shop. After the last war the Reich was unable to pay a bill of thirty-two billion dollars, a trivial sum compared to the cost of this one.

The value of reparations would lie in their punitive content, or in the restraint they placed on the future activities of the German nation.

In practice, reparations do not quite work out in this fashion. If they are to be paid in goods they result in economic weakness and unemployment in the creditor countries.[1]

The German economy, on the other hand, would be forced to become more efficient and hence increasingly powerful, a result which would be enduring.

As the capacities of the German production machine rose to keep pace with the demands placed upon it, the economic level of the German workers would have to be raised in accordance. The Germans would require shipping, raw materials, food, and undoubtedly considerable loans to maintain the industrial circuit intact. The more Germany's productivity was raised to keep pace with the reparation demands, the more potent her industrial plant would become in relation to that of her enemies. Fully as important, the German character and capacity for sacrifice would harden, while that of the beneficiaries of her labor would deteriorate correspondingly.

If we expected production from German factories, the destruction caused by bomb damage, wear, and lack of proper replacement parts, would have to be repaired. This necessarily must be at the expense of further backing by the United Nations. The effect

---

[1] How this worked out after the last war may be seen by reference to the Dawes Plan, under which more than half of Germany's annuity payments were to be made in kind —mostly in coal. Following the coal crisis of 1920, England found herself in the extraordinary position of refusing to accept further deliveries because they were putting her coal industry out of business.

would be to make the Reich once again one of the great industrial Powers in order to extract the largest ransom of which her productivity was capable.

Unless all international commerce were to cease, reparation payments in money would have the identical effect as if they were in goods. The German Government would have to realize these funds by taxing its people, or by borrowing. This would assume a prosperity sufficient to involve a large surplus. If the surplus did not exist, the German State at once would become bankrupt. If the surplus does exist, German industry accordingly would be powerful.

There is only one way in which this merry-go-round of incredible fantasy could be kept turning—that of balancing off the amounts paid out, with an inflow of foreign loans. These manifestly would have to be made by the United Nations, under threat of impending collapse of the German economic apparatus and resulting political demoralization. The net effect of the Versailles reparations demand was precisely this, amounting to a gigantic swindle by the creditor nations against themselves.

During the period up to the advent of Hitler, the amounts borrowed by Germany exceeded the reparation payments made by her by more than one billion dollars. With these funds the Germans built a first-class industrial plant enabling them to compete in markets all over the globe and to seize the economic hegemony of Europe. In addition to constructing canals, roads, hydroelectric power lines and other productive works, Germany built great athletic fields, fine municipal buildings and even model apartments for the housing of workers.

Altogether, through a succession of altering supervisions and controls forced on the Allies by events, the reparations scheme finally came to nothing. It was founded on the usual contradictions. The view was compelled to be that Germany was only capable of paying if her economic structure was restored and her credit expanded. The result was to place the key to the situation directly in German hands and to turn the Allied triumph into a Pyrrhic victory.

During the course of the tug-of-war over reparations payments,

Germany engineered the disastrous inflation of 1923. This strata-
gem which led later to the most serious consequences for the Reich,
was initiated to defraud the creditors of Germany by artificially
reducing the value of the mark. It resulted in the ruin of the German middle class, but it enabled the German State to render the
payment of reparations farcical, and wiped out Germany's internal
debt. The effects also were felt by Germany's chief industrial competitors, the United States, England and France, who soon found
that this depreciated currency enabled Germany to undersell them
on the markets of the world.

In this single action, the German talent for unlimited excesses
carried even to the point of catastrophe, becomes clearly evident.
The present German national debt is increasing at the rate of four
billion marks a month. When the war is over the Reich will be
skating on the thin ice of bankruptcy. If reparations again are imposed by the victorious Allies the compulsive impulse to repeat the
currency inflation of 1923 would be automatic.

It is apparent that reparations cannot be fastened upon a people
unwilling to cooperate in their payment. Even the Dawes Plan
which sought to achieve this object by a series of direct federal
taxes under Allied supervision, turned out to be an abject failure.
The Germans continuously protested their incapacity to pay what
amounted to two and a half billion marks a year, yet during the
period of six years from the time Hitler came to power until the
Germans overran Poland, they were able to squeeze out an extra
ninety billion marks with which to build the German war machine.

V

The only course which can possibly serve us is to put an end to
German aspirations by putting an end to Germany's ability to make
war. What we do beyond this will be unnecessary and irritating.
Anything less would be dangerously inadequate.

The proposition is this: Here is an incorrigible military State
which has forced on us the most radical of all expedients—total war.

If we have been willing to undertake this terrible ordeal to save ourselves from ruin, we should not shrink from one further step, the destruction of the physical base from which this outlaw State draws its power.

Every other contemplation is useless.

The factual matter is that we will not be able to cure the German malady by any of the conventional poultices. We cannot divide Germany into parts. We cannot legislate. We cannot police. We cannot educate. We cannot cow or bribe this nation into becoming a safe and respected member of society. Germany even cannot be left out of Europe, which must become united if it is to remain a factor in history.

The only recourse open to us is to perform a radical surgical operation by which this State will become impotent and incapable of further criminal assault against its neighbors.

Most of the pattern by which this may be achieved, already has been outlined for us in the German projects for the reorganization of Europe. It is only necessary to revise the nomenclature in these plans, substituting for the words, Poland, France, Czechoslovakia, Holland, Belgium and Russia, the word, Germany.

It is axiomatic that if any permanent solution is to be found for the German problem, it must be the result of Germany itself becoming a mandated area to the balance of Europe. It would then be administered and policed by Europe, thus insuring some degree of permanence and self-interest in the job.

Whatever the political form of the new Europe, Germany should be an area without political rights. It appears to be a reasonable expectation that a State which has made a cult of brutality, debauched its own youth, slaughtered its neighbors, and has sought to demoralize the entire world in an effort to achieve its desires, should be placed in long term restraint. Our nation did so with the Indians for reasons which were not nearly as good.

This time there must be no German army and no German police force. All the policing which is to be done should be done by Europeans of other nations.

The Germans should be forbidden to have either arms, submarines, or airplanes. As part of the disinfecting process, education should be under the thumb of a European commission. All radio broadcasting stations would necessarily be the property of United Europe.

No plants for either the manufacture or assembly of airplanes should be allowed within the territorial confines of the Reich. The ownership or use of any kind of aircraft, military or civil, by German citizens should be expressly forbidden for at least a generation. All airlines should be foreign owned, making it impossible for the airlines to become a refuge where groups of former fighting pilots of the Goering stripe can be thrown together to plot the new military renaissance of Germany.

A renewed German military threat must come from the air, which is the key to warfare of the future. On the point of German air facilities the attitude of the United Nations must be rigorous and inflexible.

The disarmament of any modern State lies in the erasure of its heavy industry and the alienation of its sources of raw materials. Wanting these, no fighting machine in the modern sense can be created. Orators may rant and political agitators conspire, but it would be impossible for a nation thus handicapped to organize for war.

Without this prospect of arms, even psychological warfare loses most of its value, and the temptation to utilize this insidious long-range arm would be materially lessened. The Germans are a practical people and they could not see themselves spending great sums in organizing the destruction of others without being able to turn it to their own advantage.

It is clear that the act of disarming a nation otherwise industrially competent, is apt to prove quite meaningless. Such a policy would represent a contradiction in logic since the future possession of weapons is dictated by the existing ownership of blast furnaces, electric power palnts and heavy industrial machinery.

Actually, the effect of disarming a great industrial Reich may be that of fastening on ourselves a ruinous type of military complacency, together with an armory of weapons which the turn of years will prove to be obsolete. The German armed forces on the other hand, trained to new efficiencies by years of severe restriction, would discover means to make the best use of those opportunities which presented themselves, as they did in the years before the present struggle.

The mere possession of her great chemical and dye trust easily could be the key to a successful blitz war waged by the Reich no more than a decade from now. The same raw materials which form the cornerstone of the chemical industry in time of peace, are intimately associated with the making of war. Such harmless materials as nitrogen, cellulose and chlorine "constitute the fundamental chemical necessities of a belligerent nation." [1] The huge German dye trust of I. G. Farben represents in itself a military potential of impressive dimensions. Without any serious difficulties in conversion, its plant could be turned to the manufacture of high explosives and lewisite, mustard, phosgene and other gases.

Any kind of aircraft manufactory can be turned overnight to the uses of war. The great blast furnaces of the Ruhr, the lignite plants, the powerful hydroelectric stations, the great coal mines and steel mills, and the intricate network of railroads and *Autobahnen* make the renaissance of a new and more formidable military Germany a matter more of will and intention than of opportunity.

Germany is second only to the United States in the chemical and electrotechnical industries, and is first in Europe in the production of machinery and motors of all kinds. Its system of railroads is area for area the finest in the world, giving it a mobility in its internal communications which has played a large part in every modern war in which the Reich has been engaged. The United States is not a military nation in the classic sense. Yet it was able to mobilize the greatest striking apparatus in history within a breathtakingly short period due to the presence of a similar industrial potential.

[1] Hessel, Hessel & Martin, *Chemistry in Warfare*, p. 131.

The plan to control Germany's industry by restricting her foreign trade, or by setting up a commission of foreign trustees to rule it, will fail. This type of thinking is a relic of the finance-capital age which reduced all power equations to legalisms. It smacks of the outmoded absentee landlord principle. In actuality it is impossible to control the industrial and physical resources of a great nation against the aroused will of that nation.

Practical reasoning can start with the fact that the Reich is an over-urbanized country, seventy per cent of whose population lives in cities. This imbalance is the very heart of the highly geared German economic structure, but is not, however, an *a priori* requirement for a happy and industrious Europe.

There is no reason on earth why this overwhelming concentration of industry cannot be reduced systematically. The Germans themselves have shown how easily this can be done when as a protection against air raids they moved whole industries into Silesia and back of the Sudeten mountains.

A large part of the German plant can be dismantled brick by brick, and machine by machine, and carried over bodily to ruined France, Yugoslavia, Poland and Russia. A portion of this would amount only to the recovery of their own property by the original owners. Another portion would be in the way of restitution for the losses inflicted by the German marauders.

German tracks could be taken up and relaid in Poland together with German rolling stock and repair shops. Complete machine tool industries could be sent to the U.S.S.R. together with stockpiles of raw materials. Russia will want great numbers of locomotives, trucks, and technical equipment. France and Poland could use precision machinery of all kinds.

The precedent for this large-scale dismantling and re-erection of industries is ample. Germany itself removed much of the factory equipment of France and Poland into Austria and Moravia. The Chinese transported the equipment of 1,354 factories under the most heartbreaking circumstances, into the Free Provinces. Much of this heavy machinery went on human backs or by junks through the rocky gorges of the Yangtze River.

Russia moved many industrial establishments out of the pathway of the German advance and reconstructed these in the East. Trains travelling at express speed, day after day, carried machinery, tools and skilled workers. The Soviet press mentioned factories in which departments had started functioning within fifteen days of the arrival of their equipment. The Voroshilov Mills were reported to have been transferred from Dnepropetrovsk in September and to have started turning out shells a scarce month later. The big Kirov Armament Works at Leningrad were evacuated to the Urals. Its thousands of workers were flown to the new location and were soon turning out giant tanks.[1]

The underlying weakness of such a program derives from the continued possession of raw material sources which cannot be removed and must remain the inalienable possession of the peoples who live on the earth's crust above them. If the existing industries were dismantled it would only be a matter of time before they were replaced.

The key to permanent economic disarmament, therefore, lies in still one additional measure, that of alienating the German people forever from primary sources of industrial power, such as coal and iron.

Seventy-eight per cent of the coal mined in Germany comes from the Ruhr or Rhenish Westphalia which together with the rich Saar valley forms part of the general Rhineland region. The Ruhr occupies an area of only some 965 square miles, but holds the greater portion of the heavy industries which compose the German war potential. This bustling region is described by the *German Official Guide Book* as "the largest workshop in Europe." It consists of a continuous mass of factories, dwellings, industrial plants and mines. Within its confines is concentrated two-thirds of the

1 Harvey and Ruggles, *The Eastward Course of Soviet Industry and the War,* pp. 24, 25.

Reich's coke, iron and steel, and an agglomeration of industrial energy quite without parallel anywhere.

The political amputation of this strategic area from Germany would not prove permanent as was evident in the case of the Saar valley after World War I. The severed fragment would remain a central cause of agitation until it was permitted to join with the Reich again.

The key to the operation lies in still another realm, that of bio-politics.

The Germans themselves have shown by their mass population transfers how a permanent solution can be effected. One of these was the expulsion of over 1,500,000 Poles from the incorporated territory into the Government General, on the heels of which came an opposing wave of *Volksdeutsche* to occupy the population vacuum which resulted. At least four million were earmarked for removal in West Poland alone. The German blueprint contemplated the expulsion of the entire Czech nation and its dispersal somewhere in Russia or Siberia. A mass migration of Netherlanders was planned to the prairies of Western Russia, their places at the mouths of the Rhine, the Waal and the Maas to be taken by Germans.

Another measure involved the repatriation to the Reich of the solid body of Germans in Italian-owned Trentino. The Russians removed the entire population of the German Volga Republic sending them to areas in Asia.

Another historic precedent under peaceful auspices, was the large-scale population exchange which took place between Turkey and Greece in 1935. By these agreements 1,300,000 Greeks were transferred from Turkey to Greece, and 400,000 Turks moved from Greek territory to Turkey.

The task of the United Nations should be to shift all Germans from the left bank of the Rhine and from the Saar and Ruhr valleys. These regions should be settled with Frenchmen, Belgians, Hollanders or others who may be induced to locate there. The German population thus would be permanently removed as a source of trouble to Europe without destroying any of the foundations on which European prosperity rests.

The return to France of Alsace-Lorraine should be followed by the removal of the Germans who have been brought in, and the repatriation of the French who have been cast out. The natural frontiers of Czechoslovakia should be restored. The Germans inhabiting the borderland Sudeten areas should be shifted back to within the borders of the old Reich.

It is self-evident that the Poles who have been thrown out of Silesia, Poznan and other provinces, should be brought back and the Germans who have taken their places expelled. It seems also both just and reasonable that Poland be compensated for the eastern lands which will be taken from her by the U.S.S.R. This could be done by granting her East Prussia and those portions of the Reich east of the rivers Oder and Veisse, which would mark the boundary between the two States. By settling these zones with Poles, another sore point on the suffering body of Europe would be finally and lastingly excised. Here is the home of the Junkers, the great landed gentry, and the original seat of the metastatic German cancer. The East Prussian island which now is washed on all sides by the Polish sea, would disappear and become Slavic again as it was before the days of the crusading Teutonic Knights.

No part of this program is in any sense beyond the resources of Europe. The removals conducted by Hitler have been handled under the most cruel and heartless circumstances, and at a moment when his entire economy was burdened by the needs of war. In peace and under kindlier conditions, this historic shifting of populations could be accomplished with little in the way of real difficulty if it were the will of our peacemakers to do so. There would be fair compensation for the businesses, homes and factories evacuated, and the re-establishment of the emigrants in other parts of Germany. Many hundreds of thousands would leave voluntarily. Six and a half million White Russians are said to have emigrated after the Red Revolution, just as another eight million Russians fled in advance of Hitler's armies into the interior of the Soviet Union.

Whatever has been taken from the other countries by chicanery or force should be returned to them, though it may prove a practical impossibility to restore the property stolen from private individuals, or even from nations. All transactions by which Axis nationals acquired property in foreign States during the period of the war, should be considered invalid unless the buyer can be shown to have been himself a refugee from the oppression of his own government.

The libraries of the countries which have been overrun should be restocked from books held in German libraries. Such possessions as clocks, household furnishings and clothing, except for those required by the German population to sustain life, should be sequestered and rushed to the suffering and starved peoples of Europe. All German valuables, both private and public should be seized. These baubles have little to do with the ability of the German people to maintain existence, and the effect of their loss on Germans morally cannot be overestimated. It would bring home to these people the fact that crime is not profitable and that war is no longer an honorable and paying institution. It will indicate that any further attempt to rule the world by conquest will not fail to bring its meed of trouble to the Germans as well as to others.

Germany it is true would decline from her position as the richest Power in Europe, but she would by no means be poorer than the nations which surround her. Both Poland and Yugoslavia will have infinitely less resource remaining and will suffer more during the coming decade even under the best conditions.

The power plants and the lignite areas of Central Germany would continue generating the electricity required for handicrafts and light industry. The new immigrants cast into the center of the Reich would find much of the country thinly populated and badly in need of agricultural workers. The Reich would have no more need to import from other countries the millions of laborers who now work in her factories and farms. The result to the Germans would be far more humane than the fate they meted out to the Czechs, Poles, and Yugoslavs, or to the three million Jews whom they wantonly destroyed.

Almost one-third of Germany's soil still is covered with forests, which are capable of yielding valuable products to a country operating on a semi-agrarian base. Less than half of the area which might be intensively worked is at present under the plow. The German earth is not extremely fertile but it is well able to produce all of the food and fodder crops necessary to keep the German people in health.

On the whole, an amputated Reich still would remain a favored country, containing ample resources for a population content to live modestly as do those of Poland, Yugoslavia, France or Spain.

VI

A final provision will have to be made to liquidate the Pan-German zealots who otherwise will be the core of German resistance to any enduring peace program. These include the large landowners, the big industrialists, the Pan-German intellectuals who dominate the judiciary, civil service, schools and colleges, and the army officer caste.

Short shrift should be made of the big Junker land proprietors whose property should summarily be expropriated and operated as giant State farms in the interests of the whole Continent. A similar fate should await the leaders of industry, who must not only disgorge the gains they have thieved from all over Europe, but their holdings in Germany as well. The latter should be administered by a commission set up for this purpose by Europe and should be regarded as being held in trust for whatever State is eventually to be established.

It is mandatory that provision be made for the permanent isolation of the more dangerous of the Nazi characters. It is almost useless to expect that these criminals will be brought to the bar of justice and tried for their crimes. If the past is any token, few will suffer penalty despite the unpardonable nature of their offenses.[1] The punishment of isolated ruffians may be expected to be taken care of by outraged individuals. The U.S.S.R. will hang a few more for the political effect it will produce. The rest will escape.

The single sensible remedy which remains is exile.

All leaders of the Nazi Party from the smallest district functionary to Hitler should be removed from Europe and exiled in some colony such as Devil's Island or Madagascar. To these should be added all professional army officers. All of these persons should be transferred without their wives, since the intention is not the colonization of Germans but a cure for the European carcinoma.

It is also important that the entire top layer of the police organization, as well as the teaching profession, be purged and removed from any position of influence.

The list of those to be exiled might come to a quarter million men, who are to be permanently separated from Germany and live out celibate lives, as did Napoleon Bonaparte, in the comparative peace and quiet of a faraway reservation. Their existence will be not much different from that of the 1,900,000 French war

[1] After World War I the Anglo-Americans also proclaimed impending punishment for the war criminals, but lacked the moral strength to enforce these declarations. Thus, the Allies fell between two stools, angering the Germans and at the same time encouraging them to believe that the West had lost the capacity for rule and was bogging down in a morass of sentimentality and weakness.

Under Article 227 of the Treaty of Versailles, William of Hohenzollern, the former German Emperor, was publicly arraigned for "a supreme offence against international morality and the sanctity of treaties." The Versailles Treaty gave the Allies the right to bring before military tribunals those accused of having committed "acts in violation of the laws and customs of war" and to bring them to quick trial.

A calendar of accused persons was prepared, and the depositions of witnesses taken. Among those on the list of accused Germans was Marshal von Hindenburg, who later as President of Germany was to appoint Hitler as Chancellor of the Reich.

Though they had solemnly obligated themselves to deliver the criminals, the Germans reneged on one excuse or another. The Allies did not insist. After two and a half years of horsing around, four minor defendants finally were placed on trial in Leipzig. The judges were all Germans, as was the court. The accused, who were guilty of particularly heinous and sadistic offenses, were given minor prison terms.

prisoners whom Hitler continued to detain in German camps long after the armistice agreement with France. The exiled Germans would be considered the wards of European civilization as long as they lived.

As a final measure it will be necessary to deal with the cultural institutions of Germany since it is here that the paranoid thinking which has colored German belief is incubated. Dr. Brickner remarks in the *American Journal of Orthopsychiatry* that "even customs and institutions which might be safe enough in other cultures, would none the less require abolition in Germany." [1]

Every cultural institution which has germinated the ugly pattern of German racialism must be removed from the horizon of the Germans. This plainly includes the universities, which have been the nursing point of Pan-Germanism for two hundred years and have been perverted irretrievably to Nazi ideology.

To an American the closing of an university is a harsh and reprehensible act. The word university has taken on a sacred meaning as of something untouchable and beyond all political motivation. In Germany the university is one of the principal centers of Pan-German political power. From its halls all free academic minds have been driven long since.

The entire teaching profession of the Reich early was coordinated by the Nazis into their system. Only the "reliable" elements were allowed to remain. There is no one on the teaching staffs of these schools whose presence would not constitute a point of infection rather than a benefit to the new Europe and the world.

German political philosophy teaches that men have no rights but only duties. This doctrine very well could continue to apply to Germans, who in the future would have duties but no privileges. They would have to make restitution to Europe, morally and materially, for the grave hurt they have inflicted on the body of

[1] Dr. Richard M. Brickner, "The German Cultural Paranoid Trend," *American Journal of Orthopsychiatry*, Issue of October, 1942.

civilization. This is a responsibility which must be accepted by the Reich and is part of the cleansing process which finally may see her emerge as a law-abiding unit in the world community.

It has been suggested by Moscow that in lieu of reparations, which are impractical, man-hours be substituted, and that giant work gangs of Germans be put to work to repair the Continent. This would have the further advantage of restoring the demographic balance of Europe by keeping the Germans temporarily from their women, as Hitler did with the French war prisoners.

The Russians are known to require some ten million German workers for a period of a decade or more to repair the damage the Nazis have done to their country alone. In addition to rehabilitating war-torn cities and industries, there are great tasks which could be undertaken and which would benefit all Europe. One of these is the construction of the Canal des Deux Mers, which would create a new and vitally important sea channel between the Atlantic and the Mediterranean by way of Bordeaux, Toulouse and Narbonne. Another would be the Gibraltar tunnel by which Africa would be linked directly with Europe by railway and road connection.

The Germans are already familiar with such work gangs in the shape of the millions of shanghaied civilians and indentured prisoners who work throughout the Reich. German service in similar labor battalions would be an act of retributive justice of which no one, least of all the Germans, could complain. It would serve one other important purpose. A sudden demobilization of the German army would release millions of turbulent jobless men into a scene of revolutionary activity which might surge beyond all control. In the sanctuary of the proposed labor corps these men would be far removed from the influence of agitators and the temptations to trouble.

In the mild penance involved in their period of labor, they may be found like Ernest, in Hawthorne's immortal story, *The Great Stone Face,* to have rehabilitated their own character and to have risen from the ignoble estate of superman to the dignity of man.

Only by these stern measures can the classic domination held over the German mind by Pan-German and imperial tradition be at last liquidated and made harmless. The degree of privation and hurt it involves would be the reply of Europe to the cold-blooded looting of its cities, and the wanton cruelties by which the painful gains of many long centuries have been laid in waste.

To act thus with decision in the settlement of this problem will require the highest courage and the greatest statesmanship. Its successful completion depends on the will to adhere to it rigidly. There will be many pressures and views exerted, some maudlin and foolish, and some dishonest, to ease the retribution which must fall on the Reich, and to stay the relentless measures by which alone permanent peace can be assured. In a democracy of blocs and blustering minority groups, capable by their agitation of destroying any statesman, these may prove difficult to resist.

XIX

REORGANIZATION OF SOCIETY

WHAT time holds in store for the world is difficult to predict. The future is like a stage on which the props are all set and the lines rehearsed, but which is still hidden from the waiting audience.

Those who knew the situation of Russia in 1917 could have guessed that she was nearing the end of an era; but who could have predicted the transformation of the somnambulant empire within the short span of a generation into an industrial giant ruled by a regime which, though the most repressive in history, has received an unparalleled devotion from its subjects? Or who could have foreseen the shattering events which followed both before and after the Battle of Britain, in which the course of history was turned as certainly as it had been twelve hundred years before at the Battle of Tours where it was decided whether Europe was to be Christian or Moslem?

All that can safely be said is that the world has been shaken by a revolution in its politics, economics, communications and weapons which is forcing us to revise all of the historic conceptions to which we are used. What emerges from there is anyone's guess. The only certainty is that the present political pattern of the world belongs to an outmoded design which is on its way out of history.

The existing political shapes have passed their period of usefulness and are doomed to be smashed by the tidal wave of change which is breaking on their bulwarks. Unless they place themselves of their own free will in adjustment to the new conditions, they will be compelled to do so later by the logic of revolutionary force.

Any factor which makes human existence more organizable, which annihilates the power of distance, which adds to the force and mobility of weapons, which opens up areas for settlement and exploitation previously inaccessible, or which in any material way changes the relation of man to his environment, causes a change in the relationship of power and compels a readjustment of social ideals to conform with the new facts. If these changes are sufficiently great, the net effect is to deal a lethal blow to the political forms by which life previously had been organized.

The once invincible brontosaurus and saber-toothed tiger yielded to functional and environmental changes which made it impossible for them to survive. In our own time the passenger pigeon and the great auk had been unable to master the new problems circumstance created for them. The passenger pigeon was doomed the instant men with guns set foot on this continent.

In the sense that the State is an organic structure performing a living, breathing function, it, too, is subject to the barometric changes in condition which suddenly may be brought to bear against it. Any fundamental alteration in the rhythm of its existence renders the State archaic, and powerless to resist enemies it scarcely regarded before.

The old institutions rarely possess the good sense to modify the rigid legitimacies on which they rest, and to adapt themselves to the new dispensation. Social acceptance is a grim, hard business. It rests on usages which remain long after the fury of revolutionary change has foredoomed them to extinction.

The irrefutable logic of the present situation is that with us, without us, or against us, war will be abolished sooner or later by one means or another. Wars have no practical value to any of the contenders and run counter to every basic need of the machine age. If they are not terminated by the method of pacific adjustment, they are certain to be abolished by the alternative of complete victory by one Power and the resulting annihilation of the others.

We are compelled to accept the fact that if we are to enter the portals of universal peace we shall have to come up the road the hard way. There will be no panaceas or easy solvents for the complex difficulties which block the road. There will be only laws of probability, and it is from a judgment of these that we will be compelled to chart our course.

We have seen that no reliance can be placed on peace treaties and coalitions. It seems clear that no confidence can be rested in a peace negotiated by the conventional give and take diplomacy. The principle of self determination no longer applies either to the individual or the nation. The society of man is maturing and what was once sweet and engaging in its youth is now in grave danger of becoming simpering and ugly.

There is not, in fact, a single problem among those with which we must deal that can be solved by the old means of power diplomacy, or by our withdrawal behind the barriers of the two oceans which wash our shores.

There are no short-cuts to world reorganization, and to peace. There is no solution which does not demand courage, sacrifice and good sense. Above all, there is no form of peace which can be created independent of the existing pattern by which power is defined. It cannot be hamstrung by political convictions which have lost relationship to the realities of this century, or have become stratified into outlived forms.

We cannot answer this riddle by dream projects, but only by political progressions which follow each other logically and without violence to the conventions and inner rhythms by which society is governed. This should be the function of politics, which must be live and virile, and not a mere liturgical shape, if it is to be meaningful to human existence.

Political wisdom should assume that social bodies are not rigid and brittle, but possess, like organic tissue, extensive possibilities for compensation within their own structures. Even where social structures fail, and are visibly evolving into new and strange configurations, the metamorphosis need not arise from spectacular and flaming collapse. The journey to the new level of existence could as readily be made in graduated stages as a matter of painless evolution.

The choices before us are simple. Either we must admit that the problem is by its nature insoluble and improvise our course as we go along, or we must set ourselves to some preconsidered program whose aspects we have weighed carefully in advance.

If we commit our policy to the latter plan, we must come to the conclusion that peace is not favored by self-serving declarations, or sonorous legalisms. There is only one condition which favors peace, and that is the necessity for it. Wherever peace automatically is profitable the odds favoring its existence become overwhelming.

The institutions which are to be created should not abandon the past but use it as a bridge to the future. Though we are to move with bold sureness, it must be with sufficient caution to see our way with clarity. We must take into consideration the nature of man, his psychology, the traditions which fetter him to his organic beginnings, and his ineptitudes as well as his capacities.

While it is difficult to project the precise type of world order which will function and at the same time be achievable without destructive violence, the general outlines of a mature and adjusted world are not difficult to perceive. They relate to the new needs of both mass-man and mass production, and to the liquidation of those inequalities which cause the nations to be a menace to each other.

As we have seen, it was only yesterday that the city-States of Naples and Venice were live and vibrant economic organisms, perfectly capable of sustaining themselves. The Apennine Peninsula could consist of eleven kingdoms and republics, the names of some of which, like Modena and Lucca, are scarcely recognizable today. Yet these were not consolidated into the kingdom of Italy until the year 1860. Today that kingdom itself is too small to exist as a separate State on the earth's surface.

France is no longer made up of separate peoples, such as the Provençals, the Bretons and the Burgundians. The more than three hundred German enclaves, city-States and kingdoms disappeared before the social reforms of Napoleon. Transylvania, Wallachia, Moldavia and Montenegro vanished as free States during the course of the modern wave of political reorganization which swept Europe.

In view of these aspects of history, it is obviously fantastic to speak of States as if they were inalienable entities anchored forever in space by divine law. The fact is that States were made to serve the interests of men, not men those of States, and these States could no longer do so. During the centuries, not only have the boundaries of States shifted and changed, but new States continually have come into existence which never existed before, and old States, seemingly firm and imperishable, have disappeared forever from the map.

A prime example is Poland whose borders shrank and expanded with rhythmic regularity and involved territories alternately claimed by Russia, Lithuania, Prussia, Austria, Czechoslovakia and the Baltic States. When Poland no longer existed, the borders of Germany, Austria and Russia, which then touched on each other, bounded what these nations believed to be their unalterable patrimonies, guaranteed to them by international law and the beneficent intention of the Lord Jehovah.

Despite the stress placed on these claims to permanence, it is plain that national boundaries are not static, but are always in a state of flux. In the last analysis, they are compelled to yield to new economic, cultural and military facts as these appear.

II

If the world slate were wiped absolutely clean of all the traditional factors which now apply, and an appraisal made in the interests of mankind generally, it would be found that there is more than enough to settle comfortably all present-day problems resulting from the material wants of all peoples.

The world stores of coal and the various metals, if they were the common possession, would last into any calculable future. Even on the mooted question of oil, which is unevenly distributed over the globe, it is estimated by geologists that sufficient quantities exist to meet the normal peacetime needs of the earth for well over a thousand years.

The horizon of material resources will expand as the physical sciences continue to plumb the uncharted mysteries of the universe, taming them to the use of man. The great storehouse of our terrestrial creation may yet prove to be the tropics. In the deep, rich soil of these regions, with their steaming rains and hot sunshine, may be found that alchemy which will provide the world with its principal wealth and raw materials. Another untapped depository of natural wealth which only awaits the ingenuity of man to mine it, is the ocean. From the waters of the sea we now extract magnesium and certain chemicals. It contains many other elements, including the different metals, in fabulous abundance.

A study of meteorology on whose profound secrets only a glimmering of light has been shed, will enable an understanding in the controls exercised over weather. Crop failures would become a thing of the past, and the ability of the world to support large populations greatly increased.

The relation of crop abundance to distribution could be solved by the new methods of transportation and storage, bridging the terrible question of famine which has plagued most of the earth since the day of Adam.

Each new electric process or source of industrial power adds heavily to the available wealth by which the material needs of men are satisfied. The discovery by the exiled Austrian physicist, Felix Ehrenhaft, of the existence of a pure magnetic current, may result again in a revolution in our technology, once more altering the relationship of man to the universe around him.

The German geographer, Penck, who has examined the question with care, has declared that the earth is capable of supporting comfortably a population up to eight billions, or nearly four times that at present.[1] While this assessment is regarded by many American geographers as being on the optimistic side, time undoubtedly

[1] Prof. E. G. R. Taylor, "Living Space for All," *American Foreign Service Journal.*

will show it to err on the side of conservatism, as new processes and methods make themselves felt.

The per capita requirement of land decreases steadily with the progress of civilization. The amount of land required by primitive tribes, such as the American Indian or Arab Bedouin, is immeasurably greater than that needed to support a settled people. Fifty thousand Australian aboriginals might live precariously on an area which would support a hundred million Europeans with ease. The use of intensive methods of agriculture, the growth of industry and the utilization of science generally, all have a deep effect on the nature of the problem.

However one regards the matter, there is room for all nations on the earth to exist on a high standard of comfort and nutrition without cutting each other's throats to achieve it. The problem, therefore, is not one of available means for survival, but of making sense out of the political and social pattern by which the existing resources are distributed. It relates to the establishment of a self-regulating equipoise in raw material holdings, power sources, and strategic space.

The first concern of any rational planning intended to meet the situation, must be the emancipation of men from the antique framework of the archaic State. This problem refers not alone to accessibility to markets and mineral wealth, but even more to the gross disparities between theoretically equal States. Under any circumstance, these unequal and economically unsound sovereignties will have to be liquidated, to be replaced by units capable of sustaining themselves in the present state of world development. These should have a population and economic potential enabling them to balance off each other without the usual provocations which weakness invites.

If the entire surface of the globe could be divided into half a dozen more or less equal political units, each possessing the mineral resources, space, climatic conditions, and people necessary for a self-regulating existence, the entire problem of peace and war would be well on its way to an enduring solution.

The existing areas of contention would be greatly minimized. The justification for war, whether based on the weakness of adversaries, the lack of essential materials, or the need for markets, largely would diminish, and perhaps disappear.

The possibility of creating a workable world organization would be infinitely enhanced since half a dozen sovereignties, more or less equal in their economic and military strength, could easily come to an understanding which would be impossible on the part of seventy, totally unequal in power as well as in the nature of the problems affecting them.

If the world could be so redivided, the areas of agreement would become relatively simple and could be well defined. War between such Power Aggregates would not be inviting and would logically be resorted to only under the most extreme provocation. Under no stretch of the imagination could it result in a blitzkrieg victory or in any overwhelming material advantage to the victor.

Each of these great Aggregates would be suitable to the technical age. Each would possess the bulk of the required raw materials it needed in its industry and would be capable of absorbing in its internal markets almost the entirety of its production. In no one of the new political divisions need dependence on external markets or raw material sources precipitate a crisis.

The differences of these units with each other could be resolved by simple agreement, since they would no longer be complicated by the fears, suspicions and temptations provided in the present political splintering of the world.

By taking a global view of the problem, it could be settled on a broad basis rather than by the piecemeal pressures of recurring power growths. The objective would be to settle at their source all of the dangerous questions and paradoxes which unite to create instability, derangement, dislocation and disorder in the world.

Each of the proposed Aggregates would hence be the universal State in miniature, capable of bringing into equilibrium all of the organic processes by which a modern viable State is organized.

An alliance of any nature between the United States and the

British Empire, even if some of the countries of Western Europe were to be included, would not serve any of the purposes for which we are striving. Nothing would be permanently determined. We would inherit the disabilities and quarrels to which the Empire is subject throughout the world, and within the scope of the agreement still would remain competitors and rivals.

The Russians, Latins and Asiatics would look with suspicion on the formation of this bloc, which they would feel to be an ill-concealed effort to set up a world government in the hands of the Anglo-American peoples. The dark races would regard it as a scheme to continue the pattern of white ascendancy. It would be resisted almost immediately by counter measures on the part of the other nations and would create a new international lineup by which the contending forces shaping themselves for World War III could be judged.

A sound working proposal would involve organizing the world into a limited number of self-contained Power Aggregates, each capable of sustaining itself through its own markets and resources. Each would possess the bulwarks of space, population and industry which would make quick military decision impossible and would cause wars to become unattractively costly and long-drawn out.

Each of these Aggregates would be completely federated, with all independent sovereignties within its boundaries erased. To do otherwise merely would bring into existence loose confederations of States, which in effect would leave the world exactly where it was before.

These Aggregates then would be brought together in a loosely joined world order, settling their fundamental questions by agreement, a process which is no longer possible in a world affected by the present unequal distribution of political, military and economic power.

The world divides naturally into five such Aggregates each with its connate set of interests. One of these Powers, the U.S.S.R., already possesses most of the attributes of a perfectly balanced modern economy, requiring only access to the warm waters and the acquisition of tropical areas. The others would consist of a United Orient, a United Europe which would cluster around the Mediterranean, a Union of the West in which would be consolidated North and South America together with the British Isles and Australasia, and a mandated territory of Africa.

The entire operation could be set into motion by a courageous act of leadership which need only involve a settlement agreement between three Powers, the United States, Britain and the Soviet Union.

If the three major partners of the United Nations could come to an agreement which would commit them to a permanently stabilized future, the remaining States of the world would have no other choice than to adjust themselves on terms best suited to their geographical positions.

The necessary preliminaries to the new world order would be: 1. A declaration by Britain and the United States in favor of a Union of the West, with their representatives taking the necessary measures for the prompt amalgamation of the English-speaking nations as the first step in this direction. 2. An announcement in the name of the American, British and Soviet Governments, supporting a European Union and declaring it in existence.

The United Europe would follow the successes of our arms as the social reforms of the last century accompanied those of Bonaparte. With no obstacle in its path, the unification of the Orient would ensue with almost mechanical sureness.

If any of the existing nations were to remain as independent fragmentary and unattached economies, they would become bones of contention between the big Aggregates, who would set themselves to the creation of gigantic military establishments, and plant capacities out of joint with their own internal needs, thus becoming not collaborators in a reorganized world but violent and distrustful competitors as before.

It should be the concern of mankind to see that no such areas of potential conflict exist. No State should be allowed to remain outside of the global settlement by which the major power problems of the world are to be reconciled.

III

Any arrangement which did not satisfy the legitimate aspirations of the Soviet Union, and into which she did not enter with whole-hearted conviction, would not have the slightest chance of success. If the Soviets did not agree, any effort to coalesce the States of Europe into a working unit would fail miserably.

In such an event we would know that another war would not be far off, and that we would not be able to prevent the Soviets from overrunning all Europe. It would have to be conceded that all effort at real conciliation had failed, and a strong policy on the part of the West would become mandatory.

The result would be unmitigated disaster.

Moscow could agree to such a simplification of the world map only if all the authentic needs of the U.S.S.R. were fully met, and if participation by the Soviet Union did not place it at an ultimate disadvantage. The U.S.S.R. will have to be considered from the start as a partner in this enterprise, rather than as a potential enemy who must be contained between brackets by the cunning devices of the old diplomacy.

The Soviet Union should be allowed to retain the three Baltic States of Esthonia, Latvia and Lithuania as well as Eastern Poland. She should be permitted to repossess the old Russian province of Bessarabia, which should be extended east to the Carpathian Mountains which mark its natural frontier, taking in the old Rumanian territory of Moldavia to the Buzau River, and thence to the lower mouth of the Danube at Sfantul-Gheorghe in the Dobruja.

The difficult position of the Kremlin in reference to an ice-free port on the Atlantic would be rectified by granting her the Norwegian city of Tromso, together with the Finmark and the Finnish province of Oulu north of the Kitinen and Kemi Rivers, so as to provide a continuous landbridge to the Atlantic.

Moscow should secure the harbor position at the head of the Persian Gulf for which it always has hungered. The annexed portions would include that section of Iran which runs west of a line following roughly through Meshed, Isfahan and the coastal city of Hindiyan. This border also might be rectified eastward through Iraq to the Tigris River to its juncture with the Diyala, and thence to the present Persian boundary. It might include the eastern foothills of the great chain of Turkish mountains facing the Valley of Kars, which run contiguously into the Caucasus.

To protect the route through the Persian Gulf, the Soviets should have complete possession of the principality of Oman from the peninsula of Qatar to the port town of Khaluf, including all of the islands which lay off the coast and dominate the approaches to the Gulf of Oman.

In Asia, the Mongolian Republic of Tannu Tuva, which is already absorbed into the Soviet economy, should officially be awarded to the Soviet Union. The bad military position of the Soviet Eastern Provinces in Siberia should be corrected by the cession of the northern part of Manchukuo, following along the line of the Nonni and Sungari Rivers to Sansing, and from there to the town of Mishan on Lake Khanka.

The southern half of Sakhalin Island must, of course, be returned to the Soviets. The military position of the Union would be immensely improved if it were permitted to annex the northern Japanese island of Hokkaido, together with the Kurile string of islands which runs like a chain of sharp knives from the tip of Hokkaido to the Kamchatka Peninsula, hemming in the vital Sea of Okhotsk.

The Eastern frontier of the Soviet Union then for the first time would face on the warm waters of the Pacific.

A Soviet empire of these dimensions would have everything it required for its happiness and well-being with the single exception of tropical territories capable of growing such products as rubber, spices, quinine and kapok.

This lack could be rectified by giving the U.S.S.R. possession of the major islands of Borneo, Sumatra and Java, taking in all of the minor islands from Natoena in the South China Sea to the Riouw Archipelago, Bangka, and Billiton.

The west and south approaches to the Soviet Indies would be held in their entirety by the U.S.S.R. from Simeuloee to Christmas Island, and would include the Cocos Islands in the Indian Ocean. To these holdings should be added the strategic Nicobar group which guards the entrance to the Bay of Bengal, north of Sumatra. The Laccadive, Maldive and Chagas Archipelagoes, which would lay directly athwart the Soviet route to the Indies, logically should become Russian possessions.

There would be another and accruing advantage to Russian presence in the Indies. The possession by the Kremlin of a vital interest in the South Seas interposes her between the Orient and any possible renewal of an Asiatic drive to the south. A military attempt by a renascent Asia against any of the islands of the Malay Archipelago would threaten to outflank the Soviet possessions and automatically would force intervention by Moscow. In itself this factor renders the possibilities of such an assault remote, unless Asia were to find herself in a position to conduct a simultaneous attack on both the Soviet Union and the West.

After the rectification of its boundaries as proposed, the total area of the Soviet Union would be 9,525,000 square miles, and its population somewhere close to 335,000,000.

IV

The second of the great power forms which would be erected would be that of Europe, or the Union of the Old World.

The proposal for a European Federal Union is not a new one. Count Coudenhove-Kalergi for more than a generation led a crusade for a united Europe. In 1929, the French Foreign Minister, Briand, proposed a union to be made up of European States which were members of the League of Nations. The member countries were to retain their entire political independence, but on the economic side there was to be a "rational organization of production and of European exchanges."

These mild attempts at European unity met a stone wall of resistance. Clashing racial egos, jealously guarded national interests, vested privileges, and the pure inertia of ingrained habit, made the voluntary coalescence of the Continent an impossibility. Only some cataclysmic event such as the present war, which shatters traditional boundaries, ancient hatreds and fixed economic interests, is capable of setting the stage for a United Europe. Otherwise none of the problems involved can be brought into perspective, and the clash of conflicting interests continues on in an interminable jangle.

Today it is clear that there no longer is collective security in Europe. The small States are absurdly small and fantastically archaic in terms of any rational modern economy. They do not coincide with present-day economic or military logic. They are unequal in power and on the verge of utter exhaustion. Such a condition can only bequeath Europe the most turbulent period in its history and pave the way for some conqueror who will seek to create with tanks, bombers and flame throwers, that union which democratic convention had failed to bring about.

Any such attempt must galvanize the world again into global struggle. Unless there has been an agreement all around for a fair division of the surface of the globe, there cannot be a European federation which does not immediately upset the power equilibrium and subject the balance of creation to grave dangers.

It should not be necessary to await the arrival of some new Napoleon to bring order out of chaos and consolidate the vaulting dreams of Hitler into reality. An organized Europe on a free and democratic basis is possible now. It would remove one of the chief obstacles to a safe and sane international world order.

The objection to this outcome does not lie in the unalterable opposition of Europeans. It lies chiefly in the suspicions of Moscow and the reluctance of conservative-minded Washington and Imperial London to really resolve this dilemma in broad terms.

The free republic of Europe would have existed from the moment we declared it and accepted the premise of its existence. Had we proclaimed such a cooperative commonwealth we might have been able to rely on the enthusiasm and good sense of the European peoples to accept this result as an intelligent and final solution to an everlasting problem. Europe is ready for union. It requires merely a declaration and the setting up of a center of authority to galvanize the entire Continent into hope, and to substitute fervent belief for an otherwise dreadful picture of poverty and bleak despair.

If instead of this creative enterprise we continue our present course of attempting to deal with the many governments in exile, or to invoke the conventions by which opinion is habitually expressed, we shall have resigned ourselves to the craft and sterile chicanery of the professional diplomat. These will twist and scheme as various sets of interests and pressures are exerted upon them, until all opportunity for settlement blows up in smoke.

The situation is complicated by the habitual nervous fears of the major Powers. Among these are the chronic suspicions of the U.S.S.R. and its genuine uneasiness lest any settlement place it eventually at the mercy of rapacious Powers. The project also would run contrary to established American policy, which is that of making common purpose with the existing order against the disturbance of revolutionary change.

To the British, a united Europe portends the most imminent and violent danger to their islands. The unity of Europe has been the nightmare of British politics, and it has been the historic objective of their policy to prevent it.

The view currently held in Washington and London is that nothing should be done and that matters gradually will work themselves out during the transitional period.

This would seem to involve a dangerous philosophy and the ultimate in risk. Europe would become perilously exposed to both the violence of external conquest and revolution. We must face the inevitable fact that in any circumstance we will be in trouble and that our nation no longer can dissever its politics from the ultimate fate of Europe.

No part of this plan can be brought about gradually, either by the concurrence of the various nations and governments in exile, or by general conference. Here it would be certain to be sabotaged by a wide variety of interests, who would conspire, maneuver and plan with all the chronic infelicity which has caused European diplomacy in the past to assume the unpleasant guise of diabolism.

The argument that the complexity of European ambitions, races, cultures and religions would place insuperable obstacles in the way, does not appear to be a sound one. Before Garibaldi unified Italy by force, the governments of the peninsula were always at odds with each other.

Before the consolidation, Venice, Sicily, Tuscany, and Piedmont differed strongly from each other in points of view, institutional forms, and what appeared to be their national self interests. Each of these States possessed its own government, diplomatic corps, tariff and coinage systems. "It is harder," lamented Cavour, "to harmonize the Italian North and South than it is to fight with Austria." Even today the quip exists that Northern Italy would rather fight the Neapolitans and Sicilians than France and Yugoslavia.

From the same reasoning advanced against European federation, Brittany would have to secede from France to become part of a Celtic empire of Cornwall, Wales, Ireland and Scotland. England itself being largely of Anglo-Saxon-Norman derivation, could be claimed by Germany.

Under any thesis of absolute boundaries based on race or culture, the oldest permanent frontiers of Europe, those of the Swiss, are incomprehensible. They encompass fragments of France, Italy and Germany which under any academic conception could not possibly belong together. There is as much reason for a united Europe as there is for a united Switzerland with its German, French, Italian and Romansh tongues and cultures, or for that tremendous mélange of races and tongues which constitute the Union of Soviet Socialist Republics.

The nationalism of Mazzini and Kosciusko was quite a different thing from the suicidal sickness and mania which since has settled over Europe in the name of national aspirations. With almost a single voice Garibaldi, Bolivar and the other great national liberators spoke in the name of human brotherhood, international collaboration and freedom. To them the liberty of their own countries meant the freedom to participate in a cooperative world. Today every frontier in Europe speaks not for its unity and free intercourse, but for separatism, suspicion, hostility and discord.

A Europe to be free must be without Francos, Salazars, Bourbons and Hohenzollerns, as well as without Hitlers, Mussolinis and Antonescus. There can be no vestige of the old order left to which reactionary elements can rally to defeat the purposes for which the Union was organized. These elements must be destroyed as they were in Soviet Russia. The new broom must sweep with utter cleanness when Europe receives its fresh start in history. These antiquated ideas no longer can serve the interests of the Continent and it is preposterous to continue wedded to them, or to clothe them with a sanctity independent of their usefulness.

It is not even required that unity be arrived at by mutual consent, which may mean mutual haggling and distrust. The unity of the States of Soviet Russia which is enforced by the mailed fist is superior to the unity of Czechoslovakia in which the Germans, Slovaks and Ruthenians were continually conspiring and rebelling against the State.

Force as a unifying agent in a great cause where the interests of mankind as a whole are to be served, is not inadmissible. With few exceptions it was the agency by which all great consolidations have been effected. The unity of the United States was preserved by force during the American Civil War. Suez and Gibraltar were seized by the British after negotiations failed. In the present war when it came down to the critical question of Greenland and Iceland, we did not stand on the order of our asking but sent in troops to occupy.

When the interests of the American hemisphere demanded it, we have not hesitated to ride roughshod over the independent rights of nearby States such as Nicaragua, Cuba and Haiti, and to dictate their administration under the thinnest of disguises.

There is hence no need to adopt a sanctimonious attitude toward the realities which we must face tomorrow. Where the essential welfare of the world is concerned, European boundaries are no more inviolable, and have no more title to exist in perpetuity, than some patent right which has run out and in the interests of the total community has become part of the public domain.

It is argued that tradition, local pride, and other immovable considerations would prevent any actual federation and loss of individual independence or identity. These considerations need not be regarded as a genuine barrier to the political coalescence of Europe. In a commonwealth where these processes offer no common danger to the community, cultural particularism might be encouraged rather than discouraged, as it is in Switzerland and the U.S.S.R. There is no reason why a man cannot be a Frenchman and a European at the same time, just as Stalin can acknowledge himself a Georgian and yet remain ruler of all the Russias.

In a free and united Continent, lingual and cultural diversities would be an asset and not a cause for malediction and bloodshed. Europe would be able to turn to the measures which make productive logic and creative sense. Problems of currency, of communications, of air and road traffic, and of a balanced urban and agricultural development, could be handled on a sane and organized basis.

The fact that Europe has been a net importer of food and raw materials, and exporter of manufactured goods, would necessarily weigh heavily in the plans of a federated Continent. France, Poland, Hungary and the Balkans are capable of greatly intensified agricultural development. Agrarian Hungary, Yugoslavia, and Bulgaria would no longer have to come hat in hand, seeking preferential treatment for their products from the great mass production States. They would not need to fear being drawn into the orbit of some powerful industrial neighbor who would thenceforward dictate the real terms of their existence.

No one would gain more than the fruit, grain and dairy countries, who would find free markets everywhere throughout the Continent and no longer would be forced to distort their natural economies in an effort to mend an almost grotesquely helpless position. They would have no need for some artificially stimulated industrial plant, alien to their resources and market opportunities, and could develop their territories along profitable and sensible lines. There would be no more reason for Bulgaria to take desperate and costly steps to rectify her industrial weakness than there would be for the great corn-growing state of Iowa.

There will be no have-not States in a cooperative Europe, since the development of the Continent would be based on a truly interdependent economy. If the manufacturing of airplanes were concentrated in Northern France and Belgium, it would make little more difference to Yugoslavia than it did to the American state of Kansas when this great industry was located almost altogether on our East and West Coasts.

The European space aggregate we will refer to as the Union of the Old World. An intelligent rationalization of its boundaries would spread them over three continents, giving the Union access to great grain producing lands, and to all of the tropical products required to sustain its economy in balance.

Our mapmakers should recognize that Europe is an appendage of Asia, and neither from the geographical or economic view can be considered as an organism complete in itself. The Mediterranean Sea is not the southern border of the Old World but its very center of gravity. It was so in ancient times when this largest of inland oceans was the central highway of a natural grouping, not called Europe, Africa, or Asia Minor, but Civilization.

The new Europe would extend from the western frontier of the Soviet Union to include the balance of the present continent. Its natural southern border is the Sahara Desert, which stretches like a forbidding and impassable sea across practically the entire north of Africa. It is the historic boundary between black Africa and the Mediterranean world, which bred its Rameses, its Cleopatras, its Hannibals and Hamilcar Barcas as well as its Caesars, Alexanders and Helens.

Even today the Mediterranean civilization of North Africa has more in common with Spain, Italy, Greece, Turkey and the Near East than it has with Africa south of the Sahara. This fact so impressed the historian, Michelet, that he once wrote: "Africa begins at the Pyrenees."

A natural grouping of the territories to form the Union of the Old World would take in all of the Mediterranean regions, including Asia Minor and Arabia.

The Mediterranean basin is one of the rich possessions of mankind. It is warm, fertile and everywhere habitable by men of European race. It offers ideal conditions for either air or sea traffic. In the great coastal section of North Africa known as the Maghreb, the settlement possibilities for white men are fairly comparable to those found on our Pacific Coast. The Valley of the Euphrates in Iraq and the fertile reaches of Syria alone could keep sixty million people in comfort.

Arabia is largely an unknown quantity, but it is certain that the long coastal strip of the Peninsula, together with the oases and potentially fertile wadis, will support densely settled populations. The builders of the Iraq pipeline demonstrated the presence of a huge water table below the entire surface of the Syrian Desert, boring producing unlimited water at an average depth of six hundred feet.

American engineers sent to Palestine proved that artesian wells sunk according to modern methods, struck water even in the apparently hopeless hill areas. With the construction of stream regulation works and an extensive system of dams and water channels, it is safe to believe that there are few sections, even in arid Libya and the apparently waterless interior of Arabia, which cannot be transformed into garden spots.

Freed of confining boundaries, North Africa and Arabia should become thriving centers of a civilized Union of the Old World, enclosing an inland sea which will be what it was in ancient times, not a source of separation and disunity but a great binding highway between various portions of the same universe.

On the southeast, the Union would take in Turkey, which is essentially a European nation. By its possession of Arabia it would have access to the Indian Ocean and front on the southern seas.

Below the natural boundary of the desert is still a second boundary consisting of the badlands and impassable equatorial forests of Nigeria and Central Africa. This region, which holds the far western hump of the Dark Continent, also should belong to the Union of the Old World. It is the natural supplier of rubber, coffee, quinine, tropical woods, spices and other products needed to maintain a healthy and thriving economy. Providentially it contains tin, zinc, nickel and other mineral products required for the proper maintenance of industrial Europe. It is one of the potential sources of phosphates, which will be badly required in Europe's intensive agriculture.

As modern methods of sanitation and transport open up new techniques for conquering the tropics, the highlands of Nigeria, Rio de Oro and French Equatorial Africa can become healthful and thickly settled communities.

The southern border of the Union would include northern Africa to the mouth of the Niger, thence to follow the Yocaba and the northern boundary of Nigeria to Lake Chad; from there north to the Tibesti Mountains, and would include the provinces of Libya and Egypt.

Thus the new Europe would possess every known factor which could contribute to her prosperity. The geology of the big Peninsula itself shows an immense wealth of mineral assets. To these would be added the tropical products of Africa as well as the immense natural granaries of the Maghreb and Middle East, together with some of the best fisheries of the world.

In Europe proper would be one of the great industrial concentrations of the globe, enabling an easy flow of commerce and raw materials which could make the Union of the Old World almost entirely self-supporting.

The new frontiers conjoined with her ancient realm would absorb Europe's surplus population for any predictable period which can be visualized. She would possess every climate and virtually every known resource, and would occupy a defensible military position which could be compared to any. Her wealth in water power, coal, iron and oil would be sufficient to support a prosperity incomparably superior to anything the old Europe has ever known.

The Union would have a population of some 350,000,000, with a land area of about 6,800,000 square miles. Its peoples have already demonstrated a talent for organization, for industrial energy, and technical know-how. They can be depended on to throw themselves with ardent enthusiasm into an effort to make the most of the new situation. Their hustle and zeal would make itself felt in a majestic system of intercontinental roads, airways, engineering works, industries, and thriving farm and urban communities, capable of providing history with some of its most glowing pages.

When the tariff walls and barriers which now throw the Continent into a hopeless jumble, disappear, Europe will possess the productive capacity by which with a little initial help from us she can undertake her own rehabilitation. If the national restrictions which now garrote the Continent are removed, it is not unreasonable to predict that within the space of a very few years Europe will have forgotten her present afflictions. A unified Europe would not only find her production restored but amplified on a steadily increasing scale.

V

If by a final stipulation with the Soviets, an organized Europe can be brought about together with a unified West, universal society could safely gamble on allowing an early consummation of what will be inevitable anyway—a united Orient.

Thus the policy which is now pursued by the West would exactly be reversed. Under the present dispensation the United States wishes a China strong enough to police its part of the world, prosperous enough to provide a market for American goods, but not powerful enough to challenge either the commercial or military supremacy of the Western nations. London wants a weak China because of India and its interests in the Malay States, the Indies and Australasia.

An influential section of American opinion is willing to risk most of the dangers which would attend the emergence of a strong China, in order to contain Russia in Asia and to deter it from seeking any major expansion in Europe under threat of bringing on a world coalition against it on all its borders.

All of this partakes of the old diplomatic power thesis by which the world was perpetually kept in a state of precarious equilibrium. It will have to be abandoned for the safety of the human race on this planet. There is no better time than now when under the stress of ideals invoked by a horrible war, men the world over are willing to agree to a permanent if radical settlement.

The factors which have applied to Europe, to the Soviet Union, and which, as we shall note, will apply to the West, will have to be applied also to the Orient. It will be necessary for the Orient to be self-contained, capable of expansion into frontier districts, and to have access to the entire catalogue of raw materials required to maintain a competent industrial husbandry.

The Orient will require immediate solution to two urgent problems. The first is the need for feeding its starving, poverty-stricken masses. The second is some badly needed help from the Western nations in the way of scientists, technicians, organizers and machinery.

Only in this manner can the Orient modify the inevitable turbulence which will exist wherever starvation and ignorance accompany a dramatic transmigration from one stage of civilization to another.

If this transition is made with our help, the Orient will develop a set of vested interests complementary to our own, and will not be harried into uncompromising resentment over Caucasian possession of valuable territories in the Southern Seas. If the Orient, however, emerges despite the white man, or only with his grudging consent, it will do so by a *tour de force* accompanied by hatred and contempt. The full power of Japanese propaganda will have lingered and grown. The white man will be considered an usurper throughout Asia, wherever he stands in the way of the ambitions of the East.

An agreement now would harden all attitudes and fit them into the most desirable grooves. By giving the East room for development and by identifying its interests with a continuation of the *status quo,* the crisis between East and West could be put off indefinitely.

From the military position, the Orient with its vast resources in men would be surrounded by a wall of steel in the shape of political aggregates even larger in extent than Asia and capable of rendering any war so costly as to prevent it altogether.

The new Asian aggregate would consist of the entire body of that continent south and east of the Soviet border. It would include China and mandated Japan, India, Ceylon, Hong Kong, Thailand, French Indo-China, the Malay States, the southeastern two-thirds of Iran, Afghanistan, Nepal, Bhutan, India, Burma, Korea, Sinkiang or Chinese Turkestan, Tibet, Mongolia and Manchukuo. It would have an area of something over eight million square miles, and a population of 1,100,000,000.

Properly the Commonwealth of the Philippines and a considerable share of the Indies should be bound into this Asiatic complex, with which their physical interests most easily would be affiliated.

However, as long as it is the policy of the West to attempt to hold Australia and New Zealand, it by necessity must have possession of the seven thousand islands of the Philippines, together with all of the non-Soviet Indies to the south. Ownership of these as we shall see, would enable us under modern methods of military defense-in-depth to throw an efficient chain of mail around the otherwise unprotectable English-speaking Commonwealths.

A move in the direction of conquest by the Orient, immediately would threaten the position of the important Soviet possessions of Sumatra, Borneo and Java. If the islands held by the Union of the West once were taken, the Soviet Indies no longer could be retained and would drop like tree-ripe fruits into the gaping mouth of the Oriental colossus. We could reasonably expect that the normal balance of power in this giant sector would find the interests of the Soviet Union primarily linked with those of the West.

As we have observed, there is no type of peace which may be formulated that possibly can exist independent of the distribution of power. The more even the equilibrium effected and the fewer inconsistencies, inequities or contradictions involved, the more certain is the continuation of peace. Therefore, the demographic disequilibrium which exists in favor of the Orient must be balanced off, at least until such a time as a clearer relationship between the East and West makes the delimitation of all boundaries desirable. This can be achieved solely by utilizing that concomitant source of power, space, bolstering the weakness of Western manpower by purely geographic and strategic considerations.

Thus the Orient may not be allowed to control the Pacific south of Formosa. With the exception of Ceylon and the Andaman Islands in the Bay of Bengal, the approaches to its southeastern coast would be all patrolled by great stationary aircraft carriers in the hands of the Soviets and the West.

In all other respects the life of the Orient would be normalized. She would be unified and free from outside interference. She would have her great factories, forest and mine areas, her bustling cities, her grazing, grain and fruit lands, and reasonably good outlets for her surplus population. In Iran, Afghanistan, Central Asia, and in the rich lands of Indo-China and the southeastern peninsula, the Orient might find room for upwards of a half billion people.

With the acquisition of Japan and Manchukuo, the East would gain highly industrialized centers capable of being the levers by which the industrial revolution could be quickly accomplished and the present technological backwardness of the Orient overcome. The millions of Japanese who cannot possibly expect to survive on their isolated islands, would be provided with an outlet by which their energy, talents and knowledge of machine techniques could be turned to the benefit of the whole Orient.

Japan, it may be assumed, will be for a considerable period a mandated territory with no rights of citizenship, and governed for the common advantage of the general Oriental community. Its population may have to be reduced to half of what it now is, to keep it from attaining the boiling point after the permanent dislocations which will be the result of military defeat.

Instead of being the center of a tremendous empire which it could exploit to its own advantage, Japan would have to turn its energies to the advancement of Asia, for the good of all its inhabitants. Rather than the privileged supermen of the vainglorious Co-Prosperity Sphere, the Nipponese would be strictly on probation, enjoying the liberty of the paroled convict who still has to prove his capacity to serve the purposes of the community at large as a free and responsible citizen.

Japan would have a long road of atonement ahead. If it could not prove its worth as an autonomous law-abiding province of the Orient, it would be dealt with, with that inscrutable firmness of purpose of which the East traditionally has been capable.

VI

One of the great question marks which would remain in the world would be that of the unhappy bulk of anonymous dark people who inhabit Africa.

In the architecture of a permanently stabilized international society, provision will have to be made for them.

As we have observed, the outstanding political phenomenon of this century has been the coming to power of the anonymous massman as a correlative of the mass production and urban age. Africa is no exception to this rule, which is affecting all the continents and is reducing the fortunes of mankind everywhere to a stereotyped pattern dominated by the mechanics of the machine era. The Africa of the kraals, of mysterious depths which only occasional hunters penetrate, is finished for all time. With it will disappear the private and pastoral Africa, which for better or worse is destined to feel the full magnetism of those towering forces which have created the industrial revolution in the West.

The induction of the Negro into the highly geared industrial apparatus which is sure to be built to exploit the resources of Africa, will introduce a social storm of tempestuous dimensions. It will be found in Africa as elsewhere that the age of industry is the age of equalization, in which the organized mass workers develop a new and terrible power capable of overturning any regime, and all rulers.

It is desirable also that the unhealthy relationship of the races in certain parts of the world be modified by provisions which take them into account. As we have noted, social ostracism is the result of habits deeply engrained in the tribal past. It cannot be permanently abrogated by the use of pure logic, moral demands or some legal mechanism. To be altered it requires that the Negro be placed in a reasonable state of balance to the rest of mankind, in short, that he become a power factor some place where his race is in the majority, thus introducing a new item of self-interest in the relationship of nations with their Negroes.

This would involve a basic change in the political status of the black man as a world dispersed entity. He would acquire a bargaining position due to his possession of a political and economic center of power. He would be able to undertake his own peculiar culture and political development.

There is no other place where this might occur except in Africa. Here the Negro is heavily in the majority and either eventually will be exterminated in a bloody war, or will dominate the Continent.

It seems not only equitable but common logic that this problem be settled now, and that all of Africa south of those sections which are to be incorporated with the Union of the Old World, be constituted as a provisional Negro commonwealth. This would embrace 7,240,000 square miles of territory containing a population of close to 100,000,000.

From the territorial view, the Negro empire would be comparable to any of the other space aggregates. It would possess every climate from tropical to temperate, with capacities for supporting an ultimate population of four to five hundred million.

There is no resource required for sustaining a prosperous and thickly settled population which is not present on this rich continent. Africa's mineral wealth leaves little to be desired. The fisheries off her coast are excellent, and every crop which can be grown in the tropical, semi-tropical or temperate climes will bear abundantly on her farms and plantations.

The underlying question would be the capacity of her people and their ability to administer this area efficiently as part of the world stream of power forces.

There can be no pretense that the Negro, by and large, today is equal to the social standards of the cultivated European. On the other hand, similar criteria could be applied to a large portion of the Caucasian race. The yardstick, therefore, must be not "each according to his capacities or his virtue" but rather "each according to his needs."

The question, hence, is not one of absolute abilities. If that measuring stick were to be used, the industrial capacities of Germany would entitle the Reich to rule Europe and would give it an unquestioned superiority over Poland, the Baltic republics and its other neighbors.

If we are to be guided strictly by such reference as exists, the Negro State cannot take its place among the world communities. The Negro Republic of Haiti has not been a great success. Neither has the Republic of Liberia shown the enterprise and talents which would enable it to rank amongst the first-class modern nations.

The case may be very different in a large territorial aggregate containing wide resources of climate, soil, raw materials and population. The assumption must be that such a State would succeed at least in attaining a competent, semi-industrial position.

If by virtue of corruption or absolute inferiority the black man is not capable of maintaining himself under civilized conditions, the result will be fully as tragic under the present dispensation of white rule, where by his very presence he would debauch the political institutions under which he lived, and represent a continuous menace to every standard, industrial, cultural or social, by which the white race maintains itself.

It must be acknowledged that there would be the most serious difficulties in connection with the establishment of a major Negro commonwealth. Questions would exist in almost every possible direction. Nevertheless they would have to be solved.

Africa itself is a complete grab-bag of black and negroid peoples living in all stages of civilization, governed by the widest possible variety of cultures and religions, and speaking a vast jumble of languages. These people would have to be unified into a more or less common sphere of culture, much as were the alien migrants to the United States during the big flood of immigration. Africa would need the sympathetic assistance of the older established civilizations in obtaining its sea legs. A special effort would have to be made to create an extensive school and university system to give the young Africans training in modern techniques of government, and in the effective handling of industry and agriculture. A progressive policy would furnish a gigantic world loan to Africa, together with the teachers, engineers and technicians required to get its development under way.

The Commonwealth of Africa would have to be mandated for an indefinite period to a world body on which the other four Power Aggregates would sit. It would attain full status in the councils of the world only when its ability to manage its own affairs became apparent.

Africa's needs are much similar to those of Asia. Africa wants roads, electric stations, automobiles, airplanes, and machine equipment of all kinds. Vast forest tracts and table-lands would have to be cleared. There must be an extensive cleaning out of the malarial, yellow fever and tse-tse fly areas. Africa requires induction hand and foot into the new technology. It needs to be taught a proper reverence for good government, whose lack has been the curse of the several small existing Negro regimes. It needs to develop a pride in itself and its achievements, and in the destiny of the race of Ham, seeking to produce its black savants, engineers and scientists, as well as black poets, orators and angels.

The paramount question of leadership, and the skills necessary to organize a thriving, modern society, would have to be answered by migration. There would not be sufficient time to wait on the education and amalgamation of the native tribes.

The proposed black empire would provide an unlimited potential field for Negroes from all over the world, who either were seeking new horizons or who believed themselves to be oppressed and lacking in commercial, political and economic opportunity. Here they could go to exploit their abilities and assist in the fashioning of a fine new world, not only aiding the future of their own race, but lending an element of deep stability to the whole of human society.

There is no abandonment of ideals involved in the fact of great human migrations, either for economic and social benefits, or for reasons of spiritual freedom. We have the example of the ancient Israelites who moved out of Egypt into the Promised Land, of the Huguenots, the Pennsylvania Quakers, the Puritans, the Maryland Catholics and the persecuted Mormons, all of whom moved onward to form their own communities.

Black Americans could supply to this struggling mass of black peoples, moving blindly toward the light of political unity, the necessary technicians, editors, organizers, engineers and business men. Several million colored men and women schooled in American laboratory and factory production, and themselves products of the machine age, would be the most valuable product which could be exported to the new Africa. They would give the new State the leadership and the know-how it would require.

A group of picked, educated and skilled American Negroes could be allowed to immigrate there under guaranteed conditions. Later, after these pioneers had prepared the way, a great portion of the Negroes from the American hemisphere might find in the Dark Continent the unlimited opportunities discovered by the early English and Huguenots in the United States.

As the country attained prosperity and grew under the magic of its own expanding dynamics, the Negro peoples of the European section of Africa who would prefer to live under conditions envisaged by an all-Negro community, could be brought to Negro Africa in an orderly migration underwritten by the other great commonwealths. *This would be regarded as part of a general plan for settling all great central issues and creating a safe and integrated world.*

Fifty million East Indians also could be settled in Africa, where they would possess equal rights with the native Negroes in what is certain to be a rapidly developing and prosperous economy.

Africa cries out for colonists who would assist her in bridging the intervening gap between colonial stagnation and the industrial civilization which is one day certain to come. The ability of such races as the Indians and Arabs to absorb themselves into African life has been proven by long experience. Arab blood runs everywhere throughout the Continent. In the Union of South Africa there are already several hundred thousand Indians who have become a progressive portion of the population.

In addition it would be an act of the highest statesmanship if fifty million Chinese and Japanese were encouraged to migrate to this new land of destiny. All these elements should easily be able to merge with each other, providing a melting pot on a grand scale never before visualized, creating a new racial grouping and what should be a modern and efficient commonwealth.

Oriental peoples from the hot weather regions of Asia should be the perfect migrants for the development of the wet-hot forest climate of the African Equatorial Zone. These are probably the most important portions of Africa, both from the view of their agricultural and mineral resources. As potential food producers, these regions are unparalleled. Their role as a producer of raw stuffs for the new age of plastics will be an outstanding one.

The greater portion of Africa necessary for this project is under British control. One part, Abyssinia, is ostensibly independent. Other portions are under the ownership of Portugal, Belgium and France.

In any world settlement these European States will have had their future secured and will have lost their specific identities as small imperial nations struggling to maintain a precarious place in the world. No one cares today that Turkey no longer holds colonial tracts or subject peoples in the Balkans; nor will it affect the primary currents of Italian destiny that Italy will have lost her costly colonies in East Africa and Libya.

It is providential that the current of economic logic runs parallel with cotemporary global needs, and makes the presence of Europe in that portion of Africa below the Equator, unnecessary, and in the sense of true global politics, undesirable.

Only three per cent of the production of important raw materials found in international commerce originated in colonial areas. Despite Germany's chagrin at being deprived of her colonies, she drew no more than one half of one per cent of the raw materials consumed in her factories from these sources.

As markets they are worth little. The quality of a modern market is determined not only by the numbers of people it represents but also by their productivity. If they produce little, they are poor. If they are poor, they cannot buy. Thus the possessing country often is saddled with responsibility for the economies of these satellites, which become under such conditions, virtual Frankensteins.

Britain was forced to purchase fully half of the 1942 Egyptian cotton crop despite the fact that she did not need the cotton, to save the growers from financial ruin. She was compelled to buy large stocks of unneeded West African cocoa after the European markets were lost.

The impending development of synthetic replacement materials by manufacturing countries, will tend to accelerate the deterioration of the colonial system, threatening it with an era of falling prices and rising native unrest.

The ownership by European States of faraway colonial preserves involves an increasing list of difficulties and disadvantages. In terms of modern manufacture and production such possessions are valuable solely when they are occupied by a population kindred to that of the possessing country, and where no penalty need arise through assisting the natural process of industrialization.

Modern techniques of manufacture and distribution demand the active and willing participation of both producer and consumer. They cannot flourish with an inert, poverty-stricken, resistant native population except by the imposition of a complete slave economy under total military tutelage.

The conditions created by modern existence increasingly place a premium on a high state of productivity, making marginal factories and marginal workers as undesirable as marginal land. Today the collection of tribute from barbaric native peoples is a petty business which requires more in the way of machinery to protect it than can possibly come in profits. All told, Britain's overseas territories have cost a good deal more than they have been worth in trade. If military and naval expenditures, and cost of administration, are taken into account, the colonies are run at a heavy deficit.

Colonies do not even offer military security in the sense of guaranteed access to raw materials. The picture can be seen with some clarity from the experience of the United States which received its rubber and tin from the Malay States and Netherlands East Indies, despite the fact that it did not own these territories. When the United States lost its access to these supplies after Pearl Harbor, Britain was cut off at the same time, without reference to the fact of ownership.

If Africa is to be held by its present European owners, or under some scheme such as that now entertained by the British, it will have to be heavily settled with whites, much as were the Dominions, and will interpose an entirely new area of explosive conflict into world affairs.

If the overall problems of global peace are to be composed, the system of white imperialism in Africa must come to an end.

The single exception which would render a forthright solution difficult lies in the existence of the Dominion of South Africa.

In reordering the political lines of the globe, the Dominion could become an outpost of the Union of the West or of Europe. The objection to this status would be the relative weakness of this region by comparison to the surrounding areas, a situation which would grow worse as the years wore on.

South Africa represents one of the most valuable parts of the African temperate zone, and one of its most natural areas of development. Subjoined to Africa as an alien particle, antagonistic to the black majority, it is a certain source of trouble and friction.

In the very territories of the Dominion itself, if the Bantu and other black races are to be given equal rights under the law, as ultimately they must be, the present racial balance of power on which South Africa depends would be irretrievably destroyed.

If South Africa is to remain a white enclave in a black world, its black majority will have to leave for the north by an assisted migration to avoid what otherwise would be a certain focus of trouble.

The question of Africa is made more torturous by the imperial view held among Boer nationalists, who consider all of sub-Saharan Africa as part of a future Boer rule. In this empire the color bar would operate with rigid immovability. There are no more determined racists in the world than the Afrikaaners, who tend to make of their Boer inheritance a sort of fetishism. The effect has been to make the Boers easy victims of Nazi propaganda.

That this excessive ambition on the part of a people scarcely numbering more than one million, never can be realized, is apparent. That a struggle between white South Africa, and the black peoples fired by the holy zeal of a war for liberation, could not fail to embroil Europe and possibly Asia, seems no less evident.

The problems posed by white mentality in South Africa no longer can be reconciled with the trend of events indicated for the future. They are utterly insoluble except by heroic measures in which the Caucasian position will remain under constant hazard.

A rational measure which, however, would be instantly resisted by whites everywhere, would be to regard the matter not as a provincial issue but as part of a broad global settlement to be approached in much the same spirit as the Greco-Turkish population exchange of 1922. The two million whites of South Africa are but a minor handful in comparison to the billions of the world's population. They could be transferred to European Africa, to South America, Oceania or Australia by orderly international processes which would offer them fair compensation for the wealth and opportunities they might have left behind.

Such a determination would be a wise and statesmanlike decision though it would go hard with the pride of the white race. Except for the larger numbers concerned, it actually is no different than the inevitable removal of white plantation owners from Tanganyika; or the equally certain relinquishment of the Belgian Congo by the nineteen thousand Europeans who now rule its thirteen million Negroes.

Whether in this or some other fashion, the problem should be faced squarely. Whether it involves Utopian measures or not, the world must assist with all its might in a proper solution of this question. If the black peoples are to be economic misfits and political failures, the world will have them on its hands no matter how it is figured, since they live on this terrestrial sphere and not on Mars.

X X

THE UNION OF THE WEST

THE Union of the West would consist of a unified North and South America, the British Isles, Iceland, Greenland, Australasia, and the islands of the Pacific south of Formosa and west of Borneo and Java. It would possess a population of 358,000,000, and a land area of twenty million square miles, a great portion of which, as in the case of Greenland and Australia, would consist of desolate wastes.

Within the Union there would be only one citizenship irrespective of the divisional boundaries by which the various parts were identified. In this empire, it would make little difference if an article were fabricated in London, Chicago, or Rio de Janeiro. Whether aviation manufacturing were concentrated in California or Bolivia would be of little more than local consequence.

The safety, wealth and prosperity which would dignify the entire system would be the common property of all. As a unit of production and military power, the Union would conform to virtually every principle by which power is contained in a modern sense, and would be wellnigh invincible. In almost every respect it would be self-sufficient. It would present far more attractions for peaceful trade than for some aggression which, even if successful, would all but ruin the conqueror.

The Union would be multilinguistic, much as is Switzerland and the Soviet Union, though English would tend to dominate. It would contain some two hundred million English-speaking people, seventy million who spoke varieties of Spanish, thirty-five million whose native tongue was Portuguese, nine million users of French, several million who spoke German, and still other millions who used native Indian or Polynesian-Malayan languages such as the Araucanian and Tagalog.

Such a Union is a basic prerequisite to any rationalized world order. If it is too late to place into effect a five Power world, and if the Soviet Union were to seize on the present disturbed situation to remake Europe according to its own vision, we would possess no alternative. The creation of the West into a self-contained fortress would be enjoined on us.

II

In committing herself to union with America, Great Britain would rectify a classic blunder in history and would enter a new phase of economic prosperity and security such as she has never enjoyed before.

She would become at once the virtual crossroads of the world, the spearhead of the trade between continental America and Europe. Through her cities and harbors most of the European commerce with the West would be filtered, giving her a genuine and permanent importance far removed from the dangerous imperial juggling by which her factories are granted priority in the rapidly closing markets of Asia.

London no longer would need to fear the inevitable confiscation of its investments in divers parts of the globe, nor the final closing off of Europe under a single autarchus control. She would have the great markets of the Americas and Oceania at her disposal, and guaranteed access to all the raw materials required by her factories. She would not be forced into a crushing armaments race to defend either her own island or her increasingly threatened possessions.

Britain, in short, instead of depending on battleships, and the chicanery of diplomatic maneuver, would rely on the intelligence and genius of her people and their ability to compete. She would gain in return, peace, and as great a measure of safety as ever can be expected in this imperfect world.

The Dominions would operate in the same relation, and would become portions of a rationalized economy enabling them to receive both immigration and finance assistance as well as military security.

If we are able to effect a consolidation with Britain and her Dominions, those possessions which fly the British flag would be added to the Union automatically. The islands under Japanese sovereignty, such as the Marshalls and the Carolines, we could seize outright. The French and Dutch possessions could be purchased or exchanged for Lend-Lease much as we purchased the Virgin Islands from Denmark. The future of both Holland and France would be that of Europe, and they would cease to exist as imperial States.

If Australia is to be part of the West, she would become another Polish Corridor and could not be held at all unless every one of the northern islands from Timor and New Guinea to Luzon in the Philippines, were combined in a single system of defense like a series of hardened steel plates each imposed upon the other.

This hedge of defenses would reach in a solid phalanx to Batan Island off the coast of Formosa, and to the little atoll of Hatizyosima lying just south of the main Japanese island of Honshu. Only the proposed Soviet ownership of Sumatra, Java and Borneo would represent a break in the pattern of control.

These Pacific bases are useless to Europe. The States under whose sovereignty they now exist could make no pretense at retaining them against a major aggression from any of the Powers bordering the Pacific Ocean. The only way these islands can be held is for one Power to hold them all, industrializing them with special reference to the war industries, settling them heavily with its millions of prospective immigrants, and dotting the entire area with military bases and airfields so as to build a complete barricade-in-depth.

Such a defense would be almost an impregnable one and would be next to impossible for an enemy to breach.

These stations, many of which figure as mere dots on the map, dominate the communications of the Pacific Ocean. If they were properly organized for a combined air and sea defense, no attack on us from the East which did not proceed over the Arctic Circle would be remotely possible. As long as we retained these outposts, we would possess the capacity for retaliatory action, forcing any enemy to immobilize large portions of his military establishment for the defense of his own coasts.

We are not a geographically conscious people and the size of these sea-girt chains are difficult for us to visualize. The total group of islands extends over an area three thousand miles deep and five thousand miles wide. New Guinea alone contains over 242,000 square miles. Even the minor Celebes hold over 38,800 square miles. The New Hebrides chain stretches over a length of almost six hundred miles of ocean and holds a land area of 5,800 square miles.

The best interests of the natives themselves will demand the incorporation of these places in the trading empire of the West, where their resources will be developed and their rights respected. The attitude of the islanders very well may be expected to follow that of the Hawaiians, who after the deposition of their queen Liliuokalani in 1893, voluntarily sought annexation to the United States.

In any circumstance, as the world's greatest military Power devoted to a frank course of protection for our own shores, we should have little difficulty in achieving possession.

A similar attitude should apply to the island system of the Atlantic. Foreign ownership of any area in the Caribbean would be as unthinkable as would a renewal of Spanish possession of the Netherlands, or British control of the northern provinces of France. The Caribbean islands have little commercial and no military value to any European State unless they are to be used as the springboard for attack upon our cities.

Possession of these islands by European Powers in the air age would act to nullify our control of the Panama Canal and could provide an aggressive State with the opportunity to organize an invasion of Latin America while we were engaged in repelling attack from another direction.

In the north, Iceland and Greenland are the direct stepping-stones to invasion and would have to come permanently under our flag.

The Azores, the Madeira, Canary, and Cape Verde Islands, are all submarine fueling stations and jumping-off places for concerted air attacks on our shipping. As stations from which a quick counter-offensive can be launched, they would be material deterrents to any aggression which might be planned against us from Europe. The distance to the nearest American port, Cape Race in Newfound-land, is less than a thousand miles from the Azores. In our hands the Azores would be an impressive fortress, a chain of unsinkable aircraft carriers which first would have to be reduced before any attack on us from the Atlantic side was possible.

In addition to their military value, the islands of the Pacific possess great economic possibilities. They would represent an empire of vast potentialities for the expansion of American finance and enterprise—a new frontier which would add materially to the prosperity of the American Continent as well as to that of the islands themselves.

The wealth of the Malay Archipelago is fabulous, as almost any schoolboy knows. Even such a comparatively unknown outpost as New Caledonia is enormously rich in minerals, possessing great nickel mines and deposits of mercury, silver, manganese and chrome ore. In the countless islands of Oceania, which dot the Pacific with almost the luxuriance of the stars in the sky, America will find a new impulse to its boundless energy. Here are countless and vastly magnified Hawaiis, reservoirs of natural riches, future centers of commerce, and potential vacation spots and dwelling places, which speedily will be developed as air transport and radio places a man-ageable harness on distance.

With control of these islands, we would dominate all approaches to the central power point—the American Continent itself. By the juncture of the United States and Brazil, the Union would have in its possession two of the great concentric circles whose merging dy-namisms hold the key to world traffic.

Our advance bastions facing both Europe and Asia would be

commercial as well as military strongholds. We could not be surrounded or decisively attacked unless all of Eurasia came under a single control. As long as we held Australia, the islands of the South Seas, Britain, Greenland and Iceland, we would be able to effect a fair balance of power against any of the contingencies whose future development can be foreseen.

If at some future point, the Union were compelled by events to withdraw into a policy of isolation, it could be almost perfectly self-sufficient, functioning as a separate and self-contained universe.

III

The addition of Latin America would cause the Union to become by far the largest and richest empire ever to find itself under a common political rule.

The creation of an integrated economy for the Americas automatically would wipe out problems whose difficult nature scarcely can be minimized. We would no longer need to be concerned with the question of penetration by Old World Powers, or the fear of European airline franchises by which the renewed struggle for control of our sister continent would recommence.

A glance at the map will show that the strategic center of gravity of the Western hemisphere is the Caribbean Sea and adjoining Gulf of Mexico. These waters form the natural pivot of inter-American military defense. They are destined to become, like the Mediterranean, one of the great trade centers of the world, a huge bowl lined with prosperous and populous cities, connected with each other and with the balance of the two continents by a network of air, sea and land routes infinitely superior to any which now exist on the globe.

Just as Ottawa, Toronto and Montreal fall naturally into the trading territory of the American eastern seaboard rather than into that of Britain or the Canadian West Coast, the natural sphere of economic interests of Florida and our Gulf States comes within the trading area of Mexico, Central America and the northern tier of

South American countries rather than with our West, Middle West and Northeast.

If all constricting boundaries were removed, Los Angeles, San Diego and San Francisco would become virtual extensions of what would be a rich Latin economy to the south, and would be the feeding points by which Oceania would connect with the twin Americas. Separated from the balance of the United States by arid and thinly populated regions, the developing industries of southern California would find their natural outlets as well as sources of supply elsewhere than in what is now the continental United States.

Miami, Florida, would become the very core of the Union's communication system, a South American metropolis at the tip of North America, and one of the great cities of the world. Participating in its prosperity and power, and linked to it by every device of self-interest, would be such cities as Havana, El Salvador, Mexico City, San Antonio, Port-au-Prince, Guayaquil, Belem, Iquitos and Pernambuco.

Villages whose names are now scarcely known would become metropolises of international importance. The Gulf and Caribbean region would become the seat of prosperous cities and blooming countrysides, a veritable paradise in which could be housed comfortably the entire population now existing in the combined Americas.

The Caribbean thus is destined to become the beating heart of the twin continents, and the dynamic center of hemisphere defense. Until they come under a single control, the Isthmus of Panama and the Caribbean Sea are the most vulnerable points in our hemisphere, exposing North and South America to the dangers of being cut off from each other, and making everpresent the possibility that our vital industrial and factory centers in the East and Middle West will find themselves suddenly under the guns of invading bombers.

The two Americas fit perfectly into a single scheme of economy and are natural offsets to each other. The experience, know-how, finance and immediate industrial powers are in the hands of the

English-speaking colossus to the north. Latin America on the other hand is our true source of rubber, tin, quinine, coffee, beryllium, tropical oils, and other essential products. The reversal of the seasons alone would make it possible in the age of air transport to supply the North American table from the truck gardens, farms and orchards of the southern continent, a process which would exactly reverse itself as the seasons changed.

Together, North and South America possess every attribute and property needed to support a great civilization. They embrace every possible resource of agricultural and mineral wealth. With the buttressing islands of the two oceans they form an ironclad military defense system. They contain the three greatest river systems on the globe—the Amazon, navigable for two thousand miles by ocean-going vessels and draining an area larger than the continental United States; the magnificent Missouri-Mississippi, mother of the American Middle West; and the impressive Rio de la Plata, which is to the far south what the Nile is to Egypt.

Though in some important respects the two continents are competitors, this need not be a deterrent to the plan of union. We could learn from the U.S.S.R. that in any well-managed economy there must be alternate sources both of manufacture and supply. It is folly to allow vital elements of the American industrial machine to remain beyond the reach of our commercial and military control. A part of the billions we have spent in importing rubber, tin, silks, quinine, tea, manganese and other products from the tropical regions of the Old World, easily could be expended in the development of Latin America, where they would redound to the general benefit of the entire West.

It has been predicted that at the current rate of use many of the vital mineral resources available to the United States soon will be eaten up. We may be approaching the time when, like Japan and Britain, our mills and factories will be dependent on outside sources for much of their supplies. There are some signs of an impending oil scarcity. The present unremitting drain on certain critical materials such as bauxite, lead and zinc is bringing our reserves

of these metals near to depletion. Even our abundant high-grade
iron ore may become scarce in another few decades.

A coordinated industrialization of Oceania and the Latin South
would prevent our being forced into an imperialist course to supply
these wanted materials. In line with the best of modern industrial
procedure, factories would be located at sites adjacent to raw material and power sources, rather than concentrated in a few jealously
guarded industrial centers. This type of development eliminates
uneconomic hauling costs and makes for a sound economic and
military balance. This is a course already sensibly followed by the
Soviet Union, and sure to be emulated by China.

In Latin America exists all of the natural conditions required to
create an impressive industrial civilization. Her only serious mineral lack is coal, a defect which may be remedied by further exploration. Her potential sources of water power are ample. Her petroleum reserves are believed to be enormous. In the Venezuelan State
of Anzoategui, alone, are said to exist deposits totalling two billion
barrels.

The riches in valuable timbers are inexhaustible, and the deposits of iron, copper and other minerals, among the most extensive
in existence. Bolivia is the world's second largest producer of tin.
In Brazil the known deposits of manganese in the single area of
Minas Geraes are some twelve million tons of forty to fifty-five per
cent ore. The Brazilian State of Goyaz is estimated to possess more
than four million tons of high-grade nickel ore, a resource which is
backed by the presence of practically unlimited reserves of lower
grade ore in Cuba.

Once Latin America were merged with the Union of the West its
development would be spectacular. The Latin countries quickly
could take over all manufactures connected with light industry,
both for export to Europe and to supply their own needs. The capital and skilled managers and operators required would be supplied
by Britain and the United States. We could go even to the point
of dismantling our own excess plants and moving them into Brazil,

Chile and the Argentine in order to obtain a better distribution of effective industrial potential for the entire Union.

Brazil by virtue of its geographic position is destined to become one of the two great jumping-off places from which the combined commerce of the Americas will be hauled to Europe and Africa. It would be to the interests of the Union to rush the industrialization of the eastern hump of Brazil as rapidly as possible, seeking to add twenty-five million to her population within a decade. Brazil would become an integral portion of a live and throbbing defense area synchronized by swift communications with the populous sections to the North and South, rather than as it is at present, a wild far-away, thinly populated and scarcely defensible outpost.

Large-scale agriculture could be created throughout Latin America, as could smelting operations, the manufacture of synthetics, and the processing of food. Foundries, shipyards and airplane manufacturing plants could be established where strategic value made them desirable. The making of cotton, wool and silk fabrics, as well as leather goods, pharmaceutical specialties, and alcoholic liquors, could be undertaken.

The annual five-million bag coffee surplus of Brazil could be turned into a powder for the manufacture of plastics. The luxuriant tropical forests with their more than eighty kinds of valuable woods, present unlimited possibilities in a chemical and bonded-plastic age.

To the industrial power and rich natural resources of the United States would be added those of Great Britain, making possible a rapid tempo of expansion in Latin America, as well as in the erstwhile British Dominions and Oceania. This would be a development participated in by equals, and not another aspect of imperialism.

On A-day, the United States will have in its possession an enormously distended industrial plant together with new techniques, which either can be used for the benefit of the whole hemispheric economy, or which could represent a fatal overexpansion capable of precipitating an industrial crisis of unprecedented dimensions throughout the West.

Europe and Asia exist as doubtful outlets for this surplus of goods and services. Their markets will have dwindled to almost nothing, and their ability to pay for what they receive will be isolated to a long-range and hence highly debatable program.

In South America, we would have a perfect outlet for our radio, automobile and aviation equipment, or even for the heavy machinery and plants themselves, where they would create new markets and become an extension of our own economy. By being a portion of our estate they could in no possible way jeopardize our future. They would open up for North America and Britain extensive new frontiers which would be a stimulus to the spiritual side of our civilization as well as to the industrial and mercantile side. The effect would be to create new enthusiasms in a civilization in danger of constriction through the failure of its own powers.

The result could be compared only to the tremendous impulses and ideals which accompanied the opening of the West. It would without question usher in the greatest flowering period the Americas are destined to know.

There would be a feverish expansion in every direction. Great investments would be made under the aegis of the common government in the opening of virgin territories, the building of new cities, dredging of rivers and creation of new industries. Prosperous, thickly settled countrysides would appear where once existed only pampas and tropical forests. Something of this phenomenon is seen in the miraculous tempo of construction in the Soviet East, and the mushrooming development of the cities of the Ural Mountains region and Central Asia.

Roadbuilding on a large scale would open up a demand for trucks and passenger cars. As Latin America's economy expanded, occupying continuously higher plateaus of activity, the demand for industrial equipment, typewriters, engines, tools, equipment and machine apparatus of all kinds would rise rapidly. With it would come a pressing need for executives, managers, engineers and technicians, chemists, doctors, surveyors and other skilled men.

This lack could be supplied by the United States, Canada and

England out of the expanding groups of trained men, many of whom will be jobless when wartime industry begins to shrink. These men would function in a manner comparable to those we supplied the Soviet Union during the early period of her industrial growth, but on an immensely grander scale and on a basis of permanence.

Everyone will benefit from the powerful dynamisms which will have been set into motion. In the warm glow of these reciprocal activities our own prosperity will be reflected as if in a mirror. At the same time the standard of living throughout these backward areas will increase immeasurably.

In the drainage system of the Amazon River alone, are opportunities sufficient to engage our energies for a generation. This rich, empty and almost unprobed territory is without roads, capital, industrial credits, or the facilities and skills required for modern manufacture. Not even its opulent agriculture can be exploited, except in a minor fashion, for want of technical skills, machines and colonists. Such problems as these must be attacked on a massive scale. They are problems involving the participation of government, as well as private capital.

The reorganization of the West will eliminate the unregulated competition which formerly existed between the United States, Britain and the Latin American countries, making it unnecessary for these States to engage in cutthroat rivalry with each other.

IV

The Americas south of the United States' borders are broken into twenty independent republics. Functioning also as separate organisms are British Honduras, the three Guianas, owned by England, France and Holland respectively, the divers French, Dutch, and British possessions of the West Indies, and the British-owned Falkland Islands.

Their combined land area is in the neighborhood of 8,700,000 square miles. They contain a population variously estimated between one hundred and ten and one hundred and twenty-five million. In most of the countries no accurate census ever has been taken.

As they now are constituted the economies of the Latin American countries are even more unbalanced than those of Europe. Most of these States rely on the United States directly for subsidies. Their industrial plant is on the whole negligible, their populations small and scattered, and their armed forces capable of little in the way of real resistance.

All of the armies of the Latin American countries put together scarcely could total more than one and a half million effectives. They are pathetically wanting in modern armament, and possess only token air forces.

On the sea they are equally weak. Their combined merchant marine would scarcely do credit to a single European country such as Holland or France. Their total naval establishment could offer not even a pretense to effective operation under present conditions of warfare. Any one of the major Powers could conquer the entire continent in a matter of months if it were not interfered with by the United States of America.

From the economic view the weaknesses of these States are even more glaring. Venezuela depends almost entirely on oil and does not even produce the cereals required for her own bread. Brazil, with the most varied resources of any country on earth, has seventy per cent of her export trade concentrated in coffee, cotton, cacao and vegetable oils. Colombia depends on coffee for sixty-one per cent of its exports. Eighty per cent of Cuba's shipments abroad consist of sugar and sugar products. Ninety-two per cent of the exports of Bolivia are composed of tin and other minerals. Even modern and progressive Chile, with an export of $141,000,000, has forty-eight per cent of this in copper bars and twenty-two per cent in nitrates.[1]

Such an economy as these figures indicate is unsound and dangerous in a modern world. No State is capable of maintaining itself as sovereign and independent on such terms as these, and in order to exist must find itself increasingly under the thumb of powerful

[1] All figures are for the year 1938.

neighbors. By their very existence such nations give rise to the evils of imperial rivalry. They become tempting morsels over which the larger Powers struggle for political and economic dominance.

It goes without saying that we cannot allow the recovery of the influential position once held by Europe in South America, or agree to a straight out-and-out competition with the new Powers of Eurasia for the favors of our southern neighbors.

Before World War II, Latin America shipped about fifty-five per cent of her exports to Europe and only thirty-five per cent to the United States. The situation has altered to the point where today the United States in many respects holds powers of life and death over these republics by being the principal purchaser of their exportable products. By the mere ability to fix prices, Washington would be able to determine the economy of many of these nations. We have controlled price agreements covering Chile's entire output of copper, manganese, mercury, cobalt, lead and zinc; and similar agreements with Peru, Brazil and others for such strategic materials as antimony, copper concentrates, zinc and vanadium.

The logic of intrahemispheric unity is borne out by still an additional fact: not only has there been an acceleration of trade by the Latin countries with the United States, but a great increase in their commerce with each other. By far the largest share of South American business is now interhemispheric. The United States takes 96.3 per cent of all Honduras' exports and supplies 76.1 per cent of her imports. 84.3 per cent of Mexico's imports come from the United States, to which she sends 91.2 per cent of her exports. Brazil's exports to the countries of the Western Hemisphere during 1941 rose to 73.5 per cent, with the United States the favorite customer and the Argentine second. An extra six per cent was transacted with Great Britain.

As of 1939-40, sixty-three per cent of the total imports of Latin America were with the United States and Great Britain, while sixty per cent of its exports were absorbed by the English-speaking nations in exchange. When to this figure is added the considerable development of intra-State trade between the Latin American re-

publics themselves, an economy is indicated which already shows
every evidence of being self-contained. The elimination of customs
tariffs, archaic tax systems and in some cases, depressed currencies,
would go a long way toward stimulating this commerce into new
and pyramiding gains.

At the present moment each of the Latin American States is victimized by provincialisms, and a political sectarianism which in itself is often sufficient to forestall all progress. Their intellectual and
political life is in the hands of a thin crust of upper-class politicos.
Most of the population is apathetic to politics, and a considerable
proportion, particularly the Indian element, is for practical purposes disfranchised.

Ninety per cent of Bolivia's three and one half million inhabitants
are illiterate Indians who speak Aymara and Quechua, not Spanish.
Most of the people of the inland areas do not even know what
country they belong to. The greater number of the thirty or forty
million pure-blood Indians still speak their native Indian tongues,
which have never been reduced to writing.

Despite the immense wealth of Latin America, the larger part of
her population lives under the most depressed social conditions, a
prey to ignorance, illiteracy and the most ruthless exploitation.
Standards of living are low despite the misleading gaiety and beauty
of such truly magnificent cities as Rio de Janeiro, Mexico City and
Buenos Aires.

The staple diet of the poor is rice, corn and beans. There is little
in the way of popular education. Sanitation is primitive, as are
methods of agriculture. Diseases such as malaria, tuberculosis and
dysentery have been allowed to run rampant.

With few exceptions the economy of these States is feudal in its
nature and constitutes a dangerous extension of the Eighteenth
Century into the present period. Only in Mexico and Chile are
there well-developed parties in the modern North American and
European sense. Even here the contentions between reactionaries,
syndicalists, socialists and others, is not on a basis of genuine plat-

forms, but of slogans and sectarian disputes founded on little more than local pride.

In practically all of these States, existence is ruled by small groups of financiers, churchmen, hacienda owners and leading families who keep themselves aloof from the largely illiterate and untutored population. To these reactionaries the feudal order is the only concept of existence which is valid. As we have noted, they veer strongly toward Spain and tend to promote a powerful anti-*Yanqui* bloc of the Southern Americas, closely allied with Europe. They bear such labels as *Los Conservatores* and *Los Liberales*, but their views are so largely similar as to lead one to believe they can only be considered in the light of the "ins" and "outs."

Democracy is anathema to almost all of them. They believe it to be the precursor to detested socialism, trade unionism and communism. They wish no disturbance of the quiet, somnambulant life which centers around the hacienda with its willing, but lamentably ignorant and inefficient cheap labor.

The political independence of these countries becomes under the circumstances an anachronism, serving no useful purpose and merely providing an arena for the rivalry of local politicos whose antics are not much different from those of Governor Talmadge of Georgia, or the late Big Bill Thompson of Illinois, and could be continued as easily under conditions of union.

It seems unnecessary for the policies of the United States to be concerned with the views of this thin upper stratum of ruling figures. By the very nature of the circumstances which have produced them and kept them in power, they are necessarily anti-American and will remain so. Yet at the same time it is our money which finances these dictatorships. It is our Lend-Lease which supplies the arms by which their military machines are operated.

As industrialism progresses and the feudal structure of these territories cracks under the logic of the machine age, the present ruling groups are certain to be overthrown. Both the political and material economy of these States will be compelled to draw their strength from a wider participation of the masses, who will have their trade unions, political affiliations, and organized doctrinal beliefs, as in other lands.

No one would have more to gain by a razing of the antiquated structures of political separatism than the Latin American farmers, workers and business men. Only a few cattle barons and great hacienda owners, the small ecclesiastical hierarchy, a scattering of first families, and the Falangist fanatics, could fail to benefit immeasurably from the establishment of the proposed Union.

When Fascism crashes in Europe, there will be at least a temporary end to the ironclad feudalism of Latin America. Revolutionary forces will be at work here as elsewhere, seeking to modernize the State and bring it in line with the powerful currents which are reshaping human society. At that time Latin America will be ready to abandon its political separatisms and embrace the cause of hemispheric union.

Despite the present highly jealous individualism of the Latin American States, sectional independence was not the social goal of its original great leaders. In 1783, the then leaders of the Latin American revolutionary forces sent three commissioners to London in an effort to persuade the British Government to help a revolution with money and arms, "at the end of which they would gladly become British subjects." The British, who were afraid to be involved in a colonial war with Spain at the time, declined.[1]

By far the most imperishable of all the names associated with South American freedom is that of Simon Bolivar. This legendary hero is to Latin America what Washington, Lincoln and Jefferson are to the traditions and ideals of the United States. It was he who inspired and led the South American wars for independence. Directly under his leadership four of these countries were freed. A fifth, Bolivia, took his name.

The great dream of Bolivar was a unified Latin America, developing its immense resources under a central political authority comparable to that of the United States of America. Despite his distinguished military successes, he died weary, bitter and disillusioned

[1] Emil Ludwig, *Bolivar*, p. 56.

over the tragedy of separatism which was engulfing his beloved continent, exclaiming: "I have been plowing in the sea!"

In his invitation to the governments of the Americas to participate in the first Pan-American Congress held at Panama in 1826, Bolivar wrote: "The day on which our representatives exchange their credentials will inaugurate an immortal epoch in the politics of America. A hundred years after, when mankind seeks for the sources of international law, it will remember the resolutions which imparted a happier turn to its destiny and think of them with admiration. What will the Isthmus of Corinth be in comparison to that of Panama!"

The great cause for the failure of Bolivar's cherished plans of union was not local intransigence and hostility, but distance and the almost terrifying emptiness of the Continent. Transportation and communications were poor and did not serve the cause of unity. The settled South American communities were far from each other, separated by oceans of jungle and impassable barriers of mountain peaks.

As the years go on, the stature of this man who could see beyond national boundaries and provincial contentions to a system of world order, becomes even more impressive. Though wedded for the moment to local interests, South Americans will not easily forget the political ideals of their peerless leader, in whose vision both of the Americas must discover a common heritage.

V

The splicing of Latin America into the common framework of the Union need involve no inconsistency or loss of freedom and cultural independence.

Latin America would retain its identity and civilization, just as French Canada does within the governing apparatus of the Dominion. All that would drop away would be the artificial and irksome boundaries and barriers which act as breeders of ill-will at one end and prevent the natural development of these great underpopulated areas at the other. It is not even necessary for any of the partners to the Union to possess a sameness of view in reference to general political objectives. French Canada is reactionary and pro-Fascist. New Zealand is far over on the Socialist side as is Australia. Our own South is largely of Bourbon complexion, while the Dakotas lean toward the Swedish vision of an economy ruled by cooperatives. It is these differences of social view which make for a healthy political existence and lend vitality to the course of the State.

Differences in culture and race do of course constitute a problem. In this reference it must be assumed that no great benefits ever are obtained without the acceptance of certain disadvantages which accompany them. In the present instance, one of these is the differing level of wages and standards of living throughout the Americas. This problem, manifestly, is not insurmountable, and to some degree may remain a fairly constant factor without hurt. There are differences of wage scale and living standards as between one part of the United States and another, the deep South, for example, differing notably from the Middle West.

Considered as a whole, the proposed Union would possess in addition to some twenty million Malay and Polynesian peoples of partly mixed blood, about thirty million Indians, twenty million Negroes, eight hundred thousand Mongolians and thirty-six million of various degrees of Indian and white mixture. The Caucasians would number about 245,000,000. These proportions of colored to white would not differ significantly from those at present existing in the United States and its possessions.

There is no reason why a bilingual civilization in the West would not be as successful as it has been in the Soviet Union. Our own Alaska contains a loyal and useful population which is mostly Indian and Eskimo. In the Territory of Hawaii, those of white blood, who include incidentally a considerable proportion of Portuguese, constitute only a fraction over twenty-five per cent of the total. With the exception of a handful of Japanese whose disloyalties may fairly be compared to those of Germans on the mainland, the Hawaiian population has been devoted and loyal. Even the much maligned *Nisei* [1] have contributed their secret service operators and interpreters who have rendered invaluable service in the South Pacific. An infantry battalion of these men has fought with lion-like courage under the Stars and Stripes in Italy.

It may be accepted that the men of Latin America are as well endowed and as capable of supporting a great civilization as any other. Even the full-blooded Indian of Mexico, Peru and Ecuador has left ample evidence of capacity to sustain civilization. When Pizarro landed in the country of the Incas, and Cortez in Mexico, they found well-regulated societies which showed themselves perfectly capable of carrying on all the business of a well-ordered State.

The American of Latin race has marked personality traits differing greatly from those of the Anglo-Saxon. This, however, is also noticeable in the case of the French Canadian as compared with his English compatriots.

The Spanish American is said to be impractical, oratorical, quixotic and dreamy; yet he numbers among his ancestors the hard-boiled *conquistadores,* who may be compared to any of the English adventurers and freebooters. The allegedly cold, practical Anglo-Saxon has given the world some of the most sentimental and unrealistic poets in literature. One need only think of Keats, or Shelley, or the magnificent boy, Chatterton.

What we may believe is ably expressed in the words of Padilla: "We may be sure that the difference between these civilizations, far from being an obstacle, is a hope and a spiritual treasure for this continent. For what else was the Renaissance but the conjunction of two culturally differing worlds." [2]

VI

The operating mechanics which would govern the merger of the Anglo-American and Latin American societies are not difficult to

[1] Americans of Japanese descent.
[2] Ezequiel Padilla, *Free Men of America,* p. 94.

visualize. If the United States, Britain, Canada, Australia and New Zealand were to unite to form the first nucleus of the Union, Cuba, Haiti, Nicaragua, Santo Domingo, Panama and Honduras immediately would follow, since they are held by the United States now in all but name. The Guianas, British Honduras and the Falkland Islands, automatically would drop into our lap so as to give us a foothold on the southern continent.

A large scale campaign of modernization and economic development of these territories quickly would be noted by the other Latin States.

The choice before the Latin American countries would narrow down severely. If they did not join the Union on equal terms they would become, despite themselves, political satellites of that Union with none of the rights of partnership which participation would grant. They would remain a collection of weak States, totally subservient to the military, economic and political dominance of Anglo-America.

The present contentions of the American Government solemnly absolving itself from dominating these territories, is a pretty piece of humbug which is likely to fool no one. With the coming of the airplane it is unlikely that the American Government will abandon the Monroe Doctrine in favor of the unlimited sovereign right of any nation in this hemisphere. We could not allow any American State to detach itself from us and link its fortunes with Europe or Asia. The increased military efficiencies which have shattered the previously impregnable power of distance, have given the Monroe Doctrine a validity and force which events are not apt to shake.

This entire diplomatic game of pretense can have no enduring value to any of the countries concerned. They must now realize that unless a cooperative Western Hemisphere is possible a cooperative world is entirely out of the question. The Latin republics with their unbalanced economies, poor roads and communications, and rudimentary industrial development, will offer a perpetual provocation to every ambitious aggressor who happens to come along.

In order to protect ourselves from commercial and military encroachments dangerous to our future, we would be compelled to
intervene openly or tacitly against any overt action which involved
further penetration of this continent by a European or Asiatic
Power.

We no longer can think in terms of nations alone. We are now
forced to think in terms of hemispheres and even of entire civilizations. If, for example, the recent Bolivian *putsch* were to deprive
us completely of tin, the United States would have no choice but
to overthrow the government by armed intervention, as the British
did that of al Gailani in Iraq.

Circumstances may be relied upon to make the options clear to
our fellow Western States. This is a choice we might be compelled
to stimulate by encouraging parties and political movements favorable to hemispheric unity. As we have seen earlier, bloodless intervention has long been part of the technique of modern political
action.

The process of agglutination could be expected to become fairly
automatic as the people of the remaining Latin States noted the
rapid growth of prosperity and economic well-being of those areas
which adhered to the Union. The effect on the masses of Latin
America would be as of some giant lodestone whose terrific magnetism could not be resisted.

VII

One of the immediate questions with which the Union would
have to deal would be that of its paucity of population in comparison to its widespread area. All countries will be following the lead
of the Soviet Union which is forcing a strategic redistribution of
population, and is creating industries and cities in the empty spaces
of its deep hinterland. Our own view will have to be dominated by
a similar set of requirements.

The new world will be built on space resources and manpower.
The ultimate value will be people. It is only people who can make

a nation great. With them will come new dynamisms, new faith and enthusiasms, helping to tide us over one of the most uncertain periods in history.

Quite dissimilar from the present attitudes held toward great masses of potential settlers, usable manpower will be considered in future decades in terms of useful man-hours. Resources in manpower will be judged with the same jealous satisfaction as resources in minerals or soil fertility. This trend already may be seen in the incentive-breeding operative in the German Reich, and Italy, despite their claims to being imprisoned in constricted living space.

The United States will have to populate Australasia, Alaska, Oceania and Latin America. Millions of Britons and North Americans should be moved to these places in an orderly, planned migration which would coincide with State-backed development projects.

In a commonwealth as large as the projected Union of the West, by creating projects of sufficient magnitude, any amount of desired development can be brought about wherever conditions are potentially favorable.

The population needs of the Union's strategic outposts would be conspicuous and pressing. Alaska, a vast subcontinent in itself, capable of maintaining a population of over fifty million, supports only seventy-two thousand people. Oceania, including Australia, New Zealand, New Guinea and the colonies of Great Britain and France in the Pacific, has no more than eleven million inhabitants. In Australasia alone we should endeavor to settle within a decade five million people from the British Isles and another ten million from the United States.

Australia could hold two-thirds of the present population of the United States. The two islands of New Zealand could support under an American standard of living, twenty-five million people, and many millions more from the standards now applying in the East. New Guinea should have twenty-five million people, and could support triple that number if it had to.

South America is still appallingly empty. In the Argentine there are almost 215,000,000 acres which can be cultivated. Apart from the rich pasturelands of this agricultural empire, only sixty million acres have ever felt the heel of the plow, and practically none of it has been subject to intensive cultivation. There are limitless tracts in the Amazon Basin and in Patagonia which do not have a population of two persons to the square mile. As fantastically low as is the population density of Brazil, three quarters of its people are concentrated in an area within a hundred miles of the seacoast. Great empires of rich land which have scarcely been touched, and which are unequalled in climate and productivity, can be found in Bolivia, Peru, Ecuador and elsewhere throughout the continent.

If the West is to acquire the additional population it needs, it must do so soon, before Europe has settled into an habitual routine and has begun to assimilate itself to the new social circumstances this war will have brought about. We may be certain that Europe will consider its people in the light of an enduring value, much as does the Soviet Union today, and like the latter, will make it difficult for them to migrate.

Europe will have its own empty territories in Africa, the Middle East and Arabia, which it will be anxious to populate. Today there are perhaps twenty million Europeans who are uprooted and homeless, and who would remain for a period of years after the war's end, a burden on an already overtaxed community. These and many other millions in addition, could be brought to Latin America or to Oceania, where farms and homesteads could be prepared for them, or where they could work as laborers on the gigantic new projects which would follow the amalgamation of the West into a common union.

Together with the Americans and Britishers who went there, they would be absorbed by the local cultures, as were the millions who came to North America in the great migration years which have passed. Workers from the Balkans especially, with their painstaking industry and inurement to hardship, could turn these tropical valleys into veritable sections of paradise.

We should endeavor to attract all of the people from Europe we can, and to siphon them off into the empty spaces of Australia, Oceania and the two Americas. If transportation is paid, homes and land prepared, and the migration organized as a function of the State, millions can be moved in an orderly routine of settlement.

With our limited population resources, a rapidly consolidating world may compel us to adopt a philosophy of subsidizing babies as have the Germans and Russians, providing either direct subventions, or an increasing ratio of exemption from income tax for each succeeding child, in an effort to fill our empire with people and make it safe.

XXI

A WORLD AT PEACE

THE proposal to divide the world into five self-sustaining communities involves an approach to a settled international order while detouring such entangling questions as those of race and social ideology. In this respect it is a compromise between the ideal of an international society and the existing era of international discord and disorder.

Each of the proposed commonwealths would have all the attributes of the universal State and would be that State in miniature. Each would have the right to grant political asylum to refugees from the others, thus minimizing to some degree one of the most terrifying dangers of a centralized and frontierless society.

As far as Asia is concerned this solution assures the Orientals of social equality as well as an economic well-being far superior to anything they now possess. It constitutes on the part of the Caucasian races a major concession to the future of the others. Western man no longer can play dog-in-the-manger in the present-day world. The approximations which are outlined above are the *least* he can do safely if he wishes to maintain peace, together with a reasonable status in which the advantage will still all be his in the world.

The compensations to the Soviets are obvious. The weak points in their economy would have been secured and rectified. The areas of incipient quarrel would have been reduced since there would be no small nations shuttling between the U.S.S.R. and the Anglo-American orbit to create an incurable distrust and vicious competitive spirit. The voice of the U.S.S.R. would not be one in seventy, but one of five in a council of equals, in which the power interests of each would be best served by preserving the existing equilibrium.

The union of the West would alter a military picture of the most glaring potential weakness. It is only the large scale on which it is drawn which prevents it from being quickly observed. The West, as compensation for its lack of population, would be provided with a powerful military position matched only by that held by the Soviets.

For a period of years the true burden of such a setup would be carried by the Western World. This in itself is a major element in the bargain and one of the principal inducements held forward to Europe, the Soviets and the Orient in arriving at this permanent settlement.

The United States would contribute by far the greater part to this arrangement, in wealth, know-how and material sacrifice. She would receive in return, security, and permanence to her prosperity. Within the Union of the West itself, she would become the balance wheel in a commonwealth whose magnificent potentialities stagger the imagination, and would be able to guarantee to her citizens, shaken by a series of desperate wars, expensive in blood, bullion and goods, an era of rich and unrivalled development both culturally and materially.

Though the United States and Britain will be compelled to make the basic sacrifices if the balance of the globe is to be assisted back to sanity, it is precisely the Anglo-American countries who have most to lose in the event of a renewal of the present suicidal struggle. Thus the outlook would not be Utopian but strictly practical and realistic despite the political idealism which actuated it. The sacrifice and investment made would create a universal easement and stability, as well as a political balance leading to the eventual unification of the world. Nothing the United States would be asked to do would involve anything like the cost of a third world war, which otherwise is inevitable.

We should be compelled if we wished to face the situation honestly, to agree to a general cancellation of all obligations, or to a moratorium which in the last analysis would have the same result. We would cease to be banker to the world, operating on the business principle of accrued interest, since this would end only with the same type of recriminations which occurred when the Soviets cancelled the debts of the Czar, or when Britain ignored hers to the United States.

The threatened aftermath of postwar chaos demands that coincident with the first steps of reorganization, we feed Europe, Asia and the U.S.S.R. without expecting more than a token payment for these acts, and that we supply their elemental wants until they are capable of doing so for themselves. It will be necessary for us to equip these States in every regard, and in particular with the machinery required to create a competent heavy industry. For practical purposes we will have to wet-nurse the rest of the world until it is back in approximate health again and its peoples once more possess safe channels in which to utilize their energies.

Until World War II the United States had lived in a dream world of surpluses and surfeits. Our economy was plagued by the fact that we had too much of everything and could not dispose of it adequately under the profit system. That era now is well past. For a long period of years we shall have to operate under the economics of scarcity rather than that of plenty. We shall have to tighten our own belts for the purpose of assisting the rest of the world, continuing our economy on what is essentially a war basis for still a few years longer—this time in the interests of construction instead of destruction, and permanent peace instead of eternal war.

By this means we would attempt to control our destiny and through ourselves rise to new levels of well-being and happiness. A reasonable part of our energies then could be turned to the creation of sound social relationships and a decent distribution of the world's wealth to all of its citizens, so that the Four Freedoms actually could be acquired on earth rather than in the propaganda heaven.

In the nature of things there never will be an absolute equality either in capacity, will, horizon, opportunity or wealth. To maintain that immutable concepts of existence which find their expression in continuous competition throughout the organic world, can be abrogated by some legal enactment is pure academic nonsense. To secure the well-being of all, however, irrespective of deterring conditions, is shrewd wisdom. This is observable in the family, where there can be no question as to who is the bread-winner and who is not, or who contributes most to the joint prosperity, or who is the weaker and who is the stronger.

In most families, this furtherance of the mutual welfare is amply understood and is in fact the backbone of all human relationships. Children are nursed, schooled and provided for, even though they obviously are economic liabilities. Men pay alimony to their wives though their wives can no longer offer them anything but hurt, and children support parents who may be passing into a querulous dotage and whom they may rarely see.

All of these are responsibilities which could be rationalized out of existence. Many of them easily could be escaped. The fact that they are in the main observed is the true lesson for organized society in constructing its larger units, and outlines the quality of the obligations it must hold toward its members.

The introduction of new methods of transport, of improved means of manufacture, and new sources of industrial power, can raise the wealth potential of the earth to a degree which today is literally undreamt of. The question of distribution of wealth will have no such potent bearing as it has had in the past, since wealth itself is composed of the unlimited resources of the earth and will become in effect the same surfeit and common possession of all as is the case with the beauty of the sun, wind and stars.

There always will be recurring advantages to the stronger and more competent, but since man himself is the only market for his own products, the very need for rational organization should make further areas of starvation and depression impossible.

After the war it will be possible for men to live on mountaintops, favored islands, or lake shores hundreds of miles away from their work, running down to the great airline taxi centers in little helicopters or combination airplane runabouts.

Wherever scenery is beautiful or life is favored and invigorated, men will live. Electric power will be cheap and more efficient. Plastics will be abundant and will replace many common materials. Houses will be air-cooled, cities laid out for beauty and efficiency.

The living standards of present-day nations reflect the continuous state of preparation for belligerency in which their national economies are always involved, and the wasteful expenditures consequent on a hopelessly inefficient political organization of the earth's surface.

Not only is there a profligate squandering of wealth on enterprises which bring no return to society, but there results an actual nullification of man's impulse to employ his achievements for the benefit of his kind. The State thinks in terms of deadly competitions and repressions. It considers its environment as a primeval wilderness containing infinite and everpresent menace, a psychology which is imparted to its principal thinkers and most energetic men.

A small part of the effort put to the business of war would wipe out many plagues and pests which now are a recurrent feature of our existence, and would add automatically to the bankable wealth of humanity. Syphilis, crows, rats and other scourges of mankind could be eradicated. In the United States alone, rats inflict a total damage of over two hundred million dollars a year. There are supposed to be more than eight hundred million cases of malaria in the world, a disease which takes an annual tribute of over ten million lives. Its economic loss to the United States is estimated at five hundred million dollars a year. A fraction of the money spent on war would give the entire world a magnificently unified road and airport system.

The predatory instincts of aggressive men could be sublimated in long-range projects for the taming of nature, which could be attempted only on a hemispheric basis. Engineering works of massive scope could be undertaken, jungles cleared, deserts irrigated, swamps drained and the forces of natural energy harnessed, as man moved to place his environment under control.

This is a dream and a vision which well could engage the attention of men and turn them from the petty hatreds and mean conceptions to which they addict themselves under the guise of patriotism, local interest, race, and even religion. In such a world the rewards would be great, and from its tranquility and peace could develop in addition to animal comfort and security, a true blossoming of the spirit and the creative mind. This would be the first of the golden eras of man, an age far transcending any humankind has ever known.

II

For the sake of international harmony one further step must be taken. The equated federations we have suggested will have to be bound together in some sort of loose union.

The central authority of the World Union would possess no legislative or judicial or prescriptive rights, and would exercise only such executive powers as might be vouchsafed it from time to time by common agreement.

The mutual self interests which would exist between theoretically self-sufficient and equally weighted bodies should make this course entirely feasible. The inconsistencies which attribute the same sovereign power and rights to a minor country such as Bulgaria, as are vouchsafed to a giant like the Soviet Union, will have disappeared. As these discrepancies melt away there will vanish with them the rivalries and temptations induced by the presence of these minor nations, making a commitment to international order both desirable and profitable.

No persistent weakness would exist in the individual setup of these Power Aggregates which would prevent them from living peacefully, side by side with each other, as do the United States and Canada. War between them would be so costly as to result only from a provocation extreme enough not to be controllable under any system.

The solution would not lie so much in the submission of disputes to arbitration as in reducing the area of disputation. The plethora of contradicting reasons which make for quarrels in a non-integrated world cannot exist in an integrated one. There is as much difference between the two conceptions of society, and the problems which arise from them, as there is between the deadly family quarrels which used to plague the Tennessee mountains, and the quiet life of a well-ordered countryside.

Thus the whole question of utilizing force in the settlement of controversies would tend to recede since the controversies themselves would lose much of their identity.

It must be conceded that there are areas of jurisdiction which can be most competently handled by a world authority to which the participating parties have allowed certain limited powers. There are questions of complementary and adjusted currency systems, of exchange of scientific knowledge, of research into major health problems, of trade and communications. There are the interesting questions of a unified world calendar and standards of weights and measures. There is the issue of a supplementary world language. Above all, a need would exist for a recognized forum where problems of a mutually irritating nature could be threshed out.

The central world headquarters could have among its tasks that of supervising the government of Africa until such a time as the various splinters had coalesced into a single unit capable of self government. It could be concerned with the founding of an international WPB, a temporary body created for the liquidation of overriding economic, industrial and agricultural problems on a global basis. It might have jurisdiction over a central bank which would serve as a clearing house for international currencies.

Under the jurisdiction of the central executive would be an International Court of Settlement, where any global problem or complaint could be aired, and which would attempt to operate with the moral authority of a family of equal members rather than with the force of an authoritarian center.

Except for projects which had specifically received the sanction of the governments involved, the powers of this agency would be solely those of recommendation. The instant this authority attempted to substitute instruments of coercion for moral powers in dissolving contentious disputes, it would have lost its force, or would be on the way to create a single world empire. Its capacity to function then would depend on the ability of one of its members to take forcible control of the rest.

A permanent world capital could be set up on some island such as St. Helena which plays no economic or military role in the world. It would operate as an independent sovereignty and belong to no State, the same as the present Vatican City.

The business of this global authority would be determined by a council of representatives from each of the five great power groups, including Africa itself.

Under the circumstances proposed, it is unlikely that the world authority would attempt the regulation of purely domestic matters. Its function simply would be that of keeping the various central questions in equilibrium. It would determine the conditions of international service of all kinds, and the rates, and perhaps might be responsible for the proper integration of all communications, transport and mail.

It would possess no police power beyond that required to keep order on its own little island. Even the mandated territory of Africa would be ruled by reference, and the cooperation of Africa's own police. If intervention should become necessary, it would be accomplished by equal contingents supplied by the various Powers, under the supervision of a leader to be appointed by the world authority.

In the new world there would be no investment by any of the Power aggregates in each other's territories, in the shape of permanent possession. Ownership of the basic resources of any national State is tantamount to interference by outsiders with its internal economy. The natural resources of the State and the results of its labor come under the influence of foreign interests.

In important respects the situation is equivalent to the exaction of tribute by absentee landlordism. It is a relic of an age of mercantile glory which has lost its rights of ordination. Under modern social conditions it no longer can perform a useful function by which its objectional features can be justified.

Modern nations tend more and more to regard their raw materials and essential services as the inalienable patrimony of the State, which cannot be allowed to fall under outside dictation. As long as ownership implies control to any degree whatsoever, international investments must be a continuous source of trouble. They cannot be disassociated from the inherent power and prestige of the State they represent.

This will become more and more true as the forces which now bear upon society begin to mature. It was inevitable that Mexico must contest British ownership of any great portion of its oil wells, as representing a situation capable of overthrowing any government responsible to a mass electorate. Tomorrow the same attitude will be taken by the Argentine toward British ownership of its railways, and by Spain over British possession of its copper mines.

An identical result would follow our ownership of Arabian oil, or Chinese airways. These investments bring into view an automatic evil, that of identifying foreign internal processes with the private interests of powerful American businesses. They create the need for direct concern on the part of American operators in the labor and other laws of the countries involved. Questions of discrimination arise and influences of all kinds are brought to bear. If the physical properties represented by these investments are important enough, they become an extension of our own sovereignty, and as such must be protected by diplomatic and perhaps military means. The very foreign policy of our country is subject to debauchment by the powerful maneuvering of investor firms anxious to save their position by preserving favorable regimes, even where these governments are inimical to the future of our own nation.

At the end of 1940, the value of American direct investments abroad was eleven billion dollars. There was another four billion dollars of indirect or portfolio investments. In Axis Europe our petroleum companies alone were involved to over three hundred million, and our manufacturers to over four hundred million. These investments represent an antiquated view of society, and in the long run are compelled to be a dead loss to the nation.

If to these figures are added still others connected with foreign loans, which must become an onerous drag to the beneficiary governments and may be expected never to be repaid, we find ourselves in a situation which can produce no benefit to the United States and which must end finally in an abnormal relationship between other commonwealths and ourselves.

It is plain that the freezing or confiscation of American investments abroad, and the repudiation of foreign loans, is synonymous with a fantastic wastage of our soil and mineral resources as well as labor.

Such alien ownerships which remained after the world settlement, should be liquidated by the World Court on a fair exchange basis, rather than remain objects of ultimate expropriation. Loans, or long term purchases made from us by the other big commonwealths, either should be treated as outright gifts intended to tide them over an emergency, as one would assist a friend, or should be paid for in goods or in some permanently stabilized token which represents a lien on goods. Whatever the medium of exchange might be, the effect of sale should be that of barter.

Trade would be kept in balance for each fiscal period, deficits to be supplied in wanted materials by the debtor country where required. This would follow a concept of real values as being contained in things rather than in the money symbol, separating money from its self-arrogated mission as the real arbiter of international affairs. The sole criterion in all large-scale international business would be the value of the materials involved and the relative energy-hours required to produce and transport them.

To do otherwise would be to repeat the fiasco of the past decades, where we supplied Japan with scrap iron, magnesium and invaluable machinery in exchange for specie and bank notes which in the true sense never can be re-exchanged for a comparable value.

III

What political form the big space units would take is not of determinative importance. Each of the giant aggregates would choose its own style of political organization, which would be an outgrowth of its own particular type of genius. Indeed, this result hardly could be prevented. That of the U.S.S.R. already is decided. If it alters at all it will do so by gradual stages uninfluencable by us. In Asia, where no experience in democratic procedures exists, some sort of dictatorship will prevail irrespective of what assurances may be given to the contrary. Because of its inevitable character, these conditions should not prove unacceptable to us.

In the shaping of the African and European federations, however, we could play an influential part. Africa would be an unknown quantity. Europe could be expected to support institutions of a more or less free character.

These questions are on the whole not critical. They could be settled, as could those arising from a planned merger of the West, by the calling of a Constitutional Conference attended by a small group of executives from each State affected, who would be equipped with the same mandate to proceed as are generals in the wartime theaters of action. In the case of the West there need be no more consummate difficulties in the path of this program than there was in the amalgamation of the original thirteen States.

In general it may be said that no absolute blueprint need be laid down in advance, and that the forms of government required would evolve based on those we now possess.

Within the aggregates themselves, an effort should be made to place the relationship between peoples, cultures and races on a fair and reasoned basis so as to avoid the recurring abrasions which have been a constant feature of the present system.

There should be established a system of regions which will not be fettered by the present antiquated type of permanently fixed boundaries. They should exist in space in the sense of autonomous forms whose parts are capable, by election, of both expansion and contraction.

Questions which have plagued Europe for centuries could be settled permanently by the creation of State units based on communities of language and culture. The old political boundary lines would disappear and the combinations would be made so as to preserve some homogeneity in each administrative unit. Brittany might wish to be free from France. The Walloons might desire to join with Holland, or the French-speaking portions of Belgium and Switzerland might commit themselves to wholly French-speaking units.

These regions would have absolute jurisdiction over their own cultural destinies, but their political policies would be assimilated to those of the entire commonwealth, just as those of the forty-eight States of the American Union yield to the superior jurisdiction of the Federal authorities. The regions could not levy tariffs and discriminatory duties, or raise armies. Any portion of their territory could withdraw to form an enclave under different cultural guidance whenever it so chose. This is the same theoretical right enjoyed within the States of the United States of America. It was symbolized by the secession of West Virginia from the parent Virginia commonwealth.

We see an unacknowledged situation of this type in the occupation of various portions of our own New England States by French Canadians, who are now in the process of turning whole sections into French-speaking communities. These are in reality extensions of French Canada though they come under the sovereignty of the United States. This process indicates that a peaceful penetration of settled areas by new peoples and cultures, is not an impossible one.

This conception permits a reshaping of political events based on social needs as they arise. Here again Soviet Russia has taken the lead, as in the bodily removal of the entire German Volga republic, or in the establishment of the autonomous Jewish region of Biro-Bidjan in south-central Siberia.

A resiliency of this type would permit a rational settlement of irritating minority problems, and would allow for the possibility of making corrections on a mass basis wherever insoluble race difficulties occurred.

In the past this had been done automatically by the self-removal of the Mormons from the areas of persecution to regions where they could build their own free institutions, or in the similar mass movements of Quakers, Pilgrims and others to our shores. What the world should seek is not the attainment of some millennium, but a working solution of its problems on whatever rational basis which presents itself. The persistent minority difficulties symbolized in the explosive tangle of races and cultures in Southeastern Europe, should be settled by a pencil and slide rule rather than by moral preachments and diplomatic bargaining.

The tragic case of the Jews in Europe, and earlier of the Armenians, and the hopeless imbroglio of races and cultures in Central and Eastern Europe, makes it appear certain that even under terms of union a semi-autonomous territorial status must be created for all peoples who desire it. This is necessary in reference to all minorities, whether they be religious like the early Mormons, or racial like the Macedonians. It creates a sanctuary and protective center in which the minority is able to find either material refuge or psychological assurance. As far as these settlements are feasible from the engineering point of view, they should be undertaken, relieving ancient points of pressure and historic antagonisms which may otherwise be incurable.

The obstacles to such a course which cannot be surmounted by private enterprise, will be seen to be without true significance when the required measures are undertaken as a form of governmental activity. These projects should be operated with the same genuine concentration of forces utilized by governments in the critical moments of war. There is no reason why the capacities and means so scrupulously used in the making of total war should not be equally utilized in an effort to create a total peace.

This procedure would imply no essential violation of the historic concepts of freedom, equality and democracy. It adds an element of social engineering which in no sense detracts from the essential character of democracy, yet adds much to its fundamental ease of operation.

The question of the mass transplantation of human beings due to whatever reason—population pressures, economic necessity or to supply an additional pool of man-hours to empty regions—should be carefully appraised. The effort should be not only to gain valuable manpower for States which require it, but to liquidate known elements of tension. That part of the population of Iran and Afghanistan, for example, which would resist connection with the Soviet Union because of economic views, or with the Empire of the Orient for reasons of race, could be removed to suitable places prepared for them in Arabia or Northern Africa. Fair compensation could be allowed them for their holdings in business or lands, by mutual stipulations involving the joint action of the commonwealths concerned.

IV

This project for world territorial reorganization can lay no claim to perfection. Nevertheless, it would mean the taking of a tremendous stride forward on the part of the human race in terms of worldwide social organization, and would appear to remove the largest part of the instigation to international crime by adjusting the world's political divisions to its economic frontiers. The major claim to be made for this design is that it fits in with the premises of a workaday world in a technical age, and presents no obstacles to the efficient operation of the earth's machinery, or use of its resources.

It would make international piracy so difficult as presumably to rob it of most of its attractions. By equalizing the weight of the

Powers and reducing their number, it makes international collaboration possible in a world run by scientists, engineers and management executives rather than by career diplomats.

Society would have a chance to operate as a functioning organic unit devoted to its own best development rather than to the dangerous obscurities of power politics.

For a time at least, the Asiatic question would be settled, and perhaps the African one as well.

Man would be able to take his breath for the new plunge forward into eternal progression.

INDEX